A Ladder In The Dark

MY JOURNEY FROM BULLYING TO SELF-ACCEPTANCE

by **Alan Eisenberg**

Published by
Bullying Recovery, LLC

BULLYING
RECOVERY

First edition June 2015

ISBN-13: 978-1514238189

ISBN-10: 1514238187

Library of Congress Control Number: 2015909352

For my wife Janet and sons Andy and Zach.
You stood by me patiently in my darkest hours
and never asked for anything in return.
I love you all and know I owe you big time

PREFACE

I believe it is important to know a bit about the author prior to reading their words. In this case, as this is an autobiography and I am working to make a change to how the long-term effects of bullying are thought of, I want to be clear with you, the reader, of how I feel about the issue of bullying.

As much as I wish that bullying would end with more education and further learning about the damage it causes, I don't think we will see humans stop bullying, whether at school, in the workplace, in relationships, or through politics and global interactions. To me, it seems to be a human condition and no amount of education or training will put a complete stop to it. Can it be reduced? Certainly I believe that. But both the bullies and the bullying survivors have to deal with the ramifications of the effects of bullying on them.

That said, I have focused my attention on helping those that suffer with the damage caused by bullying (both the bullied and the bully) to recover through better programs of support and help. There are many groups that work on bullying prevention and I applaud them and their efforts. I think each group offers support and help in their own way.

I have chosen to focus on bullying recovery and believe we can do a lot of good as a community and society to work with and help those that are bullies and/or have been bullied to learn to recover from the psychological damage due to the suffering they endured from bullying. I certainly believe that, as a community and as a society, we can make a difference and help those suffering to find a solution and hope that the books and the focus of my work brings that needed support and relief.

As you read my story, I hope you see that there is a ladder in the dark for everyone who seeks it. It is there, but you must be patient and seek out that which you don't see at first.

PROLOGUE

The Hole

Forget Lexington!

Many years ago, as a young boy, I dug a hole deep in the recesses of my mind. I'd worked very hard to dig this hole in which to bury all of my bad memories. Time went by and I grew up. But the hole was still there, waiting for me. It had been such a long time since I'd last visited the hole, and I'd hoped that I would never have to see the place or its contents again.

The hole was invisible to the naked eye, as it was level with the ground, with a makeshift piece of plywood covering the top, and it was surrounded by a field of tall grass and flowers. Behind the field was a tree line to hide it from view and through the tree line was a large yard near where I lived, away from the view of the hole. Every time I visited this field and the hole, a strange feeling of panic would overcome me as I broke through the tree line. I would break out in a cold sweat, with my heart racing and a feeling of wanting to run away as fast as I could. It would be a while before I understood why.

I dug this deep, dark hole with my bare hands over a great expanse of time, and the pain of my raw hands at the end of the work each day still haunted me. The hole was dug almost twenty feet deep, leaving my hands bloody from the arduous task. The work was meticulously done to avoid any chance of my finding the hole again, or so I thought. There was a large shoebox I had placed at the bottom of the hole where it was too dark to see. I wrote on the top of it many years ago when I was younger. The shoebox was filled with haunting images from my life of being bullied. If the shoebox was visible, it would read, in a child's handwriting, "Alan's Bad Memories! DO NOT OPEN!"

As I completed the long task of building the hole, I covered it with a piece of untreated plywood in the hopes of no one, especially me, accidently falling into the hole. The hole was not to be accessed again. My last task was to spray-paint a message on the top of the plywood to remind myself why the hole was here if I forgot and revisited it later. I carefully painted the word on the top, then turned and ran as *fast as I could, away from this feeling of panic and from this hole in the field in my mind that I hoped never to see again. On top of the plywood in large letters, I painted a message to myself. In big childlike letters were the words, "ANXIETY" and "DEPRESSION". Below it were a few more words on the wood, to remind me of something else that was important. In smaller, but still visible letters, I added the words "Forget Lexington!*

PART ONE

THE

END OF

INNOCENCE

CHAPTER ONE

Beginning of
The End

I wanted to believe that I'd never have to worry about the hole again. I worked hard to be sure the contents of the hole would be well hidden. It would be many years before I would remember about the hole I had built in the field in my mind. But one day, I found myself wandering in the field and stumbled upon what was left of the plywood cover sealing the hole. I almost fell into the hole, as the cover had weathered over time, disintegrating, and exposing the abyss below. The words painted on the front of the plywood were not visible any longer due to weathering over time. When I caught my footing, I worked quickly to repair and strengthen the cover in the hopes that it would permanently seal the hole. I painted an extra word on top this time, in the hope that this new cover would be stronger than the last. When I had completed meticulously painting the words, the top of the cover now read "ANXIETY" and "DEPRESSION" with those words below "Forget Lexington!" With this new addition, I figured there was no way the cover would wear over time. When I was certain I had resealed the hole, I ran away without looking back as I felt that familiar panicky feeling. As I ran, drops of rain started hitting me as a passing storm was coming. The new wood cover with the new paint immediately started to wear and the paint would now smear down the cover into unreadable words.

◊ ◊ ◊

The first time I had a true panic attack was during one of my last final exams while attending Virginia Tech in the spring of 1990. I was taking the test, and all of a sudden I was short of breath. I felt like my heart was going to explode right out of my chest, and I was blurry eyed and shaking. I was not at all in control of my body any longer and felt the need to flee as quickly as possible. I ran from the room during the middle of the exam because I was sure I was going to vomit. A funny thing happened though. When I got to the bathroom, the panic subsided. Unfortunately, I recognized that feeling. It was the panic and dread that I used to feel as bullies surrounded me on the playground during my younger years. I would later learn that what was happening to my mind and body was called a panic attack. But at that moment, I was not mentally prepared to understand and had no familiarity with the term. When it ended as I calmed down in the bathroom, I went back in to my class and explained to the professor what happened. I sat back down, still feeling uncomfortable and wanting to run away. I was still shaking and trying to make sense of what had happened to me. I got through my test and handed it in. As I was leaving the class, I realized my professor might have understood what I was experiencing. It was my final exam in psychology class, and he probably knew from his own learning in the field that I'd had a panic attack. If he was aware of this, he didn't say so. However, if he had, he might have spared me from the next twenty-four years of trying to figure out what had happened.

I discovered that people rarely share with each other that somewhere between eighteen to twenty percent of our population is suffering in silence with anxiety and depression at any given time. I would spend the next several years learning this lesson myself and wondering if it was just me.

My college years prior to this moment were great, as I spent four glorious years at Virginia Tech and immensely enjoyed that time in my life. I studied media communication, a subject I was passionate about, was the General Manager of our new student run TV station, VTTV, and spent three years in the Beta Omega chapter of the Theta Xi fraternity. I was not a social wallflower and certainly felt successful in both my academic life and my personal life. I had a very active social life and was even engaged to be married during my senior year to someone I met at college.

To be truthful, I was not ready to get married, but my one big flaw was that I had little confidence in myself when it came to relationships. I had some wonderful and caring girlfriends during my high school and college years but always felt that they were too good for someone like me. I always believed they could have done much better, as inside, I felt like a loser and weakling. I also had the problem of allowing myself to be attracted to any girl who paid attention to me. Little did I know at the time, this was really an issue of my self-esteem. I would cheat on almost all of my girlfriends with anyone of the female persuasion who paid me the slightest bit of attention. I had a strong need to feel liked and to feel wanted, and I felt that need was based on what others thought of me. In addition, I had the pain of my first love cheating on me with a good friend. Deep in me, I felt violated after this and lost perspective of what love should be. After cheating, I would feel so guilty about what I had done that I would stay up at night berating myself for my actions. I hated myself and truly thought that all of my problems could be solved if I could just be more likable. But I didn't even like myself, so why would anyone else like me?

It was the wrong way to think, but, boy, it felt good at the time to be wanted by someone...anyone. I would later find out that this problem of attaching myself to anyone who paid any attention to me was a part of the damaged psyche that came about from my low self-esteem, my need to be wanted and to be viewed as perfect to the outside world. I didn't love myself. I'm not sure that during my whole life I ever truly loved myself. So I would look for love and approval from the outside. I could also easily blame all of my problems on what was happening around me and not on myself. That served me well for a few years, but this kind of thinking was fleeting at best.

◊ ◊ ◊

The term "beginning" is a funny one to me because it seems as if we have many beginnings and many endings, not one, as many believe. For example, assuming you finish this book, you will see many beginnings, as well as endings, during the course of the story. This is somewhat ironic, but also so very common. I don't believe that life is made up of only one journey but many journeys with several beginnings, middles, and endings. I learned that everything is temporary and that this too shall pass, whether good or bad. I didn't used to think this way, and then, when one thing would go wrong, it would be devastating because it seemed like the end of my journey. I learned to allow my life to have many journeys and then could see the end of them and move on.

This new thinking helped me to understand how I acted at different points in my life's journey. One of the great debates in the United States is when life begins. Some people argue that life begins at conception and from that moment on, you are a living human. Others argue that life begins upon birth as that is when the bonding experience between parent and child begins. This seems to be the argument that determines the worthiness and viability of a human life. More important to me are the experiences we have during the course of our lives and the lives we touch. Regardless of whether life begins at conception or birth, our self-worth is based on the experiences that we have during our lifetime and our social interactions.

I believe it is important for everyone to be able to tell the story of where we come from and where our lives began. If you have picked up this book, I am guessing you or someone you know is in the midst of some issue relating to the long-term effects of bullying or Complex Post-Traumatic Stress Disorder (C-PTSD), anxiety, and/or depression.

This book is not meant to be a guide for one particular situation but includes various strategies and coping skills that helped me on my path to recovery. These tools are ones I learned to enable me to see the ladder that would ultimately guide me out of the darkness into the light.

I have a story to tell deep inside my soul. I have actually been telling this story through social media from my *Bullying Stories: The Long-Term Effects of Bullying (bullyinglte.wordpress.com)* website since 2007. I thought that by releasing these terrible times, I would put them behind me. What I didn't realize at the time was that I needed treatment and support for my own trauma, although I thought I was over it. It is like the saying from the Bible in Luke 4:23 "Physician, heal thyself," meaning you must be healed to heal others. What happened instead is that I brought these memories back from a hidden place in my subconscious, which only yielded thoughts of misery and despair. I had never let go of what happened to me as a child, and it haunted me yet again. Once I discovered that I needed help, I had to step back and reflect upon my life, realize how I got to this point, and help others through their pain. This book is my story and hopefully a resource for those suffering from the effects of long-term bullying, anxiety, and depression.

These issues are treatable, and none of us has to suffer alone. Back in 2007, when this particular journey through the long-term effects of my own bullying recovery started, it took me some time to realize that I needed to go through my own recovery. This is the story of my being bullied as a child, leading to my C-PTSD; what I know happens to many survivors of bullying; and how I learned to put the past in the past and move forward with my life. It can get better, if you only let it.

CHAPTER TWO

Under the Surface Of a Life

The origin of why I dug the hole in my mind is complicated, as are many things in our lives. Childhood is the first time when we learn how to deal with our feelings. We learn that there are good feelings we want to remember, and there are bad feelings we want to forget. One day I was thinking, "Wouldn't it be cool if I could find a way to take my bad feelings and get rid of them forever?" That way, they wouldn't be able to hurt me anymore. I didn't think that it would matter if I never thought about those bad feelings again. After all, childhood is supposed to be a happy time, or so I thought. So I started to plan in my head the means to put my bad feelings somewhere far away. If I could do that, then I would be able to make my life happy and find a way to move forward. I began my search for the perfect container to hide all my bad memories away.

◊ ◊ ◊

My earliest memory in my life is from when I was about three years old and drank buttermilk that I thought was regular milk. Most of our first memories are often dramatic in nature. Trust me when I say that when you drink buttermilk expecting regular milk, it is pretty dramatic. So it was at about three years of age that my memory began, but certainly my life began before that, when I was born in March of 1968.

1968 was a very turbulent year for the United States. Civil Rights leader Martin Luther King was slain on April 4, and presidential candidate Robert Kennedy was slain on June 5. The average life expectancy was seventy years old, and in late March of that year, I was born into this world to Jewish middle-class parents in Bowie, Maryland. I was sickly upon birth with a minor case of pneumonia and had to be incubated for a few days of my life. But I would fully recover and go home a few days later. I was described by my parents as an energetic child who would ride my Big Wheels bike around the neighborhood. I had many neighborhood friends during my early years in Bowie, Maryland, and recall feeling like a leader among them. That's not to say I was always the leader, but I did not shy away from wanting to take the lead on our childhood adventures.

These times of early youth from birth to age six are what I would classify as my "happy childhood" years. I had a very close family, and we would vacation with my mother's brother and my cousins often, which was always a great time. I found that I had an affinity for all forms of media, including television, radio, and movies. These types of activities always gave me great pleasure in my early years. Going to the movies and watching television were enjoyable escapes. I so enjoyed the adventures on the movie screen, especially *Star Wars, Indiana Jones,* and *Star Trek.* The memory of watching Saturday morning cartoons in the seventies was one of the highlights of my childhood. In fact, Saturday mornings was educational back then, with *School House Rock* as a main staple. I learned so much that I remember to this day. I can still recite the full preamble to the Constitution from all the times I heard it on *Schoolhouse Rock.* *"We the people, in order to form a more perfect union..."*

Many of us who grew up in this era can do the same thing, as I recall humming it in high school as our whole class had to write the preamble in our government class.

Parenting in the 1970's seemed to be more permissive than it is today. That means that parents were there but didn't keep tabs on our every move. On the weekends, I would go out in the early morning and not return home until late in the afternoon or early evening. There were no cell phones, and calling out in a loud voice from the front of the house was the only way to get your child to come home. To be honest, I think my mom liked the peace and quiet she was afforded when we were out.

My parents upheld the traditional parental roles of the time. My dad was the breadwinner, and my mom was the homemaker raising kids. Both my parents had difficult childhoods, resulting in their own unresolved childhood wounds. For my mom, her father died of cancer when she was seven. Her mother raised two children in the 1950's as a single parent. My mother's early years were marked with transient housing and inconsistent transportation, creating instability in her life. Being a product of her generation, I often wonder if my mother's hardships left her unable to adequately meet my sister's and my emotional needs.

I recently approached my mother about her childhood and how it might have led her to seek perfection in her own children. My mother would brag glowingly about her children to others, and in many ways that made my sister and me feel like we had to be the perfect little children for her. As I discussed this with her recently, she explained some of her own childhood issues to me.

She told me she felt bullied by her own mother, my grandmother, who was a tough-as-nails woman. My mother mentioned to me how she never really felt love from her own mother. After her father died, she developed a shield of confidence and carefreeness while inside she was insecure and angry. These feelings were so much like my own feelings, but different in that she was abused by her own mother. My mother shared with me a story of how these feelings came to be.

One day, when she was a still a little girl, my mother decided to help her mother by dusting the house so that she would be able to enjoy her weekend. My mother worked as hard as she knew how as a young child to clean and polish the tables that they had. When her mother came home from work, my mother proudly announced that she had cleaned and dusted the house so that her mother wouldn't have to. Her mother looked around and pointed to a cobweb in the upper corner of the room and said, "You missed that".

My mother never dusted for her again. It hurt her badly, and she came to resent her own mother, who was not affectionate and never said "I Love You" to her own children.

As my mother grew up, she swore that she would never do to her own children what my grandmother did to hers, and she worked hard not to. Of course, this led to some other issues, such as my mother's making my sister and me feel we could do no wrong. Every time we made a mistake, my sister and I beat ourselves up over it. Sometimes, when we try to repair one of our emotional issues, it can lead to a cascading issue of replacing that emotional issue with another one that could be just as harmful. We don't mean to do this, as we believe we are solving our problems, but it is never that easy. Sometimes we are lucky to make it work, but in many cases, we replace one emotional problem with another one

As I continued researching my family's history with mental illness, my mother shared another story from her youth. After her father died of cancer at age 35, my mother was bullied by her father's mother, her paternal grandmother. The grandmother would wait for my mother after her school let out and would grab her and whisper in her ear that my mom's mother killed her father. Although she understood when she became an adult that this was unlikely, to a child of seven, as my mom was, she believed it to be true.

My mother would head home with this new information and accuse her mother of killing her father. I am sure this was very hard on my maternal grandmother and created a rift between her and my mother. She decided to take my mother to see a child psychiatrist to work out the problems. My mother is a very strong adult because of these things that happened to her, but I believe that some of my own traits come from the genetic and familial social issues that are in my family's past.

Even with these issues between my mother and her mother, my maternal grandmother always lived close to us and moved with us when we moved to Lexington, Massachusetts. I never knew of this rift between my mother and my grandmother until recently, when I asked my mother if there were any mental illness issues on her side. Although I always thought that my mother loved her mother very much, I also believed there was a secret in their relationship. As I got older, I discovered that my mom had been keeping this secret for a long time. My mom is now in her seventies, and those feeling are still there.

My dad also had a rough childhood and his own abuse issues but in a different way than my mother. When he was young, he contracted encephalitis that left his legs crippled, and he became socially isolated. During my childhood and most of my adult years, that is all my dad would share with me. The only additional information he shared was that his mother was manic depressive and in and out of institutions. I never knew much about my paternal grandmother growing up and rarely saw her, but I did know about her manic depression. I feared, through my own problem with phobias, that her manic depression would be passed down to me.

My dad was a left-brained thinker who was quiet and seemed to live in his own world when I was growing up. He was an electrical engineer and had his own bouts with Obsessive Compulsive Disorder that kept him very inwardly focused. This, additionally, had my sister and me competing for his attention, which was difficult to get. Because my dad lived in his own mind, he would make up stories he believed to be true, but it was obvious to us that they weren't. This brought our family many laughs, as he regaled us with made-up stories that he believed to be fact. Once when my own family and my grandmother were travelling to Disney World, my maternal grandmother picked up a bottle of "Bullshit Spray" at South of the Border. This is a place that everyone who drives to Disney World on Route 95 knows because you see signs for it for one hundred miles in advance.

My dad was telling so many of his fabricated stories during the drive that my grandmother was constantly spraying the "bullshit spray" at him. My dad had no idea why she was doing that, but we laughed all the way to Florida.

In contrast to my dad, I was a more creative, emotional, and expressive right-brained thinker, so we rarely agreed on much. This caused communications issues between us, and it was difficult to express my feelings to him and for him to express his to me. Despite my relationship challenges with my mom and dad, I knew that they loved me, and, at least in my early years in Maryland, that was enough.

◊ ◊ ◊

I think it is important to understand ourselves, warts and all. One of the hardest things anyone can face is themselves and their own faults. We all have faults and we all have strengths that make up who we are. One of my faults is my sensitivity to the plight of the human condition. This sensitivity is both a blessing and a curse. Growing up, I was a precocious child who felt comfortable speaking my mind.

From a young age, I was extremely competitive, hating to lose at any game my family played. I felt that perfection was what I was meant to achieve, and I worked toward that, even as a child. If my sister wrote a poem, I needed to write one better. If my sister wrote a short story, I had to write one, too. I clearly remember her writing a story called "It" (yes, before Stephen King did), and I wrote "The The". These were both our attempts to write horror stories. Another of my issues was that I always felt like I was competing, and if it wasn't for attention, then it was to win some game or some appreciation from my parents. It was never enough for me because I felt like a bottomless pit that could never be filled up with enough love and affection. I didn't understand at the time why I needed this outward appreciation from others.

So many of us think we need to be perfect when that is not a useful goal but a faulty belief brought on by a society convinced that any grade below an "A" is inadequate. Toxic beliefs about what it means to be successful contribute to low self-esteem and a sense of inadequacy. For me it was my self-esteem, waiting to be stroked by others. I was hungry for attention from everyone around me, eagerly taking in any bits of praise and acceptance I could get. I struggled to understand that self-worth actually comes from within, not from those around you. This was a lesson that would soon be taught to me in spades during my younger years.

In Bowie, Maryland, we lived across the street from a wonderful family who had children exactly my sister, Robyn's, and my age. Mary and my sister got along famously and would be best friends for years to come. I had a rewarding friendship with Mary's brother, Sam, and he and I would spend most of our time playing together. My parents were great friends with their parents, and both our families spent a great deal of time together. Sam was my first real friend and one who would never let me down. He and I would run around the neighborhood causing whatever mischief we could find, as young children do.

When I was about five years old, my parents moved us to a bigger home in Bowie, which was a little farther away from Sam and Mary. Fortunately, we found a way to keep the friendships going, mainly through seeing each other at school, or preschool in my case. It was good to be young, innocent, and free.

CHAPTER THREE

Losing the Life
I Dreamed Of

I found a shoebox that looked to be about the perfect container in which to put my bad memories. It was a plain, brown shoebox with no writing on it and seemed to be waiting for me to use in my plan to hide my bad feelings away, so I wouldn't have to think about them any longer. I found a permanent marker and wrote on the box in my young child's handwriting, **"Alan's Bad Memories. DO NOT OPEN!"** *I thought in my young mind that this was a great idea. As my childhood progressed, I would keep this shoebox of memories under my bed and add to it as I needed to. Then I wouldn't have to think about them again. As a young child, I rarely had to put any thoughts into my box as I was still so innocent. I thought I was quite a clever kid to create this box. This would prove over time not to be so true.*

◊ ◊ ◊

My first recollection of being bullied was relatively minor. At the end of my street was a place my sister and I visited called "the Dunes". In our minds, it was like the Sahara desert, but in reality it was probably just a large dirt construction zone. No matter, to my sister and me, it was the desert where we could go and have adventures.

One day, we ventured out to "the Dunes" for another one of our play adventures. As we were playing on the dirt hills, some men dressed in hunting gear and holding bows and arrows came along. When they saw us, they must have decided it would be fun to scare us off. I recall feeling immediate fear at seeing them. I felt the tiny hairs on the back of my neck go up and felt tingly all over, wanting to run away. After all, they had weapons and that scared me for some reason. That's when one of them decided to string an arrow in his bow and point it at me.

Who knows why he would do this? The man with the weapon made a threatening comment to my sister and me, telling us to leave or he'd kill us. This seemed to us like a very real threat. In the end, I'm sure it was to scare us and get a chuckle from his friends. But, again I ask the question, "Why would a full grown adult threaten children, jokingly or not?"

Of course my sister and I ran out of there as fast as we could. "The Dunes" were now ruined for us and off limits. These scary men made a choice that ruined a part of our young lives. We would never travel to "the Dunes" and play there again.

◊ ◊ ◊

When I first started school, my sister Robyn and I would take the bus with the other neighborhood kids. On one of my first days of school as a kindergartener, some of the bus-stop kids treated me to my second bullying experience. To these kids at the bus stop, I'm sure it was a joke but because I was a cocky six-year-old, I wanted them to think I was cool.

There was a manhole leading to a sewer at the bus stop. I was a pretty small kid and there were kindergarten to 6th grade kids waiting for the bus. One of the older kids had taken the heavy manhole cover off the sewer.

For some reason they chose me that day to pick on. They dared me to climb down into the sewer. Wanting to be the cool kid and impress them, I did it and then heard the most terrifying sound of my young life.

Skreeeeeeeeet!

They put the manhole cover back on and stood on it, taunting me. I was trapped. It was dark and I was petrified of this small space. Years later, Stephen King would write a book called *IT* that ironically enough dealt with peoples' fears of sewers. This began my own journey into claustrophobia.

I yelled for them to let me out. Instead the older kids sat on the manhole cover and didn't budge. I recall crying and being quite scared. My sister was yelling for them to stop and let me out. When they didn't, she ran home, telling them she was going to get my parents. Once the kids sitting on the manhole cover heard that, they let me out. As my mom came down the street, she saw nothing wrong. Wanting to be cool, I told my mom everything was fine.

Years later while in college, my friends often participated in "sewer running" in the sewers that ran under Virginia Tech. I respectfully declined the invitation when they asked me to come, as this incident had never left my mind. They would return saying how much fun I'd missed out on and I always felt like I'd missed some good times due to this incident. This would not be the first or last time my anxiety got in the way of fun.

◊ ◊ ◊

When I was almost seven years old, my dad received news that his job was moving to Bedford, Massachusetts. So we packed up and left for a place in New England, far different than Maryland, and that is where my bullying problems really began. It was hard to leave all the good friends I had made in my young life, particularly Sam. Now I was leaving to go somewhere strange and new and not at all like the life I had been used to. As I watched my home in Bowie disappear from my view out the back window of the car, I said to myself, *"I'll miss you Bowie. I'll never forget the good times here."*

We arrived ten hours later at our new house in Lexington, Massachusetts, on a very hot day in August. My sister and I waited on our doorstep for neighborhood kids to greet us upon our arrival, as we had experienced in Bowie. But no one ever came by. We walked down the street looking for kids to play with. But Lexington was not Bowie; we didn't know anyone and didn't see any kids playing outside. Eventually we met some kids, but maybe it would have been best if I had been left alone. Little did I know, the next seven years would have a significant impact on me and the direction of my life. I would put these seven years away and forget about them for a while. It was unpleasant to think about my time in Lexington, so I chose to block those years from my memory and start again, in a new location. I left those memories behind and tried to pick up the pieces of my life when we returned to Washington, DC, to live in Fairfax, Virginia, seven years after leaving Bowie and moving to Lexington. I made a choice at that moment to *forget Lexington*!

CHAPTER FOUR

Life After Lexington

I have done it! I dug the hole so very deep in my mind, the way I wanted to. I thought that there would be no way to find it again from my home in Lexington, through the backyard, through the woods, to the open field. It is so deep that I needed a ladder on the side to be able to get up and down. Once it was dug, I placed my box of bad memories at the bottom, climbed up and put a makeshift wood cover over it. It was not visible to the naked eye, because the field grasses were so tall that it was hidden among them. I spray painted words on the top of my makeshift wood cover. It said what I thought the hole was as a warning not to fall in. "DEPRESSION," and in smaller letters, "Forget Lexington." In my mind it was perfect, but as I put the top on, I could hear the memories from the shoebox, trying to talk to me in whispers from below. They would say, "Don't forget me, you loser" and "You need me or you'll be nothing," but I was sure of myself and that this was the right answer. I did not indeed need these bad memories. It was time to leave this hole and this field, but I felt this strange pull as if hands were grabbing my legs, trying to make me stay there. I felt the familiar panicky feeling again. I turned and ran as fast as I could to escape the memories at the bottom of the deep hole that I hoped to never see again.

◊ ◊ ◊

Time drifts so slowly as a young person. My seven years in Lexington were the worst years of my life. I made a conscious choice to put these years behind me and try to forget them.

But memories don't go away, no matter how much we suppress them. This was a lesson I needed to learn. I didn't want to confront what happened to me in Lexington, so I worked hard to forget them and move on with my life. I put these memories into the recesses of my mind. I wasn't aware that the damage was done though. While I fought the demons of these memories, I spent years suppressing them.

But the bullies and the town changed me. I was no longer who I wanted to be. In many ways I didn't want to be at all. So I would use a mantra every time the pain of Lexington entered my brain.

Forget Lexington was my mantra. At the time I believed it would work. But the damage was done, and the person I had become was no longer someone I liked. I worked hard for many years to forget about the people and places in Lexington, but these memories were always back there, trying to get out again. I didn't want them to, so I moved on. I was not going to talk about the past seven years. They were buried, or so I thought.

Seven years later almost to the day, we moved from Lexington, Massachusetts, to Northern Virginia. At the age of thirteen, my father's job moved us to an area called Fairfax, Virginia. I had vowed to forget the people and the bad memories of Lexington. I was going to start a new life and try to do this one right.

We had a beautiful home in Fairfax, and it was the beginning of the eighties, with puberty knocking on my door. But my days in Lexington had left me hollow, my self-esteem all but gone, and my soul blackened. I had moved to Lexington a self-confident six-year-old and returned feeling like a wounded warrior back from a long seven-year battle at the age of thirteen.

The events in Lexington left me haunted and tortured by the memories not only of the coldness of the weather, but also of the human condition. I had already decided at thirteen that I was going to change who I was. I was now more quiet and reserved, not wanting to be noticed by peers. I was a very bookish person with a dark soul inside, wounded and afraid of meeting new people and making friends who would only hurt me in the end. What happened to the boy who wanted to be king of the mountain as a six-year-old? He'd moved to suburban Washington, DC, feeling like the king's piss boy. I learned that my being such a sensitive person was both a blessing and a curse. It made me compassionate and caring towards others, but at the same time, left me at risk for easily getting hurt. To avoid this, I became introverted, keeping a low profile. It felt painful to behave in a way that was contradictory to my natural inclination to be extroverted and expressive. But it didn't feel safe to be my authentic self anymore. Not after what had happened in Lexington.

Forget Lexington!

After a while in my new home in Fairfax, Virginia, I met some of the neighborhood kids as they would come by to greet the new neighbors. These boys and girls seemed nice enough, but I kept them at arm's length. I tried to be someone they would like in order to fit in, but I felt like these friends could see through my facade. There were three boys in particular that I had met the summer we moved to Fairfax. These boys were into music and comic books, so wanting to fit in, I said I was too. It wasn't a total lie as I loved music. We formed a band, even though I really didn't know how to play an instrument. I convinced my parents to get me an electric guitar and pay for lessons so that I could better fit in. I would take lessons twice a week because I so desperately wanted to be successful, but I was awful at playing guitar. I loved music but could neither read music nor play an instrument well. Still, I tried and tried and our band would play as best we could in my basement. I was trying to have fun, to fit in and be cool, and to get the other guys to like me, but inside, I was still trying to be quiet and introverted and my authentic self was battling that. I felt it was safer to lie low, but I truly needed the attention and acceptance of these peers. For a while, it worked out as I bonded with my new neighbor friends. I might have even let my guard down a few times. That was, again, my usual mistake.

◊ ◊ ◊

Out of these friends, Josh, and I connected best. Josh was really into comic books, and while I had read a few before, I wasn't a collector. Through Josh, I saw the magic of what I was missing. Many of the Marvel comics he collected were based on characters such as Spider-Man, The Hulk, the X-Men, and Daredevil. Interestingly, the backstory of each of these characters contained an element of bullying and focused in on their ability to fight back and seek revenge. These characters were all outcasts and bullied in their own way. Years later, I would wonder if Stan Lee dealt with bullies and used the comics as a way to cope with his own struggles. At the very least, he seemed to understand my plight and what had happened to me. For twenty-minutes per comic, I could escape into the world of the superhero where I could pretend to fight these bullies and enemies.

This is when I fell in love with comics. At thirteen years old, I became a collector, and to this day, I still find excitement in the stories and identify with the characters. It became my hobby and a way to escape my mental demons for a little while. I am most grateful to Josh for introducing me to a world of fantasy that I could escape to when I felt low. Little did I know years later, as special effects caught up with the comics, these same characters would become movie franchises that allowed a much bigger audience to appreciate their stories. I like to believe that Stan Lee knew what he was creating and that comic collectors are a breed of people who escape into the stories and characters to give us hope and encourage our own ability to cope with life's problems.

As I entered eighth grade, I worked very hard to stay low under the radar of the obvious bully types at my school. I found that my survival instinct served me well. Human beings, like animals, are born with the instinct for fight or flight when faced with a threat. This fight or flight function is essential to survival. Over the many years of practice that I had with bullies, I honed my ability to take flight or avoid getting too close to others. The threat of being injured emotionally and/or physically made me keep a safe distance away from others. Despite my caution, I did develop some friendships that year. I shared many classes in eighth grade with a boy named Chris McCandless. Chris was a reserved, quiet guy like me. I had little reason to think about this issue during this point in my life, but years later Chris became quite famous as the young man who died in his early twenties in Alaska while he journeyed on his own to spend his life in isolation.

Chris was immortalized in a book and movie called *Into the Wild.**
It is the tale of a man breaking away from his previous life and starting
anew and is loved by many who identify with his plight. Often, I think
that Chris might have been suffering from some of the same abusive
scars I was. Interestingly, more recent conversation about Chris has
surfaced from his sister's suggesting that there were personal familial
problems and possible abuse that he experienced by his father that may
have led to his decisions to isolate himself from society in his post-
college years.* Chris may have been suffering from Complex Post
Traumatic Stress Disorder (C-PTSD) due to these family secrets long
before this type of issue was diagnosed. C-PTSD stems from extended
childhood abuse of some type. It seems both he and I may have had
that in common.

It was no matter in eighth grade though, because Chris and I
would bond for that one year. Maybe we both knew that there was
suffering going on behind the other's eyes. Those of us who knew the
adolescent Chris would be surprised to know he was suffering as it
wasn't outwardly shown. My friends at the time would say the same of
me as well. People like Chris and I reveal to others only what we feel
safe enough to show. You only see what is on the outside, but there is
great pain on the inside. It seemed to me that Chris McCandless and I
were kindred spirits who took different paths to deal with this burden.

◊ ◊ ◊

Through my connections with my neighborhood bandmates, I got
to know some other eighth grade boys who were jocks and into sports.
I was never much of an athlete and had been given few chances to play
anyway, so saw little enjoyment in hanging with jocks. It was too late
when I realized I wasn't going to benefit from knowing these kids.

About halfway through the school year, I was invited to a
sleepover by one of my new school, jock acquaintances. My bandmates
were going, so of course I wanted to be included. I didn't know this
particular boy who was having the sleepover well, but I went anyway.
When I arrived at the sleepover, the discussion quickly turned to

smoking marijuana and who had tried it. I thought it would be cool to say that I had smoked pot. It wasn't a lie, and in Lexington, I had done so to fit in and as much as I wanted to forget those days, my mouth was quicker than my mind. It appeared that I was the only one who had. The kid hosting the sleepover said he had some and produced a bag of the green flaky substance and rolling papers. Everyone looked at me.

"Eisenberg, since you're the only one of us who has smoked, roll up a joint and show us how it's done," ordered the boy.

As I reflect back to that time, I can't believe I was thirteen years old and rolling a joint. If I knew that my sons had done that at thirteen, they would have been grounded until they were twenty-one. But back then, again wanting to fit in, I rolled it, twisted the ends, was handed a lighter, and I smoked it. I started coughing right away. Something wasn't right, and now all I could think about was how this would not end well for me.

"Dude! That was oregano, not pot." The jock boy chuckled. "You've never really smoked pot in your life, you liar. Boy are you stupid."

With my self-esteem already fragile and my sensitivity heightened, all I could do was hang my head in shame as they laughed at me. These boys didn't know my story.

Forget Lexington!

That voice inside me told me to laugh and shrug it off. Needless to say, the rest of the night was painful for me. In fact, I was the continual butt of many jokes during that evening, and it would be the downfall of my friendships with my neighborhood bandmates. Maybe that's for the best, I would tell myself. After all, I did have other friends at school and these kids were not in any of my classes. But still their words that night stung like a bee whose nest I'd disrupted. It was the first night since Lexington that I'd felt something wrong in my gut, but I didn't pay attention to it. An old familiar panic came over me, resulting in stomach pain and making it difficult to eat. At the time, I didn't know why, but I would soon learn that this common symptom of the fight or flight reaction is essential for physical survival when one's life is threatened. However, even the slightest emotional threat to my self-worth would set off panic and anxiety, reinforcing the irrational belief in me that the world was a dangerous place.

The Monday morning after the sleepover, while at the bus stop, my neighborhood friends and bandmates began taunting and teasing me about the weekend event. There was a very sweet neighborhood girl my age named Carrie who also knew them, and she told them to cut it out. She was the first bystander to bullying I had seen, and with her words, they did stop. She was tough, and the neighborhood boys knew not to mess with her. From then on, they ignored me and didn't talk to me anymore. I was fine with that because Carrie and I became friends, and she wouldn't tolerate their picking on me. It was encouraging to witness a bystander actually make a difference in a bullying situation. This was the first bystander who had ever stood up for me.

CHAPTER FIVE

Young, Lost And Confused

Sometimes while I was dreaming, I would see the hole with the shoebox that I had left in the Lexington field in my mind. I could hear the memories trapped in the shoebox in the hole calling to me. "Don't forget me, Alan. I am still here and you will never amount to anything. No one likes you. Don't even bother to try." I would wake up in a cold sweat, repeating my mantra that I had developed since moving away from the bad memories and the trap that I had been in. "Forget Lexington…forget Lexington…forget Lexington," I would say to myself over and over, rocking back and forth. Eventually, the nightmare and hurtful words from the shoebox would fade away, and for a while I would again forget these memories I had trapped in the shoebox in the hole in my mind.

◊ ◊ ◊

The remainder of eighth grade was uneventful, as I retreated into myself and my isolation for my own safety. I was successful at not being bullied the rest of the year. I learned two important survival skills that year. The first thing I learned was to lie. If someone asked me if I had done anything risky in my past, I would lie and say I hadn't. I wanted to be another naive thirteen-year-old who didn't know anything of the troubles of the world. I didn't want to let any of my new friends know of the darkness that the human soul can hide or of my past experiences. I drowned myself in comic books and fell in love with the horror books of Stephen King. I read *Carrie*, a story about a high school girl with special powers who gets bullied for being different. She is abused both at home by her mother and by her school peers. She lies to peers at school to cover up her secrets and her life. She is a haunted soul, and by the end of the book, she gets revenge on those who abused her, including her mother. I knew after reading that book that

Stephen King "got it." He understood bullying revenge issues, and so I devoured anything he wrote.

Interestingly, Mr. King is a New Englander and captured the culture of the people I met when I lived in New England. I am a huge fan of the movie *Stand by Me,* which was based on Stephen King's short story called *The Body.* In the story, he tells the tale of a group of twelve-year-old boys who go on an adventure to find a dead body they hear about. It is an amazing coming-of-age story that truly took me back to a time in my young life as well. What struck me was the last line in the story and movie. After describing the ups and downs of the boys' future lives, the main character says, *"I never had any friends later on like the ones I had when I was twelve. Jesus, does anyone?"*

I cried after reading that line. It can be interpreted in so many ways, but the truth is that being twelve is tough on many kids, and the people we knew during those years are ones who affected us very deeply, good and bad. In that moment, I realized that I had lost my childhood in Lexington and that I could not get it back.

Forget Lexington!

The second thing I learned in eighth grade was how important it was to be a chameleon. I could change my appearance and attitude based on what I perceived were the needs of the people around me in that moment. I learned to blend in with my surroundings and not draw attention to myself. I learned to agree with people so as not to make waves. I was whoever they wanted me to be, a departure from my authentic self. While this approach did little for my self-esteem, it was another way I knew to feel safe and avoid trouble from bullies.

◊ ◊ ◊

One day I had an opportunity to experience the other side of bullying. A rumor circulated at school that a boy named Herb and a boy named Mitch were going to fight across the street after school got out. It was a big deal, and you could feel the energy of the other kids throughout the school as the news spread. I could have walked away and not gone to the fight, but I was feeling like for the first time, I was on the other side of the bullying. We all knew what would happen because Mitch was a lot bigger than Herb, and Herb would lose the fight. But Herb had to show he wasn't scared. I knew what he was feeling.

The rumor of the impending fight was so rampant that the school administration learned about it. At that time, schools were not prepared to manage an incident of this magnitude. At the end of the school day, about every kid proceeded across the street to a dirt area where the fight would take place. It was a huge crowd. The students encircled the fighters, preventing the administrators from breaking it up. I remember watching all this, feeling grateful and relieved that it wasn't about me this time. Then I saw the two boys. It was obvious to me that Herb was between a rock and hard place as he knew he couldn't back out of the fight but was likely to lose.

The two boys circled each other in the middle of the large crowd. There were shouts from the mob, demanding a fight. It started to get pretty scary. Herb put up his fists, and then Mitch raised his hand, made a fist, and brought it down on the crown of Herb's head. At that moment, it was over. Herb was down and that was that. It was anticlimactic and just plain ugly. I wanted to leave, feeling sick for Herb and because I had witnessed this fight. I walked home alone, the whole time wondering why I'd watched. I knew what Herb was feeling. I had been there before, and I didn't do anything to help defend Herb. I was thirteen and glad I wasn't that kid who got beat up anymore. I wasn't a brave bystander. I wasn't the guy to stick up for others. I was a chameleon, watching life happen before me and blending in so as not to be noticed.

Once in a while, I think about that fateful day when Herb was called to fight. I wonder if I or others had stood up as bystanders for Herb, if the whole fight could have been prevented, but unfortunately, I didn't have the courage to do what I wish others had done for me.

◊ ◊ ◊

I hit puberty in eighth grade, which came with a whole new set of issues—girls and sexual feelings. Of course the school was teaching sex education, and I realized I had those funny early crush feelings for one of my friends, a girl named Hannah.

Hannah was very skinny and a bit on the nerdy side. Those were the qualities that attracted her to me, and we became fast friends. I wanted to invite Hannah to the eighth grade dance. With the encouragement of my friends, I approached Hannah at the locker bay.

"Hi," I said sheepishly.

"Hi," Hannah said back.

"How's it going," I said, feeling my heart beating fast and the sweat forming on my brow.

"Good," Hannah said back, looking at me strangely. "What's up, Alan?"

I mustered all the courage my thirteen-year-old self could muster and quickly blurted out the question I wanted to ask her.

"Would you like to go to the eighth grade dance with me Saturday?"

"Oh, Alan, I can't," Hannah answered quickly. "I have swim practice and my parents won't let me stay out."

"Oh," I said trying to hide the deep pain that stabbed me and the feeling of wanting to run as fast as possible away from there. "OK, no problem. Thanks anyway."

I left as quickly as I could. Hannah's eyes followed me down the hall. I couldn't turn around or she would see the tears welling up in my eyes. Rejection is difficult for everyone, but I felt it more acutely than most, poking me in the ribs each time. I took a risk and proved yet again how unsafe it was to be authentic, to be myself. Hannah couldn't know how much her rejection hurt me, and it would be quite a while before I could muster up the courage to ask someone out again. But still at that moment in my life, my ego and my self-esteem were still so fragile. I didn't want to feel that way again…EVER.

I didn't ask anyone else to the dance that year. I didn't go to the dance. I stayed home, watched television, and listened to the music of the early eighties that had become my soothing companion. I drifted away to sleep that night as the band *Styx* played their latest hit on the radio in my room. Ironically, the song was called "The Best of Times".

CHAPTER SIX

In a State of
Imaginary Peace

"What is wrong with me?" I thought. A song would play on the radio that was famous during the years I'd spent in Lexington and I would be crying. "Why am I crying?" I would think to myself. My repressed memories hiding in a box in hole in the Lexington field in my mind made it difficult for me to understand why I was hurt when I heard the song. "Remember you heard that song right after you got beat up, you loser," the shoebox would whisper to me from afar. I didn't know what it all meant, to hide the existence of these painful memories. It was becoming increasingly difficult for me to ignore the whispers coming from the shoebox I buried so far away, as these memories wanted to escape. But every time they tried, I would once again start my mantra, "Forget Lexington." Eventually, my mind would quiet again, but only for a short time.

◊ ◊ ◊

Eighth grade ended with a whimper, and the highlight of the summer would be my parents sending me to a Jewish overnight camp in North Carolina for a month. This was nothing new, as this was their routine every summer. I usually enjoyed the experience, despite feeling like I never quite fit in. But off I went, and at fourteen, this time I would be a CIT, Counselor in Training. This would give me a taste of responsibility and freedom.

I enjoyed my bunkmates and relatively young, laid-back lead counselors. We talked about music late into the night. There were great debates about whether Styx's album *Paradise Theater* was better than the Police's *Synchronicity* or Rush's *Moving Pictures*. You know, very important conversations. Then there was this new Australian group called Men at Work who sang about a product called "Vegemite". Since there was no internet at the time, we would argue incessantly about what Vegemite was. Did it taste good, and why were they singing about it? Later in life, I would taste Vegemite and still wonder what all the fuss was about.

Of course, the other topic that fourteen-year-old boys talk about is girls, especially what you have done with a girl and how far you had gone. The one thing I'd learned about this subject was that everyone lies. The claims of fourteen-year-olds were rarely true. Of course, I was still lying about what happened in Lexington.

Forget Lexington!

I was still quite naive when it came to girls, but bragged along with the other guys anyway. In many ways, we made each other feel inadequate with these exaggerated stories of our male prowess. But we were of that age, and the other CIT girls were no doubt having the same conversation in their bunks. By the end of camp, each of us would choose a girl to spend time with that summer.

For me, there was one particular girl who seemed interested in me. Sandy was tall and beautiful, and I knew those teenage hormones had kicked in. She and I started "summer-camp dating" about two weeks into our month long camp. Sandy made it very clear she liked me, and I certainly liked her back. After all, she was paying attention to me. What else could I ask for?

As all fourteen-year-olds know, two weeks of dating is a long time at that age, and Sandy and I spent as much time together as possible. She was so bright and kind, and I was thrilled that I finally got to kiss a girl. We carved our initials into a tree in the old-fashioned ritual. It was like one of those romantic movies. I had feelings for Sandy that I never thought possible. I realized that I could be loved by someone, and that I could love in return. Up to this point, I had doubted that love could ever enter my bleak soul. That might be a shock to some, but for a person who had the scars of a haunting past, that is common to experience. I will never forget that first kiss with The Police singing in the background, *"Every breath you take. Every move you make. I'll be watching you."* Music and I are old friends, and I am grateful for the ability to recall times in my life based on musical moments. My memories are both a blessing and a curse. While I enjoy recalling particular songs from a sweeter time, I can also be haunted by memories of songs triggering less pleasant moments.

Forget Lexington!

I did forget Lexington, for that moment. As summer camp wound down, the inevitable goodbyes started. Saying goodbye to Sandy was one of the most difficult times in my young life. We snuck off for one last kiss, and we promised to write and call each other. Then, each of our parents arrived to pick us up and take us home. Sandy kept her promise, as we stayed in touch for the next two years. We would never see each other again, though.

Sandy taught me that no matter how briefly people come into your life, they can have an amazingly positive impact on you through the way they express their emotions to you. I later heard that Sandy attended Massachusetts Institute of Technology (MIT). I imagined she would be most successful, as bright as she was. Over thirty years later, I remember fondly my first love, Sandy, and the two weeks of summer that seemed to go on forever.

When I returned home from camp, I had the rest of the summer to consider who I was going to be in high school. I decided that my safest bet would be to continue with my quieter, chameleon-like ways, doing what I needed to belong. The high school was built right next to the junior high, but it might as well have been a world away, because junior high school kids never travelled over there. I knew there would be many more students at the high school, as my class size was about 650 students. I felt very nervous to walk the halls of the big high school with the typical cliques: the tough jocks; the smart nerds; the popular, beautiful girls; and also the dark, depressed loners. Most of what I knew about high school came from John Hughes movies like *The Breakfast Club*, and that made me think I was in for one wild ride over the next four years. I was still very cautious about who I should be and where I would belong.

CHAPTER SEVEN

New School
New Life

I didn't realize it, but time was taking its toll on the cover on the hole with the shoebox in my mind. I sensed that the plywood lid covering the hole in my mind had become so brittle that it had fallen apart and now the hole in my mind was exposed. The shoebox was no longer covered and no longer protected. More and more of my bad memories from the box in the hole were able to leak out, due to the wearing out of the hole and a little crack that formed in the box of memories. It was getting harder for me to forget Lexington. But I would keep trying to forget the past and move on with my life. "I am a teenager now, and my childhood didn't matter to me," I thought. I wanted to be invincible and strong and forget about all of the bad memories of my childhood. I wasn't a child any longer and wanted to be someone else. But the shoebox was still there and now the hole was open and there was no warning on top. The whispers that said, "You're a loser. Why do you bother? Nobody likes you..." were leaking out. But I held them at bay...at least for a while.

◊ ◊ ◊

An important event happened to me right before the end of eighth grade. My sister, who was a high school junior, encouraged me to check out the Drama Club that she was in at the high school. She had found her place at school through the Drama Club. She would come home very excited about drama and talk about this wonderful teacher, Ms. Joan Bedinger, who everyone called Ms. B. She had been the drama teacher at the high school for almost 20 years. After school, my sister would regale me with stories of how cool Ms. B was and that her favorite word was "moment". Honestly, I had little idea what my sister was talking about. My past experiences had taught me to be cautious about sharing too much with my teachers, but now Ms. B told my sister that she wanted to meet me.

I worried like crazy about what my sister had said to Ms. B. Did she tell her about my years with bullying and who I was now?

Forget Lexington!

Despite my apprehensions, I walked over from the junior high to the high school while the Drama Club was building sets for a show called *Cabaret*. When I entered the enormous auditorium, Ms. B immediately greeted me. She acted like she already knew me and said that my sister had told her all about me. She made me feel special and welcomed right away, a rare experience for me. She asked me if I was going to register for drama class in the fall. Before that moment, I hadn't thought about it. But after the visit, I decided I would indeed like to have a class with Ms. B.

I was shocked that this teacher took such an interest in me. Little did I know, I was meeting not a teacher to whom I would grow close for the next four years, but a mentor who would also guide me to my place in high school and ultimately to my chosen career. I wasn't yet aware that several of the students rehearsing before me then would later become my friends.

When I began high school, I looked forward to drama class and knew it would be a part of my life for the next four years. There was a term for us: *drama fags*. But I didn't mind, as I found a place to belong and wasn't targeted by bullies. Every production we created brought in a packed house full of students and parents who seemed to enjoy our performances immensely.

Drama didn't usually attract the popular kids or the jocks, but the ones who were quiet loners, flamboyant, closeted gay teens, and the un-athletic. We seemed to be individuals who didn't quite fit in elsewhere. No one was turned away from Ms. B's class, and everyone had something to offer, including me. I knew I had found my group for the next four years. While they weren't exactly like me, I sensed that we definitely shared some commonalities. We didn't talk about whether we had been bullied in our past. It wasn't like that. It was more about the fact that this group accepted all who came to them. There was no popularity contest. There was no bullying in the group. You could be who you wanted to be as an actor and an individual.

I realized I had a gift for acting, having practiced for years being a chameleon. There was one particular girl in my class who was known as the high school gossip. In order to be her friend, I started gossiping too, and was often caught gossiping with her while the person we were talking about was right behind us. That was another lesson I would learn. Every time you gossip about someone, they seem to find out. I was behaving badly. But my automatic reaction was to do what it took to make friends. This was a habit I would learn to change with more conscious thinking, but then it was about being liked by all and changing to please others as needed.

My participation in Drama Club and the plays made four years of high school fly by. Ms. B took a liking to me, and I was able to work on every play we ever put on. Ms. B had a knack for treating fourteen to eighteen-year-olds like adults. Ms. B gave us opportunities to excel and encouragement to do more than we thought possible. I saw Ms. B work with kids who were shy and turn them into extroverts on stage. I saw her take the young man I was and make him forget about his days of being bullied for a while. She made me believe that I could be liked, that I could be successful, that I was talented, and that I could do anything I wanted in life. That is the magic of a mentor. She made me who I am through her teaching, and friendship.

At the age of fourteen I was building sets for *You Can't Take It With You*. Then at fifteen, I was starring in *The Wiz* as a character she allowed me to create from my imagination and write the script for. When I was seventeen, she asked me to be the assistant director for a show called *Mame*. I recall those days clearly, sitting next to Ms. B and learning about how to lead a team to success.

She taught me how to make people feel confident when they doubted themselves.

She taught me how to make people forget about bad times and escape into the fantasy of the acting world.

At the end of that production of *Mame,* Ms. B presented me with a silver cup inscribed with the words "My Right Hand". I have never received anything so meaningful as that cup and those words. Ms. B changed many lives during her tenure as a teacher. All can benefit from seeking a mentor, a special person who can guide and help them succeed.

Ms. B knew that I thought the world of her. She was rarely far from my thoughts when I needed a good pick-me-up. In 2008, long after my four years of high school were over, I received the news that Ms. B had died. Even though I hadn't seen Ms. B in almost ten years, two days before her passing I was talking to my mother about wanting to visit her. Ms. B had developed dementia and was in a nursing home when she passed. My mom called me to tell me she saw the obituary about Ms. B in the paper.

At my workplace today, I continue to display and cherish the varnished silver cup that says "My Right Hand – 1986" on it. It was so special, and Ms. B was so special to me that I still keep that memento near to me, and I would protect it with my life.

During my freshman year of high school, my sister drove me to school, since she was a senior. I couldn't imagine taking the bus anymore, as I feared bullying from my former neighborhood friends. Driving to school, for me, felt safer. Once my sister graduated, I was grateful that Bill, one of my best friends whom I'd met through drama, took over driving me to school. He would pull up to my house every morning in a bright orange Volkswagen Karmann Ghia. The doors no longer opened, so we had to get in and out of the car through the windows. We thought we were so cool in that car. Bill worked behind the scenes for the drama productions and through our long hours of rehearsal, we became good friends.

Bill had a heart of gold but a slightly pessimistic attitude. I took his lead and complained about people, school, and whatever else Bill wanted to complain about to placate him. It was and still is his way. Despite his tendency to complain, I considered Bill a friend and confidant, and appreciated the reciprocal friendship we had that made us always available to each other. I accepted him for his strengths and vulnerabilities as he did me. He was both trustworthy and caring and had his own family struggles with a brother who had a drug problem. I wondered if his pessimism and complaining was about how unsafe he felt in the world and if that feeling had been brought on by his brother's problem. Maybe that is why we got along so well.

Then there was Eddie, the goofy and funny friend who made sure everyone was having a good time, whatever we were doing. Eddie was very religious, and his faith brought to him the belief that life is good and God is good. He had what I didn't have, faith that no matter what happened, God would have your back.

I'd certainly had years where I had a great faith in God that he would take care of me, no matter what. But back in Lexington, I had begun to lose that faith and started to question why no one, not even God, had my back anymore. Why would he allow me to experience such abuse?

◊ ◊ ◊

I would soon meet my best friend in the world, a person who would remain my friend through the present day. I met Terry during my sophomore year of high school in geometry class. He was a funny guy, joking around and falling asleep in class to the chagrin of our teachers. My friendship with Terry is the story of how a single friend can lift you up out of the darkness from the depths of despair. It seemed like the torture and cruelty of bullying would haunt me forever. When you are young, that's the way it feels. Time passes so much more slowly. If you have a relatively happy childhood, this is a great thing. When you are in the midst of being bullied every day, starting a new day can be extremely challenging and even undesirable and for some unbearable. Studies show that approximately 160,000 kids stay home every day from school due to bullying.* It was three years after I moved away from Lexington and the bullying that I met a friend who helped me realize that the painful days were behind me and more encouraging days were ahead. I had to be patient and wait, but it did happen.

Terry and I didn't start as good friends, but acquaintances who saw each other only in class. We connected with different groups of friends. Outside of drama, I had very little involvement in other school activities. Terry changed all of that.

He dragged me to our high school football games. Terry was the guy who painted himself in school colors and cheered loudly. Sometime during my senior year of high school, I realized he had become my best friend. It was ironic to me to see a large photograph of us in the homecoming page of our senior yearbook, because it was hard for me to believe that life could feel so awful at one point and completely different at another point.

The reality that Terry and I wouldn't attend the same college and see each other as much after high school graduation hit me hard. Although Terry and I attended different colleges our first year, he planned to transfer to my college in our second year and even ended up living with me once we were attending the same school. Our friendship continued to grow while we lived together. He became the brother I never had.

I often reflect on how fortunate I am to have Terry in my life. Having this light in my life could only have happened after working through the darkness of my bullying experiences. What if I had given up on believing it could get better? I know Terry wouldn't believe this, but in some ways, he saved my life by showing me that a friend can be trusted and loyal for an extended period of time.

I remained friends with Hannah as well, the first girl I asked out, and we both participated in drama class together for all four years of high school. I always felt close to Hannah and eventually did take her to a dance, but we never really *dated*. In fact I would say that Hannah and I had reached a point in our relationship where we feared dating might ruin the friendship we had.

We comforted each other when other dating relationships ended. In fact, her entire family embraced me as if I was their kin, and I would turn to them for advice and support during my high school years. But, the one subject that I never talked about with them was my bullying experience. By this point in my life, I had almost forgotten those years and the suffering I had endured.

Forget Lexington!

I had also met and started dating a girl named Rebecca from my drama group, who was one year behind me in school. She was in drama class with me, and I thought she was the sweetest girl in the group. When I found out she liked me, I was on cloud nine. We dated for six months before high school ended for me, even attempting to continue the relationship while I was away at college. But a strange thing happened. The closer we became, the more frightened I became. Looking back, I realize my low self-worth could not tolerate this happiness. Perhaps I didn't feel I deserved it, even though I believed that I had let go of the past. I would wonder later if I sabotaged the relationship and hurt her so that she wouldn't hurt me first. I wish I could have told her of the damage that was done to me and the way that I reacted when anyone liked me. I went into fight or flight mode (obviously flight!) to seek the safety of the familiar when in a panic. To run and hide was the easiest and most natural thing I could do.

Growing up is hard and for some reason, it's really challenging during high school years. When I arrived home from school, I felt the need to strip off my fake chameleon personality and show my family my true self, the unhappy one who was angry at the world over what had happened to me.

Forget Lexington!

I often yelled at my parents and took out my frustrations on them. For many of us who are frustrated with ourselves, we end up hurting the ones we love. This is likely because we trust that they won't leave us. I would find out later that it is a psychological term called displaced aggression. That term means that you are incapable of taking out your anger on who you really want to, so you take it out on someone either weaker or who won't leave you, like family. I'm sure that's where the saying *you always hurt the ones you love* comes from. It's not that my family life was bad, but I was an angry young man and didn't know how to express my feelings very well. After all, nobody really taught me how to deal with these frustrated feelings, and there was little belief at the time that bullying could lead to any kind of mental disorder, like C-PTSD. It's normal for families to have ups and downs as we grow up; however, I felt an additional challenge, based on my past bullying experiences. I didn't feel able to share the true depth of my anxiety and frustration. My sister had left for college, and as much as I loved my mom and dad, I felt more and more alienated from them and spent the majority of my time with friends.

CHAPTER EIGHT

Gaining a
Life Lesson

I realized I needed more than one box of memories, because the box of bad memories I had left in the hole in the Lexington kept trying to speak to me. Now that the shoebox was exposed, those memories would still scream to me to listen to them. I found another shoebox and put my good memories in there and put it under my bed. I had hoped with my good memories closer, it would speak to me louder than the shoebox of bad memories that I left so far away. It worked for a time, where I could hear the good memories speak to me under my bed while I slept. "The past is behind you, Alan. You are strong and confident. Keep moving forward," they would speak to me. But every so often, I would again have a nightmare about the hole in the field in Lexington where the shoebox of bad memories was now exposed, with no cover on the hole. Over time, the cardboard shoebox would soften from the rain, which made it easier for the bad memories to escape.

◊ ◊ ◊

As the summer approached and I prepared to transition from high school to college, I had some of the more interesting experiences of my young life. First was the graduation tradition we called "beach week" in Ocean City, Maryland. It was a rite of passage for Northern Virginia youth at the end of high school. I had a friend whose parents owned a one room condo in Ocean City. They let my friend use it for the week. I don't think they realized that he would invite twenty of us to stay there as well.

One of the girls who was staying there, named Melissa, was a girl who I'd had a crush on for some time in high school, but I always figured that she wouldn't date someone like me. I had told my friends that I was nervous about her being there because I'd had a crush on her for so long. Of course when they told her that, the same old problems reared their heads.

When Melissa found out that I had a crush on her, she decided to act on it. We were on the beach one day, and she told me that my friends told her I liked her. I was still dating Rebecca, but I was fixated on the fact that Melissa liked and wanted me, and that night Melissa and I slept together. I wish I could say I felt guilty, but I yearned to be needed and didn't think about those I would hurt.

Of course, irony would play its part in this as well. Melissa was only using me, not realizing how much that would hurt me. The next morning, she acted as if nothing had happened and then went on to find another boy to be with. I felt cheated (even though I had done the cheating), taken advantage of, and even rejected. It really hurt me, because I had spent all that time wanting her to like me in high school, but I also realized that I had hurt my relationship with Rebecca. I didn't feel very good about myself at that moment.

When we returned from the trip, I shared with my friends how upset I was about what had happened. Melissa heard that I'd told the story of what had happened between us and was furious, which put a rift in my friendships with this group. To this day, when I see them on Facebook and at reunions, the relationship is strained. I learned a valuable lesson, best summed up in this quote.

"A mountain is composed of tiny grains of earth. The ocean is made up of tiny drops of water. Even so, life is but an endless series of little details, actions, speeches, and thoughts. And the consequences whether good or bad of even the least of them are far-reaching."

~Swami Sivanand~

Of course my selfish demeanor and continued low self-worth never took into consideration Rebecca or playing it safe; I chose not to share it with her. I was off to college anyway in a few months.

◊ ◊ ◊

The summer still had one lesson to teach me. I had no job lined up between summer and the first day of college at Virginia Tech. One of my high school acquaintances, Karl, was going to be a counselor at a camp and asked me if I wanted to do that, too. Having no money, I of course said yes.

Karl failed to tell me that it was a camp for children with disabilities. He also failed to say that we were supposed to be twenty-one to work there, so we never mentioned our age on any forms or to anyone.

When we arrived, the first week was a total immersion program into learning sign language and how to care for children with spina bifida, muscular dystrophy, cerebral palsy, and traumatic brain injury. The counselors were from all over the world, and we bonded during that week. I was put into a bunk house with two other counselors who were both very nice and taught me how to work with the children.

The first group of children we encountered were ten-year-olds and were a terrific bunch of children. We did have one child, though, who was deaf and refused to use sign language because he was homesick. Unfortunately we had to send him home. We had several other children with either muscular dystrophy or cerebral palsy as well. All of them had a great disposition and were so different than the kids I knew when I was ten.

Forget Lexington!

We had another child named Johnny who was hit by a car at four years of age and had a traumatic brain injury. When Johnny arrived at camp, he had impaired speech and could not walk. We were told eventually he would fully recover, but it would take years. While we worked with him that summer, we watched Johnny as he took his first steps out of his wheelchair. Upon his parents' arrival, Johnny surprised them by lifting himself out of the wheelchair and taking a few steps to hug them. There wasn't a dry eye among the witnesses of that moment. It renewed my spirit and gave me a better understanding of life.

Sometimes, when I am feeling particularly sorry for myself, I think back to when I was eighteen and remind myself of the gift that working with these children gave me. When you need to appreciate the life you have, imagine the struggles of people less fortunate than you. You'll notice that it gives you a perspective about your own struggles at that moment and how what you might be going through is not nearly as hard as what some others are. This helps you to appreciate the life you do have, even with your troubles. I find it to be therapeutic to work with others who need my help. For me it was inspiring to spend time with children who weren't limited by *I can't*, and who were encouraged to believe *I can*.

One young lady named Patty, who was about thirteen and had severe cerebral palsy, truly impressed me. She had no control of her muscles and was non-verbal. Many assumed that because of these limitations Patty also had an intellectual disability. With Patty, nothing could be further from the truth.

Because this happened before personal computers were readily available, Patty had a cardboard pad called a communication board with letters on it. With great concentration, she could point to a letter and start to form a word. A typical five-minute conversation would take her thirty minutes. Consequently, few counselors had the time. But there was a spark in Patty that I saw when I met her. During our activity time, I sat with Patty while she conversed with me on her communication board. She knew everything going on with everyone at the camp and had a great sense of humor. Of course, many would see none of this. But we connected through the communication board, often having a good laugh. She would even laugh in her own way, which I learned to recognize.

I often wonder what she does now. Is she in a group home where she is cared for? Do her parents still care for her? Does she try to write like Stephen Hawkings? I can't get the answers to these questions, but I know that I learned a great deal from her about the strength of the soul that we each carry. Imagine trading places with her and how you would handle it. Life does deal us bad hands in some cases, but learning to play with the hand you've been dealt is a skill that makes all the difference.

◇ ◇ ◇

I found myself in a familiar situation, as some of the female counselors indicated their interest in me. Feeling desperate to be needed and wanted, I took several opportunities to soak up the attention without considering the consequences. I did realize I made primarily emotional decisions versus more logical, rational ones, but this is the way I still coped with my past.

Forget Lexington!

I can't regret any decision I made as a young man as it was all part of growing up. But Rebecca was still waiting for me at home. In fact, her family was vacationing close to the camp, and one day, while I was working at the camp, Rebecca called me. She told me they would be driving by the camp, and she wanted to see me for an hour. I stood stunned, knowing that I had cheated, and that the other female counselors would see her with me. I felt like a jerk, a loser, and a louse.

Rebecca arrived very excited to see me. We hugged and kissed and had lunch together. I could feel the steely gazes on my neck and felt guilt welling up inside me. Rebecca's family wanted to get back on the road, so we said goodbye after an hour. There were tears in Rebecca's eyes.

What have I done? I thought to myself. *I hate myself. I'm a jerk and who wants to be with a jerk?*

I was too young to understand that people only learn from their mistakes and while I never wanted to intentionally hurt anyone, I still felt empty inside and, at this point, there was no satiating me. I didn't like myself, and when you don't like yourself, you can't give to others. I saw Rebecca when I got back home from camp and before I left for college. I promised her we were still together and we would work on the long-distance relationship. Of course I said I would always be faithful to her. However, I lied and had already broken that promise several times now. Inside, I was ripped apart, but I had yet to discover just how much.

I was totally co-dependent upon others. I allowed what others thought about me to affect me so much that I didn't know who I really was anymore or how to act like my authentic self. Inside, I loathed myself, but outside, I tried to be funny and adventurous and sometimes even self-confident. I hoped that the next four years at college would give me an opportunity to grow and gain self-awareness. At least I still had some hope.

CHAPTER NINE

Reaching for the Stars
While Gasping for Air

Life was going my way and I actually had to get extra shoeboxes to fill with my good memories. Of course, there were still the occasional bad memories, but I let them linger longer and didn't feel the need to bury them in a hole. My childhood was behind me, and I was bound and determined to have fun and look forward, not back at the past I'd buried. Once in a while I would hear a voice speaking from the shoebox trying to tell me something. "You're a thief, a cheater, a liar, and a loser!" But I learned not to listen, and with much practice, I was able to ignore the knocks on my mind's door. "Go away!" I screamed at these bad memories, and for the most part, they would...for a time.

When I started at Virginia Tech, I felt gloriously free. I looked forward to the adventure of college and knew that I wanted a career in broadcast media. I had known this since the end of high school when PBS came to film a show at school and included drama kids as extras. I enjoyed talking to the crew behind the cameras and knew that's what I wanted to do. It fascinated me, and I thought I could actually make a career out of it.

I lived in an all-male dorm my freshman year and knew a few high school friends who lived there too, including my roommate Dan and my friend Mark, who lived down the hall. Mark had been in the high school band and in college played in the orchestra during performances. I knew Mark as the preppy, sweater-wearing guy who was nice and friendly to me.

I visited Mark down the hall, knocked on his door, and what I saw was a whole different person. Mark had got a Mohawk haircut and was wearing jeans and a leather jacket. When he'd lived at home, Mark had seemed more reserved and conservative, but once he got to college he changed drastically. To say I was shocked would be an understatement. We chatted for a while about the old friends we knew and where they went to school. I didn't say anything to Mark about his change or why he chose to make this change. I knew it would be inappropriate to bring it up.

After chatting for a while, I went back to my dorm room and only saw Mark sporadically for the rest of our college years, and when I did, we engaged in only minor chit-chat. I don't even know if he graduated from Virginia Tech.

What I do know is that a few years after my graduation from college, I found out through a friend that Mark had died. He had been walking on train tracks and listening to music with headphones. His death was ruled an accident, and they chalked it up to the fact that he was listening to music and didn't know the train was coming.

Here's my problem with that story. I have also walked on train tracks when a train is coming. I know how they rumble long before the train arrives and how you know to get off several minutes before the train comes. I struggle to believe that Mark didn't know the train was coming, because of my own experience. I often wonder if he was troubled and why he'd decided to make such a radical change to himself after high school. I would've liked to know what Mark was experiencing that day I spoke with him in his dorm. I only wish I'd known him better.

◊ ◊ ◊

Early in my freshman year, I decided to write to my parents and tell them how I felt about leaving home to go to college. Knowing my mom was extremely sensitive, I knew that it was particularly hard on her to have an empty nest with my sister and me both gone. I wrote her a letter because I wanted to feel independent. She cherishes the letter to this day, but for many years, I hated what I wrote. It is only recently that I understand why she kept it. I wrote it to think I needed a clean break from my parents, but my mom knew what I wrote was my continued cry for loving attention. I can't figure out if I'm happy she kept it or embarrassed that I wrote it. In the letter, I wanted to thank them for their years of helping me grow up. I shared with them the following words from my eighteen-year-old self:

Mom and Dad:

Hello! I should probably be doing my homework (which I have mostly done), but instead I chose to write you (aren't you lucky). I couldn't even put into words how happy I am to be here. I'm sorry to say it, but I feel very little homesickness. But, I think I have been ready for college for quite some time now. I find that living on my own is what I have been looking for, for quite some time. The times I have shared with you in the past are times I have and will never forget. But, I have realized that, when I left the house that Saturday 2 weeks ago, it was the last time I would ever call that place my home.

Now, don't get me wrong! I'm not saying that I could never call that house home again, but now VA Tech and Vawter (my dorm) are my homes. This is where I live. This is where I shall grow up for the next couple of years. I realize now, though, how much I truly love you guys. Through the good times and the bad, I will always have memories of fights and love and us sharing things. Time and distance can never keep us too far apart.

I want to tell you now that, as parents, I wouldn't want them to come any better than you. No matter how much bullshit I said, you really know I never meant any of it. I do tend to say stupid things sometimes, but then, don't we all?

I've made some great friends here already. Of course, they are all from Northern Virginia. But, hell, half the people here are from Woodson (my high school). I feel so at home here. Like this is what I should have done from the start. I forget quite a lot about my friends in Northern Virginia. You were right, it is very easy to forget about those people. But I know that they will always be my friends if I want them to.

By the way, I saw Ed yesterday night. We talked for a long time, but he is a cadet, so I can't get to know him too well.

I wanted you to really know how happy I am here and that I do think about you. I love you two so much. I'll go do my homework now.

Your loving son,

Alan

It was hard for me to forgive myself for the way I'd treated my parents as a teenager. I was rebellious and got into trouble as a result of peer pressure. My low self-worth made it difficult to enjoy being around my family at times, as I took out my frustrations and irritability on them with my displaced aggression. This letter was my way of releasing the guilt I felt about my behavior. I blamed my past for it all.

Forget Lexington!

◊ ◊ ◊

I became great friends with my hall mates in college, and we hung out and talked music all the time. One late evening, there was a knock on my door and a very drunk guy walked in, asked me what I was doing in his bed, and then kicked me out of my own bed. His other drunken friend was yelling in the hall looking for him, so I called him over. The new drunk guy told the other one who was now in my bed to get out, because he no longer lived there. The first guy then remembered he lived off campus and got out of my bed. The other drunken guy apologized to us and then handed my roommate and me cards to get into a fraternity party.

His invite to that party would be the beginning of my fraternity experience. I joined this fraternity the following year with my friend Terry and some other people I had met. I had my *"Animal House"* dream, and it was good. But as I joined the fraternity, one of the things I dreadfully feared was hazing.

While I had become accustomed to being bullied as a way to ostracize me from my peers, hazing was a type of abuse that enabled me to be included in the group. Hazing is more ritualistic in that it tends to be an organized group activity creating experiences that humiliate and insult others to encourage their participation as a group member. Many of us believe that hazing is a part of fraternity life. It scared me and I almost backed out of pledging a fraternity several times due to this fear. When we made paddles as pledges, I wondered if they would be used on us. My fears were not realized, as we experienced no hazing in this fraternity.

Not everyone in the fraternity was nice. One person in particular, an older brother named Sean, a senior, seemed to enjoy bullying new members. Pledge brothers frequently hung out and socialized at the fraternity house. The house was open to all members at all times. In the basement was a bar area for conversation and socializing. Early during my pledge period at Theta Xi in my sophomore year of college, Terry and I arrived at the house and went downstairs to the bar in good spirits, enjoying this new home away from home.

Sean was at the bar. He was alone, drinking a beer and wearing a yellow construction hat. I hadn't talked to this particular person much before, but as Terry and I sat down, Sean stared at us. It was pretty uncomfortable. He antagonized us when we asked him why he was wearing the construction hat.

"You want to know about the hat?" Sean sneered at me.

"Yeah. Why are you wearing a construction hat?" I said.

"This is my *I hate people hat*," Sean snarled. "Wanna guess why I'm wearing it?"

This was getting pretty unpleasant. I didn't bother to ask him, but he was going to tell me anyway.

"When I'm wearing this hat, it means you should go away, because I'm not going to be responsible for what I do next. Got it?!" he threatened.

Sean looked as if he was going to get up, but instead we got up and left him to play king of the mountain at the bar and feel like he had won that battle. Sean appeared to be an angry person, preferring to sit alone and stew in whatever was bothering him. What he really managed to do was alienate new people. He used power and intimidation to keep others from getting close to him. When he wore that hat, everyone left him alone. I couldn't imagine someone not wanting others to like him, since I'd spent much of my energy trying to pull people in. He used his energy to push them away.

Bullies do not exclusively use physical violence. They can do plenty of damage through words that can ruin your reputation or sway others to believe that what they say is the truth. Sometimes this can be more damaging than bruises from the schoolyard. Sean at the fraternity was one of my first recollections of someone's using their reputation and words to hurt me. The increase in social media and cyberbullying in recent years illustrates how powerful an impact bullies can have, hiding behind a screen and doing damage that has even led to suicide.

During that first year of college, I tried to keep my promise to work at a long-distance relationship with Rebecca. As far as I knew, she was faithful to me and would visit me every few months during my first year. I admit to trying to be faithful and wanting to be, but yet again failing when someone of the opposite sex showed me the least bit of attention. Being in an all-male dorm helped minimize the temptation, but I still felt the desperation to be liked.

The fraternity and my second year at college put further strain on my relationship with Rebecca. I had tried to convince Rebecca to apply to Virginia Tech and join me, but her father, who was in the military, was being deployed, and she chose to relocate with her family to the Middle East. Eager to please when she prompted me, I agreed to remain faithful, although I was already living a double life. The first time I telephoned her overseas, I received a bill for thirty-six dollars for that one call. Now that might not seem like much, but to a poor college kid like me, it was significant. To save money, Rebecca and I decided we would occasionally mail cassette recorded tapes of ourselves talking to the other person. I was already moving on and assumed she was too, simply because she chose to travel overseas with her family instead of going to college with me. I assumed incorrectly.

Around the middle of my second year of college, I met Susan, a shy, pretty young woman who attended our fraternity parties. When I drank, I would let my guard down and be much less inhibited. She seemed to be attracted to this side of me. I devoured the attention, and for the next six months, Susan and I were inseparable. I truly believed I was in love with Susan—a love stronger than I had ever felt. During this time, Rebecca and I stopped communicating for several months. I kind of forgot about her as I found someone else to pay attention to me and assumed the same went for Rebecca, as her recordings would talk about her having a guy friend she hung out with. When I returned home that summer, Rebecca called me one day. She wanted to meet up to talk and I agreed.

We met at a restaurant, and Rebecca looked very happy to see me. I was excited as well but for different reasons. In my mind, this was a great opportunity to end the relationship, face to face. As Rebecca began to speak, I discovered how wrong I was. Clearly she was still committed to our relationship and even mentioned that she was considering applying to Virginia Tech for next year.

I told her about Susan, how I was in love with someone else. I went on and on about how great my life was at college and wasn't thinking about Rebecca's feelings at all. I give Rebecca credit as she maintained her composure, but I could see the damage was done. It was another mistake I was going to have to chalk up to learning. She quietly got up, hugged me, told me she hoped I was happy, and then left.

I watched her leave the restaurant, feeling that I was not a very nice guy. The familiar sense of self-loathing reared itself once again. The voices in my head spoke to me about the kind of person I was. This was still not who I wanted to be.

Later, I got a call from a mutual friend of Rebecca's and mine. He threatened me, telling me if I ever tried to contact her again, he would come take care of me. I felt a pang of regret for hurting another person, especially one who cared so much for me. I know that I was selfish and that my own self-worth was damaging my relationships, but I still felt there was no being satiated when it came to my need to feel wanted.

Karma always seemed to have a way of catching up with me as well. When I returned to Virginia Tech in the fall for my third year, Susan was behaving strangely towards me. I knew deep down what was going to happen but didn't want to face it. Susan told me she was too young to commit to me and wanted to see other men. I begged her to reconsider. I loved her. I stayed up all night calling her and sitting outside her dorm when she didn't return my calls. I cried and beat myself up a lot that night. When she finally responded to me, she told me that she was with one of my fraternity brothers that night. I felt heartbreak for the first time. I suppose I got what I deserved, and I learned something about myself. I can experience love, which can be both a great joy and also quite painful.

◇ ◇ ◇

To distract myself from the pain of my breakup, I focused more on my other passion in college, broadcast television. In the beginning of my junior year of college, several students and I established a new cable television station on campus called VTTV. It started as a class project the previous year and eventually became a student operated station. When elections were held for this newly established organization, my peers chose me to be the first General Manager of VTTV.

While I was flattered to be elected, I was terrified deep down of having this responsibility. But the part of me that was eager to please, accepted this proud honor to be head of the organization. It reminded me of earlier days when I was *king of the mountain*. Even so, I had my doubts about my ability to manage that role. With this newfound responsibility, I would discover that managing conflict is a key part of being a leader, and I had never learned how to handle conflict well. This was a problem I had been dealing with most of my teen and adult life. My trust and faith in the goodness of people had slowly slipped away during my youth. I could only see conflict as threatening and unsafe. If you had a conflict with me, I would react with fight or flight (or *freeze*). I had the option to fight back, run away, or do nothing and freeze. I called this feeling that I had the *perceived threat syndrome*, because there was this part of me that believed any threat, physical or emotional, was dangerous and required immediate action. Yet, emotional threats are not dangerous or a threat to one's survival. But during my early childhood years, I became conditioned to react to them as if they were indeed dangerous. It is not the most effective way to deal with conflict, but it was the only way I knew to stay safe. The cost of poor conflict resolution skills would be the loss of friendships and a professor's trust.

I had a very good friend at VTTV named Chet, and he would be my second in command at the TV station. Chet and I shared our love of comic books and the way we could lose ourselves in them to escape our lives for some time. I sensed that Chet had some demons in his past as well. I would find out many years later that Chet had dealt with abuse at home by his step-father. He no longer talks to his family, which I always found sad, as I had such a good relationship with mine. I often wondered if Chet might be gay, as he showed no interest in dating women and would comment about my looks, which was a bit uncomfortable, yet validating as well.

The VTTV group was generally a fun group to be a part of. But there was one particular woman named Nancy whose strong personality and confidence intimidated me. To be honest, these kinds of people scared me in general as they shared traits with many bullies from my past.

Forget Lexington!

Imagine my surprise when this self-assured, confident woman showed an interest in dating me, so we began a relationship, as I still liked the feeling of being needed. Nancy was a year older than me and graduated the same year we started dating. She was into radio and decided to start her career in Washington, D.C., near where my parents lived. A part of me enjoyed the attention Nancy paid me, but another part of me was not interested in being with her. The desperately needy part of me was not willing to give up someone who cared about me so much. So when Nancy graduated, she asked me if I thought she could live with my parents temporarily while she saved up for her own place. When my parents obliged, I realized the trap I'd set for myself.

Nancy now lived in my home, and as soon as I returned to college my senior year, I knew I didn't want to continue the relationship with her. But every time I tried to break up with her, I was distracted by her ability to make me feel worthier when I was with her. When I returned home for winter break, Nancy had hinted that she wanted more permanency to our relationship. I thought myself truly unlovable, especially after what had happened with Susan the year before and my issues of low self-esteem. I actually justified my next action by thinking *she might be the last woman to love me.* With this thinking in mind, I bought her a ring and asked her to marry me.

Instead of breaking up with her, when I returned for winter break, I proposed to her. Of course, Nancy said yes. I was in such a rush to be loved forever and really didn't trust that anyone else would love me. My self-worth was based on Nancy's perceptions of me. The minute I slipped the ring on her finger, a part of me I knew I didn't want this.

When I returned to college to finish my final semester, I spent much of the time trying to figure out how to get out of what I'd gotten myself into. *How did this happen?* I asked myself. I thought about various ways I could call off the engagement, but Nancy was living in my home now, and I felt stuck and very alone. I believed this was the life I deserved, nothing better. Then, Nancy told me she got a new job in Atlanta, Georgia, and that we would be moving there. I had never been to Georgia, but she rented an apartment for us, and she logically expected me to relocate there following graduation.

I felt a complete loss of control over my life. This was about the time I experienced the first panic attack that I would have in my adult life during that infamous psychology final. College was ending. I was engaged to someone I didn't want to be with. I did not have a job. I was moving to a strange place. I was leaving the comfort of Virginia Tech, my fraternity brothers, and VTTV friends. I didn't know what would happen next, and this made me quite anxious. I felt inadequately prepared to manage all these transitions in my life and express my true desires. I got through my final exams and arrived at graduation.

The convocation was delivered by a graduate of the broadcast communication department. She told us that most of us would never work in the field that we'd studied for four years, and that Sears or Walmart were hiring. I don't know if she was trying to be funny, but at that moment I said to myself that, come hell or high water, I would always work in my field of study. Her speech was a disappointment, and it hurt to hear these words from her. To me, it felt like a form of verbal bullying to our whole group.

After graduation, my parents helped me move my belongings to Atlanta. We arrived at the apartment Nancy had leased for us, and my parents, God love them, were saints, said goodbye, and went on their way. I know they knew I was unhappy, but they let me make my own mistakes, which allowed me to feel more like an adult. I appreciate that my parents supported me, no matter what. But there I was, panicky, miserable, and alone with Nancy, the only person I knew in a strange place. I looked for a job in my career field and did get one. I worked at Blockbuster Video for minimum wage. I was truly miserable inside and felt worthless, but tried hard not to show it.

My friend, Terry, and I had discussed plans for backpacking across Europe immediately following graduation before settling down with jobs. I thought, *when will I ever have a chance like this again?* But Nancy didn't like the idea of me going, and I felt like I had to do what would make her happy. After all, we had plans to marry after moving to Georgia. I shared my disappointment with Terry, and he went on the trip without me. It is difficult not to regret the choices I made, the adventures I missed out on, and the emotional pain that followed.

After a month of living with Nancy, a part of me mustered enough strength to assert my feelings of dissatisfaction and unhappiness in the relationship. Now that I knew I wanted to speak up, I had no idea how. I had no skills in conflict resolution. As the anxiety of my situation grew inside of me, my instinctive fight or flight kicked in. I instigated an argument that escalated to the point where Nancy finally told me to leave. It was an ugly ending and one I did not handle well. At one point during the argument, I felt so victimized that I reached for a knife from the counter.

Why would I do this? I wouldn't hurt Nancy. But I was angry and scared and feeling out of control. I saw Nancy's face when I reached for this knife as some sort of protection. *Why did this feel like a familiar reaction for me? Why did I perceive Nancy as a threat?* I put the knife down, not knowing what had possessed me to pick it up in the first place. In the back of my mind, there was a memory of a weapon, but at the time I couldn't place why. I couldn't remember ever wanting to use a weapon like that. I couldn't remember what would lead me to such behavior. But it did move the issue forward, with Nancy's kicking me out of the apartment and my leaving and heading back to my parents' home in Northern Virginia.

Even though I ultimately got what I wanted, I seriously hurt Nancy in the process. I had no skill at being able to say no or part ways maturely. Part of me felt so cruel, and another part felt incredible relief. This was very confusing.

CHAPTER TEN

Every Experience
Offers a Lesson

The shoebox full of bad childhood memories had softened from the exposed weathering after the plywood top disintegrated, and those bad thoughts were leaking into my consciousness. I still worked to hide them, but they were coming back, little by little, and affecting my personality in ways I didn't understand. "You are a pathetic twerp!" they would say. "Why would anyone like you? You are a loser, remember?" my thoughts would whisper to me. I was angry and I didn't know why. I was feeling like I needed to be perfect. I was distrusting of others. "This isn't the new me!" I thought. "Why am I letting these memories back into my life?" I thought I had left them behind. I thought they couldn't affect me any longer as long as I made the hole and buried them. I was wrong and would soon learn that was not the way that life worked and that my attempt to hide memories in a hole as a child might have long-term ramifications as an adult.

◊ ◊ ◊

I returned to my parents' home near Washington, D.C., feeling defeated. My mom asked me what was wrong because I was so bitter and angry about so many things. I didn't have an answer. I mostly stayed alone in my room or found other distractions, anything to avoid thinking about my situation.

Job hunting served as a decent distraction. I had my first interview at a small video studio down the street from me. Boy, was I excited as this was the exact kind of job I wanted! In fact, I bought a new suit so I could look sharp and professional for the interview. The day of the interview, I was pretty confident. I had done my research, learning about the small video production studio with a minimal staff. It reminded me of my summer and college experiences working in small video production studios. Eager for the interview, I arrived a few minutes early.

The studio occupied a small space in a plain-looking, multi-floor building. When I arrived, there was no receptionist. I was to meet the general manager of the studio. Someone came out to tell me to take a seat and that the general manager would be with me shortly. My interview was at 2:00pm, and I sat down to wait at about 1:50pm.

Tick-tock…2:00pm…tick-tock…2:15pm…tick-tock…2:30pm… tick-tock…2:45pm…tick-tock….3pm.

I waited and waited. No one came out to see that I was still waiting or to tell me when I would be seen. Since it was my first interview, I didn't want to make a scene, so I sat there, unsure about the best protocol in this situation. About an hour after our scheduled appointment, the general manager finally came out. No apology, just a wave to come back to his office.

He sat behind his desk. I sat in a chair facing his desk. He was all smiles. He was looking at my resume and asked me to discuss my experience with him. I told him about my summer work at a production studio and my experience at college with the student station. I began to share with him what I was looking for in a position.

"Hold it there…" he interrupted me. Then he said something that I will never forget.

"Let me tell you something about working in this field, because you don't know anything about working in this field. You college kids think you've learned something. You put together this resume that says you have experience. You don't have anything. You don't know anything. You don't even belong at this interview. If you want to work here, what you need to do is go work for free for a few years in New York or Los Angeles. Be a gopher and get coffee while learning this business. Then, maybe you can come back here and interview with me."

It felt like a fist hit me in the face, no different than being bullied. I think I was in shock for a minute. I felt my now familiar panic and anxiety, while my face turned flushed. I turned and left, never looking back, still shocked and amazed. What a bully this guy was. Did he call me for the interview, knowing I had limited experience, only to shame me for applying? Did he plan to leave me waiting for an hour in the lobby with little respect for my time? There are more professional, kinder ways to provide feedback to a prospective employee. Somehow though, this motivated me to try harder to succeed. Part of me was used to this mistreatment, but another part of me was stronger now and not willing to be defeated by his bad behavior. I would later learn that there is a form of bullying called "workplace bullying" and that it was more common than I had even known. As I began my website of tales of bullying, so many people shared their experiences of being bullied in the workplace. It was another form of bullying that adults experience.

I thought back on this sometime later and recalled something I heard an industry leader, Dick Clark, say in an interview. He told a story about a time early in his career when many people would not give him a job and were cruel, slamming doors in his face. He created a list of all these people. When he became successful, he taped that list to his desk. People on that list who didn't give him a chance would eventually seek work with the now successful Dick Clark. Dick Clark refused to meet with or do business with any of them. The lesson: Do not abuse your position of power, as it can change at any moment. You never know when the roles may shift and you may need the help from someone who you turned away when they needed you.

I did eventually find a job and began working for a small cable television station that showed all old movies and television shows. I was making commercials and producing shows, which was exactly what I wanted to do in my early career.

It worked well for me to move in with my sister who had an apartment closer to where I worked. One night, one of my former fraternity brothers, Jim, called to say his girlfriend and he would be in the area, and asked if I wanted to meet them at a bar. He told me that one of his girlfriend's former college roommates would be there, too. I remember that night vividly because initially I had plans to meet another friend to catch a movie about the band The Doors and then meet Jim at the bar.

When I arrived at the bar, I saw Jim, his girlfriend, Becca, and a beautiful woman with them. We went through the usual introductions, where I learned that the woman with them was Becca's old college roommate, Janet. Awkwardly, I used one of the worst opening lines in history. I asked Janet what she did for a living. She politely answered, and I could immediately tell that Janet was both shy and fairly quiet. But the more we drank, the more I got to know her. I was actually smitten with Janet and her shy personality.

Janet and I began dating. She was so different from the other women I had dated. I was never sure how much she liked me, as she was more reserved about her feelings. She finally told me she loved me when I was cleaning out the back of her car after her friend Becca had thrown up. It was a boost to my self-worth to hear her say that as I was doing her this favor of cleaning the car. I knew I loved her too, because she made me feel good about myself. Janet had been married previously for a brief period. Somehow that made me feel like she knew what she wanted, so it made me feel more secure about the relationship and myself. I felt that Janet knew what I was in my soul, and I trusted her to be able to know things about me that I hadn't shared with others at the time.

But I still felt like I could lose her at any second because, well let's face it, who really liked me? I didn't even like myself that much at the time but kept my happy face on. Three months into our relationship, I asked her to marry me. It's hard to believe I was ready to propose marriage after three months, but she said yes. We actually spent the next year and a half planning the wedding. This time I wanted the wedding, and I wanted to make my relationship with Janet work forever. I decided then and there that I would give all I could to Janet and believed that love could be real, not just fleeting.

Our wedding was a lovely occasion and a very happy time in my life. It was all I had hoped it would be. Our early life together was quite positive. The only problems I seemed to have were the occasional panic attacks at stressful moments such as job interviews and a bit of claustrophobia and anxiety when on a plane or a train. I didn't think much of these issues at the time. I pushed my displaced anger about my youth deep down, but when feeling *unsafe*, reacted in my *perceived threat syndrome*. Janet would learn I was highly reactive, easily stressed or panicked, and easily angered, although never violent to her or anyone else. These all were foreshadowing what was to come. But, for many years, these were infrequent and low on my scale of life problems.

Early in my career, I wanted to gain more real experience, and I found much enjoyment in directing a local cable television show called *Krazy Greg's TV Platter Party*. Krazy Greg lived the fifties lifestyle and had Dick Clark as his hero. For a while, I thought Greg was putting on the Krazy Greg character, but I was wrong. He lived that way every day. I know that Krazy Greg had a difficult and somewhat abusive childhood, too and suspect he may have created the Krazy Greg persona as a coping mechanism. Janet's cousins were really into the fifties, so they actually danced on his show and that made it a more bonding experience for Janet and me. Then one day a few years after I started working on the show, the producer called me. Krazy Greg had committed suicide, and he asked if I could meet him at Krazy Greg's house.

I drove to Krazy Greg's house in a state of shock. His mom was wandering around in a funk. Krazy Greg had shot himself in the head in the van that he carried his production gear in. The mortician had already removed his body, but no one had cleaned out the van. His mom asked us if we would do it. Cleaning up after a suicide is gruesome. It pained me to learn that Greg was in quite a bit of emotional pain and probably depressed. He made what he must have felt was the only choice, and it was the first time I realized how fragile life was. Greg's suicide was now the third death of a friend I had to deal with, along with the death of my friends, Chris McCandless and Mike. I didn't quite know how to make sense of these young lives lost.

In addition to these friends' deaths, one of Janet's college friends, Stephanie, who we frequently spent time with, had a terrible tragedy not long after Greg's death. Her oldest son, Zach, who was nine years old, was hit by a car while riding his bike. We found out he died by reading it in the newspaper. There was no comforting Stephanie after this loss. No mother should lose a child, and, while she had four other children, the devastation of a young child's loss is nearly impossible to recover fully from. Even for me, seeing her child in the small casket put me into a funk for quite a while. In his memory, Janet and I chose to name our younger son, Zach.

Janet and I raised two wonderful sons, born four years apart. We were able to move from a townhome to a single family home and increased our standard of living as we developed successful careers. We enjoyed an active lifestyle, being involved with our sons' activities including sports, boy scouts, and Jewish education.

◊ ◊ ◊

About ten years into my career, I switched from broadcast video to a career in this newfangled thing called the internet. I believed that internet video and training with multimedia eLearning was going to be big. One day, fraternity alumni requested that one of my fraternity brothers, Fred, and I create a video and multimedia presentation for one of our alumni reunions.

Fred and I worked well together. He and his wife owned their own small video and multimedia creation company. After we worked together on the reunion project, he asked me to work for him in the multimedia area of their company. Without hesitation, I said yes. I hadn't yet thought about what could happen when you work for friends and how my past youth experiences might affect this decision.

For nine years, we worked well together and the company was financially successful. I was promoted from a multimedia producer to the Chief Operations Officer of the company, although I wasn't sure I was competent enough for the position. I loved the job and I loved working for my friend. I was naively committed to this being the last job I would ever have. As much as I enjoyed the job, though, I struggled with the leadership role. I found it challenging to supervise and discipline subordinates because I wanted everyone to like me. Fred noticed this, as did his wife, who co-owned the company with Fred. It was commented on in my evaluations at times. But I truly felt like I had *made it* in my career and had a career surrounded by friends that I would work for and with for a very long time.

At one point while working for Fred, I had an opportunity to travel for business for two weeks to Bangkok, Thailand. I certainly was not a worldly traveler and was quite nervous about going halfway around the world, but knew that I would regret not taking the opportunity. The trip was to webcast the international AIDS conference. I would have an opportunity to see and hear people like Nelson Mandela and Richard Gere. It was quite an exciting opportunity and one that I knew might not come again.

I purchased some books and tried to learn as much Thai language and culture as I could. But no book could prepare me for the culture shock of seeing the Buddhist culture of Thailand, a culture and philosophy so different from the western cultures of Judaism and Christianity that I knew about.

Bangkok was a city as busy as New York City in the United States, yet no one was blasting their horns at each other. There were Buddhist shrines on almost every corner, where people would light incense and candles. The kindness of the Thai people was another culture shock for me. I wondered when I would be taken advantage of as a tourist or mugged because the people were so kind and helpful, but nothing happened. It was just the way of the culture and the philosophy of the Buddhist people.

In many ways, during those two weeks I felt a strong kinship to the philosophy of Buddhism. I wasn't aware at the time how much it would affect me later though. I knew that the kindness shown and the peacefulness of the culture were attractive to me. I learned at one specific moment how much different the American and Thai cultures were.

My travelling companions included a New York City videographer named Paul and his wife. Paul was a kind man in his early fifties, but had that rough New Yorker attitude that said *don't mess with me*. The AIDS conference was at a large convention center, and at the end of it, we were packing up all our video gear as the Thai workers took down the temporary walls that were our workspace.

At one point, one of the Thai workers was taking a piece of metal off one of the walls in the area we were packing up in and it fell on Paul's head. I am sure that it hurt Paul, and he screamed out at first in pain and then in a string of expletives at the Thai worker who had dropped the metal. Paul started after the Thai worker and was very upset, acting like he was looking to challenge the Thai worker to a fight or possibly take a swing at him.

It was at this point that I saw the strangest and most unexpected action from this Thai Buddhist culture. Unlike what my expectations had taught me about situations like this in the Western world, where it would either be a fight or the Thai man would run as fast as he could to get away, the Thai man who dropped the metal bowed his head down. As Paul kept up his rant, wanting to goad the Thai man into a confrontation, a large group of Thai security guards came over. The man who had dropped the metal on Paul started to back away as this group of Thai security guards made a tight circle around Paul. The security guards were shoulder to shoulder, refusing to allow Paul out of the circle they had formed around him. Then the security guards bowed their heads down as Paul turned his attention to them. Each time Paul tried to break out of the circle, the guards, with heads still down, would hold hands together and prevent him from breaking their circle. Paul continued to yell at the guards, but they stayed in their circle with their heads bowed down.

Eventually, Paul realized that nothing was going to change for him, and he quieted down and relaxed. As soon as the guards saw he was done with his anger and ranting, they broke apart and left. The worker who had dropped the metal was nowhere to be seen.

I had never witnessed the beauty of peaceful, non-confrontational solutions to an angry person. I was both in awe and amazed at this aspect of the Thai culture and Buddhist philosophy. I know that there are always exceptions in every culture, but in my two weeks in Thailand, I only witnessed kind, helpful, generous, and gracious people. I realized that the world isn't full of hatred and that some cultures try to cultivate peace as a way of life.

I visited the Thai Grand Palace on my last day in Thailand. It was a beautiful, golden, ornamental palace with great Buddhist statuary showing their reverence. On my way out of the palace, I picked up a couple of miniature statues to remember their culture and philosophy and what I liked about it. I learned much on that trip to Thailand, but for me, one of the biggest lessons was that I could live a more peaceful life by learning about how this culture found a way to handle situations in a more quiet and dignified way. In many ways, when my plane took off, I realized I would miss Thailand and the people who showed me what peaceful living and mindfulness look like. I wish I'd had the wisdom to remember what I had learned there before I needed it in my own life.

CHAPTER ELEVEN

Carrying the Weight
Of the World

The shoebox of bad memories had worn down over time and the lid was now wet with precipitation and a rip in the cardboard formed at the top of the shoebox from the softening. From this new rip, bad memories were able to escape and return to my conscious memory. It was like being slammed to the ground as their grip on me tightened, like that of a snake wrapped around my arm. They spoke to me, the stories of my youth, ridiculed me as a worthless being but begged me to let them back in. I felt like enough time had gone by that I might be OK to let them back in. It was in the past now. So I let them in, thinking I was prepared to face these memories of pain. I would find out that I was far from prepared and that my child brain could overpower my adult brain, with the result being a return to my past and my feelings of inadequacy. I was now going to remember what I'd tried to forget.

◊ ◊ ◊

There were a few triggers in my life that started me spiraling down the hole that I had built for myself. In the back of my mind, I was still blocking my youth in Lexington, not yet willing to confront it. I still blamed much of my negative behavior on a youth full of being bullied.

The first trigger I recalled was when two teenagers, Dylan Klebold and Eric Harris, went into their high school in Columbine, Colorado, and killed thirteen people, twelve students and one teacher, and injured twenty-one more before killing themselves. There was no definitive conclusion that bullying had anything to do with what Klebold and Harris did, but it brought back for me some of the feelings of needing revenge that I experienced as a young teen.

The second trigger was the shooting at my Alma Mater, Virginia Tech, where a student named Seung-Hui Cho went into one of the buildings and killed thirty-two people, wounded seventeen more and then committed suicide. Cho was diagnosed with severe anxiety disorder and was known to be bullied in his high school days and made fun of for his shyness.

These incidents both upset me greatly and made me want to take action to try to help change the future behavior in the area of bullying. I decided that I would create my website on a familiar subject for me: *"Bullying Stories: Dealing with the Long-term Effects of Bullying"*. It was this website where I hoped that releasing all my own bullying stories and letting others know that adults are still affected by bullying would help.

A part of me had come to terms with the bullying in my youth, but only that it was negatively affecting me. There was another part of my mind that was still burying these memories away, not wanting to remember the pain. But once I opened the memories back up, it was like opening Pandora's Box. The memories flooded into my consciousness, some taking control of how I felt. I wanted so badly to do some good by sharing my own experience, and the thought of helping others made me feel good. So I started writing on my site, and other people added their own stories.

Then I took another risk after all my stories were out. One of my high school drama friends had become the new drama teacher at my old high school. The school, as were many others, was having a bullying issue, and she suggested to me that we work with the drama kids to create a play using some of my life stories. At the time, I thought this was a wonderful idea.

I spent a few months working with the drama kids and my friend, the drama teacher, and we created a play called *"Standing By"* that they rehearsed and then performed for the school. As I watched these kids perform the painful issue of bullying, suicide, and even reenacting some of my stories, I wept from the pain of watching the experience. Although I was so proud of the work and to see the play, it still hurt so much to watch the stories acted out and relive these moments. Looking back, I only wish I had been more prepared to create and experience this play.

But between the new website, a few speaking engagements and newspaper and radio interviews, I had begun to experience a slow burn of the return of panic and anxiety that would ultimately lead me down a darker path. I had thought that I was in a place to handle creating this website, but as people shared their stories and as bullying became more front-page news, I felt more saddened and pessimistic about the world and was forgetting the good things I had. Even though I had a good job and what most would see as a good life, I started to feel empty inside. I was struggling to find my happiness again.

About a year after starting my website and feeling this lack of happiness, it became quickly apparent to me that I was heading for trouble. As I look back to try to understand what happened next, I only saw the negative side of my life again. My company had lost our major money-making contract. We shrunk from a forty-five person company to about fifteen people because the work wasn't coming in. But I was confident they would never get rid of me, their friend and fraternity brother. I had worked so hard climbing the ladder there. My secure position and income allowed for my wife to work part-time, and life was great.

Then, one day, Fred said to me, "Let's go for a drive."

I remember him driving to a remote empty parking lot near a 7-11. He looked over at me and told me he thought it was time for me to look for a new job.

"Are you firing me?" I asked nervously.

Fred hesitantly looked at me and then looked down. "Yes," he said.

I felt faint, with my heart beating rapidly and panic kicking in. I tried to talk Fred out of letting me go, to no avail. I felt alone and betrayed by my friend and fraternity brother, and angry at the cards I had been dealt. I thought that after nine years of giving my life and career to my friend's company, I would settle into this work forever. That's the way that I wanted my life to go, and I had no backup plan. I forgot about all the blessings I had in my life and could only focus on the curses.

It was difficult to hold a balanced view of my life. Everyone has ups and downs and learns to cope. But I would have nine good experiences, one bad one, and the bad experience was the one my brain held onto. The only way I knew how to cope was to run and hide. Escape. Protect myself from the pain. Kind of like how Roger Waters built *The Wall* in the classic Pink Floyd album of the same name. This classic rock opera tells the story of a character who, having experienced childhood trauma, built a wall around himself to protect him from his own demons from his past. One interpretation is that he built the wall in order to feel safe and protected from the pain of his world. Eventually, the wall crumbles, perhaps a hint that one cannot hide behind a wall forever.

This most recent rejection and panic attack from losing my job was really the final straw in my long-standing battle to keep my shoebox of memories sealed deep within the hole. At some point, I realized I created this website because I couldn't *Forget Lexington* as I thought I had. I had never confronted what happened to me in Lexington.

It was at this moment that I realized I'd lost perspective on my life. The life that included great positive moments, such as my time in high school drama class, my best friend who only lived a few houses away, all the fun I had in college, finding my soulmate, and having two wonderful boys with her. It felt as if in a moment, all of that had been wiped from my mind and I had been left alone, in the dark, with no way out. I was forced to confront the memories that had simply been hidden from my awareness all of these years as I found great moments of happiness. But at that moment, I could not see my happiness, but only the bad times that continued to haunt me. I let my memories of my youth back in. I was able to find new work quickly, but still missed what I had with my friends at my old job. The new job was just another job for me.

I'd take a trip with my family to a lake soon after I was fired. I remember that, no matter how much beauty was around me or how much my family loved me, I felt totally alone and hated myself and the world for the cards I was dealt. I lost all perspective of my good life. It was gone in an instant and my child brain started to take over where my adult brain used to be. It called out to me the words I didn't want to hear again.

Remember Lexington!

PART TWO

DARKNESS GROWS
WHERE
NOBODY KNOWS

CHAPTER TWELVE

Only Just Learning
The Lesson of Life

Before the hole was dug in my mind and before the shoebox was buried; before the dark and bad moments of my life, I had built a utopia. It was a beautiful place with a wonderful house, a large yard and a protective area of trees along the perimeter of the land. My utopia would speak to me, telling me not to travel outside the perimeter of the protection of my yard, but I could see a beautiful field on the other side of the trees. I was young and I was full of hope and confidence. I was not scared, so I travelled through my yard, through the thin forest of trees and came upon a beautiful field of tall grasses full of flowers and dandelions. It was peaceful here for a moment, but then the hairs on the back of my neck stood up, and I felt scared. I started to sweat a bit and felt my heart rate increase. I turned and headed back through the trees to my yard and home. Once past the trees, I felt safe again and my heart slowed down. I stopped sweating and the hairs on my neck rested again. "What was that?" I asked myself. I heard no answer back.

◊ ◊ ◊

It was a hot August day, and I was six years old when we moved to Lexington, Massachusetts. It was so hot that my parents stuck my sister and me in a cool bath while they unpacked the car. My sister and I were excited to meet the kids on the street, like we had done in Bowie, Maryland. We walked down the street looking for kids our age to play with. I remember that first day, heading home, disappointed that we didn't meet anyone.

When I finally met a new neighborhood friend, Kyle, I found he was a mischievous kid a year older than me. Kyle had a younger sister, Lauren, who would also hang out with us once in a while. Kyle introduced me to a few more neighborhood kids, like Tommy, Sherry, and Mary. Everyone seemed nice enough, but more serious and hardened than the kids I knew before I moved. Maybe it was due to being older or the culture and lifestyle in New England. I can't say for sure.

What I do know is that while I had started to make friends, it didn't take long for trouble to start for my sister and me, and in some ways, for our whole family. I was still a naïve, confident, if not cocky, six-year-old when I left Maryland. Being in Lexington required me to grow up much faster than I wanted to, stripping me of any confidence and self-esteem I'd brought with me.

CHAPTER THIRTEEN

Very Bad
Vibes

More bad memories needed to be added to the shoebox of bad memories under my bed. In this new place I moved to, I was adding memories much more often. As I tried to sleep, the shoebox of bad memories under my bed would whisper to me and want me to remember. I didn't want to remember and covered my ears. I could still hear the whispers coming from the shoebox, and they would grow louder and angrier. I needed to find a better place to put these bad memories. I needed to sleep, but these whispers were keeping me up at night with rumination of things that happened to me. I thought it prudent to find another place far away from my bad memories. "Hopefully I can do this soon?" I thought, wanting to put these bad memories in a place where they couldn't hurt me any longer.

As my family settled into the new community, we joined the local synagogue, which was walking distance from my home and where my sister and I would go for religious school. Most of my parents' friends were families affiliated with the synagogue, but my sister and I wanted to meet more kids in our own neighborhood. Days after our arrival on the block, I was walking to Tommy's house. On my way to Tommy's house, Sherry and Mary, whom I had only met a few days ago, approached me from their yard where they were playing. They looked me straight in the face and said, "You killed Jesus", spit on me, then ran away. The only thing these girls knew about me was that I was Jewish. They'd already made the decision that I was not worthy.

What did I do?

Why the hatred?

Suddenly, I was ashamed to be Jewish. I know I did nothing to provoke these actions and can only assume it was something they were taught to believe. As the spittle traveled down my face, I realized they also weren't taught how their actions would impact others' feelings. It hurt me, and I became ashamed of my identity. This was the beginning of several experiences that would lead me to dig the hole deeper and deeper in which I could safely hide.

◊ ◊ ◊

In the weeks before school started, my mom wanted us to practice walking to our new school, Franklin Elementary. The school was about a mile away from home, which meant we would be walkers and not ride a bus. Behind our house was a small grove of trees that opened up to the top hill of a farm that had cows; to the left was a junkyard. We discovered that on nice days, we could cut through the farm, go up the hill and cut through the grove of trees to get back to the house. We had to watch out for mating season, as they would bring in a bull that would chase us if we cut through there. I had a few close calls with that bull.

Franklin Elementary had an enormous playground area with plenty of playground equipment, swings, and slides. My sister and I immediately ran to play on the equipment. There were already two boys playing on the equipment. They were about twelve or thirteen years old, much older than my sister and me.

For no apparent reason, they began teasing my sister, calling her names. We were playing by ourselves, not even near them. They followed us as we tried to get away from them. My sister told my mom, who, confident as ever, got up and confronted these two boys.

Then something happened that I didn't expect. These two boys began taunting my mom, calling her a wicked witch and singing the song from *The Wizard of Oz*. My sister and I were terrified at the time as we saw my mom being taunted by these kids. She was trying to protect us. As mom chased after them, they ran from her in circles as they were much faster than her. She couldn't catch them.

The two boys continued their laughing and taunting as my mom finally gave up, grabbed our hands, and walked us home.

It was unsettling to think about my mother as powerless to protect us from these two bullies. I no longer saw my mom as my hero. As these bullies took away her power as a protective mother and safe adult, I felt the loss of believing that she could save me from a bullying situation. Perhaps no adult had the power and ability to stop bullies. I considered this frightening thought that no one could keep me safe. I was on my own.

CHAPTER FOURTEEN

Enemies All
Around Me

A deep hole! That's the solution I needed. I could dig a deep hole in my mind and put the shoebox of bad memories that was under my bed so far down this deep hole that they couldn't whisper to me anymore. I would keep all my good memories, but put these bad memories down in a hole where no one would be able to find them. I thought long and hard about where to dig this hole. "Where is a place that no one knows about?" I thought. Then I remembered the tall grass field outside the protective tree perimeter in my mind. If the grass is tall and the flowers and dandelions untouched, then probably no one knows about this field. I will dig my hole there and put my shoebox of bad memories there. That will protect me and let me sleep better. I can forget about it over time.

◊ ◊ ◊

When I began second grade, I felt out of place in a school full of strange kids whom I didn't know. But I was still quite cocky and figured I wouldn't have any trouble getting along with peers. My teachers all had funny New England accents, and it took me a while to get used to understanding what they were saying. I made it through the first half of 2nd grade without incident. My first New England winter passed by, leaving a cold chill in the air that would soon move to my soul.

One morning, I awoke with a swollen eye from some kind of irritation. I didn't want to go to school with the swollen eye, but my mom wouldn't let me stay home. I decided I would wear sunglasses all day at school, so that the other kids wouldn't see my swollen eye. To be honest, I was kind of looking forward to the attention I would get with everyone asking me what had happened to my eye.

When I arrived in class, one of the students immediately teased me about my glasses. My teacher instructed me to remove the sunglasses. I replied to the teacher that I needed to wear them for my injury, but she didn't seem to care. This was not going as planned, and the attention I received was not good. Everyone was staring at me, chuckling and whispering to each other. I even fabricated a story that the doctor told me I had to wear the sunglasses. I was trying to save face, but it was too late. She called me over to her desk and demanded I remove the glasses. I did and she saw my swollen eye.

The swelling in my eye was reduced, but she let me keep the glasses on. I was so humiliated, sulking back to my seat hiding behind the dark lenses. I felt like I was the center of attention in a way I didn't want, and alienated at the same time. It was clear to me I wasn't in Maryland anymore. One classmate, Bob, took a special interest in me following that incident.

◊ ◊ ◊

The playground at Franklin was quite large for an elementary school and spanned over three sides of the school grounds. Teachers remained outdoors with students but were oblivious to what was going on around them while they chatted to one another.

In a secluded wooded area toward the back of the schoolyard was a large wooden playground with multiple platforms to play on and a pole for sliding down. My new school friend Jimmy and I were playing on the wooden structure when a bunch of kids, led by Bob from my second grade class, approached us. They ignored my friend Jimmy and surrounded me on the deck. The hairs on the back of my neck stood up, and my pulse started racing in a typical fight or flight mode.

This fight or flight instinct is known to all animals, including humans, as an alert to physical threat or trouble It's an easy feeling to recall, because decades later, when I had my first panic attack during that final exam in college, it felt the same. It became a familiar feeling that I would experience over and over again, even when I wasn't being physically threatened.

When I was surrounded by my peers, the name calling started. "Hey iceberg!" a play on my last name, "Bob wants to fight you. What are you going to do?" Bob was a big kid for his age with a tough demeanor. I did not want to mess with him and had a bad feeling about him from the beginning. The kids kept squeezing in on me. I didn't want to fight and said so.

They didn't care, and I couldn't get away from them as they had me surrounded and trapped like a caged animal. Bob balled up his fists and began punching me. I didn't fight back because I had never been in a fight before and didn't even know how to fight. I worried if I fought back, it might make the situation worse. The part that sticks with me is how quiet it was, while I was taking my beating. The kids weren't yelling or cheering, just watching me get beaten. I think they expected me to fight back.

I fell to the ground in a ball and felt a few kicks from Bob. When he was finished, the kids walked away. Once everyone left, Jimmy approached me again. No adults were anywhere to be seen. They didn't even see it as they chatted on the schoolyard steps. The entire incident lasted a few minutes, but felt like an eternity to me. I felt powerless to stop it.

I know I was crying, but I didn't want anyone to see me. My dad never gave me the impression that I had to "suck it up" and be tough, but I knew that boys shouldn't cry. There was even a song on the radio around that time with the lyric *big boys don't cry*. I didn't want to be seen as a little baby, so I turned away.

Don't get me wrong. It's not like I wanted to be quiet about this, because I didn't want it to happen again. To this day, I can only assume I was targeted by Bob for wearing the dark sunglasses and probably being new and different. Did I act a certain way? Was I still an outsider to this community?

I went home and told my mom what had happened. With the best of intentions, mom told me that the best thing to do would be to keep quiet and not fight back. She told me to never fight back because that would make the situation worse. While I listened to her advice, I regret the next few years of not fighting back. It is not right for young boys to fight, but the settling of problems with fists is something that has been passed down from generation to generation. It was and still can be the "kids being kids" mentality of many adults. At some point, I can only hope that the thinking that boys will be boys or even kids will be kids will be changed.

For the remainder of second grade, I was Bob's punching bag. At some point, I asked my teacher if I could stay indoors during recess due to the constant bullying from Bob, but she said everyone had to go outside and play. When Bob felt like picking on someone, he always seemed to beeline to me, and I was just taking it. His cadre of followers, most of whom I assume followed him so they wouldn't take the same punishment, started hitting me as well. I spent much of my time avoiding getting pushed around on the playground. I remember what mom told me, "don't fight back"...and I didn't.

It was hard to avoid the kids at recess. There were too many places for them to attack me without being seen. I wanted to be left alone to play with my friends. One day I was with my friend Jimmy on a metal piece of equipment that was shaped like a rocket ship we could climb on and into. It was cool looking at my age, and we could come up with all sorts of adventures we could have on that pretend ship, and we did. It was nice to escape to outer space playing on that. Of course, that fun would be ruined by Bob and his friends.

One day I was high atop the rocket ship with Jimmy when Bob and his friends came over. They began taunting me, telling me to come down and fight. I remember the feeling of fight or flight panic come over me. I was probably six to eight feet above the ground, but it might as well have been 20 feet to a small kid like me. They were beneath me, climbing up from the inside and grabbing my clothes to pull me down.

I remember feeling scared that I would fall head first onto the ground. I couldn't hold on anymore and slipped, hitting the metal on the way down to the ground. When I hit the ground, I wasn't sure if I was hurt or not, but faked that the wind was knocked out of me and I was hurt. I laid on the ground moaning. The kids began kicking me in my side and accused me of not being injured. I just lay there. Finally they gave up on me and left.

I was bruised. Not as much physically as mentally. I had to fake being hurt for them to leave me alone, and even after that, they still kicked me and sensed I was faking it. I didn't play on that rocket ship after the incident. I wanted to, but didn't want to be caught in that situation again. Eventually Jimmy and I drifted apart as friends. I don't recall how much longer we remained friends, but I sensed he wasn't as excited to hang out with me after that incident and my new bully victim reputation. Maybe that was my feeling ashamed, but I'll never fully know the answer.

◊ ◊ ◊

The bullying was so bad during the first few years at Franklin Elementary. It wasn't just Bob. Another boy named Mitchell got wind that I was the "boy who wouldn't fight back" and began picking on me, and tripping me in the hallway. When Bob wasn't beating on me, Mitchell took over. When the last bell rang at the end of the school day, I became panicked, knowing that either Bob, Mitchell, or even some of the other known school bullies would beat me up on my long walk home.

There were plenty of opportunities when the adults in my life let me down. Looking back, I would chalk most of that up to either a lack of understanding of the issues of bullying or the "kids being kids" mentality that I think a lot of adults hold about issues of bullying and fighting.

One of the most disappointing and discouraging experiences, reminding me how alone and helpless I was, occurred after a rather brutal confrontation with Bob that left me bruised and with a bloodied nose. It's hard to believe no teachers witnessed it, but I have to admit that many of these fights probably only lasted a minute or two. Since I was not fighting back, it was pretty much one punch and I was down.

After this particular incident, I believe the school was finally catching on that I was getting bullied. This conclusion became apparent to me when I was told the school principal, Principal Brown, wanted to meet with me. I don't think I had ever met Principal Brown before, and was ridiculed for being called out of class for the meeting. I vividly remember how nervous I felt sitting outside Principal Brown's office. There were children's books there, so I picked up a *Curious George* book. In this book, Curious George is in the hospital when he stumbles upon a canister of ether. Sucking up the ether, George drifts off into a dreamlike state. At the time, being able to "float away" from all of this seemed pretty appealing. It seemed as if I was sitting outside Principal Brown's office a long time, and the waiting only heightened my anxiety.

Finally, Principal Brown's door opened. She was a tall and slightly cherubic woman who seemed to tower over me. When Principal Brown called me into her office, I sat down, still wet from perspiration, feeling panicky and in tears. Principal Brown asked me several questions about what happened, about why I think I was being picked on. I don't ever recall her asking about how I felt, and she didn't even involve my mother. I'm not sure whether that would've been helpful or not. I proceeded to spill my guts about the boys who were bullying me, particularly Bob. She assured me she would take care of it and that I shouldn't worry about it. Then I was dismissed. I was more terrified than ever. Should I have told her Bob's name? What was she going to do? What should I do?

The next day it started. Now Bob and his cronies were really mad at me, because they had heard about my conversation with Principal Brown. Now I was a RAT! As usual, there was minimal adult supervision on the playground, so for the next several weeks, I played in closer proximity to the teachers outside. Principal Brown never called me in again. I was treated as if I was to blame for the problems and was referred to the school psychologist, who I had to start meeting with several times a week.

Nothing was resolved by my meeting with Principal Brown. The only follow-up on her part that I could tell was seeing me as the one with the problem who needed counseling. As far as I knew, the bullies never received counseling. I sensed that Principal Brown might have even been avoiding me after that meeting. Just as neither my mother nor the teachers could protect me, this reinforced my belief that I could not trust adults and the school system to protect me. I was truly alone to deal with this on my own.

CHAPTER FIFTEEN

Rolling Downhill
With No Way to Stop

I was still looking for a safe place to rid myself of the bad memories in the shoebox. At first, I thought maybe I would put them outside, in the yard away from the house. But at night, as I tried to sleep, I could still hear their whispers outside my bedroom window. "Loser! Liar! Wimp!" they would yell to me. I kept trying to move the shoebox farther back, but each night, I would wake in a cold sweat, the voices in the shoebox wanting to come back to me. I needed a better place. I needed a place farther away from me where I could forget these memories.

◊ ◊ ◊

By fourth grade, I began to tire of the endless bullying and beatings and was eager for a solution. A healthy dose of fear alerts us to a potentially dangerous situation to which we need to pay attention. Human beings have been that way since the existence of our memory to allow for survival. But living with fear on a daily basis is terribly damaging. It grips you, making you believe the world and everyone around you is unsafe, as you prepare for fight or flight. You behave in ways that do nothing but promote pure survival from moment to moment. You react in ways that are out of character and irrational and that leads to your mind racing. For me, the fear of being bullied deprived me one of the most valuable things in my childhood…TIME! I spent so much time trying to survive that I missed out on many simple childhood pleasures.

We all have to live knowing that each minute of our lives is one minute closer to our deaths. Practicing mindfulness teaches us to live in the present moment and make the most of our time, not *kill it* or wish it to move faster. But as children, we feel like we have all the time in the world. A year feels like an eternity, and a summer could last forever. As I look back, I realize how much time I actually lost due to fear of being bullied. As a child of only eight or nine years old, I wanted out of the daily bullying so badly that I created a new daily routine after school. When the three o'clock bell rang, the last thing I wanted to do was leave school with the other kids because I worried the bullies were out there waiting for me. I lived about a mile away from the school, as I said earlier, but as a kid, it felt much farther than that. When you are little, everything feels bigger. The school was surrounded by wooded areas, plenty of places I could be pulled into and beaten up. But one day, I waited about 10 minutes until all the kids and buses had left. My bullies were so patient; I knew they were still waiting for me, so I came up with an idea. I ran out the side door of the school and into the tree line.

I cut through the forest, which was three quarters of the way around the school and came to a dirt road that was a good two-hundred plus yards away from the school. I walked this new path and came out farther down the street to avoid the bullies.

I did this every day for over two years. I calculated the number of minutes I wasted avoiding the bullies. Based on the ten minutes I would wait and the extra fifteen-to-twenty minutes it would take me to get to the path from the tree line, I lost thirty minutes a day for over two years, just to avoid bullies. When I do the math, it appears I lost over eight days of my life in avoiding being bullied. It pains me to look at the time lost in my youth, so often spent as a stalked animal trying to survive. I don't think I noticed the lost time, as I was trying to stay safe. This took a significant toll on my self-esteem, unable to help but question whether I was even worth saving. I truly began to loathe who I was now and feared going to bed each night, knowing the energy it would take to survive the next day.

◊ ◊ ◊

One of the common results of bullying, I noticed, appeared to be the "turn of the friend". As I progressed through elementary school, it seemed difficult to trust those who I once believed were friends. In a safe, secure friendship, there is reciprocity in trust, sharing, and support. It never dawned on me that a friend could turn his back on you and become your bully. I understand this happens often with girls who are bullied by someone who was previously a friend, but certainly boys experience this as well. For me, it was one of the few friends I had at school for over two years, named Luke. He and I had a friendship that lasted several years.

Luke and I often played together, but one day, Luke turned on me. It wasn't like we drifted apart as friends do over time. This happened on a dime. Perhaps Luke realized I was unpopular, and he needed to join the more popular crowd intent on bullying me. I am unaware of anything I did to trigger it, but Luke began tripping me in the halls and beating on me. I did not see that coming. I thought Luke was my friend. Franklin Elementary, in their infinite administrative wisdom, decided once again that *I* was the problem and that I was the one who needed to see the school counselor twice a week. It seemed I was the one to blame for getting taunted and teased, tripped and beaten. The counselor did try to help, encouraging me to talk about what was wrong and why I was sad. But this only made me feel more like I was the one with the problem, as opposed to those who behaved so badly towards me.

Back in those days, bullying was viewed as the victim's problem, and there seemed to be a belief that resolution came from helping the victim to change his or her character, personality, or behavior. This was long before the days of addressing and reporting bullying in the news. The sessions I would have with the counselor were very generic; I was asked "what's wrong?" and "why do you feel sad?"

The last thing I wanted to do was rat on my peers, especially since I couldn't trust the school administrators or teachers to help. One brutal experience on the playground occurred when Luke pushed my face down in the dirt where an animal had left its feces. I returned to class covered in dirt and feces, and in tears. My teacher immediately sent me to the counselor's office. The counselor questioned me about the incident, but I didn't want to talk about it. He pushed and pushed so I told him what happened, but not who was involved. He basically demanded that I give him a name. When I told him it was Luke, I begged him not to approach Luke. I told him about my past friendship with Luke and how it suddenly ended one day.

Now, I was more scared than ever of retaliation, but a part of me was hoping I could trust this adult to help. At this point, I had been working with this school counselor for several years and he had yet to let me down. With high hopes, I returned to class. Later in the day, I was sent back to meet with my counselor and found Luke sitting in the office as well. My heart was racing. He and the counselor looked at me and smiled. I will never forget that. Of course they had talked and the counselor had confronted Luke.

It seemed Luke explained that we were friends, but we had a fight about something. It was all a misunderstanding. While Luke and my counselor talked, I sat in a frozen panic, unable to move. They talked about how it was all "water under the bridge," and Luke and I could be friends again. Luke manipulated the situation, saying he wanted to be friends again but not really meaning it. The counselor believed every word he said. The counselor made us shake hands and make up.

You would think an adult administrator would know better, but thirty years later, I watched the movie "Bully", and there on film is the vice-principal of the school doing the exact same thing and believing he had solved that particular bullying problem. I was shocked that he believed a handshake could end the torment of bullying. As the counselor dismissed us, he looked pleased with himself, perhaps feeling like he had done a great job with us. As we got up to leave, the counselor made the biggest mistake of all. He sent us away at the same time, and I knew what was going to happen.

When Luke and I left the counselor's office side by side, he was acting like my buddy. Then we rounded the corner and that was it. He threw some hard punches in my gut, and I collapsed on the floor. Class was in session, so there were no witnesses. He said some nasty things to me and walked away while I tried to catch my breath. Was there ever any doubt that this would be the outcome? That was the last time the counselor heard from me about any of the kids who picked on me. If he asked me about Luke, I lied and said it was all fine and we were friends again, which couldn't be further from the truth. I didn't need that type of counseling again.

Even at 10 years old, I knew what was going on and had a feeling I knew what would happen. I could see this counselor had no idea how to manage this situation to keep me safe. Today I believe that the adults are the ones who need the education on these matters, not the kids. How the adults in my life handled these situations could have made a difference. Adults need to pay attention to the fears that children express and respect those fears.

Perhaps adults forget what it was like to be a child. Perhaps adults struggle to manage their own fears, making themselves less available to the children who need their help. The idea that "kids will be kids," letting them work it out themselves is not effective. Kids cannot work out conflicts if they have not been taught the skills to do so. This only reinforces to the bully and victim that adults are powerless to help, and that the world is indeed an unsafe place.

◊ ◊ ◊

While Luke was now my enemy and bully, I did still have friends at school and in the neighborhood who would stick with me no matter what. Kyle and Tommy were still two of my best friends. I never lost faith in that friendship as they stood by me, even though I was being picked on a lot. At any time, they could have easily walked away from me, but they didn't and I found comfort in that.

We joined the Cub Scouts together in third grade. It was interesting, because even though some of my bullies, like Mitchell, were in Cub Scouts with us, there was little opportunity to be bullied when adults were present at meetings and events. As an adult, I became a Cub Scout leader and felt empowered to be the set of eyes watching and making sure no one got bullied in our pack. I watched later as both my sons fell in love with scouting and achieved the rank of Eagle Scout. Boy Scouts has a mixed reputation, but many of the skills taught in scouts are life skills, such as independence, leadership, and self-confidence. All of these would have been great lessons for me in my youth. But as a child, I didn't make it past Cub Scouts.

I participated in Cub Scouts for two years as a Wolf and a Bear. During those two years, my father chose to be the Scoutmaster and wore a full Indian headdress to meetings. This embarrassment was more ammunition for my bullies. As time went on, I felt like I needed to change my reputation of being the "boy who didn't fight back." As exhausting as it was to avoid bullies after school by taking my detoured path, the playground at recess was an unavoidable opportunity to be beaten up.

I decided the next time a bully started in on me during recess, I would fight back instead of letting someone beat the piss out of me, no longer remaining the pacifist my mother raised. Truthfully, I have always hated the idea of fighting, ever since I was a little boy. Unfortunately, our culture has raised boys to believe that the best way to resolve power struggles is with their fists.

In Massachusetts, the winters can be quite cruel and long. I often joke now that there are two seasons in New England, winter and August. Teachers were required to provide outdoor play even through the winter months. The snowman building contest was a big deal, and my friends and I had planned our snowman idea well in advance to try to win the contest. We created a giant snowman head with a very large nose. We thought it looked hilarious. We spent most of our time trying to make the nose as big as possible, without it breaking off.

Right before the end of the contest, Mitchell came over and knocked the nose off the snowman's head after what felt like hours of building it. That moment was the straw that broke the proverbial camel's back. I jumped on top of Mitchell and began punching him in the face. After a few quick punches, I leapt up, ran all the way home, and never looked back, for fear that Mitchell was right behind me.

My sister, Robyn, who attended the middle school next to Franklin, was walking home a few minutes later. One of the teachers who knew she was my sister stopped her to tell her what had happened. She ran home after me. When she got home, I was hiding. I was petrified that Mitchell would come after me and kill me in my own home. I'd never hit anyone before, and looked down at my bruised and bleeding knuckles.

Years later, I would see Jean Shepherd's classic tale of bullying and what happened to the boy in the movie, "A Christmas Story". When Ralphie, the movie's protagonist finally fights back at the bully, he just loses it. He keeps punching and punching him, unleashing a slew of expletives. I often thought at that moment in the movie, if his mom didn't stop him from beating up the bully, Ralphie would have kept at it until the boy was either unconscious or dead. Just like Ralphie knew when he had hit his breaking point, I found myself in the same position. I recognized that feeling and remembered how that movie made me think, *A-ha! I'm not alone in this.*

When Robyn found me, she calmed me down. But I had a bigger problem ahead of me. That same night was the Cub Scout Blue & Gold Dinner. Mitchell would be there, and I would have to face him. Of course, my father would accompany me, but he was not aware of the previous incident. He would be busy as a Scoutmaster, and I didn't talk to him much about what was happening to me. The only thing I wanted to talk to my parents about was when we would be moving again.

So, off we went to the Blue & Gold Dinner, with me scared out of my wits having to face the boy I'd hit and run from. When we arrived, I scanned the room and saw him. There was Mitchell...with a black eye. I figured now I was in real trouble. I wasn't proud of punching him in the face, giving him a shiner. I felt sick seeing him and thinking about what I had done. But he came up to me, and as he approached, I wanted to run away.

Mitchell simply said, "Hey, Alan." That was it. *Hey, Alan.* Like we were old friends and nothing had happened that day. Like he hadn't knocked the nose off of our snowman, and I didn't just lose myself and beat him up. I'm sure I replied with something like, "Hey" back to him, but who knows? My heart was pounding so fast and fear gripped me. My survival instinct for fight or flight was telling me to flee as soon as possible. Seeing Mitchell at the event was enough to set off my panic button. But he simply walked away, and my fears of being gravely injured from the exchange gradually subsided.

And that was it. . .

Mitchell never bullied me again. Now I had to deal with the question: *Did my fighting back stop him from bullying me?* If so, how many more fights was I going to have? Unfortunately, *a lot more* was the answer. It's not fair that fighting back seemed to be the answer. In order to survive the bullying, I began defending myself with my fists, and it would only escalate from there. Over the next few years, I found that fighting back was indeed more effective than using words to stop the bullies in elementary school. Not my best years and to this day, not something I am proud of.

CHAPTER SIXTEEN

You Can Only Kick
A Dog So Much

I walked patiently through my yard, through the thin protective tree line, to the field of tall grass and flowers. This is a perfect spot to put my box of bad memories. I was the only one who knew where this spot is, and I can come and add memories here anytime I want without anyone's finding out. I thought myself quite the clever kid, until I again felt the familiar hairs on the back of my neck rise, my heart race, and sweat start dripping from me. I wanted to run at this moment, but I knew that I had to bury the box there. It would take time to dig a hole deep enough to hold the contents of my box of bad memories. I found the spot I wanted, fighting my own desire to run far away from the sense of danger that seemed to be around me. I cleared only a small spot of the tall grass, making sure it was still surrounded on all sides so as not to be seen by anyone. After clearing the spot, I was ready to dig. I looked down and realized I would have no tools to help me dig but my two hands. This was going to hurt.

◊ ◊ ◊

The moment I decided to fight back, my bullying situation changed drastically. By this point, I felt broken and needed the bullying to stop. Childhood innocence was lost to the years of bitter cold that not only the weather brought, but the kids who came into my life as well.

I may have succeeded in getting Mitchell to stop bullying me, but I had never fought back against Bob, whose beatings I had tolerated for almost four years now. Even though Bob was much bigger than me and looked tougher, I realized that I had no choice but to fight back.

I can still see the location of this fight. It was on the side of the school away from the teachers who were supposed to be supervising the students' playing. Of course, Bob's group of cronies cornered me in and then the well-known fight circle formed. It's funny how kids can sense a fight coming, and they naturally form a circle around the fighters to keep the adults away.

Bob started in with the insults and punches as he had always done with me. He didn't expect that today would be the day I would fight back. When I threw my first punch, I connected with his chin, although not well. It was clear I caught him by surprise, but he began swinging at me anyway. We grabbed at each other and tumbled to the ground where we wrestled, beating on each other. The kids screamed and yelled as their adrenaline kicked in and the true animal aggression of the human being came out. We are all only slightly above our animal cousins, right?

Now this went on for a few minutes until finally an adult realized the students were all clustered in this one area. The kids alerted us as the teachers approached, and the fight ended. The adults had witnessed nothing. And no one would admit to anything.

But I know, as dirty and bruised as I was, that I did fight back this time. It was even more effective that my peers witnessed it. Bob did not bully me anymore after that day. Of course, just because Mitchell and Bob stopped tormenting me doesn't mean there weren't others. But, I was no longer a victim of these two boys' bullying.

A part of me holds them in my memory as mean, vicious boys whom I had hated. That's the thing about memories; they are based on how you perceived things at the age you were when the memory was formed. That child part of me had such fear and contempt for these boys. As an adult, I would learn to have compassion for the troubled souls who went through their childhoods bullying others to prove their worth. I often wondered what became of them as adults and would later find some answers through the magic of social media.

I was eleven years old now and becoming bitter as I faced bullies on a daily basis. Despite having been successful at earning enough respect to no longer be bullied by Mitchell and Bob, my sense of self-worth was so very low. I didn't like who I had to become, a fighter, in order to avoid the bullies. I wasn't able to be true to myself, to meet my needs. This was not a good way to enter into my teen years. For someone with low self-esteem, going through puberty was probably even more painful that it would usually be.

◊ ◊ ◊

Having low self-esteem due to my continued insecurities from the bullying and my sensitivity to what was happening to me, I made poor choices that I thought would make me more well-liked by others. I would do almost anything a friend or potential friend wanted me to do in hopes of not having to deal with disappointing them. This included dare games with sexual overtones that some kids engage in around puberty. I later learned I was not alone in the sexual experimentation that I engaged in and that the embarrassment and shame I felt was shared by many who rarely speak of such things. For me, it was a way to help me feel wanted and loved, feelings I was struggling with at the time.

Kyle was still my best friend, and I spent much time with him and his family, as well as his friends Sherry and Mary, the two girls who had spit on me for being Jewish and told me I killed Jesus when I first arrived in Lexington. I imagine that they had forgotten about this incident as they did not treat me as anything but a friend by this time. I, of course, had not forgotten what they had done and struggled with how to be friends with them now and forget their behavior from some years ago.

Kyle was a year older than I was and hit puberty earlier than I did. I felt inadequate in my still child-like body next to his as he developed. Because the rest of the group had started puberty, I felt like I could not keep up with the others. Sherry and Mary had already started to develop as well, as girls usually develop earlier than boys.

One summer day, before I entered sixth grade, I was over at Kyle's house, playing with Kyle, Sherry, and Mary. Kyle had told us of a game he heard of called "Five Minutes in the Closet," where you spin a bottle, go into the closet with the person the bottle pointed to, and take off your clothes. I was uncomfortable with the idea, but no one else seemed to object. I was worried that, if I didn't go along with it, Kyle might be mad at me. I didn't want to lose him as a friend as my self-worth was already disappearing quickly. Besides, I kind of liked the idea of getting attention from a girl, so maybe it wouldn't be so bad. Kyle started the game and spun the bottle. When it stopped spinning, it pointed at me. Well, we both knew two boys were not going into the closet together, so Kyle decided he and Mary would go in the closet first. Kyle told me to keep time and let them know when five minutes were up. As Sherry and I waited outside, we could hear whispers from the closet. I was getting panicky, feeling nervous, and somewhat excited at the same time. After five minutes, I called "TIME!" alerting them to come out of the closet.

Then it was Mary's turn to spin the bottle. The bottle spun quickly, then slowed down and pointed at me. My heart was racing, and I wasn't sure what to do. But when Mary headed straight to the closet, the new expert of the game, having gone in the closet with Kyle, I followed. When we were in the closet, Mary told me that Kyle showed her what to do. She started to remove her clothes, and I did too, not wanting to look like I didn't know what I was doing. This was the first time that I'd seen a naked girl, and eleven was probably much too young. Mary, who was also eleven, explained that the boy lays on top of the girl, so I did, neither of us knowing what we were really supposed to do.

I remember the awkward feeling of that moment, wondering *How long do I lay on top of her?* It felt wrong to be doing this. I worried that I was hurting Mary, but she said she was okay. Then it struck me again how odd it was to be looking into the eyes of this girl who had spat on me a few years earlier. She looked at me and all I could think of was how much she'd hurt me before. I started to feel anger and even disappointment at the fact that this moment seemed to mean nothing in these girls' lives.

"TIME!" I heard Kyle shout from outside the closet.

I felt ashamed of my activity and the whole situation and wanted to go home. I really was disgusted with myself for not asking the girls if they remembered what they did to me. While the spit of the past could be washed away, their words still stung me. I made up some excuse that my mom needed me to come home, so I left.

This first sexual experience left me confused and ashamed. My introduction to sex was not about attraction and intimacy, but a game about peer pressure and wanting to be liked. We would play this game many times at Kyle's house. Because of my low self-worth, I didn't think I could speak up about not wanting to play. I didn't want to be the odd-man out. I wanted them to want me to be a part of it. I grieve the loss of childhood innocence, feeling sad about how quickly I had to grow up at a time when I should have been much more carefree.

◊ ◊ ◊

Kyle, Tommy, and I built a fort in the woods outside of Tommy's house that summer. The fort was built for only two reasons, to have a place to stash Kyle's adult magazines such as *Playboy* and *Penthouse*, as well as cigarettes that we would steal from our parents. I didn't worry about becoming a chain smoker like my parents, so if smoking and drinking made my peers accept me, I was in.

The three of us would meet at the fort, look at *Playboy*, and smoke cigarettes. I was twelve years old. It shocks me to this day the things I chose to do at such an early age. I wanted so much to be liked that I sacrificed much of my authentic self to try to fit in, although I would discover as I got older that many teens deal with this experimental time in their life. But at the time, I didn't know that. I was so conflicted about what was right and wrong that I often did the wrong things in order to be accepted.

As normal as it is for a teenager to rebel against social norms and family values, I was conflicted about my behavior. Peer pressure is so very powerful, enabling us to do things we wouldn't usually do in order to feel a sense of belonging. I felt terribly guilty about distracting the bookstore owner as Kyle shoved adult magazines under his jacket and left the store. Though we never got caught, there are times when I wished we had.

One time Kyle thought it would be fun for us to go to the record store to see how many cassette tapes we could steal. Since it was the dead of winter, we wore bulky winter coats. We rode the Lexpress bus for a quarter to the record store in Burlington, Massachusetts. When we arrived at the store, I felt I owed a debt to Kyle. Since he stole the magazines, I should probably help him with this venture. Once we were in the store, we each began shoving cassette tapes inside our coats. I probably had grabbed ten of them, and as God is my witness, I looked down at my belly and looked pregnant. There were no security tabs on the merchandise that would stop us at the door, so we held our coats tight and walked out. We boarded the Lexpress for home and that was that. I was now a thief, which I needed to be okay with if I was to keep my best friend.

When I got home, I unloaded the cassettes I had stolen. I still remember some of them, like *The Eagles Live* album and *The Kinks Live* album, as well as The Who, a group I was really into at the time. But I knew what I had done was wrong, and I worried the police would be at my door any minute. I took the ten cassettes I had stolen and threw them in the trash. I felt completely dirty and ashamed. Later, Kyle would ask me to bring the ones I stole over to his house. I always had an excuse for forgetting them, and finally, he stopped asking.

Following that incident, my self-esteem continued to cascade into a downward spiral, and I often felt angry without knowing why. But self-worth is a funny thing. Most of us know when we have it, but we forget about it when it isn't there. My self-worth was quickly eroding.

◊ ◊ ◊

The mind of a broken child is a funny thing, and the confusion which comes from the tween and teen years of childhood is one of a loss of innocence and a realization that the world can be an ugly place. I had already experienced enough ugliness to last a lifetime. At that time in my life, my self-esteem and self-worth was all but gone, and I was simply hanging on to life by a few strands. These few strands would continue to be stretched farther for a few more years in Lexington. There were many days ahead when I had doubts about being able to survive any further bullying and torture at the hands of the school bullies. I wanted to feel good, to feel liked, and to feel wanted. But as time went on, I found that it was harder and harder for me to believe that anyone could like someone like me. Obviously, there was something wrong with me and not the other way around. Such is the mind of one who has been broken down to believing what others tell him about himself. I had all but given up, and it was looking like the bullies had won.

CHAPTER SEVENTEEN

I Believe I Lost
Myself Somewhere

Every day that I returned from school in Lexington, I travelled in my mind to the clearing through the thin tree line, where the grass was so tall, except for the area I had cleared to dig my hole. I had only my two hands to dig with, so I began to scoop the earth slowly and painfully with my hands to begin the process of creating a hole for my shoebox of bad memories. I would still feel the familiar danger prickles on the back of my head, but I had focused work to do. I dug more with my hands as the hole took shape. I worked until my hands were sore and bloody and my body exhausted. I hadn't dug very deeply and was disappointed. I would have to wait longer to remove the shoebox of memories from under my bed that was keeping me up at night with their whispers asking me to "remember."

◊ ◊ ◊

Sixth grade was my final year at Franklin Elementary School. Using my secret detour for leaving school and staying close to teachers during recess helped reduce the incidents of bullying. I discovered recess was a good time to read a book on the steps next to the adults.

Despite Kyle's having moved on to the middle school, our friendship continued but was impacted by a new cadre of friends Kyle had. I noticed the change when Halloween came. Historically, Kyle, Tommy and I would go trick-or-treating together. But this year it was different. I had planned to trick-or-treat with Kyle and Tommy, and some of their friends. Kyle called and told me to meet them at his house down the street. I got dressed in whatever bloody costume I thought would be cool when I was twelve years old. I remember making the blood out of corn syrup and red food coloring. I got all ready and headed down the street with my flashlight to Kyle's house. When I got there, his mother told me they had left five minutes earlier.

I was devastated that they had left without me. Hanging my head in disappointment, I began walking away from Kyle's house and back towards home, all the while fighting back the tears. Then I heard it. Some laughing was coming from the bushes. Then they called my name. It was my friends. As I approached the bushes, they ran. I tried to catch them, but it was dark and they hid again. They were laughing and calling my name, but wouldn't let me catch up to them. Eventually they ran into the woods and disappeared. I remember thinking that if they were joking around with me, they'd come out. It didn't feel like a joke to me, and they never came out. Feeling very hurt and sensitive about the whole thing, I went home. My mom asked me what happened and why I wasn't out trick-or-treating. I made up some story about not really wanting to go out this Halloween and turned on the TV to watch a movie called *Phantasm*. I remember watching it, because I remember that night. They don't go away easily, those painful memories. That was the last Halloween I went trick-or-treating. I told myself that I had outgrown it at twelve years old, the only way I knew how to deal with the hurt.

When I saw my friends the next day, they acted as if it was all a big joke. Their minimizing of it made me feel like I was overreacting. But my survival instincts were so sharpened from all the years of bullying that it was difficult to take a joke when it was on me. It was all I could do to protect myself from harm--physical or emotional. Years later, my wife would reintroduce me to the joy that she felt Halloween is as we took our kids out trick-or-treating. I learned to feel safe celebrating Halloween and am glad to have been able to enjoy it with my children.

Many years after that, Kyle and I had a chance to talk about this incident. He mentioned that he remembered the incident as their being goofballs to me. I was quite surprised he even remembered it, and I think if he knew of the pain I was going through at the time, he might have acted differently. But that's in the past and can't be changed now.

It wasn't all sad to be truthful, as I have another memory about that night. That same Halloween, my dad thought it would be fun to dress up to answer the door. He bought a gorilla suit to wear. I don't think he read the tag on the costume carefully, because it was a female gorilla suit. We could tell because it was…well…it had boobs on it, and it was pretty obvious to all who saw him. So there were some laughs that night, and the strange looks we got from the kids and parents when he answered the door are fond memories that I hold today. It is interesting to note that I wouldn't have those good memories if I had joined my friends that evening. It is ironic that different decisions lead to different outcomes, and it's easy to dwell on the negatives without remembering the positives of that time.

That is why family is so important to me today, because my parents and sister would always try to pick me up when I fell. Those are memories that I cherish, and they help me to laugh through the painful times. How odd that we need to go through pain in order to get pleasure in life. It's one way to think about how our universe is indeed balanced the way it needs to be.

◊ ◊ ◊

Soon after Halloween, I made a new friend when a boy named Ryan moved from England to Lexington during my sixth grade year. Having just moved, he was unaware of my reputation as the bullies' punching bag. We quickly became friends and spent time playing at each other's house. We enjoyed making stop-motion movies with our *Star Wars* figures for endless hours on weekends. His camera had a frame-by-frame setting that enabled us to make these movies. When I was allowed to spend the night at Ryan's house, I stayed up all night for the first time. We shared many of the same friends, and for almost a year we were best friends. While I still endured my share of being beaten up and bullied, Ryan's imposing height made me feel protected.

I was eager to finish Franklin Elementary and move on to the middle school where I hoped for a fresh start getting to know new kids from other elementary schools. I figured if I could survive this last year at Franklin, life would be better. For a while, I did find that to be true. But so much damage had already been done. I spent recess reading

Hardy Boys books next to the adults to ensure my safety from bullies on the playground. I took the long path home to avoid bullies beating me up after school. And I had learned to fight. Basically, I changed so many things about myself that I wasn't sure anymore who Alan really was, other than a bitter and angry twelve-year-old boy.

As the school year ended, I looked forward to summertime. Ryan and I would meet up at the Reservoir, which is what the local swimming hole was called in Lexington. That was the community pool, or as we called it, the RES. We made films and hung out. I got to know Ryan's parents pretty well spending so much of my time in their home. I observed them to be an average, calm and well-functioning family.

Then, one day in late summer, Ryan stopped calling or returning my calls. It was like, all of a sudden, he wasn't my friend anymore. Unfortunately, as good as my bully radar had become, I didn't see this one coming. Out of all the people who'd picked on me, beaten me up, and manipulated me emotionally, no one surprised me more than Ryan. This is part of a misconception I had because I had always believed that bullies were being bullied at home. As far as I could tell, that was not happening at Ryan's house, because I thought I knew his family pretty well. Of course, I don't know what his life was like when I wasn't at his house.

In my hope of all hopes that middle school would be different, it wasn't. Ryan was going to make sure that my last year in Lexington was going to be my worst year of all. I was going to learn that once you crumple a piece of paper, it is hard to make it look the same again. That's what bullying is like. We are all like a piece of paper, and once it gets wrinkled, those wrinkles begin to feel like a permanent part of who we are. I wanted to throw my paper into a deep, dark trash can. I spent many years believing that these scars would not fully heal, but trauma is not an incurable disease. Pain from trauma yearns to be felt, confronted, processed, and healed. It is only then that one can feel resolved to move forward. But, at this time in my life, it felt like it would be impossible to let go of.

CHAPTER EIGHTEEN

The End of Days
Approaches

It became a daily ritual to return to the field and continue to dig farther in the ground with my bare and now raw and bleeding hands to create the hole that would hold my bad memories at bay. I still could feel the panic as I entered the field, but it had become such a common feeling for me that I barely took note of it anymore. It was an uncomfortable feeling, but at the same time, now a familiar part of this place that was built in my mind. As the hole became more formed and deeper, I found that I needed a way to get into the hole and dig as it had become deeper than my arm's length. I looked around the field in my mind for anything that might help me. At first I didn't see it, but it was there, lying in the field, not 20 yards away with the sun gleaming off it. A perfect ladder that I could now drop in the hole to get in and out. The ladder was a shiny metal one that could extend to about 20 feet long. It was perfect as if it were meant for me to find all along. I dropped it in the hole and continued to dig and dig, knowing I could get back out of the hole with the ladder. Soon my bad memories would have a new home, and I could get the rest that I so desperately craved.

◊ ◊ ◊

Jonas Clarke Middle School in Lexington, Massachusetts, was a progressive and modern school for its time. The walls of the classrooms could be collapsed in order to create a more open learning environment between two classes. There were many aspects of Clarke that I liked. My teachers treated me well. I remember, in particular, my social studies teacher, Mr. Wood, who was a kind, young man. When Mr. Wood invited our entire class to his wedding, I felt respected and mature, something I hadn't had the opportunity to experience very much. I also remember my English teacher, Mrs. Handly, fondly. I remember that Mr. Wood's and Mrs. Handly's classrooms were right next to each other with the removable walls and we would often have a combined class by opening the wall between the two. Since I enjoyed both their classes and these teachers, this was always a great treat for me. Overall, the school staff was excellent, but they were unable to keep me safe from the bullies. Since the middle school was right next to the elementary school, I continued to take the winding path through the woods to get home and avoid any possibility of bullying after school.

I met some new friends in middle school. Some I had already known, like Glen from the synagogue Hebrew school. Because we attended different elementary schools, Glen and I only crossed paths during the years we attended Hebrew school. He didn't know I was tormented by bullies because I was actually popular in Hebrew school. It was weird to live that double life, being liked for who I am in one setting, and being tormented for it in another. Glen introduced me to Aaron, who was a friend of his from elementary school. In turn, I had a couple of friends, Bruce and Evan, with whom I had several classes, and we became close friends.

I have fond memories of volunteering with these boys to be the Audio/Visual (A/V) helpers. There were many advantages to doing this job for the school, such as getting called out of class to deliver A/V equipment as needed, and hanging out in the A/V room unsupervised whenever we had free time. We felt important and needed, something I very much appreciated during these tough years. It was definitely a nerdy group to be in, but it was MY nerdy group.

At this point Ryan stopped speaking to me, even if I saw him and said "hi" in the halls. I couldn't understand what I did wrong. I later found out that he had met and befriended many of the bullies who'd tormented me. I am sure, at some point, they told him all about me and that he shouldn't hang around with me.

I remember one of my friends telling me at lunch that Ryan wanted to fight me. I was completely clueless as to how this had happened. The last thing I wanted to do was fight Ryan, because not only was he much bigger than me, but I still thought he was my friend.

He was someone I had trusted not to hurt me. My classmates told me that Ryan wanted me dead, among other things. I did not have any classes with Ryan, so we had little interaction for a while. That would change. Ryan intimidated me, and I didn't want to fight him.

I began receiving prank phone calls when I arrived home from school. I was a latchkey kid, being home alone or with my sister in the afternoons. Hearing the heavy breathing on the other end of the phone was very unsettling, and I began having nightmares about a confrontation with Ryan. I was tired of the bullying and tired of the fighting. I felt I had little left in me to handle this. If there was ever a point where I wanted to end my life, this would have been it.

But I was fortunate to have a close family, and, even as alone as I felt, I didn't want to hurt them. I didn't give a damn about myself, but I couldn't take the idea of my mother seeing me dead. I would learn later that others confronted this demon called *bullycide* in different ways and that it would be more prevalent than it should be.

There is no easy way out of these bullying situations when you are twelve or thirteen years old. I was trying to be more mature and handle it on my own. Part of me felt that telling adults would be immature at this age. Mostly, I had hoped it would go away. But it didn't.

Ryan found a loyal following from his friends who also started taunting me. One of these boys, named Joey, I recall, fit the mold of the *Loyal Lieutenant*. Joey was a small kid for his age who was always standing under Ryan's wing, but was one of the more vocal boys. It is interesting to notice how the smaller kids align themselves with bigger kids, a purposeful maneuver and a theme often portrayed in movies, TV, and books. Of course, the most famous Loyal Lieutenant was portrayed as the bully's sidekick in *A Christmas Story*. I think, once again, the author of the story, Jean Shepard, got that part exactly right.

Ultimately, Joey was offered to me as the boy I would have to fight first, to prove my strength to Ryan. Refusing did not seem to be an option for me anymore. I had tried so many times in the past to get out of fighting, but I never seemed to succeed. At this point, I had resigned myself to having to fight to stay in step with the bullies. Even though I felt pretty confident about defeating Joey, due to his size, I worried about who I would have to fight next. Would no one be there to defend me? Finally, the date was set for when I would fight Joey, the Loyal Lieutenant. There was a system to this, mind you. It usually happened at lunch in the cafeteria. Word of the fight would be passed around the lunch tables.

"Hey, Alan. Joey said he wants to fight you tomorrow in the woods behind the school."

That would be told to me by one of my friends, who was told by one of his friends, who was told by one of his friends and so on. Since there was no recess in middle school, fights were planned for after school. Careful planning was now part of the bullying game. The entire seventh grade knew that there would be a fight and would be waiting. It sucked for me more than ever! I hoped that fighting at least made me look like I wasn't afraid, but of course I was terrified. The date was set for after the weekend, and I needed be ready because this fight was only the beginning.

◊ ◊ ◊

I was so nervous about the upcoming fight on Monday that I was distracted from my Bar Mitzvah preparation. A Bar Mitzvah is a traditional rite of passage into adulthood for Jewish boys at the age of thirteen. The ritual for girls is called a Bat Mitzvah, and both require significant preparation. My peers and I celebrated this journey to adulthood by attending lavish receptions on a par with weddings. It is where I learned that alcohol could dull my pain.

At most of these events, alcohol, including wine and champagne, was served to those over 21 years of age. The kids got savvy at snatching alcohol off the tables when adults weren't looking and sneaking off to drink it. The first time I was truly drunk, I was twelve years old and throwing up into a toilet at the synagogue. But the alcohol did indeed numb the pain I felt when worrying about bullies. In fact, I felt very little when drinking alcohol.

Following one of these receptions, Glen asked if I wanted to hang out with him and spend the night at Aaron's house. Aaron, Glen's friend, had access to marijuana, as his older brother was a pot dealer. It felt good to be invited and included, so I went.

I had never seen drugs or been around drugs before. Aaron had a bag and it contained what looked like green flakes. He had something called rolling papers and showed us how to take the green flakes and roll them into the paper to make what looked like a cigarette with pinched ends. He lit it, inhaled deeply into his lungs, and passed it to Glen. There I was, twelve years old, sitting in a circle, being passed a joint. When it was my turn, I took the tiny cigarette between my fingers, being careful not to drop it, and put the joint to my lips. As I inhaled, I coughed, feeling the strong, burning sensation in my throat.

Aaron asked me how I felt. I was still drunk on champagne and now getting high on marijuana, and I was twelve years old. All I knew is that the combination of both of these made me forget the upcoming fight planned for Monday, and anything else I might have been stressed about. In addition to dulling my pain, I thought it was cool to hang out with Glen and Aaron, doing things that older people do. As sad as it is to think about the choices that I was making, I have learned to honor the part of me that was desperate to escape the pain that paralyzed me with fear for so long. It was the best I knew how to cope with my situation, given what few tools I had. My pain was real, my self-esteem was at an all-time low, and anything that could make the pain go away was something I wanted and needed.

Of course, my problems didn't magically disappear, but for a while, it did make me forget. That is what I wanted, and sitting there, drunk and stoned, I realized what people mean when they say *hit rock bottom*. I felt a complete loss of control and loss of hope of living the life that I wanted to live. I was now living the life that I believed would make others like me or at least make the pain go away. I was twelve, and not so sure anymore that I would make it to thirteen.

CHAPTER NINETEEN

Growing Reality
Of Fear for My Life

The hole in my mind where my bad memories would be placed was getting quite deep now. The twenty-foot ladder was now only just able to reach the top of the hole. I had made the hole so deep, yet worried constantly whether it was deep enough to hold those memories, without them finding a way out of the hole. I looked at my bruised and bloodied hands. They were cramped from all the digging, and the dirt could never seem to be washed from under my fingernails, no matter how hard I scrubbed. When I looked at my hands, I somehow always had a piece of the hole with me, no matter how hard I tried to get it off me.

When Monday arrived, I dreaded the reality I had to face that day. The Loyal Lieutenant, Joey, was mouthing off about how I was weak, and that even he could take me because I was now "the boy who didn't want to fight." I knew full well that he was goaded into saying these things and that Ryan and that gang put him up to it. This boy was much smaller than me and for the first time in my bullying experiences, I knew that I had the upper hand. So, I told my friend Glen to tell them that I didn't want to fight him. That he wouldn't win.

Of course that did no good. That just egged on the group more. I look back and think how cruel it was for Ryan to push this kid to fight me. He had to know what was going to happen. Or did he really think that I was so weak that the little guy would beat me? The message came from one of Ryan's friends that the fight was on, and we would meet in the woods behind the school after dismissal.

As a walker to school, I saw no way out of this situation. I had to go past the woods to get home. I guess I could have tried to sneak out of school early, but I wasn't willing to do that. The biggest fear I had was that the rest of the gang would start punching me when we got there. But for the first time ever, I had some loyal friends of my own who were willing to protect me from that. That was a small comfort, but knowing the fight was going to happen anyway was still very unsettling.

When school let out, each of us with our gang of friends met up out in the woods behind the school. I am almost sorry to say that my friends were not much better than the bully's friends at this point. My friends were equally taunting me to start the fight, which I didn't want to do in the first place. But it was better than not having friends with me, and I knew the fight would happen anyway. We got to the clearing in the woods. As much as I didn't want to fight, I mustered up the parts of myself that were confident and cocky enough to get through this to make them leave me alone.

So, there I was facing Joey, the Loyal Lieutenant to Ryan. The boy was a good bit shorter than me. His gang was goading him on. He looked at me and tried to goad me into the first punch. I told him I didn't want to fight him and that he should "throw it." It took a while for the first punch to be thrown. The gang of kids encircling pushed us toward each other. His first swing started the fight.

He was smaller and weaker than I. I easily threw him to the ground and pinned his arms with my knees while sitting on his chest. He couldn't move. The fight was pointless. But now, the crowd of kids on both sides was incensed. They wanted to see the fight finish. My adrenaline flowed quickly and my heart was pumping. I leaned down to Joey and whispered to him.

"Just say 'I give up,' and I'll get up," I begged him.

"No way," Joey yelled back at me.

So, I did what the crowd expected. I punched him in the face. I wasn't running from this one and I didn't have to, as I knew this was a fight I would win. However, it was maddening how unfair this fight was. I felt like I was the bully here. But he would not give up, and his friends kept goading the fight on.

I asked him again, "Do you give up?"

"No way!" His confidence was unwavering.

I hit him in the face again. By this time my first punch had left his lip swelling. This one injured his ear. The next one created a black eye.

I was sick to my stomach, instinctually fighting for my survival. Having taken a beating from me, Joey finally surrendered. Even after I climbed off him, his friends continued to goad him into going after me. I gathered my friends together, and we started to walk away.

"I'll kill you, Eisenberg," Ryan threatened me.

I didn't look back. I didn't want to see the face of my former friend stabbing me with his ugly threats. Maybe I should have because in a few short weeks, I began to believe he meant it.

CHAPTER TWENTY

Enter the Bully
And its Name is Me

It was finally time. I had dug the hole very deep and also wide enough for me to climb down the ladder and sit if I needed to be away from the world above with the bad memories. I took the shoebox labelled "Alan's Bad Memories! DO NOT OPEN!" and brought it to the hole that I had dug. The whispers from the box were screaming in my ears as I carried it, causing my ears to ring. The whispers were telling me not to take them away, but I knew better. "You're still a loser. No one likes you. You are just a bully's punching bag," they would say to me. I didn't want these memories. I wanted a perfect life, and the way things were going, I needed to put these memories away. I carefully climbed down the ladder with one hand, holding the shoebox with the other, desperately working to keep the lid from coming off. I reached the bottom of the hole, placed the shoebox in a corner and sat for a moment, exhausted from the climb down. I had to cover my ears now, because the whispers from the shoebox were now shouts and louder than ever. Even with my hands over my ears, I could still hear them begging me to let them out. Telling me who I really was inside.

◊ ◊ ◊

After the fight with Joey, Ryan's Loyal Lieutenant, I was getting daily threats from Ryan via his gang of friends. Ryan would send one of his cronies over to me, and they would always say the same thing.

"Ryan is going to kill you!"

I truly started to believe them. After all, I had embarrassed him by beating his Loyal Lieutenant and while I usually didn't see Ryan at school, I saw his cronies, leering at me, putting a finger shaped like a gun to their heads, and pretending to pull the trigger while making a firing sound with their mouths. To say I was exhausted and scared of the bullying that was happening to me would be an understatement.

But before dealing with Ryan, I found ways to distract myself with other matters.

Glen, Aaron, and I continued to get high from the marijuana Aaron's brother provided us. Looking back on it, I am amazed how we were able to get away with sneaking into the boys' bathroom at school and smoking pot. One day, the school librarian asked the A/V Club (Glen, Aaron and me) to work on a mailing that was to be distributed to parents of the students. I don't recall whose idea it was, but either Glen or Aaron thought it would be funny to scribble drug innuendos on the mailing and seal them. Of course, I didn't object and probably thought it was funny too.

"Spark 'em!"

"We're high as a kite!"

"Marijuana is fun!"

"Light 'em up!"

Those are only the ones I remember. We thought we were pretty funny and creative, and that the kids would get a kick out of it. We were wrong...dead wrong.

A few days later, Glen, Aaron, and I were called into the Vice Principal's office, only to find all of our parents waiting there for us. The letters from the mailing we desecrated were in a stack on the Vice Principal's desk, along with very angry notes from parents. There was no question who was responsible for this. As a result, the three of us were reprimanded and suspended for three days. It struck me odd that no one questioned whether or not there was any drug use going on, given the innuendos in the mailing. My parents were none too happy, but they didn't ask me about drug use. During those three days, Glen and I got together and talked. He was the first to admit that he didn't like smoking pot. I confessed that I didn't either. We agreed that getting in trouble was enough to deter us from hanging around with Aaron and getting high. I didn't want to be "that kid" who was using drugs. I am grateful that Glen had the courage to speak up. It gave me the courage to do the same and change my behavior. No more drugs for me.

◊ ◊ ◊

I found it interesting how I could suffer so much in middle school, but have fun and be popular in Hebrew school. I liked how it felt to be a part of the group and not be picked on. To be included and accepted. But when you have been victimized as much as I have, it is easy to lose perspective of what is important to you. Spending time in Hebrew school was truly a gift, but I did something that was less than gracious.

The world of bullying isn't black and white. There aren't simply "the bullies" and "the bullied". The world is full of grays and questions that are debated endlessly, with answers that feel like they change with the blowing of the wind. While much of my identity developed because of my being "the bullied", I saw how easily I could identify with being "the bully" as well. Does being bullied increase the chances that one will become a bully himself? It was confusing to understand what was happening to me.

Prior to Hebrew school, my classmates and I played indoor dodgeball for about a half an hour. I did my share of goofing off with Glen and my other friends in Hebrew school, being reprimanded for being inattentive. It was so vastly different from what I experienced at middle school. Since I wasn't the one being picked on, for once it happened to someone else. His name was Daniel, and I can't really say why he was chosen. Maybe he was a little bigger than us. Maybe he was the one who always raised his hand and acted smarter than us. To be honest, it wasn't like he was bullied every time we went to Hebrew school. Most of us grew up together and got along.

But Daniel was the butt of many jokes, and reflecting back, I see how unfair it was. On one occasion, I participated in a cruel prank. We placed about ten tacks, pointing up, on Daniel's chair. I totally believed he would see them there long before he chose to sit down. But for some reason he got distracted while talking to someone and didn't see the tacks. I still have that awful image of Daniel setting his full weight into his chair, onto the tacks. His face turned a crimson red, but he bit his lip, trying hard not to cry in front of us. I was in awe of how he didn't react by jumping up out of his seat. It was like he was defeated. The teacher noticed him turning red and tears welling up. The teacher asked Daniel what was wrong. He couldn't speak to answer or he would start crying. Daniel simply stood up and walked out of the room with all the tacks stuck to his bottom. It was at this point that the teacher realized what had happened.

As Daniel left the classroom with tears welling up in his eyes, the other kids snickered with laughter. *At least it didn't happen to me* was all I thought. Then the teacher spoke up. He said he didn't want to know who did it, but that they should go help Daniel. A few of the boys who were involved, as well as myself, left the room to help him. At this point, I realized what I had done and felt remorse. This was not at all funny. We went into the bathroom and there was Daniel, tears streaming down his face.

"Why did you do this?" he begged for answers. The boys and I could say nothing. I think we all felt the same. I don't know who was more embarrassed, Daniel for being the victim of this malicious prank, or us for dehumanizing our classmate. I cringed as I helped pull the tacks out of his sore bottom, knowing I was hurting him again. I felt terribly ashamed that I was the bully this time. The boys and I returned to the classroom, but Daniel never returned to class that day. We never picked on Daniel again.

For all the shame I felt about my behavior, I am grateful to have had the opportunity to reconnect with Daniel as an adult and express remorse for my actions. He was so happy to hear from me, said that he didn't even recall the incident, and we talked for hours. Over the last few years, we have seen each other a few times, and I proudly call him my friend. It doesn't change what happened, but it allowed me to come to terms with and accept what had happened thirty years earlier.

CHAPTER TWENTY-ONE

The Moment I Saw My Life End

Once I felt the hole in my mind was deep enough so that no one would find my memories, I dug it wider, so that there was plenty of room to hide in the darkness. It was hard work to dig the hole in my mind. I was a child when I started digging this hole, and with each rung down the ladder, I would age back to the child I was when I started digging, no matter how old I was. At the bottom of the hole, like Peter Pan, I never would grow up and neither would my box of memories.

"Ryan is going to kill you this week for what you did to me," Joey threatened me, and I believed him.

I gave Joey a message to give to his boss. "Tell Ryan that I have a knife, and if he comes after me, I will use it," I warned. The idea that I needed a weapon to defend myself just came to me. I hoped this new information would deter Ryan from wanting to fight me. But a knife seemed so violent and dangerous. It wasn't really my style. I didn't want to hurt anybody.

When I arrived home from school that day, I searched for something to use that would fit and be hidden in my pocket, and serve as my protection. Then I saw it, as it caught a gleam of light shining in through the window of the kitchen. It was my mom's metal fingernail file. It was small enough to tuck away and pointy enough for protection. As I practiced carrying the file in my pocket, it poked me and hurt. A part of me knew it was wrong to carry a weapon to school, but another part of me didn't care. I wanted to feel safe. Carrying this file made me feel safe...at least for a few days.

The threats on my life delivered from Ryan's friends continued. And I repeatedly warned him that I had a knife, hoping to deter this confrontation. By the end of the week, I thought I was safely avoiding Ryan and the bullies by taking my special detour through the woods. But Ryan had found out about that path. I didn't know how, but he had. After a 30-minute walk around my hidden path, I emerged at a point where I could see the road, and there, looking down at me, was Ryan. There were no cronies, no friends to support either side. It was just Ryan and me. I was petrified and reached into my pocket to wrap my fingers around the cold steel of the file for security.

"I'm going to kill you," Ryan said to me, calmly, almost deadly. My heart was pounding. I didn't want to fight him. I was tired of fighting. I pulled the file from my pocket. At the top of the path, where it met the road, Ryan immediately threw down his backpack and took a swing at me with his fist. I instinctively lashed out at him with the file. My adrenaline was rushing and I was shaking. I lashed out again, and this time made contact with him, cutting him in the midsection of his side.

I saw the shock and surprise on his face, and then he screamed out in pain. Catching him by surprise was my only chance to escape. I was sick to my stomach about having used a weapon against another human being, but I felt I had no choice, like a cornered animal. I turned away from Ryan and took off running down the road to my house.

When I quickly turned my head to look back, I saw Ryan running after me, not giving up that easily. He was angry and I assume in pain. I had no idea how much damage I had done when I slashed him with the file. I turned and ran as fast as I could. I ran out of worry about what I had done. I ran out of fear that he WOULD kill me if he caught up to me.

I ran the whole mile home at my best top speed, with adrenaline running through me. I felt like I was going to throw up. Ryan ran after me the whole way, too. I was lucky, because my grandmother was at my house recovering from surgery a few days earlier. There was a long driveway leading up to my house that felt like it went on forever. I called out for my grandmother as I ran. Ryan was right behind me. My grandmother must have heard me because as I reached the front door, she opened it, welcoming me to safety.

From the other side of the screen door, Ryan was yelling that I had stabbed him while I stood safely next to my grandmother. He was still screaming when she yelled back at him to leave, protecting me. As he was leaving, I saw blood on the side of his torn shirt where I had slashed at him with the file.

As an adult, I often wondered about my peers in the same situation. Did other kids bring a weapon to school for protection from bullies, feeling the same way I had, fearing for their lives? Some kids even resort to carrying a gun. Is fear that strong that it can guide us to make these decisions? Since that day with Ryan, I have never carried a weapon. I also don't recall ever being that frightened again.

It is difficult accepting the choices I made and the impact my actions had on my life and the lives of others. I know I didn't do much damage to Ryan, but it was enough for him to finally leave me alone. I had tried to warn him through his buddies. I had tried to avoid him by taking a detoured path home. But when confronted, I did the only thing I could do, survive. You would think that would feel like a victory, or even relief, but it didn't. It sickened me to have to harm Ryan. I'm not so sure that Ryan didn't get off easy, because I think I felt more pain than he did that day.

CHAPTER TWENTY-TWO

So Much Pain
So Much Lost

Although I dreaded the task, I had to track through the yard, beyond the tree line to the field of long grass and flowers to return to the hole and add more bad memories to my shoebox. As I approached the hole, I could once again hear the whispers of the memories in the box, and the familiar sweat, rapid heartbeat, and fear would come over me. I slowly made my way down the ladder to the shoebox lying in the dirt below. I would have to take off the lid to add these new memories and knew what would happen when I did. The soft whispers coming from the memories in the shoebox would be screaming at me. I would have to use all my strength and concentration to keep them in the box as I added the new bad memories there and then close the lid as quickly as possible. The sound of the bad memories when the shoebox opened was deafening and would leave a ringing in my ears for hours. I pushed the new memories in the box, closed the lid and climbed up the ladder as quickly as I could in my weakened state, as this process drained me of my energy. As I got through the tree line, the whispers did subside, although I could still hear them, even at night, calling to me from the hole.

◇ ◇ ◇

After the incident with Ryan, I was never quite the same at school. I stopped going to the A/V club and became a bit more introverted. It wasn't safe taking my detour home from school, so I needed another excuse to stay after school.

I still found some solace spending time with my favorite teacher, Mr. Wood, in my social studies class. We did fun things in his class, like drawing a giant mural of the world on the classroom wall. Students were permitted to stay after school to work on the mural, which Glen, our classmate Carl, and I would do. I was in Mr. Wood's class when the first space shuttle was launched, and I recall all of us, including him, watching in amazement. Talking with Mr. Wood distracted me from the horrors of bullying I experienced that year. It all culminated for me at the end of that year in what Mr. Wood wrote in my yearbook. He wrote:

> *"This has been a great year for me, Alan, and believe it or not, you are one of the reasons. Not often does a teacher and student relationship progress to one of friendship. I guess that's how I feel ours has gone. I think you are a super guy. You've made some difficult moments enjoyable because of your personality. God bless you."*

I have no idea if Mr. Wood knew anything about what I was going through, but these words really helped me at that time. I was contemplating my life's worth and thinking that maybe I didn't belong on this earth, but these words helped bring me back to reality. I still look back on them today to remind me that all was not bad during those years and that, even in my worst of times, I could have some positive impact in this world. Mr. Wood's validation of my self-worth made a significant difference in my life. The world benefits greatly from teachers like him, who help mentor students through the tough times.

Years later, as I continued to think about what Mr. Wood, my first mentor, did for me, the magic of social media connected me to a picture of Mr. Wood today. He looked older, of course, and was now working as a school principal. I hoped the staff and students at that school knew how fortunate they were to have an administrator like Mr. Wood. I wished for them to benefit, as I did, from his ability to connect with and support young people in need.

◊ ◊ ◊

To every yin there is a yang. And for every effective teacher in my life, there were also ineffective ones. In seventh grade, I would experience both the kindness of my social studies teacher and the bullying of my art teacher.

One thing I noticed about myself was that I went from being a very outgoing and vocal six-year-old when I moved to Lexington, to being a withdrawn and timid thirteen-year-old who constantly worried and felt threatened about bullies. As I look back at pictures of myself during those years, I see a smiling young boy at seven and then a serious and disheveled thirteen-year-old with dark circles under his tired eyes. In many pictures, I recognize that I am always wearing a Grateful Dead shirt that had a skeleton surrounded by flowers on it. I had my mom buy it for me when I first saw it at a store. I knew I had to have it, because it said the words that I had said to myself many times in my days in Lexington. I know that I will be more grateful when I am dead. I thought that someone reading my mind had had the same thought. I loved the picture on the shirt and the saying. It would be some years later before I actually figured out that the Grateful Dead was actually a band and I was wearing a band shirt.

For a fleeting moment, when putting on the shirt, suicide would cross my mind. I didn't know what my purpose in life was anymore, other than to be picked on, punched, and scared all the time. As an adult, I know that this is a time that many bully survivors go through and it is one of those decision moments. At this point in my life I contemplated the idea of suicide for a little while, but I could never hurt my family by leaving them with a suicide, and that is what kept me going.

Certainly puberty and other factors played a part in the rebellious angst that I was starting to feel more in my life, but I can honestly say that I think my social environment also had a lot to do with it. I had, during this time of being bullied, developed a personality that was defensive and untrusting. I did not look like a student who a teacher would be happy to have in his class, as I appeared unhappy, angry, and probably stoned. I wonder how much it was a factor when I walked into my art class in seventh grade.

For me, art class was a nice break from the stressful work of the core classes in middle school. As a creative person, I always enjoyed art and how it allowed me to express myself. My teacher, Mr. Whitlock, was a man in his late fifties or early sixties. Early on in art class, I noticed that Mr. Whitlock took a great disliking to me. He was very critical of my work and would say it aloud to me in front of other students. He would often hold up a piece of artwork I had done and use it as an example of the "wrong" way to do the project, along with pointing me out and showing my low grade to the rest of the class.

Mr. Whitlock gave me terrible grades and many times ignored me if I had my hand raised for a question. I would even stand at his desk, wanting to talk to him about how to do a project or my grade, and he would simply not look up and ignore me, so I would return to my seat defeated. There is little doubt in my mind that he was picking on me. Given my sensitivity at this time in my life, it's possible I was hyper-aware of this and maybe more judgmental than I would be otherwise, but he definitely treated me differently.

I regularly attended class as expected and completed projects by the deadline. Because art is subjective, I didn't understand how I could be given a low grade if I completed the assignment; my artwork earned C's and D's, while my classmates earned A's and B's. When the grading period ended, the quarter grade was unsatisfactory to my parents. At that point I explained what I perceived to be going on with this. I told my mother that Mr. Whitlock would not tell me why he was giving me bad grades, so she scheduled a meeting with him.

My mother returned from the meeting feeling angry about what he had to say about the grades and me. She was not that upset with me, but she was upset with him for the way he rudely treated her and talked about me. Mr. Whitlock told her I paid no attention in his class and didn't follow directions that he gave. He continued to single me out with criticism and bad grades. I recall on the last day of the school year, my mom picked me up from school and took me to a restaurant for ice cream. When we got there, ironically enough, my art teacher was seated in a booth eating across from us. He sat there and stared at my mother and me. We stared back. It was very eerie, like each one was waiting for the other to make a move. It was unfortunate that a class I anticipated enjoying became a class I loathed attending. What it was he didn't like about me, I still don't know. But I do know that I was in a very dark place that year. I think it was outwardly obvious to him that I was in this place. But I wasn't a mean kid. I wasn't a delinquent. I was having a rough time, and he did nothing to help make that better.

CHAPTER TWENTY-THREE

Body Blow
Knock Him Out

I didn't understand why, with all the work I had done, that the voices of my bad memories continued to speak to me from the shoebox so deep in the ground. Then it struck me that I was leaving the hole open and the shoebox memories were leaking out. I needed a cover for the hole and went back to the field beyond my yard and tree line to search for something to cover the hole. As if planned, I found a piece of plywood lying only a few feet from the hole that was big enough to cover it. I didn't remember seeing that before. As with the ladder, it seemed to be there to be noticed when I needed it. I took the cover and placed it over the hole. I had to adjust the ladder at a bit more of an angle to keep it lower than the cover, so the cover could truly seal the hole that contained the shoebox of my bad memories. As I placed the cover on the hole, it sealed it perfectly and the whispers coming from the hole subsided. But my feeling of panic hadn't, and I was again sweating and feeling my heart beat in my chest rapidly. I still had to place one more bad memory in the hole before trying to leave it permanently. Unfortunately it was one memory that I never wanted to put in there, because it was the last of my Lexington bad memories and its name was Carl.

◊ ◊ ◊

In the Jewish tradition, I would become a Bar Mitzvah at thirteen years of age. I studied Hebrew and the Torah for years in preparation to become an adult in the eyes of God. While this day is very exciting for most boys, I was not looking forward to it because I didn't have many friends with whom I could share this special occasion. .

But as the Bar Mitzvah date approached, I did invite Glen, Kyle, Tommy, Aaron, and my new best friend from social studies class, Carl. I promised them it would be fun, and there would be champagne, as we had seen at other Bar Mitzvahs. The ceremony was conducted at the synagogue, and the reception was celebrated at a nearby hotel.

When we arrived at the hotel, I noticed that my table (the kids' table), did not have champagne on it like the other tables. I was upset and embarrassed because I had promised my friends, who probably didn't care. But I did. I wanted to make them happy, make them like me more. When I asked my parents if we could have champagne on the kids' table, they were hesitant. When I became even more upset and began to cry, my mother gave in and placed a bottle of champagne on our table. I stopped crying but felt like a loser. I had made a promise to impress my friends, and it didn't turn out the way I'd anticipated. I was embarrassed for both wanting this champagne for my friends to drink and not having it and worrying that I would lose my friends over it.

Despite the alcohol incident, my Bar Mitzvah was a lovely event, and everyone seemed to have a good time. Carl brought the biggest gift to the party for me and had the widest smile during the entire event. I was so happy to have a new best friend, really the only gift needed at that time in my life.

A few weeks after my Bar Mitzvah, my father came home from work one day to report that his company was transferring him to an office in Northern Virginia, near Washington, D.C., and that we would be moving in the summer. My sister was upset because she had made great friends in high school. I, on the other hand, was ecstatic and dreaming each night of starting again, away from the bullies. That was the good news. The bad news was that I would be saying goodbye to a newly made best friend.

◊ ◊ ◊

There was more good news: The bullying appeared to have ceased, because now I had the reputation as "the boy who stabbed Ryan". I was mostly a pariah now at my school, except for the few friends who'd stuck by me. One day, though, Carl and I had an argument. Though I cannot recall what precipitated it, there was indeed a confrontation with someone who I thought was my best friend. Carl decided that the argument warranted a fist fight after school. Every time I took a swing at Carl, my mind flashed to all the other punches I had thrown in my mission to survive the bullies. Carl spewed ugly and demeaning slurs at me, and I returned just as many, destroying the last bit of our friendship. It ended as quickly as it had begun. I took my long mile walk back home, thinking to myself *I simply have to survive another few weeks and then I will be out of here. Out of this hell I was living in.*

Carl and I never spoke again. It didn't upset me though, as I was numb to the pain by now. One friend after another had abandoned me, and the few remaining, I lacked any trust in anymore. I couldn't wait to get into my parents' car and leave Lexington for good.

When we arrived in Northern Virginia, we were fortunate enough to stay with Sam, my first childhood friend, and his family while my parents searched for a new home. I recall being with Sam in his bedroom reflecting on how it had been eight long years since we had seen each other. He seemed to have had a relatively happy childhood and was well adjusted as a teenager. This was in sharp contrast to the person sitting across from him whose innocence had been lost much too early. He had gotten new music from a band called Rush, who had released an album called *Moving Pictures*. We sat in his room, listening to the album over and over again. It was an easy way to pass the time without having to talk about much.

Later that night, Sam's parents set up some old eight millimeter films they took of us when we were just little kids. As I watched those films and saw myself on the screen, I no longer had any idea who that happy-go-lucky boy was. There was darkness to my sense of self and personality that made it difficult to connect to these early childhood memories with Sam and his family. As much as I wished to rekindle my friendship with Sam, too much had changed, and we no longer had that commonality to have a close friendship again.

My family was now relocating to a new home in Fairfax, Virginia. Our home in Lexington, Massachusetts, sold quickly, and in no time, we were packing up the moving van. I recall that the night before we moved, my family had to stay at a hotel. At the dinner we had that night at the hotel, I ordered a drink called a Tom Mix, which was a non-alcohol version of the Tom Collins drink. When the waiter brought us the drinks, I took a sip of mine and immediately tasted the alcohol. The bartender had mistakenly made me a Tom Collins. I drank the whole thing, without letting on. It felt like my last rebellious "screw you" to Lexington. My sister, Robyn, was in tears, saying she didn't want to go and leave her friends. She even grabbed hold of the house in protest. I wasn't going to show it, but I was jumping for joy in my head, eager to start anew. I was already in the car with my seatbelt securely fastened, wondering when the hell everyone would get in the car and get me the hell out of here.

Away from all the bullies.

Away from all of these painful memories.

As I watched my house in Lexington, Massachusetts, disappear from my view out the back window of the car, I said to myself, *"I'll forget you Lexington. I'll leave those memories behind.*

In my mind I had one more visit to the hole to make before I left Lexington. I didn't want anyone else to find it or accidently fall in, so I brought some shotgun orange spray-paint up from my yard, through the tree line, to the tall grass and flower field in my mind. I leaned over the plywood cover of the hole and painted the word "DEPRESSION" on it, thinking I was warning others that there was a deep depression in this spot, so they wouldn't fall in. I turned to leave but decided to write two more words, just for me, to remind me what was in this hole, "Forget Lexington".

PART THREE

DIGGING IN

THE DIRT

TO FIND WHERE

I GOT HURT

CHAPTER TWENTY-FOUR

Events That I
Could Not Control

I was now an adult and even though I was able to keep the shoebox of bad memories in the covered hole out of my mind for many years, there were times when I saw myself standing over the hole and reading the smeared and barely visible words on the weather worn plywood cover, "ANXIETY" and "DEPRESSION". The words were taking on a new meaning for me, and I could still hear the quiet whispers of the memories deep down in the hole begging me to let them out. Instead of letting them fully out, I stood over the hole, unable to run away any longer and with my own anxiety keeping me frozen in my spot. My ears were ringing loudly from the cacophony of screams from the bad memory box, and I couldn't see in front of me. Fear gripped me and I was frozen. What had I done? The memories I didn't want were now screaming for me to listen to them again and again.

◊ ◊ ◊

After my move from Lexington, I had many great years, successfully keeping those awful memories buried. But I noticed I struggled with anger and anxiety from age thirteen through my adult years. It was a slow burn from anxiety to depression. I sequenced the events leading to my fall from anxiety to depression more recently in trying to figure out how I got to this point.

Symptoms of Anxiety Leading to Depression

1. Around the age of 21, I panicked during times of major change and transition, feeling the need to flee from crowds or avoid crowded situations. I thought it was strange, but ignored it as I was a problem avoider.

2. Around the age of 22, I developed gastrointestinal and upset stomach problems during times of stress which led to my

having my first gastrointestinal evaluation. No medically significant findings reported, but I would still suffer often.

3. At 22 years old, I experienced my first panic attack during college exams. Panic resulting from the brain's signaling of an emotional threat occurred often, making me fear danger when there really wasn't any. As years went on, these attacks would happen infrequently to me, but would still reoccur, particularly at times of stress.

4. On April 20, 1999, two boys named Dylan Klebold and Eric Harris walked into a school in Columbine, Colorado, and opened gunfire on the students with seemingly no remorse. Captured on video was a horrifying scene as they hunted down and shot their classmates. A commission was held to study how this could have happened. Stories of rampant bullying in the school were confirmed, and it was reported that both Klebold and Harris were victims of bullying. This is not to say that bullying was the root cause of their actions, but it did bring to light the larger issue of bullying as a problem. In the end, bullying was ruled out as the cause of their action, but what did come out of it was that the school had a bullying issue that others brought up when talked to.

5. On September 11, 2011, my world was rocked as I watched the World Trade Centers in New York collapse. I felt tremors in the building where I worked, as the residual effects from the plane crashing into the Pentagon a few miles away were felt. I worried that I would never see my family again. I began to worry all the time after that and had an anger in me that burst out to affect my family.

6. At my Alma Mater, Virginia Tech, on a sunny day on April 16, 2007, a young man named Seung-Hui Cho went into a classroom building and gunned down thirty-two people before

turning the gun on himself. During the investigation that followed, fellow high-school students of Cho shared with reporters witnessing Cho being bullied, repeatedly ridiculed for his shy demeanor and his accent. He would also share his view of the Columbine shooting as heroic.

7. In May of 2007, wanting to make a difference on the issues of bullying based on the attack at Virginia Tech and my knowledge of what had happened to me, I created my website chronicling my bullying experiences in Lexington as a way to release the countless stories bottled up in the dark recesses of my mind. I thought it would be cathartic for me and also help others to feel like they weren't alone in being bullied as a youth. It was effective for others, but was not cathartic for me.

8. During the next few years, between 2008 and 2012, I was interviewed by newspaper reporters and radio show hosts, and spoke in public on the long-term effects of bullying. Whenever I spoke about it, I became triggered by the memories that I had really not confronted, finding myself in tears during each interview or presentation. I was trying to support others on a journey that I hadn't fully healed from myself. I learned why the Bible contains the saying "physician heal thyself." You truly cannot help others until you have helped yourself.

9. In June of 2009, when I was laid off from my dream job, I was once again triggered into the fight or flight panic that was now constantly occurring. Emotional threats felt as dangerous to me as physical threats. My brain didn't know the difference, and I developed what I call my perceived threat syndrome, seeing many things in life as threats to my well-being. Any shot to my self-esteem, loss of a job, abandonment and betrayal by friends, or rejection sent me into a panicked state with the sole purpose

of surviving.

10. In the summer of 2011, while viewing the documentary *"Bully"* by Lee Hirsch, I found myself sobbing throughout the film. I cried, because, as I watched it, I realized how little had changed from the time I was bullied as a child to how bullying is being managed in the present. I felt deeply for the people in the movie and felt that no matter how hard I tried, I had lost hope that I was making a difference in the world of bullying.

11. I noticed in early 2012 that my anxiety increased dramatically. I had to sit in the aisle seat at the movies or on a plane, for fear I would have to escape quickly. I had daily panic attacks, even when out shopping or getting a haircut. I was constantly trying to escape from invisible demons in my mind. A dark room frightened me, and sitting in a crowded theater for a movie, play, or show put me into a sweating, heart racing panic attack. I had bouts of secluding myself at home, not wanting to go out or see anyone and experiencing a low mood. The anxiety made my life so unmanageable that I needed to seek professional help. My physician prescribed medication and diagnosed me with General Anxiety Disorder. Then, in September of 2012, I struggled with the normal transition of missing my eldest son when he headed off to college. I didn't know how to grieve the loss, as acknowledging any feelings felt unsafe.

12. In late 2012, I experienced a significant loss of appetite all the time and constant stomach aches. I lost over twenty pounds in a month and felt very weak. I was sent to a gastrointestinal specialist who ran several painful tests on me. My son drove me to my appointments because I'd developed a fear of driving. The only medically significant finding was some acid reflux occurring in my esophagus. Yet the persistent stomach pain

continued.

13. Around the same time as the stomach aches, my sleep was restless, as I tossed and turned throughout the night. I awoke fatigued and lethargic. I felt nervous throughout the day and took to my bed as soon as I got home. I didn't want to talk to anyone. I felt very down on myself, like a big loser working at a job I no longer enjoyed. I worried that my wife and children were going to abandon me and that I would lose my job. Depression was setting in, and I didn't know it because I had never felt it before. My thoughts became very dark, very fast.

14. In December 2012, I received an offer to return to Lexington, Massachusetts, because they had discovered my website and stories, to speak about my years of bullying there. I wanted to go so badly and close that chapter of my life. I was to give my speech in March 2013. But as the date for the trip approached, things turned from bad to worse, and my anxiety had become a problem all the time. My fight or flight mode was constant, and I was a nervous wreck. I couldn't even attend any social event or meeting at work without having a panic attack. I wasn't eating, I wasn't sleeping, and I wasn't talking. I was only hurting. I went back to my doctor because I was sure I was dying of stomach cancer or something, due to the increased pain in my stomach. I was to travel back to Lexington to speak in a week. My doctor put me on a stronger anxiety medication, gave me something to help me sleep and the name of a psychiatrist to call.

15. I called the psychiatrist, Dr. McDonald, and he agreed to see me right away. I was glad, because I needed to travel to Lexington and speak and felt I could not do that without help. I had been missing work from my anxiety and fears and needed to settle back down. I didn't know what was wrong with me. I

drove on a wintery day to this first psychiatrist's office, and that is where my real troubles began.

This is the list that would lead me to my ultimate diagnosis and force me to face the things that I had feared for much of my life. Just as my paternal grandmother had suffered from depression, I would find that depression does run in the family. It never leaves me, the feelings I had at the beginning of my fall into depression and a total loss of belief that my life had any further worth. As I said above, I ended up at my doctor's office in a panic, and he gave me the name of a psychiatrist to go see right away along with some anti-anxiety medication. I recall going on the long drive to this psychiatrist's office. I went in and the first thing they did was tell me to pay them two-hundred and fifty dollars up front. I paid, feeling as if I would pay anything at this point to feel better.

I was sent to a waiting room where there were a number of other patients. I felt like they were all staring at me. My legs could not stop shaking, and I was so scared and nervous about this visit. My stomach was in knots, and even though I had every test result telling me nothing physically was wrong, I still felt like something was wrong with my stomach and that I needed to go to the bathroom all the time. Finally, after waiting several nerve-wracking minutes, I was called in to meet with Dr. McDonald, the psychiatrist.

I walked in and sat down and that was it. I completely broke down, cried my eyes out and told him what was going on with me. In fact, what I really said to him was that I didn't know what was wrong with me. I was so confused. I told him about my upcoming trip to Lexington, my loss of weight, the pain in my stomach, and my constant fears. Dr. McDonald only listened to me for fifteen minutes. He explained that I had depression and that my symptoms were common. Dr. McDonald asked me if I felt suicidal. I said I didn't think so. He asked me if I had weapons at home. I told him I didn't. He wrote me a bunch of prescriptions, some for depression and some for anxiety, gave me his card with his cell phone number, told me to cancel my trip to Lexington, because I told him I didn't want to go, and sent me on my way.

Fifteen minutes was all I got, and he scheduled me for my next two-hundred and fifty dollar session two weeks from then. I went to the supermarket and filled my prescriptions and took them right away. Dr. McDonald warned me that there would be side effects to the medicine. For me, that would be an understatement.

I made my first big mistake by looking up all the side effects on the internet. I was going crazy looking at all the information about the side effects of the medicine. Besides the usual trouble sleeping, loss of libido, ringing in ears, I began to experience, or so I thought, another major issue that only a few subjects had. I was pacing around and around my kitchen table. Two days later, I called Dr. McDonald and told him I was having this pacing problem. He told me to stop taking the medicine immediately and set an appointment for a few days later.

I knew then that I now had two major problems. One, I was back to where I started, and two, I could not afford to pay another two-hundred and fifty dollars so soon. I decided, in a momentary lapse of calm and rational thinking, that I would reach out to two people I trusted. The first one was Adam Blum, a great gentleman who worked for Jewish Social Services that I had worked with on some of my bullying presentations. The other was my Rabbi, my trusted clergyman, who was also my friend and a great supporter of my bullying initiative.

Then, what I can only explain as karma or, some might call it, kismet happened. My friend, Adam, at the Jewish Social Services sent me a list of three psychiatrists who took my benefits and who he thought were good. Then my Rabbi told me of a synagogue member who was a psychiatrist; he thought this practitioner would be a good fit for me. This psychiatrist, named Dr. Rosenbaum, was on both of their lists. I called Dr. Rosenbaum's office and was told he was booked and wouldn't be able to see me for two more months. I truly felt as if I did not have two months to wait and was so confused about the way I was feeling. I honestly wasn't sure I would be able to survive another two months.

I called my Rabbi again, crying and begging for help. He calmed me down and said he would reach out to the psychiatrist on my behalf personally to try to help me. About fifteen minutes later, I received a call from Dr. Rosenbaum. He was cheery and friendly to me and listened to me as I explained myself for a minute. He told me how the Rabbi had called him and how if he had known I was a congregant, he would have made a consideration. Dr. Rosenbaum told me to come see him the next day and gave me the address of his practice.

At the moment he gave me the address, I sensed that finally something was going right, and I started to calm down. I believe in faith and I believe that things happen for a reason. The address of the psychiatrist was an office space on the same floor that my company had vacated only a year before. He was literally working in my old office space now, and somehow I saw that as a sign, like kismet, that my solution was in front of me.

The next day, I went to the familiar building where I used to work and climbed the familiar steps to this new office space. There was some comfort for me in doing this routine, and I walked into Dr. Rosenbaum's office where my desk used to be only a year earlier. How strange and yet comforting to know that there might be some logic to this. I was met by a much happier person in Dr. Rosenbaum, who put his arm around me as if we were old friends and escorted me back to his office. I sat in his office and this time calmly told him what I was feeling and what the past history of the last few months of my anxiety and depression had been.

Dr. Rosenbaum told me I was showing many of the signs of classic depression, brought on by the anxiety I was experiencing. He explained that many times, anxiety and depression go hand in hand. He heard my tale of bringing the bullying days back to my mind and agreed that it could have had an effect on me. He honestly explained that there was no quick and easy cure and that the first step is to try some medication to stop the constant anxiety attacks and worry so that I could be treated further. As Dr. Rosenbaum wrote these different prescriptions, he explained to me in detail what the side effects might be and that I should expect to be patient for about six to eight weeks for the medicine to really work. He escorted me out, telling me to call him any time I needed to talk and he would be there for me. I felt I was on my way to a cure. I really had no idea at the time that it would be two years of hard work and learning to find my path to feeling better and learning techniques to stop the pain and depression.

CHAPTER TWENTY-FIVE

The Great Depression

I stood in the field in front of the thin protective trees, beyond the yard that had held my demons at bay. Those bad memories were trapped in the shoebox down the hole for a very long time and were not happy to be there. It took much of my strength over that time to keep them there, and I felt weak with exhaustion. As I stood over the hole with the barely readable weathered plywood, holding my ears as the bad memories from the shoebox screamed to me, I felt faint. The world in front of me went dark, and I fell, splitting the plywood spray-painted with the words "ANXIETY" and "DEPRESSION". The depression warning was no longer the hole; it was how I felt inside. As I fell down the over 20 feet I had dug out with my bare hands as a kid, the shoebox of bad memories began screaming at me to open it. I landed with a loud thud in complete blackness, for the light was too far away at the top. I could not see, and all I could hear were the screams of my bad memories. I felt around and placed my hands on the shoebox I had left there long ago as a child. The shoebox, worn with time, broke apart in my hands and disintegrated, leaving me with my bad memories alone at the bottom of the dark and dirty hole. They were shouting at me. "Loser, Thief, Liar, Wimp." All I had was darkness and the incessant screaming of my bad memories. My good memories were far away now, no longer within my earshot, so I couldn't recall them. All I heard were the hauntings of my past. A past I had worked so hard for so many years to forget. But I could no longer forget the memories, and they screamed so loud at me that my ears begin to bleed. I heard, felt and saw nothing else. I was truly lost in my own place, all alone, with my bad thoughts.

◊ ◊ ◊

In the time since I had my first major depressive episode, I have learned that many people I knew had also had their bouts with depression. In fact about twenty percent of Americans are supposedly suffering with a form of depression at any given time. That number is probably low as many men don't report it and some people turn to drugs and alcohol to reduce their feelings of stress, never seeking the help of a professional mental health expert or doctor. There are also peak times that depression can hit, when you are in your teens, around mid-life, and as you move to retirement age.

I do believe, however, that you cannot explain the feelings that come with anxiety and depression to someone who has not experienced it. It is that way because it's hard for anyone who hasn't had it to understand that a person with depression and anxiety doesn't want to feel this way, does want to go and have fun, but their mind tells them they can't do it. It was a very confusing time for me as I felt completely trapped by my depression and was close to giving up.

I also learned that depression and anxiety, like any other learning process, requires time to comprehend. At least it did for me. Those four learning processes that I would go through with my depression for me were:

1. **I didn't know what I didn't know** – I had this terrible feeling that I had never felt before and had no idea why. I was scared and terribly lonely, even with my family and friends around. I did not want to communicate with anyone and wanted to be alone. I was so scared because I could not explain this loneliness and emptiness inside to anyone.

2. **I know what I didn't know** – After looking on the internet and meeting with psychiatrists, I now knew that I had serious anxiety and depression. It wasn't going to go away tomorrow, and I could not hide in a corner or work around it. I was going to have to go through it.

3. **I learned what I didn't know** – for the next two years (yes, two years), I would go through a period of discovery and self-evaluation to learn about what was going on with me, what

caused it, and how I would eventually solve it. I would study from books by authors who wrote on the issue. Some books and some websites were helpful. Others would make me more worried.

4. **I became an expert on what I didn't know** – Well, expert might be a little strong. I feel like I have read every possible book and learned every possible thing I could about what went wrong with me. But even with all that knowledge, I still felt like a stranger in my own body. It would be quite a while to find my new *normal.*

During the beginning of my journey through anxiety and depression, I would come to a realization that mending the mind is much like mending a broken bone. Many times, when you break your bone, you need to have the bone set back in place by a professional doctor or specialist, wait for it to heal, and then begin therapy to increase your strength and heal completely.

When you break your mind, I found it to be much the same process. You must work to set your mind back into a place where it can heal. I found that I needed the help of a professional, whether a psychiatrist, psychologist, licensed clinical social worker, or life coach; there is someone out there to help. Then the long waiting period starts as, for me, I walked through my four stages of depression. This was a long two-year process, and I was impatient about it, but the time was needed and it is one that I would never regret.

During the first few months of my depression, I had an accident (actually, I dropped a boat on my foot) that did truly break a bone in my foot and keep me from walking for over six weeks. In some ways it couldn't have happened at a less opportune time as I was in the throes of a major depression and anxiety episode. At the same time, it forced me to sit and simply have to confront myself head on. I couldn't go to work at the beginning and had extreme physical pain to go along with the mental anguish I was suffering. But I was also stuck with myself, and I had a lot of time to think.

It was some time during these six weeks of physical healing that I realized I didn't want to sit around and watch television by myself. I missed the freedom I had lost and the sense of happiness about life that I used to have. I realized that I would have to heal, like the bones in my foot; I would have to heal my mind as well. I knew that exercise in the form of physical therapy would be required to get my foot back in order, and I found an old Yoga DVD that my wife had. I put it in and made a daily routine of doing all I could through that DVD. I looked forward to my daily thirty minutes of Yoga and the peace that I began to feel doing the routines. It would still be a long recovery, but this was a first step, figuratively and literally, to getting better, now both mentally and physically.

I had also read a lot of books on the subject of anxiety and depression. Almost all of them spoke of journaling your thoughts. But I was not much of a diary keeper and was quite confused about how to best keep a journal. I had read somewhere that I should rate my General Anxiety Disorder (GAD) discomfort in a journal but mistook this to mean to journal about it. I looked back on some of my early entries and realized some of the great mistakes I was making. My entries read:

12/3 – GAD level 7 out of 10: Ear ringing started again. Sleep got bad again. Will I ever get better and why can't I stop this from happening?

12/4 – GAD level 8 out of 10: Ear ringing and headache with the bad stomach ache and sleep problems again. Not sure of the reason why this is happening. I am trying to stay positive. Went to bed around 9:30pm and was up and down all night.

12/5 – GAD level 8 out of 10: I am down again. Ear ringing and headache are constant. I feel lightheaded. I am lost in who I am. Oh well! It is what it is and I need to try to rise above.

But what I failed to realize at this point is that I was making it impossible to rise above my problems because I would write all negative things and then read them back, keeping all my negative thoughts in the forefront of my mind. How could I possibly see any good if I didn't think any of my days had any good in them?

This is before I learned about gratitude journaling. In the early days of depression, we tend to focus on the bad. The good, while it might be there, is nearly impossible to see. This is where I was and it would be some time before I would learn about gratitude and dealing with putting this negative, pessimistic side behind me.

I had to come to terms with the bullying that had happened to me and my own actions or inactions in some as a child. But still, my child brain was constantly telling me what a loser I was and how much I hated myself for what happened to me as a child. My adult brain was now in the back of my mind, hiding, and it was hard to bring it forward. But I worked hard with both my psychiatrist and through the internet to discover more about what I was going through. I quickly found out that I wasn't alone and that there were so many people on the internet sharing stories of their anxiety and depression, with exactly the same symptoms as me. While there was some comfort in reading those stories, this was not a cure and in some ways made me obsess more about my issues.

While I was waiting for the medication to work, I decided to look for other ways to help myself. I signed up with an anxiety group through something I discovered called *Meetup*, a website I found that had help. I wanted to go to a meeting close by so that I didn't have to travel by car—something that would only trigger my anxiety. I found out that the group met at a close-by library. I made an account and waited for a meeting to be set up to be invited to. But no one did set up a meeting. My impatience kicked in, and wanting to take action, I set up a meeting at the closest library to me. To my amazement, about ten people signed up to attend.

As the meeting approached, I realized that, because I planned it, it was my meeting to run. So my first group therapy was going to be led by me. I pondered how crazy this was, since I knew so little about what I was going through. But the meeting day had arrived, and I figured it would be like what I saw in television or the movies, where we would all tell our stories.

I arrived at the library early and set up the room, arranging folding chairs into a circle. People started arriving, and I noticed the great variety of anxiety-ridden people walking into this meeting. There was the young man in his twenties, who was very muscular and tough looking. There was the old man, who was a pensive thinker. There was a woman who looked like she was heading to the gym right after the meeting. There was another middle-aged man who was very quiet. There were several women who sat in their chairs and kept their heads down. I counted nine of us, but remembered that ten signed up. We all looked very different from one another, but we all shared a secret called anxiety and, for some, depression.

Based on the website, it was my job to start the meeting and explain the rules. I told everyone we were going to share our stories and offer feedback. Since I set it up, I thought it only fair that I start to share. I told my story in great detail of how I started with my anxiety and depression and the stories of where it came from. The young man with the muscles talked a lot as well. He shared that when people see him, they think he is tough and strong, but that inside, he feels weak. The old man asked me what I was doing to get better. I shared my doctor's visits with the group.

Several of the group asked if I was changing any of my life patterns. The muscled young man asked me if I worked out because going to the gym helps him a lot to relieve stress. Since I had mentioned my stomach problems, several people asked me if I had changed my diet yet. I hadn't even thought of that. About half the room shared some of their stories, and I found out how similar I was to them. The fears of crowds and of feeling trapped and claustrophobic were common problems shared by all. There were a few in the group who said little to nothing but just listened. I have no idea if anything said helped them in their current state. Someone else in the class mentioned how much yoga and meditation did for them. I took copious notes. Then, as quickly as it began, the session was over and everyone left quietly.

I didn't know it until I got home, but the tenth person who was supposed to be there was out in the parking lot of the library where we had the meeting. I found this out when I went back to the *Meetup* website and saw what she had written. She had shared that it was all she could do to force herself to drive to the library, but her anxiety was too much to let her get out of the car and come to the meeting. She could not face us yet. It was at that moment I knew that I, like my own bullying stories, did not have anxiety and depression as badly as many other people. Although I was suffering, it actually brought me some relief to know that I was not at the worst point, and like the bullying I endured, there was always someone out there with a worse story than mine. It was at about that moment that I truly convinced myself that I could get better.

CHAPTER TWENTY-SIX

The Slow Return
From the Abyss

As I sat afraid and chilled at the bottom of the hole with my crumbled shoebox of childhood memories, I let them overtake my mind, making me believe that the only memories I had were these bad ones and that I was really everything they called me. I all but forgot the good memories that I had built over time that were still under my bed, collected and far away. As I sat on the wet, hard ground, I listened to these bad memories screaming how bad a person I was. All the things that I had done, like stealing, lying, using a weapon, and smoking. I didn't want to believe that was me, but my defenses were now down, and I was stuck facing the reality of these moments in my life, no matter at what age they happened. I was paralyzed with fear and panic and unable to move. I was blind in the dark bottom of this hole I had built for myself and could not see any light or any way out of the hole. I felt I would be here for the rest of my life and that my good and happy life was over. I would never get it back again, and now I questioned whether life was really worth living.

◊ ◊ ◊

As promised by Dr. Rosenbaum, I wasn't going to be cured overnight. I was an impatient and angry man at this time, still dealing with the depression, although the anxiety had lifted somewhat about four months into my medicine and psychiatric treatment with my doctor. My stomach still hurt, but my doctor told me something interesting. He told me at one of our sessions that there is a nerve that travels from a portion of the brain to the stomach called the Parasympathetic Nervous System, and when you enter fight or flight mode, that nerve tightens your stomach as a way to gain the energy needed to fight or flee. I fully believed him about this and convinced myself to try to start to eat again, even though my stomach would protest. After some amount of time, my stomach gave up fighting me, and I enjoyed eating again. Eventually I would start to gain weight back as well.

I listened to what my psychiatrist was teaching me and also took to heart what I learned in the group therapy session that I led. Although I had not attended another group session, I started gradually changing some habits in my life.

My first change was nutrition. I wanted to eat better and healthier and since I was having so many stomach issues, I decided to work on that first.

I read somewhere that a "green smoothie" that was made of kale, bananas, apples, flaxseed, and fruit juice helped some people who were depressed with stomach issues. I ran to the store and bought all the ingredients for my green smoothie. I made one and, surprisingly, it did not taste bad. In fact, it tasted pretty good. At that moment I made my first life change, which was to make a green smoothie every day I could and have it for breakfast. I could feel the energy of the fruits and vegetables helping me a little. Maybe it is psychosomatic, but to this day, I make one every morning and love them. If there is a time when I cannot make one in the morning, I feel as though I missed a great energy start for that day.

The second change was much harder for me, the idea of exercise. I knew what a runners' high through endorphins was and had learned through many of the books and talks with my psychiatrist of the importance of exercise and nutrition in recovery. But I had always hated exercise and felt it was tedious and boring. I wanted to feel better though, so I came up with a solution.

My work offered a free gym on the first floor. It wasn't much, just some elliptical and treadmill machines. I packed a change of clothes one day. I made a mix of "workout" music on my iPhone. Right after work ended, I went to the gym and started on the elliptical machine. I did twenty minutes the first day, and it was miserable. I hated every second of it and didn't want to go back. But then I remembered something my psychiatrist said to me. He said that *"when your mind tells you that you don't want to do something is the exact moment when you should try to do it"*. You have to work through the problem and not go around it. So I did keep going to the gym, and eventually I would find the endorphin high that comes from a cardiovascular workout.

The workout started to clear my mind and bring my adult brain back to the front, at least for the time I was exercising. I went from twenty minutes on the elliptical to alternating between the elliptical and treadmill. Eventually twenty minutes became thirty minutes. It was then that I started to enjoy the workout time. It was time I spent with myself, learning to like myself again and feeling like I was doing something to help myself. This would eventually lead me to join a bigger gym across the street from where I lived, because they had more equipment, and thus I was able to add more variety to my workout. They also had classes, like yoga and aerobics. I began to do weight training as well, as I had gained some weight back, particularly in my midsection. In a few months, I was working out about five to six days a week and truly found happiness in working to stay healthy and knowing I was doing something for myself.

I had a great friend who was always posting her pictures of running in events around the community. There was a 5 kilometer race (about 3.11 miles) coming up close by, and I decided to sign up to run with her. I needed a goal for my workout at the gym and figured I would train to run in my first 5k race. I convinced my younger son to run with me, which forced me to have to go to the event. Without him, I probably would have backed out. I was having extreme anticipatory anxiety the day of the race and didn't want to go. But, not wanting to disappoint my son, I went.

I was so nervous and there were so many people at the race. I felt like I was waiting forever for it to start, and then the gun went off and we were running. It was a cold April morning, and it felt great to breathe in the fresh oxygen-rich air. I was not winded and was able to do a consistent jog the whole way through the 5k course. I even sprinted at the end, filled with a euphoria and energy that I had not felt in a very long time.

At the end of the race, all participants got a shirt and a medal. I hung the medal prominently in my room so when I felt low, I could look at it and remember that I can still set goals that make me feel like I can accomplish things I put my mind to. I had trained so well that I even beat my younger son. The experience made me feel like the hard work I was doing to get better was paying off and my happiness was truly coming from my accomplishments, not through trying to please others.

◊ ◊ ◊

Finally, I started yoga and meditation. I found these activities to be quite simple. First, I started with that terrible yoga DVD my wife had. It was simple yoga, but it would take my mind off my problems for thirty minutes each day. Eventually, I learned that my gym had one-hour yoga classes, so I started one. The instructor was wonderful at helping to bring peace to the room and to me. It truly was and still is a magical experience of self-awareness every time I go to the yoga class.

Meditation was a bit trickier as there are a lot of ways to meditate. I downloaded all of the apps on my iPad that did meditation. There was guided meditation, where a person talks you through relaxing and focusing on positive affirmations, and there was unguided meditation. After many failed attempts at meditating through apps, I found one called "Calm", which cost about ten dollars a year, but had guided meditations of different durations for every type of anxiety and support need under the sun. I found it to be money well spent and do about ten to twenty minutes of guided meditation with the "Calm" app as many days of the week as I can.

I was making progress, but my impatience still grew, and I struggled to leave the confines of my home or work. I felt unsafe in any other location and wanted to leave quickly to the safety of my home. The full anxiety and depression would still take a lot of time to get over, and I was now a reading junkie, trying to learn all I could.

I continued with my gratitude journaling, every day writing about three things I was grateful for before bed. I learned to better my technique in writing my gratitude. It could be as simple as "thank you for waking me up to see a new day" to as complex as "I figured out a large problem at work and people congratulated me". It didn't matter, as long as it was about good things only. The idea of the gratitude journal was to get my mind out of its pessimistic "everything sucks" state and train it to see more optimistic ideas. Each morning I would read what I wrote the night before, to both end and start my days on positive notes. I must fully admit this is no easy task, but eventually, I felt my mind shift over.

It was about then, around eight months into my psychiatric treatment and use of the medication that I met with my psychiatrist, Dr. Rosenbaum, again. I had explained all the things I was doing to try to get better, but while I did feel a little better, I was still feeling depressed. He said that it was great to hear that I was taking on trying to get better myself and that is exactly what most people do not do. He was encouraged enough that he suggested it was time.

"Time for what," I asked.

It was time to start seeing a therapist instead of him. Dr. Rosenbaum wanted me to meet weekly with a therapist in the practice named Dr. Patterson. Dr. Rosenbaum made an appointment for me to see him the next week. This was yet another beginning to my recovery that I wasn't expecting and in some ways was dreading.

CHAPTER TWENTY-SEVEN

Eventually a Solution
Starts to Appear

I sat at the bottom of the hole I had dug below the field of tall grass and flowers for what felt like an eternity. As the voices of my bad memories continued to scream at me and remind me of how horrible a person I was, whispers from my good memories were finally reaching me, speaking softly in my ear from far away, where I had safely tucked them. Eventually, after a long rest, I had gathered some strength to search the hole I was in, looking for a way out. The disintegrated shoebox of bad memories could not be put back together, and those memories were following me as I felt around in the dark depths of the hole. I could not see, but in the back of my mind I tried to remember that I must have made a way out of the hole. My hands felt along the cold, wet mud of the walls. "There must be a way out," I thought. I had some hope to cling to as I continued to feel the edges of the hole I had dug with the same hands that made this hole in the first place. I started to truly wonder if there was a way out.

◊ ◊ ◊

I was still unhappy and nothing, not even my loved ones surrounding me, changed that or made me feel any less alone. Every day, I was feeling unhappy and still dealing with depression and some of the anxiety. I had another visit with my gastroenterologist and told him about the anxiety and depression and that, even with this knowledge, my stomach still hurt and I was having trouble sleeping with the hurt stomach. He explained to me very gently that this was not uncommon in people with anxiety and depression. He said he often prescribed a very low dose of an anti-depression medication that both helped sleep and eased the stomach discomfort. I was nervous about taking yet another medication, but talked to my psychiatrist, who thought it a good one to take in conjunction with all the other medication.

I started to take this new medication, and for me, it was a miracle from heaven. It not only helped relieve my stomach discomfort, but also put me right to sleep for an entire night, which I had not done in a very long time. Waking up that first morning after a full night's sleep was refreshing and strengthening. For the first time in almost a year, I felt like I could face the day ahead.

My medications were now helping me to sleep and focus. The only current side effect was a ringing in my ears and a bit of a tension headache. Both of these would come and go over time, but I learned to accept them as part of my cure. The day, though, had finally arrived to go see my therapist for the first time. I had read much about therapy and the different ways it could work with someone with my problem. I knew that Cognitive Behavioral Therapy was big, which is the idea of practicing and doing the things you are afraid of to break the fear. I walked into the same familiar office space where my psychiatrist now was and where I used to work. The therapist, Dr. Patterson, came out to greet me.

I remember being very nervous during our first session about what would come to be eight months' worth of forty-five--minute weekly sessions with Dr. Patterson. During the first session, Dr. Patterson was just getting to know me. He asked me what my biggest anxiety was.

"I am constantly afraid I am going to crap in my pants," I told him.

Dr. Patterson shot me a glance, and I could tell that he had maybe heard this tune before.

"And what makes you think you are going to crap your pants, Alan?" Dr. Patterson inquired. "Have you done that before?"

I thought for a minute and realized I have never crapped my pants before. In fact, I'm not sure I had too many close calls, unless I ate something wrong and would have to rush to the bathroom.

"No," I answered him.

"And what would you do if you did have an accident in your pants?" Dr. Patterson asked me.

"I guess I would leave where I was, hopefully be able to get home and change."

"So, let me get this right," Dr. Patterson stated. "You have never had an accident in your pants, but if you did, you think that you'd be able to get home and change for the most part."

He had me there. I answered my own question in my mind.

"Yeah," I said. "But I'd be embarrassed."

Dr. Patterson looked at me inquisitively. "I understand that, but do you really think that people would not have sympathy for you? Why would you be embarrassed?"

He got me again. The therapy was forcing me to confront these fears, and he was helping me to understand the unrealistic nature of my thoughts. It was certainly a wake-up call for me and a time for me to face myself.

Over the next eight months, we would talk about the bullying events of my childhood; we would talk about ways to handle stress, anxiety, and my depression. I would become braver over the next eight months, starting to travel again and taking risks to work through these feelings. Some days would be very successful and some days would be failures. I learned that it was okay to have the feelings of success and failure and that the main thing was to never give up and try to always work through the anxiety and depression and not fall into the trap of letting it control my ability to live my life.

The early days were a struggle, and I would find that I would get sick with worry when we traveled the first few times and my stomach would be disrupted. But the more I traveled, the less I had the problems. My cures certainly didn't come overnight, and I would still have to focus to go to the gym, eat better, and meditate. Along with this, I was trying to fill my mind with positive affirmations to turn my

Alan Eisenberg | 157

pessimistic brain into more of an optimistic, if not realistic, brain. I hated myself less and less and eventually started to switch to liking myself more and more.

Everyone is different, and how long someone may or may not need therapy and help from professionals depends a lot on how an individual can and will get the help they need to overcome their issues. Throughout my therapy, Dr. Patterson had given me the most wonderful gift of advice and solutions in order to help me overcome a lot of my feelings about my past. But no matter what Dr. Patterson said, it was my job to listen and do my homework. It took a lot of work on his part and a particularly large amount of work on my part, as I continued to read and listen to books about how to get better.

◊ ◊ ◊

Ironically, soon after I started my therapeutic recovery work, I received a call from an old high school friend, Ron, whom I hadn't talked to in a very long time. He had returned to Fairfax, Virginia, after moving to Georgia and then spending time in the Navy. I recall how we both somehow admitted to each other we were having some issues around our mental state.

Ron's issues were a bit more long lasting and dramatic. He had Bipolar Disorder that caused him to have very extreme highs and lows. He had been dealing with this disorder a long time and struggled to hold a job or keep his focus. We talked at length about what we were going through.

During one of our conversations, Ron shared a word with me that he used often to remind himself of what he had to do to get through his life with Bipolar Disorder. The word he invented and wrote for me on a piece of paper to keep in my wallet was CANEI.

Of course, the first thing I did was ask him what it meant. CANEI stood for "Constant and Never-Ending Improvement". I thought about this and liked the concept very much. It took away the perfectionist reality that I was wanting to live in and also told me that this was not something to cure, but something to work at all the time.

After Ron shared this with me, I began to use it and even say it in my daily life. Interestingly, Ron gave me the word when he was in an up state in his bipolar condition and feeling good. I was in a down state in my depression. But as time moved, Ron would call me when he was down and I would simply tell him to remember CANEI. He would tell me that was helpful, and we learned to use his word to help both of us get through our tough days.

◊ ◊ ◊

At around the eight-month mark with my therapist, I had realized I was coming into his office feeling happy, self-confident, and more like me. I believe Dr. Patterson agreed when I suggested that I stop therapy for now and see how it goes on my own. Our meetings had turned more into conversations about my success, and it was time for me to try to return to the world without the therapy.

As I left Dr. Patterson's office on my last visit, he simply told me that he was happy for me, but that if I was ever again feeling low or bad, to pick up the phone and call and we would resume where we left off and work again to help me recover my authentic self. As Dr. Patterson's door closed behind me and I left the office, I noticed that I felt different. As I entered the elevator, the door reflected my face back to me. I was smiling and I was happy. It had been such a long time since I had seen that face on me, and at that moment, I felt so empowered to move forward with my healing.

◊ ◊ ◊

I had read and learned about belly breathing when I felt anxious or nervous. It seems that you can practice deep breathing into your belly instead of breathing into your chest, which is shallower. As I practiced this technique and learned more about the proper way to do it, I saw how it calmed me down some. It took a long time and a lot of practice, but breathing into my belly deeply and not into my chest had a calming effect on me.

I was meditating almost every day for ten minutes at this point in my recovery, which was about a year and a half after my depression started. I was spending about one to one and a half hours at the gym five or six days a week. I did yoga at the gym one day a week. I drank my smoothies every day I could, and I felt like I was a different person. I was someone who actually liked *me* again, who could spend time with *me* and enjoy it. Slowly the fog of depression lifted.

While the depression and anxiety wasn't completely gone, I was functioning now and ready to move on to the next part of my journey. It was time to completely put the past behind me and allow myself to accept the bullying years that I'd suffered through. This was yet more work and more time that I needed to spend recovering, but I was ready to take it on.

CHAPTER TWENTY-EIGHT

Recovery
And Repair

As I reached in the dark with my hands, along the dirt wall that was my hole, I felt cold steel like that of…that's right! I had found a ladder as a kid and put it in the hole to escape. I had forgotten this over time and now remembered that I had found and put the ladder in the hole so that I would be able to climb out. I looked up and the top of the ladder was reflecting the light of the sun. It looked far away from where I was, but I was sure that the warm glow of the sun was at the top of the ladder. With that hopefulness, I began my slow and careful ascent up the ladder, my bad memories still screaming behind me as I climbed. The ironic thing was that, the higher I climbed, the quieter the screaming became. The bad memories followed behind, losing their powers with each rung I grabbed.

During my recovery period, I was challenged a few times. Some of the challenges were things I put in front of me and other challenges were surprising to me. I have already mentioned that Daniel found my story and I had reconciled with him, building a surprising new friendship. That moment with Daniel, repairing the damage of the past, helped me immensely.

Then Kyle discovered my site and contacted me to tell me he'd read the story of what happened that Halloween. He wrote to me about that incident, now thirty years old, and he shared that, although as he remembers it, it was just Halloween mischief to him, he was sorry that it hurt me.

I then reached out via Facebook to Carl. I hadn't spoken to Carl since I had left Lexington and honestly it only occurred to me to contact him via posting some old pictures from my Bar Mitzvah. It led to another moment of apology on both our parts. Old wounds in me were healing day by day. So it is interesting that, at about this same time, I was asked by my synagogue to deliver a sermon about bullying because the Rabbi was out of town, but he thought it would be good for me to deliver this message.

I was very nervous about being on stage in front of a bunch of strangers and telling my story again. But I was healing now and so I wrote a particularly special piece about the need to say the words *I'm Sorry*. I made my way nervously up to the podium that Friday night at services. I felt the beginnings of my anxiety and started shaking a bit, but cleared my throat and began delivering the speech I wrote as best I could. This is what I said:

"The bible reading this week is Aharei Mot, which in Hebrew means After the Death. This is because it takes place right after the death of Moses' brother Aaron's two sons. The reading is also maybe even more significant, because it is also the origin of the Yom Kippur ritual.

Interestingly and possibly even intentionally, this reading takes place about 6 months after and equally six months prior to the Jewish Yom Kippur. It's as if to say that we should remember that making atonement is not just a once a year event. It has always been a challenge for me to understand the idea of the once a year atonement that Yom Kippur is. I know that some of us believe we have the other 364 days to build up our mistakes so that once a year we can ask for forgiveness, and even then, we only ask it of God. While in other religions, they go weekly to confess their sins and ask for atonement, but again, only from God. Why from God, as if he is going to tell the people who most need to hear it?

Why do we struggle to say the words Ani Mitzta'er ... Hebrew for 'I'm sorry'? Why is this so hard for us to do? And what does it mean to others when you say it to them, sincerely, and meaningfully?

David Brin, an American science fiction author, has one of my favorite quotes on the subject. He said: 'Why must conversions always come so late? Why do people always apologize to corpses?' The author and abolitionist Harriet Beecher Stowe said it as well when she said, 'The bitterest tears shed over graves are for words left unsaid and for deeds left undone.'

How often I have seen this as the truth. How many of us regret the moments we didn't say I'm sorry. I was 21 when my grandmother died. She had lived within driving distance of us my whole life. I had spent summers with her and shared many special moments with her during my childhood. When I was 21, I was in college, and she and I had drifted apart. For many reasons not spoken, we had argued recently and I didn't apologize. And then she was gone and I could no longer tell her what I wanted to.

Zay Moykhl! That's Yiddish for "I'm sorry" and a language she spoke often to me. Unfortunately, it was typically to tell me that I was Meshugeh (crazy). Being a fan of movies, I often quote them, sometimes to the pleasure or dismay of others. I find comfort in the lines from movies, because they help me to understand that others go through what we all do. When it comes to this idea of waiting to say you are sorry, I drift to an unlikely movie, <u>The Sixth Sense</u>*, which is mistaken as a scary movie, when it is really about discovering the power to help others and do good. And no, it's not that the guy is dead at the end. And if I ruined that for you, you should have seen the movie 10 years ago anyway. At the end of the movie, the boy who has the power to talk to the dead tells his mother that his grandmother, his mother's mother who had passed away years ago, has been talking to him. The boy's mother and his grandmother had a falling out years before and the mother was suffering with guilt from it. He tells his mother that the grandmother wanted to tell her something. It was an answer to a question the mother asked every time she visited her grave that went unanswered. The answer from the grandmother was "EVERY DAY". The boy asks his mother what question she asked when she visited the grandma's grave. His mother says the question is "DO I MAKE HER PROUD?" At that moment in the movie, the mother is able to release the pain she had carried with her all those years.*

But in life, we don't get to talk to the dead, and they don't get to answer us. It is ironic that this is the week I have been invited to deliver this sermon, because I contemplate this question often when I speak about bullying. Since 2007, I have chosen to take on the cause of helping others cope with the pain and suffering they feel from being bullied. I speak to groups and have a website of stories and information to try to help others. I started this to help myself, because I too had been a victim of bullying as a child and knew the long-term suffering this was bringing to others. I realized that the theme I would share when I spoke was one of trying to teach and promote empathy and find forgiveness. Because it is in heart and head that we carry the burden of the pain of cruelty and also the guilt of what we did. I had no idea in 2007 how this decision would change my life.

I decided my first action would be to write down all of the stories I remembered from those years of bullying. I grew up in Lexington, Massachusetts, in the 1970s, and this is where it all took place. This is important later. I wrote my stories on a website. I did it for me to release these things and put them to rest. But it would not be so easy. A few years later, I was invited to speak about my stories. This was also very difficult and the pain of those memories would come back to me. You see, I believe we never really forget the wrongs done to us, we store them in the back of our minds and put them in a deep place. But they build over time, and without the apology, without someone making amends, I believe they make us a harder person. But over the last five years, it seems many have found my site and find hope in the words posted there. What I never expected was that those people I knew in Lexington would find my stories as well and that I would have to confront these words . . . 'I'm sorry'.

The first person to find his story was actually my best friend from those years. I knew he had found them because he started replying to other posts with his memory. But he hadn't found his story. You see he had hurt me as well. One Halloween, he and my other friends had taunted me from the woods and ran off, leaving me to walk home alone, no candy in my bag. Looking back as an adult, it doesn't seem that bad. But our memories are from the age that things happen. He read his story and then I received his note directly to me…30 years later.

He wrote: "For what it's worth, and what I recall of that night, it was just kids being kids… I think we were all just being goofy with the mischief of the night, being Halloween and all…and I will say I am sorry if your feelings were hurt." For those young people in the audience, can you imagine getting a note from your friend 30 years later, apologizing? I couldn't and was embarrassed I had put him in that position. But you know what, I felt a little better. I called him, and we talked for hours after that. We still do today. A little repair. Prosti…That's Russian for 'I'm Sorry'.

I had hoped that would be the last. I never really expected anyone to read my site anyway. Who am I? I'm just someone trying to work his way through life. I then was looking through my old Bar Mitzvah book one day and saw that there was a boy in it from Lexington named Carl. I knew his name, but only vaguely the times we spent together. We found each other through Facebook one day, and he wrote to me recounting all the good times we had. He particularly reminded me of the time we blew up our toys with firecrackers. Don't tell anyone I did that though. He wrote: 'I must say that you moving away was one of the saddest events to me. We became such good buddies so fast. I have an unbelievable amount of memories hanging out together, doing sleepovers, and just being generally mischievous...'

It bothered me not to remember him as well as he remembered me. His memories were so vivid of me. Then I discovered why. In his second note, his explanation told me when he wrote: *'I remember being incredibly sad when you moved away. I got over it of course, but there's always been something about it in the back of my mind that's bothered me. Specifically, what happened at the end of 7th grade when we had a fist fight at school. As far as fistfights went, it wasn't unusual. Even for friends, because usually they can move on and endure that kind of stuff. But what's bothered me since then (and I was just thinking about it only a couple of weeks ago before you contacted me) was how that injured our friendship, and then you moved away before we could really set it completely right. That was a mean day for me, and one which I really wish I could have back.*

And since a window of opportunity doesn't always open for long, I have to use our reconnection to tell you now how incredibly sorry I still am for what I did to make that fight happen, for every blow struck against you, and for whatever mean (and I mean in the low-class, uncaring, dirty, and despicable sense) action or words that were used by me, before or after. I've always known that my part in that event was a sin, and one which I still hold onto. I have never forgotten about it.'

Thirty-two years later and that guilt was still with him every day. Because the pain of losing one more friend during those years was too much for me, I had tried to forget this moment. We talked and shared our feelings. He was able to say sorry in person, and I did too. Even though I didn't remember the fight that well, I was sorry. I began to wonder, what if I hadn't made my site and found him? Would that still haunt him to the end? Do we all have that inside us? But for me, this was a little more repair.

Finally, I want to share this more recent story that took place in December. By far, it was the hardest story for me. You see there was a moment in time when I was the bully and the guilt was in me. During Hebrew school class one day, we put tacks on one of the kids' chairs, not a few, like ten. We thought it would be funny. When he sat down, it wasn't. I felt bad about doing it. See, he was the one who got picked on then, and I was the one participating in it. I shared that as well on my site. Well, it seemed in the five years since I'd started it, my site and stories had been read by many and at what would have been the 25th reunion of the high school in Lexington, Massachusetts, it seems they were talking about me, the bully expert who writes about the bullying that happened there. It seems to some, I was a local hero to write about what happened to not just me, but I would find out to many. It seems that the boy, now a man, who was the victim of the tack attack, Daniel, heard as well and found his story on my site. I knew he did, because I heard from his friends, who wrote not too kindly to me. It was my turn to have to reach out and say I was sorry. I was racked with guilt...thirty-one years later. I called him. I said the words...'I'm sorry'...I expected anger. What I got was a wonderful conversation with an old friend who was happy for my call and for sharing our stories. He had bullying happen to him far worse than me, but he used it for strength. He repaired a bit. I repaired a bit. We talk often now...it is behind us.

I feel lucky to have had these three experiences of saying "I'm sorry." Many of the negative feelings that I started with five years ago have left me. I think in some way, I have helped others do the same. I saw the documentary called BULLY that came out. I wish I could tell you much has changed, but it seems like not a lot. In it, an awkward 14-year-old named Alex is beaten daily on the bus and ignored by all. His mother asks him 'doesn't it bother you, doesn't it hurt you?' He just says in calm anger, 'I really don't think I feel anything at all anymore.' So what happens next to him, to others like him? There are many stories of children, young children who commit suicide from bullying. It is too late to say I'm sorry after that, and many are left with the guilt. I think it interesting that this weekend's reading deals with Aaron and this loss of his children. Is this where the origin of Yom Kippur starts? What does that do to an individual...to society? These are rhetorical questions I ask often as I contemplate the issue of bullying.

What difference would it make if we said 'I'm sorry' more often and meant it when we said it. As I and some of my elementary school friends have learned, it's never too late to say you are sorry. It changes lives. And I can tell you it feels good to say it and move on…

Jammer!…Oprostite!…Tevechi…Anteeksi…Desole…Gomen Nasai…Przepraszam!… Samahani…Xin loi…Ani Mittzta'er…I'm sorry."

I exited the podium, and as I looked out to the audience, there were tears and many members looking down in sadness. We do not clap during a sermon; it just ends quietly. I did not want any appreciation from others, I just wanted to release and find peace. I left the stage having accomplished another step in my recovery, by putting another set of ghosts from my past years of bullying behind me. A little more repair and I could feel my self-esteem slowly returning to my body. But I wasn't done yet, because I had only talked to old friends or people I bullied. I had yet to talk to one of my bullies, and when I did, I would find out how close the bully and the bullying victim are to each other.

At what was surely an inopportune time in my life, my father was diagnosed with non-Hodgkin's lymphoma, a form of blood cancer. This was very hard on my mother and on me as well as it added to my feelings of anxiety. But I wanted to be there for my dad. During this period of time, I was starting to learn techniques to calm myself down from the anxiety and panic I was feeling.

As my father worked through his recovery, he got the nickname, Superman, for his positive strength, something he believed would conquer the cancer inside him. His faith and belief that he could conquer it proved to be true, as he finished his first round of blood transfusions due to complications from his treatment and would then be put on a steroid regimen to help his body fight the complications.

But as he took the steroids, he found that he could no longer sleep and entered into a bi-polar manic depressive state. He began to believe that he could do and invent items that were not real. He began to lose control of his displaced aggression and call my mother all sorts of names, believing she was conspiring against him. At one point, he had convinced himself that he could invent the travel capsule item from the movie *Avatar* that allowed a paralyzed person to travel to another galaxy. He was scaring my mom with how he was acting and calling her names when she said she didn't believe what he was saying.

One night, early in my own recovery, I received a call from my mother saying she was scared of my father and the way he was acting and wanted me to come over, drive him to the hospital and have him committed for psychiatric evaluation. He had already seen a psychiatrist about this, but he was not getting any better. Our family was scared that it was now a permanent part of who he was. As I was driving over to their house, still feeling anxious and uncomfortable, I remembered some of the things I had started to learn to calm myself down.

Breathe from my belly, stop my mind from ruminating on bad things, and think about my breathing. As I approached their house, I could hear my father from the outside, ranting about something and calling my mom a bitch for not believing him. I entered their house, and my father was still pacing and ranting. He came up to me and told me that mom wanted him committed and asked if I thought he was crazy.

I was honestly wondering the same about myself. But I did now have some techniques under my belt and thought that maybe if they worked for me, I could calm my dad down. I pulled up two chairs, still feeling strongly uncomfortable myself. I asked my dad if he would sit down, but he was still pacing and rambling about how no one believed him. My mom asked him to sit down in the seat across from me. He did, and I looked at him. He was sweating, breathing heavily, and shaking. I had never seen my father like this.

He wanted to get up, and I could tell he was using all his energy just to sit there. He was rambling, and I asked him if he could be quiet for a moment. He kept rambling incoherent thoughts, and my mom asked him in a stern tone to stop talking. With all his energy, he did so. I truly wondered how someone like me, in my condition could help. All

I had were my own techniques. I asked him to close his eyes, and he did. He was struggling to sit still, and I could tell he wanted to get up and run. I knew the feeling well. I told him how to breathe from his belly and asked him to take ten deep breaths with me. He did, and slowly as we made our way to the tenth breath, he calmed down enough to allow mom to feel secure again.

I talked to him for some time to see what he was thinking. He seemed to come back to reality. I talked to my mom, and she agreed not to run him to the psych ward at the hospital tonight if he could remain calm. In the morning, they would go to the psychiatrist. I stayed for another hour to make sure he remained calm. As he started to get sleepy, I hugged him and my mom and left, shaking from the experience myself.

The following day, I received a call from my mother to tell me about the psychiatrist visit. She told the psychiatrist what I had done the night before, and the psychiatrist asked her how I knew to do that. She told him of my situation. My father was given some medication and sent off to be evaluated by another doctor, who weaned him off the steroids and removed his pancreas, which was really at the root of the problem. Once off the steroids for about a week, my father returned to his old self, no longer manic, but still with a realization that it can and sometimes does run in the family, as with his mother before him, my grandmother.

My mother was very grateful to me for helping him. It felt good to take something I had learned and be able to help another. I wasn't quite better myself, but I knew enough to be helpful when asked to step in and could now share these new stories and techniques I learned through my own personal recovery. Life can get better, if we stop fighting and let it back into our beings.

CHAPTER TWENTY-NINE

The Final Struggle
Out of the Dark

From the bottom of the ladder, the hole looked much deeper than I originally remembered. As I climbed, I could start to feel the warmth of the sun closer to the surface of the hole. Behind me, my bad memories continued to follow me as I worked my way slowly, one rung at a time, to the top of the hole. I was exhausted once again and needed to rest about half way up the ladder. I stopped and looked up and could see the light of the sun above me. I looked down into the darkness below. It was time to make a choice, and I wanted to be up where the sun was. No matter how tired I felt and how little energy I had. No matter how loud my memories were yelling at me. It was time to make a choice. I would use my last bit of strength to continue my climb up and out of this hole I had dug for myself.

◊ ◊ ◊

I had a few more surprises coming to me during my time of depression and anxiety recovery from my days of being bullied. In fact, I truly was surprised to discover the anxiety, phobias, and, of course, depression that comes as part of the C-PTSD process. The word injury is used to define this problem, as in having a mental injury the same as a physical injury.

I like that the word injury is part of the definition because as we come to realize that these are injuries of the mind, much like injuries that are more obvious, like a broken bone, then we can focus on how to mend and fix these so life can return to normal. In the eight plus years since I started my website, the bullying issue has exploded to front-page news every single day. If I wanted, I could write a new story about bullying daily from searches in the news. It is the yin/yang problem again, which is to say I am glad it is news now, but there is so much of it going on that it saddens me. But it is now an issue that we all want to solve, and that is great. The recovery from the injury of bullying and other mental illness needs to be the next item to fix, though, and sometimes I wish so hard that I had discovered my issues earlier in life. Studies have already started about the long-term effects of bullying, and I believe that psychologists and social workers are both more focused on working toward solutions to this issue. I have been researching my own set of twisted thinking problems, like my need to feel loved; being a perfectionist; all or nothing thinking; and my anger issues, heavily over the last few months.

It was some point during this time that Mom called me and during the course of the conversation about my continued work toward getting past anxiety and depression, told me of a time early in my father's career when he was put on anti-anxiety medication due to his work stress. I was shocked to find this out as it was never mentioned to me at any point. My parents had, like many others, swept it under the rug and kept it secret from my sister and me. My father was under extreme pressure on a project in his early career, and the pressure caused both my father and his co-worker to have to seek help for anxiety. Knowing that my grandmother on my father's side was manic depressive made me feel that there was more of a genetic connection to this disease of anxiety and depression.

I ended up taking a hike with my father and talking to him further about what happened. This opened an old wound up in him that he had since let scar over and now was revisiting. My dad talked to me at length about what had happened to him. It was truly a bonding experience between a father and a son, and I didn't know whether to be happy about opening this wound up for him or sad that I had caused him to bring it back to the surface, as I had felt I had done. During the walk, we also talked about how my story about working with the children at the camp for disabled kids affected him as well.

My dad and I share one specific trait together that I always knew about. He and I both had extremely short fuses and were easily angered. We both took out our frustrations and angry feelings on the ones we loved the most. I found out that in psychology, this is called displaced aggression or displaced anger and comes about when we feel powerless to take out our internal anger on someone else, like for me a bully or for him a boss at work. This certainly made sense for me as to why I had and still do have a strong tendency to *hurt the ones I love*, because of a habit I developed during my years with bullying. But what caused my dad to have this displaced anger issue? During our conversation and then through an email he wrote to me afterwards, I would find out the answer.

My father ruminated on his displaced aggression issue because in the most recent months, it had become a bigger problem as he recovered from cancer. He remembered my story from my days working at the camp with the disabled children and one child in particular who had a brain injury from being struck by a car, but was told he would one day recover. That story triggered in my father his memories of his childhood, when encephalitis at six years old caused him to be physically disabled and he would struggle to walk for many years. He started remembering how his father would carry him around and have him sit all day in the backyard, learning to drag his limp legs wherever he wanted to go. He wrote to me of a memory he had about his recovery in an email:

"...I would often climb up as high as I could into my beloved, twisted locust tree and sit there for hours, while the other kids played below. The tree was my haven away from reality, and when my mother and father would call me to come down for dinner, I would stubbornly refuse. When it started to get dark, I would climb down the tree and go upstairs for dinner. My mother would reheat dinner for me, and I would eat alone. Obviously, they realized what I was going through emotionally and tolerated my bad behavior. I did this often, from second through fifth grade when we moved to Silver Spring, Maryland, away from my beloved locust tree. I had a whole new set of friends, who never knew what I'd been through, and my life was changed forever...

Years later, when I was bipolar on steroids (during my recovery from cancer treatments), I vacillated between feeling like Superman and that angry and frustrated little six-year-old boy again. I retained much of that anger and frustration after my recovery, and I guess I was not fully recovered and still may not be even now. The doctor told me that the after-effects of heavy doses of steroids can last for over a year, and I guess my anger was one of them...

I never realized that both the physical and emotional effects of the steroids can last for more than a year, and I now realize that I have been suffering from C-PTSD for many years as well."

I was not alone.

I was never alone, and my father was actually suffering in silence as well. I was shocked to learn this after so many years. No one is ever alone, they just feel that way.

My own recovery brought out in my father the knowledge of why he also suffered from displaced aggression and anger. Sometimes, I feel a little of my heartbreak when I think of bringing these memories to the surface for my dad. But he also helped me to understand that my displaced aggression was not something that I only suffered from. Later, he would come to a therapy session with me, and we would both learn ways to try to control this anger that was in us and that was created at such an early age when we had no knowledge to understand why we did what we did.

My own suffering had a yin to its yang, which was the opportunity to bring me closer to my father, who I had long felt was so vastly different than me. I thought he would never understand the emotional toll I was going through. I couldn't have been more wrong, and by sharing my feelings and story with him, he was able to release his own inner demon that had been haunting him.

This is not to say that my dad and I have both figured out how to stop our displaced aggression issues. A lifetime of this behavior isn't going to end easily. But now we know and we share the bond and promise to work together and help each other get better day by day. I am happy that it wasn't too late for me to discover this important milestone in my relationship with my father and that, through it all, we have both a love and an understanding about who we are. This valuable lesson taught me to never think that I am alone in what I am going through and even the closest people to us may be hiding their own secrets that, if shared, can change our lives.

◊ ◊ ◊

Having recently decided that even with my awareness, I needed the mending help of professionals, I can honestly say that, from my vantage point, you can't go it alone. There are too many people that either can't afford proper mental health care or believe they can solve their own problems but get nowhere. In some cases, we see the results on the news with a suicide, or worse yet, a homicide as the result of a lack of treatment. We can't ignore this issue any longer. I couldn't let my inaction go on without some self-help either.

One day, I took a giant chance and decided it was time to look up and contact Bob, the first bully I encountered so many years ago who still haunted my mind. He was so easy to track down on Facebook, the magic tool to find everyone now. I sent him a message asking for his phone number, but I did not reveal why I wanted to call him. Almost immediately, he wrote me back with his number.

Now the hard part was that I had to pick up the phone and tell him why I wanted to talk to him. He was still the scary monster from my youth who was so cruel in my mind; I thought maybe he would be that scary monster still. But I wanted to get better, face my demons and defeat them, so now would be the time. And that monster is now from a long time ago when I was only a child. I had to continue to fight to resolve my C-PTSD.

I called the number.

"Hello, this is Bob," my old bully answered. I recognized the voice with the heavy Massachusetts accent right away.

"Hi Bob, this is Alan. Do you remember me from our days at Franklin Elementary?" I asked, body and hands shaking uncontrollably with anxiety and trying to figure out how to say what needed to be said.

Bob replied, "You know, I don't have much memory of my youth, but your name is familiar. I don't remember that much from when I was young. But it's good to reconnect."

"That is why I wanted to call you," I said.

Now was the time to reveal why I had called him. I wasn't sure if I could do it.

"I am calling you and wanted to talk to you because you were my bully."

A moment of silence and then Bob said the words as I find many I confront later do.

"I am so sorry. Oh God, I am sorry about that. I don't remember it, but I am sorry."

It is amazing when those words come after so many years. Why can't we say them when we are young? Because we don't understand yet, that's why. He was flowing with remorse. I stopped him somewhere along the way and explained that I wanted to contact him because I needed to let go of the memory I had of him from when I was a youth. Then, the other thing that often happens in these reconnections, Bob started sharing with me the whys from his end.

The Bob I was talking to now was remorseful, honest, and dealing with his own set of demons. We shared information about ourselves openly and honestly. He came from an abusive home. His young life was not easy either, and he dealt with his own self-esteem issues. I listened, learning more than I expected as he shared more with me.

He shared that he had been dealing with his own demons in life and that he was working to overcome the ones he had. An abusive youth, tough teen and adult years, and finally that he now looks to find the positives in life in hopes of overcoming what he had been through. We were kindred spirits from different sides of the bully spectrum.

Bob and I talked for probably an hour that day. I told him about my work trying to solve the bullying issue. He was so supportive and also said that he counsels prisoners at a jail on alcohol and drug issues. How ironic, I thought, that Bob was now doing counseling. I could tell as the conversation continued that he was releasing his demons, too. It was truly amazing to me to have this closure with the person I had demonized all these years. Bob is an adult, with adult struggles and now an understanding of where he comes from and why that is.

After about an hour of pouring our hearts out to each other (remember that we hadn't even seen each other in thirty-three years or so), we had to end the conversation. Bob closed out his end by shocking me again.

He said, "I can't wait to share this conversation with the men who I work with at the prison. This has been something I needed, and I am so glad we talked. Can I call you again tomorrow?"

This was a wrinkle I didn't expect. Bob needed me as much as I needed him. My role had changed from the victim to the helper and listener for Bob. I can't begin to explain how that made me feel at that moment.

"Of course," I replied. "You can call me anytime, and let's friend each other on Facebook if you want."

He did and now I had a bigger view of his life and he mine. He posts lots of positive thoughts on Facebook, as I do to help with recovery. We always put a like on those for each other. We've talked many times on the phone as well, and he has offered to do anything to help with my cause. He understands what it is like to feel alone, but no one is really alone. He gets that the demons we have to live with within our mind can be undone through help and sharing like this. He has suffered as I have, and we are both looking to help ourselves by taking action, like my calling him.

Bob had no recollection of bullying me in the end. But he was going home and dealing with the troubles he had in his home life. In a recent conversation with Bob, he told me that he never saw himself as a bully and even asked some friends, and they said he was always the one who stuck up for others, not the bully. I'm not sure what happened in those years that he and I were the bully and the bullied, but it is a question that will have to remain in the past, never to have true closure, because it is gone, as are those days.

For now, the damage of the Bob demon is repaired for me, and I can now move on. It can get better. It's never too late to decide to stop fighting and put your demons behind you. I never thought that so many years later, I would be. But I think my decision to stop running and hiding from my demons, instead confronting them, allowed me to heal much more completely than if I had tried to let them go with no attempt at closure. I have been blessed with the ability and strength to continue to fight these long-term effects that bullying burdened me with. I now sleep better at night with dreams of the future instead of nightmares about the past.

In many cases, help is but a phone call away, and you will find that sometimes…just sometimes, the demon is an angel in disguise. This, I decided was my final closure on the issue of bullying. It was time to truly let go of the past and bury it in the ground permanently.

CHAPTER THIRTY

A Space to
Breathe Again

I reached up to the final rung in the ladder. The light was now shining brightly on me, and I could feel its warm glow on my face giving heat to my bones and strength to my heart and soul. The final rung was very slippery, and my grip on it slipped off many times before I finally grasped it and lifted myself out of the hole. I laid down in the field of tall grass, flowers, and dandelions and rested for a long time, exhausted from the journey up. I could feel the full effect of healing rays of the sun shining on me, giving my body the warmth and bright energy it so craved. I was tired and worn out, but not broken. My bad memories leaked from the hol,e and I allowed them back into my consciousness, no longer allowing them to scream at me, but fully accepting them as part of my life. I accepted them and then they had no power over me and no longer screamed at me. They now lived inside me, with all of my good memories. A funny realization came to me. These voices that were screaming at me were not the voices of the bullies, but were all the sound of my own voice, yelling at myself.

I realized that I shouldn't have tried to bury the past, but to accept and learn from it. That alone made these memories into simply moments, neither good nor bad, but a part of my life that contained both. I realized they can't haunt me from afar, if I always kept them near to me, out of the hole and a part of who I am. I realize that there was never a need for a shoebox and a hole.

◊ ◊ ◊

There was one more lesson I needed to learn on my journey to recovery from bullying, anxiety, and depression. This lesson may be one of the hardest to learn and that is to consciously change the way that I think. I finally understood how important it was to fill your mind with gratitude about your life and to constantly try to read positive affirmations to get the webs of negativity out of your mind and start to think *I can* instead of *I can't.*

Meditation and yoga helped me learn to change from an impatient and angry person into one who learned to enjoy the quiet time of learning to live with myself and my own mind. There are many great people and support sites that I use to constantly keep me in check and focus on the many positives that my life offers me.

Lori Deschene publishes on a website called *Tiny Buddha,* which is filled with stories about others who have overcome hardships and tips on how to recover from these hard times. She runs a wonderful site and has several books out that are incredibly helpful in keeping my mind focused on the positives in life. Her website at tinybuddha.com has a whole section of quotes of positivity that I can turn to any time I need, and her books are filled with positive affirmations. On her website alone, you can find quotes on acceptance such as:

"The past cannot be changed, forgotten, edited, or erased. It can only be accepted." – Unknown.

"Life becomes easier when you learn to accept an apology you never got." – Robert Brault

"The intensity of pain depends on the degree of resistance to the present moment." – Eckhart Tolle

There are so many quotes that can teach, soothe and help us to recover from pain, and Tiny Buddha is, I find, a great source of inspiration when I need it.

Another source of inspiration that helps me make it through my life now is another website called *Lessons Learned in Life.* This website is full of positive quotes and lessons that help ease your mind and help you to refocus the way you think. I use it daily both to read and post positive affirmations on Twitter. Recently, the site posted a very powerful message for me.

"Breathe. You're going to be okay. Breathe and remember that you've been in this place before. You've been this uncomfortable and anxious and scared, and you've survived. Breathe and know that you can survive this too. These feelings can't break you and they will pass. Maybe not immediately, but sometime soon, they are

going to fade and when they do, you'll look back at this moment and laugh for having doubted your resilience. I know it feels unbearable right now, but keep breathing, again and again. This will pass. I promise it will pass" — Daniell Koepke

So many times I read these messages and wonder how the speaker got in my head and knew what I was thinking. They didn't get in my head, though, because I am not alone and others are thinking the same way I did. Many others do, and there is no shame in having these feelings and sharing them, so they know they are not alone.

What I have found, however, is that depression and anxiety are rarely understood by those who haven't gone through it. Depression is not sadness, and most people who have depression or anxiety would do anything to get rid of it. I don't believe that anyone wants to feel this way and even for those of us who are going through it, we constantly question why we feel the way we do.

So, as a caution, I suggest that those who haven't gone through it think carefully about what they say to an anxious or depressed person. Saying things like *you need to go outside and get fresh air* or *you'll get over it, just give it time* are not really helpful. Of particular importance is not to say *I know what you are going through* unless you actually do. Even if you do, your journey was not the same as the person you are talking to. Having sympathy and maybe even trying to help them find professional help is good. Acting as if you can understand the mind of the person going through anxiety and depression at the time is not helpful to them and probably not to you.

There are so many resources available for people with anxiety and depression, and you can always help by researching which are credible resources for someone and seeing if they interest the person going through their anxiety and depression.

Another important part of understanding is to know that many times anxiety and depression can be *cured* with medication, therapy, and self-help methods, but sometimes that is not the case. Don't assume there's a magic pill or magic therapist that will make it all better. Every person is different, and we all need to figure out what works for us and what doesn't. I found that the biggest help for me, along with the other items I named, was simply time. I needed time to process what I was going through and to figure out what types of support and therapy worked for me. Learning to be patient might have been the biggest new skill I learned during this tumultuous time in my life. I compared my depression to stages of grieving. There seems to be a series of steps one must go through to get to recovery. Each step plays a pivotal role in helping you understand what you are going through and how you will mend. But without patience and a belief that you can get better, this process will not work.

◊ ◊ ◊

Another important person in my recovery was Dr. David D. Burns, M.D. I have never met Dr. Burns, but I did read his book *Feeling Good – The New Mood Therapy*, which was actually released quite a while ago in 1980, twenty-four years before I needed to find it.* The goal of the book seemed to be to try to offer drug-free treatment for depression. But whether on a drug therapy or not, the lessons in the book helped me to discover more about myself than those in any of the other books I read.

First, Dr. Burns discussed the thoughts and feelings that go along with depression. He outlines many of them such as:

1. Sadness or Depression
2. Guilt or Shame
3. Anger, Irritation, Annoyance, or Resentment
4. Frustration
5. Anxiety, Worry, Fear, Nervousness or Panic
6. Inferiority or Inadequacy
7. Loneliness
8. Hopelessness or Discouragement

I sat reading and checked off all eight of the above items for myself. There I was on the page, and I couldn't deny it. But to add fuel to the fire, Dr. Burns then had a checklist of cognitive distortions:

1. **All or Nothing Thinking:** Looking at things in only black and white with no gray. Yup, that was me, the perfectionist.

2. **Overgeneralization:** Viewing a negative event or feeling as a never-ending defeat. I can hear myself telling my family and even me that "you never do this..." or "you always do that". Always? Am I always unhappy or am I only sometimes unhappy. My Rabbi told me this at a meeting I had with him. I told him I never feel happy. He looked at me and said, "Never?" I said, "Well sometimes I'm happy." He asked me if I expected to be happy all the time. And when I said no, he said, "As a wise man should, you are happy as much as you should be and enjoy the happiness when you do experience it." I find myself happier now just thinking of it that way.

3. **Mental Filtering:** Dwelling on the negative items and ignoring the positive items. This is such an easy thing for a depressive personality to feel and so many of us do it in order to reinforce the way we feel.

4. **Discounting the Positives:** Things in your life that you accomplish are discounted. I won a special award for the video I did for my company but still walked in the next day thinking I would be fired. Why? Because I discounted the positives in order to reinforce my depression.

5. **Mind Reading or Jumping to Conclusions:** The assumption that people are reacting negatively to you with no evidence. I was constantly mind-reading everyone around me and thinking they didn't like me or I had to impress them. It made me worried every day until I realized the only one I had to impress

was myself.

6. **Magnification or Minimization:** The typical blowing things way out of proportion or shrinking the important items inappropriately. I was king of this one. I could blow all situations out of proportion to reinforce everything I believed.

7. **Emotional reasoning:** Instead of using your mind logically, you reason from how you feel. I would constantly tell myself how stupid I was or allow myself to wallow in my own self-pity and not force any change in my life. This does not work to recover yourself.

8. **Should Statements:** You constantly say to yourself statements with "shoulds" or "shouldn'ts," "Musts, "Oughts," "Have tos" and these force you to think illogically. I was and still have to work on this one all the time.

9. **Labelling:** You are constantly criticizing yourself and your shortcomings. You say "I'm a jerk" instead of "I made a mistake". I thought of myself as the biggest loser, and not in the weight way. I was constantly trying to put a label on myself and who I was, instead of being me.

10. **Personalization and Blame:** A constant blame that you place on yourself or other people for things they or you aren't entirely responsible for. I made a great practice of this issue as well and would blame both myself and my family for everything bad in my life.

Obviously, Dr. Burns had spent considerable time with people with depression and anxiety as these, I found, would ring true for everyone I met with these issues. To solve all of these things, Dr. Burns discusses the ways to undo the thinking. I have read the book cover to cover many times and will continue to do so as I try to practice undoing this list of cognitive distortions one by one. I get a little better each time I try. I hope one day I can learn to undo the years I spent building these ways of thinking. There is great information in his book and even on the web at *http://en.wikipedia.org/ wiki/Cognitive_distortion*. It may be one of the most important parts of my recovery, to understand how I was thinking and learn to stop thinking that way.

It is work, and it is a lot of work. It is always two steps forward and one step back. But much like *The Wizard of Oz*, Dorothy always had the shoes that would take her back to her home, but she had to experience the adventure in the movie in order to grow and learn. Only then, after she experienced both the good and bad that Oz had to offer, would she be told to click her heels three times and go home. She arrived back at her home changed for the better. I think we all must experience this in our lives. We all do have the ability to change, but must experience the journey first in order to want the change.

This lesson hit home for me recently, when one of my fraternity brothers, Ken, took his own life. Ken was kind to me, funny, never mean to anyone I knew, and was in fact always happy when I saw him. Recently, though, his marriage to his college sweetheart dissolved and the business that he'd tried to start began failing. I'm sure to him nothing seemed to be going right. He left a girlfriend, ex-wife, children nine and four years old, and a humongous load of fraternity and life friends who now clean up the pieces left from this action. For me, there was always going to be another day, tomorrow maybe, when we would see each other again. Now, there is no next time.

My problem is that I know the darkness he felt surrounding him. The hole that you fall in, where you look up and don't see any light to guide you back home. Your family and friends might be down the street as are mine, but you feel so alone. There is no one to understand what you feel, what you think. *"I am alone and I don't see the way out,"* you hear yourself saying. Depression and mental illness are diseases, and we do not yet fully understand how to diagnose and help those who have these afflictions. Is it the magic pill, therapy, time, or some other magic trick not yet thought of? I wish I had the answer. I saw no scream of help from my friend before he made his terrible choice to take his life and leave all of those who cared about him behind.

But depression can rob you of logical thought. We have to pay attention to those around us. Take our faces out of our tablets, phones, and distractions and get back to focusing on raising our community through interaction. I am truly as guilty as anyone of not paying attention to those around me and having my nose in my electronic toys all day. But in my life I've lost too many friends to suicide and depression:

Chris McCandless – Yes, the one they wrote the book and movie *Into the Wild* about. The boy I grew up with from age 13-18 was not the person in that movie. I don't know what happened to him during college or why he made the choices he did, but he obviously gave up on society. I don't know what led him to do this.

Mark – A high school and college friend who was struck by a train while walking on train tracks. I've walked on train tracks. I've felt them rumble as a train approaches. You don't just get hit by a train while walking on train tracks. I don't know what happened to him, but I know that in high school he was a preppy kid, and then on the first day of college, I went to see him and he was in leathers with a Mohawk. I'm not sure he was ever able to be comfortable in his own skin. I don't know about his home life. I only know I can't see him again. He is another friend that always had a smile and kind word for you.

"Krazy" Greg – When I graduated from college, I started working as a director for a local cable access show starring "Krazy" Greg called "Krazy Greg's TV Platter Party". We had so much fun doing that show. Greg truly wanted to be a 50's record host TV star like Dick Clark was. We made a show as best we could. I enjoyed the few years that we did this. Then one day out of the blue, the producer of the show called me to tell me that Greg shot himself in the head. He was dead. I had to go to his apartment and clean it out. I had to help clean the van that he committed suicide in. I can't put into words what that was like and how much that hurt us, the ones who had to live with this as his last memory. Why did he do this? Depression no doubt played a part. He was also accused of a crime, and he also had little to no money and a hard family life. All he had was his show and reputation, and that wasn't enough for him. The note he left said the world would be better without him. It is not. It most certainly would be better with him in it and the happiness he brought through his love of the 50's. But he can never know that now.

Ken – My friend and fraternity brother. I wish I could say I knew him better, but the times we did see each other were some special times. He always made me laugh and had a free spirit about him that made you want to hang out with him. I hadn't seen him in some years, but my fraternity alumni are very active, and we all keep up with each other. Of course he was a Facebook friend and I could spy on his life through that, so I never felt like he was that far away. Now he is away permanently because he took his own life and left literally hundreds of people questioning why.

Suicide is a selfish act and one that leaves survivors with guilt and shame. Suicide due to depression happens when a lost soul hits the bottom of the hole but doesn't realize that there is only one way to go from there, and that is up. It is so hard to see the light from the bottom of the hole though. That is why there is professional help and medication if needed. I needed to make many changes in my own life to realize how valuable I was to others…to myself. I had to find the rungs of the ladder and climb out of that dark and deep hole. No one promised any of us that life would be easy. Depression does not discriminate based on your status in life, your wealth, or your career, your family life, and your success. It is a disease, like getting cancer. You have to ask for help, show you need it, and decide which process you will take to get better. If you don't seek or ask for help, you may decide that life is no longer worth living, and no one around you will be able to get what you needed.

I have talked to many people who have survived and learned to thrive past their depression, whether due to a past of abuse, bullying, or just the way their mind works. Of course, I know firsthand as well. I wish I didn't, but I do. I am lucky to have a large family around and many friends who love me. It is unconditional, and I had to live if for no other reason than because I couldn't bear to hurt them. But during that time, I certainly did not think much of myself. I needed to want to get better. I can't bring back any of the four friends I have told you about. But I can share their spirit and keep them alive through sharing this story. If one of you reads this and realizes that life is always worth living and it will get better, then it was worth writing and sharing this personal pain. I will keep going, but I will never forget those four friends and the choices they made. They robbed me of a life of positive memories that would have come once they got past their depression, issues, or whatever led them to make their choice.

I hope that you understand that life is a series of peaks and valleys, and we can only see how wonderful the peaks are if we fall into the valleys and look up. Then it is a hard climb back to the peak. But when you are back up there, with the fresh air and surrounded by your friends, family, and the doctors who held out their hands to pull you to the top, and only when you are pulled back up, can you truly look back down at the valley and say, *"Maybe one day I'll climb down again, but I know that I can get back up."*

I wish my four friends could have done that.

I no longer regret what happened to me in my past, and I no longer dwell on a future that I cannot predict. As I battled my two years of depression and my lifelong pain of the bullying in my youth, my wife understood and stayed by my side. She gave me two items that I look at each day that have sayings to help me put my mind back in the right place.

The first item is a coffee mug with a saying on it that I have learned to take to heart.

"Life isn't about waiting for the storm to pass.
It's about learning how to dance in the rain."
— Vivian Greene —

The other item is a framed picture and then a refrigerator magnet that she got me with the reminder that I use daily. The picture is at my work desk for all to see, because we all must practice it. The saying is by Eleanor Roosevelt, the first lady and wife of United States President Franklin Delano Roosevelt.

"Yesterday is history.
Tomorrow a mystery.
Today is a gift."

I like to add my own ending to that saying. I always add that is why today is called "the present", because it is a present given to us and we should treat it as such. The bullies are behind me now, and it is history.

In talking to my mother, she gave me another insight into myself and the way that I was thinking. While my mother did have a tough life, she always seemed happy. I asked her why she thought that was. She told me a story of a group meeting she was at, where the question was posed about how some of us think when someone doesn't like us. The question was, "Do you think what's wrong with me or what's wrong with them?" It seems only logical that the "what's wrong with them" people, like my mother, would feel less susceptible to self-esteem damage. She helped me to try to change my thinking in that way. I'm not going to beat myself up about the way I am, because there is nothing wrong with me. Some people will like you and some won't, and that's just the way of the world. I can accept that.

My mind eventually added back the memories that were important to me and that made me feel good about who I am. I am a good person who had some rough times and made some poor decisions along the multiple journeys of my life. Like everybody else in this blue orb we live on. I brought them all back in and relished my accomplishments again.

Memories of having a mother, father, and sister who were still close by and having my in-laws close by. I never had to be alone, because family was all around me.

Memories of working with the boys and girls at the camp for disabled children and the great feelings I had when I thought about working with them.

Memories of my friends from the drama group in high school, people who were still there to talk to me on Facebook and at reunions.

Memories of my college friends from VTTV and Theta Xi, who accepted and loved me as family and who I cared about so very deeply.

Memories of my best friend Terry, who only lived down the street and was always there. He had been my best friend for almost thirty years and shared all our secret jokes that would make us laugh. How lucky I was to have a friend for such a long time who I truly call "brother".

Memories of a wife who loved me and of creating two beautiful and wonderful boys who I raised to be gentlemen and who found their own success in life by choosing paths that I helped guide them to.

I forgot how lucky I truly was and that I had started my website about the long-term effect of bullying to help people, including myself, understand that there is nothing wrong with us and that it was normal to have some of these issues. I was just another person who wanted to help, and I forgot that I had made a difference and could continue to make a difference now that I understood these feelings.

Once all of these memories came back and after a great amount of work to quell the overwhelming depressive bad thoughts that circled my head, I slowly started to feel my self-worth return. These thoughts made me feel worthless and believe that I was not worth the work others would have to do to make me better. I learned to change from journaling daily about how I felt to journaling about my gratitude for being alive. One of the books I read explained that our brains don't control us, we control our brains. Our eyes are not truly window to reality, but windows to the reality that our brains want us to see. We can control and change that reality. By journaling positive thoughts and reading positive items, our brain learns to change its thinking to positive from negative. I learned it could be as simple as writing a "thank you for waking me up today" or a "thank you for breathing today," or as complicated as you want to make it. I now look back on these journal entries.

1/20 – 1) I solved a tough challenge at work today and it felt great. 2) I went to the gym and worked out when my mind told me I didn't want to. I did it anyway and feel good. 3) I meditated for ten minutes today.

1/21 – 1) I solved another tough issue at work today successfully. 2) I went to yoga class today and really enjoyed it. 3) I told my wife that I love her.

1/22 – 1) I am thankful to be awake today and to be breathing. 2) I made a wonderful dinner for the family and we ate together and shared some laughs. 3) I am so happy about deciding to start my new company and write a book.

When I look back at these "gratitude journal" writings, I feel good and even sense a smile on my face. It really works for me, and I could feel my brain slowly but surely turning a corner to think in a positive *can do* way. I felt my confidence as a person returning and constantly go back to my journal to recall that, each day, I do have things to be thankful for and am lucky for these things in my life.

◊ ◊ ◊

Recently I visited my psychiatrist again for our typical visit, which now only takes place every six months. I told him that I never felt better. I told him that I had reconciled with my past and that, for the first time in a very long time, I felt like my old self again and felt my depression and anxiety had completely gone away. In fact, I looked forward now to each new day and adventure.

He was happy for me but also gave me some words of caution. It was another yin and yang moment I would be learning. My psychiatrist shared with me that he had spent thirteen years working as the director of an alcohol and drug treatment center at a local hospital. He asked me if I knew who the people were that would always relapse back into drug and alcohol problems and show up again at his treatment center.

I told him "No", even though I knew what the answer was.

He told me it was the people who thought they were cured and stopped going to Alcohol Anonymous meetings or eventually got so busy they gave up on going to meetings or thinking of themselves as susceptible to a relapse.

He explained that he was so happy for me right now, but to always remember that, in the back of my mind, I should never forget that anxiety and depression I experienced. He reminded me it can happen again and that I need to continue to stay alert to how I feel. I know that he is right, and I am aware now of what it feels like to hit rock bottom. With that knowledge in mind, I must always remember what got me there and how I got out of the hole that anxiety and depression put me in.

I will continue to help both myself and others deal with the pain and suffering that bullying leaves in your soul. But I am here to tell you that you can change if you want to and that you can thrive and survive. It can and it does get better if you give it time and put in the effort.

You are not and will never be truly alone as there are many of us out there who have gone through some form of anxiety and depression and come out of the other side mentally healthier for the experience. It is not a sign of weakness that caused the anxiety and depression, but it's a sign of all the years that we fought to stay strong.

Those of us who have suffered, are suffering, or will suffer with anxiety and depression are all around you. We can hold each other up, one by one, to make a difference in the lives that we live. I am now more convinced than ever that I will not be haunted by my past anymore. After all, the past is in the past, and I am not that young boy or that teen and young adult with low self-esteem. I do not have to regret a life made up of many peaks and valleys. I simply accept the life given to me, live it in a mindful day-by-day way, and find ways to be grateful for what I do have. After all, we get only one life to live, and I shall live it not only by the length of it, but also by the width of it and hold my head high, for I am grateful to be here.

EPILOGUE

The Hole

I take the mound of dirt that is above the hole in my mind and shovel it slowly with my hands, scoop after scoop, into the hole that used to contain the moments of my past that I let haunt me. Those moments are now with me, and I no longer feel that panic I felt when approaching this place. With each scoop of the dirt filling the hole, I felt the past become a part of the earth, simply to be and no longer to dwell on. When the last scoop of dirt filled the top of the hole and I could no longer see that there was a hole there at any time, I knew it was time to say goodbye to the field by the tree line, behind the yard I had made in the recesses of my mind.

I understand now that I never should have dug the hole, but I don't regret that I did the work I had to be able to fall into the hole, climb out of the hole and fill it back in, to truly understand me. I know that one day there is a possibility that another hole could be dug again and I will have to climb out of that one. But today I doubt the hole will be dug, and I can move on with my life.

As I walk away from the old spot that was the hole, I take one more backward glance. Through the tall grass I cannot even see that the hole was there. It no longer matters to me as it is now in the past and is simply a place in my life I no longer need. I realize that my life is not the one journey that I felt guilt and sadness about, but it is many journeys with this part being only one of them. The hole is filled in and gone and its bad memories are no longer able to haunt me. I have accepted them for what they are, a small fraction of my life.

As I leave this field that had been such a long part of my life, I look down and notice for the first time that it is filled with beautiful flowers and dandelions I ignored each time I came. I pick a dandelion and blow its white floating seeds into the air, watching them as they twinkle against the sunlight that is shining in my face and eyes. Each seed has the possibility of landing and creating more dandelions to fill the field. I look around and realize it is beautiful in this field, and I wish I had noticed before the beauty that was all around the hole I had made. But thinking about that no longer matters to me. Yesterday is truly a history that no longer haunts me. Tomorrow is a mystery that I no longer ponder for endless hours. Today I am reborn with a new focus to work my hardest to live my life to the fullest. Not just the length of it, but the width of it as well. I have accepted my past and have fond memories of the good parts of my life as well as ones that I learned from, but that were not necessarily bad if they taught me something…and that's all that matters for now.

AUTHOR'S NOTE

Many of the bullying parts of this story take place in Lexington, Massachusetts. This and many of the locations mentioned in the book are real, but I do not wish to leave you, the reader, believing that Lexington isn't a beautiful place with great people. My experiences happened many years ago as a child, and I do not fault the people or town of Lexington, Massachusetts, for this. It is a wonderful and historic colonial town in the United States famous for being the "first shot heard around the world" to start the Revolutionary War. Although I haven't been back in a very long time, I am sure the years have been kind to both the people and the place.

I do know that some changes have taken place since I left. Franklin Elementary and the schoolyard where much of my bullying took place were closed and leveled many years ago. Jonas Clarke Middle School put a lengthy anti-bullying policy in place, and it can be found on their website.

I look forward to the day when I can visit Lexington again, because in between the bullying that happened to me there, I did have some good times and good friends that I will also never forget.

~*Alan Eisenberg (June 11, 2015)*

ACKNOWLEDGEMENTS

A big thank you to all the people in my life who helped bring me to this point, including the bullies in my early life, without whom this book could not have been written. Thank you to my mother and father, Roy and Carol, and sister, Robyn, who saved my life many times during my youth and probably never knew it until now. My Aunt Sue Egan for taking the time to help edit my words and offer me feedback from an honest personal family angle. My best friends, Stephen, Tim, Jody, Eddie, Dan, and Bill who have been by my side from the beginning of our friendship, never wavering and always reminding me what strong souls and true friends look like.

To my friends and supporters, without whom, this book could not be written: Tim and Ann Wierbinski, Tricia Kleber, Kelly Valenta, Darby Gippert, Alan and Sharon Steckman, Lisa Steckman, Dan Warthen, Ed Rossi, Jenie Perry, Jason Herman, Patricia Wade, Kim Boswell, Gayle Schneider, Melissa and Tom Morgan, John and Robin Muse, Chris and Diane Spina, Brendan Rafferty, Stacey and JD Thomas, Jimmy Woodson, and Valerie Jones.

To all the mentors in my life who believed in me when I didn't believe in myself and who encouraged me to move forward. Without you I would not be the person I am today. My in-law family, Earl and Marie, Becky, Randy, Jill and Jeff for always treating me as one of the family and making me feel loved. You have given me years of happy memories to cherish.

A special thank you to my friend, Laurie L. Rosen LCSW, whose editing, guidance, and advice during the writing of this book made me understand and tell a better story.

To my high school friends, Nic DiPalma for believing in my cause and providing the amazing cover art for the book, and Shane Hinkel for the photography. Thank you to all the contributors to my *Bullying Stories* website for candidly sharing your stories and helping me to understand the extent of the issue of bullying and C-PTSD around the world.

Finally, a thank you to my family, Janet, Andy and Zach, for keeping me grounded. You watched as I went through a hard recovery and patiently waited as I worked to heal myself. I love you all so much.

WORKS CITED

* Krakauer, Jon. *Into the Wild*. New York: Anchor, 1997. Print.

* McCandless, Carine. *The Wild Truth*. San Francisco: HarperOne, 2014. Print.

* Barkhorn, Eleanor. *"'160,000 Kids Stay Home From School Each Day to Avoid Being Bullied'"* The *Atlantic*. Atlantic Media Company, 03 Oct. 2013. Web. 08 June 2015.

* Burns, David D. *Feeling Good: The New Mood Therapy*. New York: Morrow, 1980. Print.

OTHER WORKS READ BY
ALAN EISENBERG
DURING HIS RECOVERY

Katz, Alice. *It's Not Personal!: A Guide to Anger Management*. Westport, CT: AJK Pub., 1996. Print.

Carbonell, David. *Panic Attacks Workbook: A Guided Program for Beating the Panic Trick*. Berkeley, CA: Ulysses, 2004. Print.

LeJeune, Chad. *The Worry Trap: How to Free Yourself from Worry & Anxiety Using Acceptance and Commitment Therapy*. Oakland, CA: New Harbinger Publications, 2007. Print.

Wehrenberg, Margaret. *The 10 Best-ever Anxiety Management Techniques Workbook*. New York: W.W. Norton, 2012. Print.

Muir, Alice Jane. *Overcome Depression*. London: Teach Yourself, 2012. Print.

Deschene, Lori. *Tiny Buddha: Simple Wisdom for Life's Hard Questions*. San Francisco, CA: Conari, 2012. Print.

ABOUT THE AUTHOR

A Ladder in the Dark is Alan Eisenberg's debut novel, but not his first writing on the subject of bullying. Alan has been contributing to the issue of bullying through a web blog he created called *Bullying Stories*. The website is about the long-term effects of bullying and he has been sharing his and other contributors bullying stories since 2007. In that time, Alan has amassed a large following on his website, to include over one million unique visits and the material on his website is used in many schools to help children learn and research about the issue of bullying. He has also written a one act play about bullying in conjunction with his old high school drama department called "Standing By". The play is available for free to download from his website at www.bullyingrecovery.org.

Alan has been featured on *National Public Radio* (NPR), in *The Boston Globe* and several other online radio and blog sites discussing the issue of bullying and sharing his perspective and story. In 2015, Alan started a company called *Bullying Recovery, LLC* to be able to further contribute to trying to help create better programs and support those that suffer with the psychological effects of long-term bullying.

Alan lives in Fairfax, Virginia, a suburb of Washington, DC with his wife and children. He works in the media communication field as an eLearning and training content developer by day and runs his *Bullying Recovery* company by night and on weekends.

21097656R00117

Made in the USA
Middletown, DE
19 June 2015

Praise for *Collaborative Divorce*

"Collaborative Divorce is a brilliant achievement and major contribution to people going through divorce. This comprehensive and deeply intelligent book will prove to be an invaluable resource for helping couples who are separating and the professionals who work with them to navigate the stormy waters of divorce with intention, integrity, and soul."

—Debbie Ford, author of *Spiritual Divorce: Divorce as a Catalyst for an Extraordinary Life*

"This practical book should be assigned reading for every divorcing spouse. It describes the advantages of a revolutionary idea whose time has come: hire professionals with a collaborative orientation and the process of divorce will be less painful and will lay the foundation for better long-term results."

—Robert H. Mnookin, professor, Harvard Law School, and author of *Beyond Winning*

"Collaborative Divorce is truly a new and better way to end a marriage or any intimate partnership. This first book on the subject is written by experts for couples who are on the verge of divorce and want to keep their integrity, come to a fair financial settlement, and help their children through this difficult transition."

—Jean Shinoda Bolen, M.D., professor of psychiatry, University of California San Francisco, School of Medicine, and author of *Goddesses in Everywoman*

"In this brave and visionary work, Tesler and Thompson chart the path to a humane and compassionate divorce. *Collaborative Divorce* is one of the rare books with a vital lesson, powerfully taught, that will make the world a better place."

—Thomas Lewis, M.D., assistant clinical professor of psychiatry, University of California San Francisco, School of Medicine, and author of *A General Theory of Love*

"A great step forward. This book will enable spouses to bypass the truly awful, adversarial process of the courts at the time of the breakup."

—Judith Wallerstein, Ph.D., author of *The Unexpected Legacy of Divorce*

"A positive and encouraging read . . . Tesler and Thompson make a good case for [collaborative divorce] resulting in more satisfied parents and happier children."

—*Parent's Press*

collaborative divorce

The Revolutionary New Way to Restructure Your Family,
Resolve Legal Issues, and Move on with Your Life

Pauline H. Tesler, M.A., J.D.
and Peggy Thompson, Ph.D.

HC
An Imprint of HarperCollins*Publishers*

A hardcover edition of this book was published in 2006 by HarperCollins Publishers.

First paperback edition published 2007.

Designed by Sarah Maya Gubkin

The Library of Congress has catalogued the hardcover edition as follows:
Tesler, Pauline H., 1942–
    Collaborative divorce : the revolutionary new way to restructure your family, resolve legal issues, and move on with your life / Pauline H. Tesler and Peggy Thompson.
    1st. ed.
    Thompson, Peggy.
    ISBN: 0-06-088943-8
    Includes index.
    1. Divorce—United States—Psychological aspects.
    2. Divorce—Law and legislation—United States.
HQ834.T47   2006

ISBN: 978-0-06-114800-2 (pbk)
ISBN-10: 0-06-114800-8 (pbk)   2006298196

07 08 09 10 11 10 9 8 7 6 5 4 3 2 1

CONTENTS

3 Assembling Your Team   65
Choosing Your Collaborative Divorce Team ★ The Collaborative
Team Agreement ★ Getting Started: Alice and Todd's Story

4 Gathering Information: A Look at the Role of the
Lawyers and Financial Advisor   88
First, the Facts ★ The Legal Side of Your Collaborative Divorce ★
The First Four-way Meeting with the Lawyers ★ Gathering
Information with Your Collaborative Lawyers ★ Understanding
Negotiations, Understanding the Law ★ Gathering and Exchanging
Information with the Help of Your Financial Consultant ★ A
Word About Timing ★ An Older Couple Works Efficiently with a
Small Collaborative Divorce Team: Ronald and Martine's Story

5 Gathering Information: A Look at the Role of the
Coaches and Child Specialist   110
Working with Coaches ★ Gathering and Exchanging Information
with Your Child Specialist ★ The Five-Way Meeting and the
Parenting Plan ★ How Long Does Information Gathering Last? ★
Coaching Opens the Door to Creative Problem Solving:
Jeff and Sarah's Story

6 Reaching Resolution   148
Brainstorming Options for Resolution ★ When a House Is More
Than a House: Adam and Sue's Story

7 Attaining the Necessary Sense of Closure   163
Finishing the Job ★ A Look at the Papers ★ Planning for the
Future ★ Your Conflict Resolution Plan ★ Using Your Team to
Anticipate, Forestall, and Resolve Conflict ★ How Your Conflict
Resolution Plan Will Help ★ Untying the Knot and Tying Up
the Loose Ends ★ The Signing Ceremony ★ An Opportunity
to Create Personal Meaning ★ A Final Meeting: Eileen and
Andy's Story

INTRODUCTION:
Searching for a Better Way

In the long run, we shape our lives, and we shape ourselves. The process never ends until we die. And the choices we make are ultimately our own responsibility.

—ELEANOR ROOSEVELT

You and your spouse have the power to divorce with integrity, dignity, and mutual respect. You have the ability to act in ways that make it possible to preserve what remains of good feeling between you, and to negotiate new relationships with those you will continue to be connected to after the divorce is final: your children, your spouse (who is still your children's parent), and the many friends and relatives who form your community of support.

Preserving what remains of good feeling between spouses during the divorce process has obvious benefits for couples with children, who may continue to come together over a lifetime of births, graduations, marriages, and deaths. It can be equally important for childless couples whose ties to one another's extended families are deep, or who simply do not wish to mar happy memories of the good days of their marriage with unnecessary unpleasantness during a divorce. For many divorcing couples, their marriage was profoundly meaningful in its time. That chapter of life can be remembered without undue pain, and even with acceptance or good will, by those who choose to part with respect and dignity. Collaborative divorce offers a model for this kind of dignified, respectful divorce for couples who want it. We know that it is possible because we have watched couples achieve it again and again. We are writing this book to show you how to achieve it yourself, whether you are only thinking about ending your marriage or a divorce is about to begin.

Does divorcing without hate sound impossibly unrealistic? Let us assure you: we base everything you will learn about in this book upon the incontrovertible evidence of our own experience and that of our thousands of collaborative divorce colleagues. In case after case, we have watched couples no different from you and your spouse say no to filing inflammatory court papers; no to taking hard-line, emotion-based positions that diminish one another's dignity and self-esteem; and no to drawing their children into the nightmare of seemingly endless conflict.

We have watched those same couples say yes to a process whereby both partners and their team of professional advisors commit themselves to resolving differences justly and equitably out of court; yes to using their best efforts to reach agreements that meet the fundamental needs of both parties; and yes to keeping at the forefront integrity, civility, and the long-term well-being of all involved as important financial and child-related concerns are resolved.

After years of handling divorce the old way, we have had the privilege every day for more than a decade of helping couples and their families work constructively and respectfully toward solutions that work—sometimes surprisingly well—for all concerned. It's not always easy, but it can be and is being done by people just like you.

This book is for married individuals and people in other kinds of intimate partnerships who are willing to consider a way of ending a relationship in a way that differs greatly from methods of the past. As you read this book, you will be invited—as we invite our own clients—to see possibilities for divorce dramatically unlike what your divorced friends and relatives may have experienced, unlike what you have seen on television or read about in novels and self-help books. We offer you what we—a lawyer and a psychologist—have learned over decades of work with divorcing and separating couples: divorce may be difficult and painful, but it also is a normal life transition that unfolds in a step-by-step sequence over a predictable timeline (a timeline that has no connection whatsoever with the timeline of court-based divorces). Moving constructively through this life transition requires addressing a spectrum of difficult but normal emotions and concerns.

Those vital human concerns are always impacted (for better or for worse) by the choices that every person involved in a divorce must make. In this book, we will show you a process—available to any divorcing couple—that invites both partners to aspire to high intentions and worthy goals, a process that proceeds with respect and concludes with civility, a process that honors human relationships and personal integrity at least as much as it values financial security and the "bottom line."

HOW WE CAME TO WORK
WITH COLLABORATIVE DIVORCE

We had learned from long experience that our culture's commonly held beliefs about marriage and divorce don't match reality. Each of us had worked in the adversarial court system for many years, becoming more and more frustrated and disillusioned with what we saw happening there. Without anyone intending it, family law courts had become a place where—in the words of one experienced California family law judge—"they shoot the survivors." We felt there must be a better way. Without knowing about each other's existence, each of us searched for, tried, and discarded new approaches to divorce as they became available. With every effort, we each learned more about the kind of help couples and their children really need as they move through divorce—and how little of that help they were actually getting.

When we finally met in the early 1990s, we were astonished to see how much overlap there was between a lawyer's perspective and a psychologist's perspective about what was wrong with our current methods of handling divorce. Though we had traveled very different paths, we had arrived at very similar conclusions about what would have to change in order for divorcing couples and their children to get reliable, consistent, effective professional help—and to avoid destructive professional help—as their families break apart and are rebuilt.

We are colleagues, not partners. We continue to travel parallel paths in our separate professional practices, but since the early 1990s, we have worked together to develop, improve, teach, and publicize collaborative divorce through a number of joint projects. Since the late 1990s, each of us in our own way has said "good-bye" to the courts and to adversarial divorce dispute resolution. Now each of us works exclusively with couples who have chosen collaborative divorce. And because we both practice in the San Francisco Bay Area, every now and then we have the pleasure of being selected by a couple to work together with them on their collaborative divorce team.

PEGGY'S PATH TO COLLABORATIVE DIVORCE

Early in her career as a psychologist, Peggy Thompson worked with many couples to improve their relationships and to help them avoid divorce. She also helped children whose divorcing parents were involved in bitter custody fights to adjust and, if possible, to maintain healthy relationships with both parents. Later, she became a custody evaluator and a high-conflict divorce counselor, working with couples involved in court-based custody battles and ongoing conflicts after the divorce. Again and again, she saw well-meaning couples in her practice move from respectful communication to pitched battles after they turned over their divorce disagreements to conventional adversarial lawyers—despite their best intentions to keep their divorces civilized and contained. All these experiences made Peggy painfully aware that everyone involved as professionals needed to approach divorce in a different way. She was searching for a better way for everyone—but most of all for the children.

With her husband, the psychologist Rod Nurse, Peggy tried first to change how custody evaluations were used, working over a more extended timeframe with families to help them see changes they could make that might improve their children's situation. But this wasn't enough, because custody evaluations were being done only after the battle lines between the parents had already been drawn.

She then formed a study group, which included a lawyer, another family psychologist, two child therapists, and a financial specialist, as well as her husband and herself, to brainstorm various approaches that might be more beneficial for families than custody litigation. From the ideas generated in this group, which met for two years, came the beginnings of the collaborative divorce model. After a long but unsuccessful search for a lawyer who would be willing to embrace that model, she was delighted when her path crossed that of Pauline Tesler, who was already fully engaged in the practice of collaborative law. That a divorce lawyer could be committed to working constructively with clients entirely outside the courts in ways that respected human relationships and avoided battle opened entirely new possibilities in Peggy's mind for effective interdisciplinary collaboration. Pauline, like Peggy, had come to feel that truly constructive divorce-related conflict resolution would require the coordinated resources of an interdisciplinary team. From their different professional perspectives, they had come to the same conclusion about what needed to be done.

Their work together, along with other dedicated professionals, led to the creation of the International Academy of Collaborative Professionals, and to the development of sophisticated training programs to teach lawyers, financial consultants, and mental health counselors how to work effectively in collaborative teams that can help divorcing couples reach far-reaching and long-lasting resolution.

PAULINE'S PATH TO COLLABORATIVE LAW

Pauline Tesler's journey from hardball litigator to collaborative lawyer began with an aching sense that something was very wrong with how the legal system handled divorce. She was winning great victories as a litigator, but whether she won or not, her clients seemed to be equally miserable. Looking for a better way took her on a ten-year quest, including study with a cultural anthropologist to explore how other cultures manage highly emotional conflict resolution.

Her attitude toward handling divorce in the courtroom changed completely when she encountered the psychologist Carl Jung's notion that every dark part of our nature that we disown, suppress, or ignore becomes part of our "shadow" and drives our behavior in ways we don't perceive. She saw that the legal system encourages the shadow behaviors of everyone involved in divorce, from judges, court clerks, and lawyers to the clients who walk through her doors (who are sometimes possessed by rage, guilt, grief, shame, fear, and remorse—the realm of the shadow).

Once she saw that, her own job description changed. In the early 1990s, she was the moving force behind bringing collaborative law to San Francisco. By the late 1990s, she stopped litigating entirely and focused her efforts on expanding the availability of collaborative law and interdisciplinary collaborative divorce in the United States, Canada, and Europe. As a collaborative lawyer, she now works to help her clients see that while spending time in the grip of powerful negative emotions is completely normal during the grief and recovery process associated with the end of a marriage, nobody can make good decisions when those decisions are made in a state of strong emotion rather than considered reflection. In her writing and training she teaches collaborative lawyers and other collaborative divorce professionals how to encourage their clients to reflect before acting, to understand the shadow phenomenon, and to negotiate solutions based on best hopes rather than worst fears.

COLLABORATIVE DIVORCE
IS BECOMING MAINSTREAM

The very first collaborative lawyer in the world, Stu Webb, began doing this work in Minnesota in January 1990. His idea made so much sense to divorce lawyers that news of it swept rapidly across the legal world of North America during the 1990s, and divorce lawyers in urban areas clamored for training. Pauline Tesler was one of the earliest trainers traveling across North America to meet this demand. As satisfied clients began telling their friends about this new and better way to deal with the end of a marriage, a groundswell of demand began rising in the late 1990s. By 2000, trained collaborative lawyers were offering this approach to their clients in most major cities and many smaller cities and towns in the United States and Canada. Now most people in most North American states and provinces can find collaborative lawyers, if not in their own communities, then close enough to make collaborative divorce an option.

Meanwhile, as more and more family lawyers were embracing collaborative law, the interdisciplinary collaborative divorce team approach was also gaining momentum. Originating with the work of Peggy Thompson and her colleagues, the collaborative divorce interdisciplinary team approach was first offered to clients in Northern California in the early 1990s. When Peggy and Pauline discovered the overlap between collaborative law and interdisciplinary collaborative divorce, they began training professional colleagues all over North America in how to take collaborative law to the next level: interdisciplinary collaborative professional teams. The excellent match between what divorcing couples and children need and what interdisciplinary collaborative teams offer is so apparent that the team model is now available in most states and provinces in North America, and divorce lawyers in Europe are now asking to be trained. Peggy and Pauline continue—separately and together—to teach collaborative professionals in North America and Europe the skills of interdisciplinary team collaboration, to work directly with divorcing clients, primarily in the San Francisco Bay Area, and to consult with both professionals and clients nationwide.

IT DOESN'T MAKE IT EASY, BUT IT HELPS

When you choose collaborative divorce, a team of professional helpers from the fields of law, psychology, and finance will provide coordinated support and guidance to help you and your partner slow down, reflect, focus on your values, aspire to high goals, make good choices, work together constructively while avoiding court, plan for the future, and reach deep resolution. In our experience, this kind of coordinated professional help isn't available anywhere else but in collaborative divorce. If you choose it, you and your spouse can count on professional advice and counsel that will always

- Encourage both of you to remember your goal: the best divorce the two of you are capable of achieving
- Educate and remind you about the divorce grief and recovery process so that you can choose to operate from your hopes rather than your fears
- Help you focus on the future rather than the past, and on your deepest personal values and goals for the future rather than what the local judge is permitted to order
- Make it possible for your financial advice to come from a financial expert and your parenting advice to come from a child specialist, so that your lawyer is freed to do what lawyers do best: help you reach a well-considered resolution
- Keep you and your spouse focused on how your children are really doing and how the two of you can help them move through the divorce with the least possible pain and "collateral damage"
- Teach both of you new understanding and skills that will help you be more effective coparents after the divorce

than you may be capable of right now as your marriage ends

- Make sure you and your spouse have all the information you'll need to make wise decisions—information not just about the law but also about finances, child development, grief and recovery, family systems, negotiating techniques, and anything else that will help you devise creative, long-lasting solutions
- Emphasize consensus and real resolution, not horse-trading and quick fixes
- Help you maintain maximum privacy, creativity, and self-determination in your divorce

USING THIS BOOK

In chapters 1 through 9 of this book, we show you exactly what to expect in a collaborative divorce. To make that clearer, we have included many stories about the collaborative divorces of couples whom we name. These are real stories about real people's divorces. Naturally, we have changed all the names and a few of the identifying details to protect their privacy. In a few instances, we have created composite stories from the actual experiences of more than one couple. These stories all show what can happen when people choose to act from their best hopes instead of their worst fears. In chapter 10, "Common Questions and Concerns," we answer specific questions about various collaborative divorce scenarios, based on actual questions clients and professionals have posed to us as they worked on collaborative divorces.

Divorce is never easy. Even collaborative divorce can be difficult and painful. Our intention in writing this book is not to pretend otherwise, but rather to offer you information, options, and tools that can make the process far better and more constructive for you, your spouse, your children, and the other people who matter to you most.

1

THE OLD OR THE NEW WAY OF DIVORCE?
You Have a Choice

The truth is that our finest moments are most likely to occur when we are feeling deeply uncomfortable, unhappy, or unfulfilled. For it is only in such moments, propelled by our discomfort, that we are likely to step out of our ruts and start searching for different ways or truer answers.

—M. SCOTT PECK

You don't need to be a lawyer or a psychologist to know that going through a divorce is one of life's roughest passages. It can cause a myriad of emotional responses that at times makes you feel overwhelmed and limits your ability to think clearly or make good choices. Unfortunately, this occurs at the very time you are called upon to make some of the most important decisions of your life.

For many people, the ending of a marriage is a time of temporary "diminished capacity." By diminished capacity, we mean a period during which the person you thought you were—competent, thoughtful, considerate, reasonable, fair-minded, resilient—disappears for days or weeks at a time. The person you generally know yourself to be is temporarily replaced by an unfamiliar and frightening self who can hardly summon up enough energy to get out of bed; wallows in fear, confusion, or anger; or jumps to hasty conclusions in order to end the conflicting impulses about what to do and how to behave.

Recovering from the shock of a failed marriage involves moving through that initial period of diminished capacity, until gradually, more and more of the time, your predivorce "best self" is back at the helm. Most people can expect to feel something like their old, predivorce selves in eighteen to twenty-four months from the time of the divorce decree, though it happens more quickly for some and more slowly for many. During that recovery period, it is quite common for people to veer suddenly and dramatically from day to day, or even hour to hour, between optimism and darkest pessimism, between cooperative good humor and frightening rage.

You may be experiencing such intense emotions as you come to terms with the possible—or actual—ending of your marriage. Most people do, at least some of the time. Keeping the focus on best intentions and good decision making in light of that reality is what collaborative divorce is all about.

Thinking clearly about what kind of divorce you want and how you'll get there may be an unfamiliar concept to you. Most people are surprised to learn that the choices made right at the start of the divorce process have a great impact on what kind of a divorce experience they will have. Even when people do understand the high stakes of those early choices, thinking clearly and making intelligent choices at that time can be very challenging, because divorce is an emotional wild ride like no other. Even very reasonable and civilized people can find unexpected, hard-to-manage emotions popping up at the most inconvenient times, particularly during the early months of a separation and divorce—exactly the time when you will be making decisions that determine what kind of divorce you are likely to get and how your divorce will affect the rest of your life.

THE EMOTIONAL ROLLER COASTER OF DIVORCE

Divorce is an emotional task unlike any other in modern society, and different people experience it in different ways. While some individuals go through nearly all of the extreme emotional states that we describe here, others have an easier time getting through this period and will maneuver these choppy waters with more skill. The important thing to remember is that all the emotions we discuss are normal, but while some are readily acknowledged by the people experiencing them, others are so uncomfortable that it's difficult even to admit they exist. The wide array of emotional states that many people experience during the early stages of the divorce process can diminish their capacity to think clearly, impair their judgment, and make rational decision making difficult or impossible.

GRIEF AND SORROW

Being sad when a marriage ends is natural. Although it's painful, grief is a healthy emotional response to the loss of an important relationship. We are hardwired to feel it, and it wouldn't be reasonable to expect otherwise. While sorrow and grief can be very hard to handle, most people do understand and accept the inevitability of these feelings.

We know from research, theoretical writings, and personal experience with thousands of people going through divorces that though the emotional impact of a divorce is as severe as that of a death in the immediate family, the grief and recovery process does have a beginning, middle, and end. Though they may seem endless, the pain and confusion surrounding separation and divorce do gradually lighten and finally go away—for most people over a period of eighteen months to three or four years following the marital separation, though recovery can be quicker or slower.

Elisabeth Kübler-Ross, a pioneer in the hospice movement, first described the stages of grieving about and recovering from a major trauma such as death or divorce:

- **Denial:** "This is not happening to me. It's all a misunderstanding. It's just a midlife crisis. We can work it out."
- **Anger and resentment:** "How can he [she] do this to me? What did I ever do to deserve this? This is not fair!"
- **Bargaining:** "If you'll stay, I'll change" or "If I agree to do it [money, childrearing, sex, whatever] your way, can we get back together?"
- **Depression:** "This is really happening, I can't do anything about it, and I don't think I can bear it."
- **Acceptance:** "Okay, this is how it is, and I'd rather accept it and move on than wallow in the past."

Understanding these stages can be very helpful when it comes to talking about divorce and decision making. It's important to know that when you are in the early stages of this grief and recovery process, it can be challenging to think clearly or to make decisions at all, much less to make them well. Identifying your present stage of grief and being aware of it is an important step toward ensuring that you will make the best choices you can.

GUILT AND SHAME

Experiencing guilt and shame is also a normal reaction to the end of a marriage. These feelings arise when we feel a sense of failure—of not having fulfilled our own or our community's expectations. In the case of divorce, people often feel guilt and/or shame because they have failed to stay married for life. That's partly a matter of personal expectations—not fulfilling the promises made to a spouse—and also partly a matter of not fulfilling what our culture seems to expect from us. If our culture's expectations about marriage and divorce are reasonable—if they fit well with how people actually behave in that culture—and we don't measure up, the guilt and shame felt at the time of divorce may be appropriate. If the culture's expectations don't match well with the reality of marriage and divorce as people actually live it, the guilt and shame can be much more problematic—difficult to see clearly, difficult to acknowledge, difficult to manage in a divorce. In addition, there are some marriages in which one or both partners have engaged in extremes of betrayal, deceit, or even criminal behavior that almost always involve feelings of guilt and shame.

Regardless of whether the feelings arise from not having met one's own or the culture's ideals or from actual wrongdoing, we know that for many individuals, guilt and shame can be so painful that they change very quickly into other, more tolerable feelings, such as anger or depression—often without the person's even knowing that the guilt and shame are there. This is why it is so common in divorce for each partner to blame the other and why it can be so difficult for divorcing partners to accept responsibility for their own part in a failed marriage.

We've encountered few divorcing people who find it easy to see or accept their own feelings of guilt and shame. These powerfully negative feelings often remain under the radar, hidden and invisible, where they do the most harm. Strong feelings of guilt or shame can make it difficult or impossible to take in more balanced information, to maintain your perspective, and to consider realistically your best alternatives for how to resolve problems.

Guilt can cause spouses to feel they have no right to ask for what they need in a divorce, causing them to negotiate unbalanced, unrealistic settlements they later regret. Family lawyers have a saying that "guilt has a short half-life," and because guilt is such an uncomfortable feeling, it can easily transform into anger. We often see people who have negotiated guilt-driven agreements having second thoughts and going back to court to try to set aside imprudent settlements.

Similarly, shame often transforms into blame, anger, or rage directed at the spouse. Bitter fights over children or property can be propelled by feelings like these, because modern divorces seldom brand either partner as Snow White or Hitler, Prince Charming or the

Wicked Witch, and therefore the anger, which needs to go somewhere, goes into fights over matters that courts are permitted to make orders about.

FEAR AND ANXIETY

Fear and anxiety are common because of our hardwired "fight-or-flight" instinct. Our bodies react to stresses (such as an angry phone call from a spouse) by using physical alarm mechanisms that haven't changed since our ancestors had to react instantly to avoid being eaten by saber-toothed tigers. You react to stress physiologically in the following ways:

- Your heart speeds up, and adrenaline pours into your bloodstream
- Your adrenaline makes your heart contract more forcefully and may cause you to feel a pounding sensation in your head
- You may feel hot flashes of energy
- Your attention homes in on the event that triggered the strong feelings, limiting your ability to take in new information

When people are under chronic and severe stress, they may have anxiety attacks, in which they tremble and their heart pounds. Or they may be paralyzed by almost overwhelming feelings of fear that seem to come out of nowhere. We work with many people who experience these feelings as their marriages end. People who feel overwhelmed or confused in this way tend to fall back upon old habits of thought and action rather than looking intelligently at the facts of their situation and weighing the best choices for the future.

OLD ARGUMENTS DIE HARD

As marriages become troubled, couples often rely on old habits of dealing with differences that lead to fights rather than solutions. If those old habits didn't lead to constructive solutions during the marriage, they will surely yield no better results during the divorce. In addition, people feeling anxious and fearful may resist pressure to move forward and resolve divorce-related issues because of feeling unready, while their spouses may be impatient, seeing no reason why the divorce wasn't over months ago. Bitter fights in the divorce courts often stem from differences such as these.

Unfortunately, both our court system and our culture at large encourage us to take action in divorces based on how we feel when we are at the bottom of the emotional roller coaster, when we are most gripped by anxiety, fear, grief, guilt, and shame. After all, that's when most people are moved to make the first call to a divorce lawyer. As a result, people are encouraged to make shortsighted choices based on emotional reactions that do not take into account anyone's long-term best interests. The resulting "bad divorces" harm everyone and serve no one well. They are very costly; they fail to plan intelligently for the future; and they inflict psychological scars on both the adults and the children. Let's take a look at how this corrosive way of divorcing came to exist in our culture.

ROMANTICIZING MARRIAGE AND DEMONIZING DIVORCE

One of the largest emotional hurdles that anyone considering divorce has to get over is that our society has romanticized the institution of marriage and demonized the process of divorce. Contemporary marriages carry a heavy load of romantic myths that don't fit the real-life challenges of living with another person once the honeymoon is over. In fairy tales, we're told that the prince and princess lived happily ever after—but those stories usually end right after the wedding. Although marriage ceremonies often include words such as "for better or for worse, in sickness and in health, for richer or for poorer," it's rare for a couple basking in the early stages of romantic love to appreciate that the window of time on their blissful feelings is closing fast. Unrealistic expectations that the hormonal excitement associated with early romantic love will last forever—and that something is wrong with the relationship if it doesn't—account for many of the divorces we see in our work with clients.

These false beliefs that people hold regarding marriage are further complicated by the unhelpful and even destructive myths that they believe about divorce. Unfortunately, these beliefs are quite widespread, often causing people to expect the worst when a marriage ends. They fill the minds of divorcing couples with fear and anger, driving out trust and hope and preventing clear thinking about how to change and adapt well during what is, after all, an entirely normal and predictable life transition. Well-meaning friends and family tell divorcing couples to expect battle and strike first, and they reject as foolish any attempts to make healthier and wiser choices about how to behave during divorce.

But it isn't simply friends and family, with their misplaced good intentions, who send bad messages to divorcing couples about how to behave. False and exaggerated beliefs about divorce are common in our culture. You'll find these negative messages everywhere once your ear becomes attuned to them: from television to films to comic strips to novels to news reports to law offices.

Here are some of these false beliefs:

- You can't expect good behavior or generosity from yourself or your spouse during a divorce
- Divorce always means war
- It is foolish to extend trust or good faith in a divorce
- If she/he has hurt you, you must retaliate
- The only smart course is to expect the worst, look out for number one at all costs, and strike first for greatest strategic advantage

Once you start listening carefully, you will hear these myths about conflict and divorce everywhere. For example, Peggy's dentist, Brad, is now married to Mary, who was divorced about eight years ago from her first husband, Edward. Mary's best friend, Rita, is now married to Edward and is the stepmother of the three children Mary and Edward had together. Edward and Rita themselves have a young son who is the half sibling of Mary's children. The two families celebrate their holidays and birthdays together and sometimes take vacations together. But what does Brad say in casual conversation with his friends and coworkers about how he plans to spend his holidays? He's embarrassed. He tells acquaintances, "Mary's family is strange." He feels he must apologize for them because he "knows" it's not "normal" to be so positive about these adaptations to changes in intimate relationships and family systems.

We, on the other hand, regard the extended family Brad and Mary have created as a sensible, mature, and very functional new system that benefits everyone—children, adults, friends, relatives, and even community (because they are demonstrating a valuable social reality: that divorce does not have to mean war). Brad would be quite surprised if we pointed out to him how much he has absorbed and accepted the negative stereotypes of divorce even as he is participating in a real-life postdivorce family system that proves those stereotypes to be false.

The truth is that divorce is statistically normal. Nearly half of all people getting married will experience it—and this rate has remained constant for more than thirty years. Understanding what's normal during predictable human transitions such as divorce helps people marshal their strength, optimism, and other resources to move through the big changes of a divorce in a constructive, healthy way, whether it was wanted or not.

THE POWER OF NEGATIVE THOUGHT

The tidal wave of negative messages in our culture about divorce equaling war encourages us to believe—incorrectly—that bad behavior is normal. Believing that it's normal to behave badly can actually *encourage* people to behave badly when those feelings of guilt and shame that they're not even aware of take over and make good judgment and self-control disappear.

Solid empirical research demonstrates that even a little negative thinking changes behavior dramatically for the worse in ways we aren't even aware of. You don't have to take our word for it; scientific studies prove it beyond a shadow of a doubt. For example, the science writer Malcolm Gladwell has gathered a number of research reports showing that even very brief exposure to negative ideas has powerful effects—even if you don't believe them or even notice you've been exposed to them.

In one experiment, researchers had students (who thought they were taking a language test) make sentences out of scrambled words full of references to old age, loneliness, and worries. The students who read those words walked out of the testing room more slowly than students who hadn't had those words in their sentences. In another study, students were put into two groups and asked the same set of difficult questions from the game Trivial Pursuit. One group, asked to spend five minutes before the test thinking about what it would be like to be a college professor, got 55.6 percent of the questions right. The other group, asked to think about football hooligans, got only 42.6 percent right.

When widespread negative thinking about divorce promotes the idea that bad behavior during divorce is normal rather than unfortunate and misguided, the resulting effects on behavior are just as clear as what the students experienced in those research studies—but far more damaging to the families involved. False messages about what's normal in marriage and divorce are everywhere, drowning out clear thinking and making people going through divorce less able to

- Understand their own feelings and put them into perspective
- Adapt well to change

- Behave with integrity
- Make healthy, well-considered choices
- Recover from the trauma of divorce
- Raise healthy children
- Recover their optimism
- Get on with their lives

So what can you do to protect yourself from the effects of the negative messages about divorce that surround us? The best protection against damaging myths is to feed your mind every day with positive information about handling divorce with grace, dignity, and creativity. Collaborative divorce teams work expressly with divorcing couples to keep them focused on the positive, on the future, on solutions—on half full, rather than half empty.

WHERE DID THESE FALSE BELIEFS AND EXPECTATIONS COME FROM?

Let's review a little history that anyone facing a divorce should know about. Until thirty years ago, when California pioneered the concept of "no-fault divorce," the legal process for granting a divorce in this country almost always began with deciding which spouse was the "guilty party." Without a guilty party, there could be no divorce. The judge then would punish the offender financially and reward the "innocent party" with money and the children. Those old concepts of guilt and fault remain embedded in our legal system in ways that are difficult to see, much less to change.

Think about it: no-fault divorces have been available for at most thirty years—a mere blip on the timeline of the long history of marriage and divorce. For centuries in the English common-law tradition that we have inherited, divorce was not possible unless you were the king. By the nineteenth century, ordinary people could in theory divorce, but divorce remained a shameful and rare event that occurred only when a spouse had behaved very badly indeed: scandalous sexual behavior, gross physical abuse that couldn't be concealed, or abandonment.

As we moved into the twentieth century, ideas of individual freedom and social change spread into the mainstream, happiness in marriage became an acceptable expectation, and the choice of divorce began to be more common. Particularly after World War II, with urbanization and the breakdown of extended families, we saw a great increase in the number of couples choosing to end their marriages. But to get a divorce, they had to lie to the courts, trumping up proof of adultery that hadn't really occurred or colluding in false allegations of mental cruelty—because without fault, there could be no divorce. This was the context in which our legislatures finally, twenty years after the end of World War II, enacted the first "no-fault" divorce laws. They were trying to make the law reflect modern expectations about marriage and the accompanying modern demand for divorce.

"NO-FAULT" DIVORCE REALLY ISN'T

While "no-fault" divorce is now available in all parts of the United States, "no-fault" is a rather misleading phrase. It's true that you no longer need to persuade a judge that your spouse abandoned you or committed adultery or mental cruelty in order to qualify for a divorce. But courts are ill equipped to deal with "no-fault" divorces because court proceedings are based on an opposition and conflict scenario in which a wrongdoer is identified and consequences are meted out. Courts as an institution are set up to find fault and allocate responsibility, and not much more. Battle is what takes place in a courtroom, and collateral damage is the rule. And you can't have a battle without an enemy. In short, the old habits and thinking of fault-based divorce are alive and well in the divorce courts, "no-fault" or not.

The adversarial nature of the legal system also matches perfectly the strong emotional need that many divorcing individuals feel to ease their pain by blaming their partner for all that went wrong in the marriage. Shame and guilt are so intensely uncomfortable that anything that soothes the pain even briefly is hard to resist, while taking personal responsibility for our own behavior is one of the most difficult things to do. Divorcing individuals can be drawn magnetically to the idea of fault. It is often much easier to attack the other partner than to accept a fair share of responsibility for the breakdown of a marriage. Spouses can feel powerful impulses to demonize and attack each other because of the guilt and shame they feel when their marriage ends sooner rather than "happily ever after."

THE GOOD NEWS: IT'S ALL NORMAL

Here's the good news: during divorce, it is entirely normal to experience a wide range of emotions. Some of them, you now know, are part of how healthy people adjust to losing a major intimate relationship. Others grow out of that welter of false beliefs and unrealistic expectations connected with marriage and divorce that nearly everyone in our society accepts before seeing them more clearly. With the right help during the divorce, you can learn to recognize and handle strong negative feelings in ways that support good decision making.

Here's another interesting fact: at some point during a divorce, many people can expect to experience not only those negative emotions we've been discussing—such as fear, grief, confusion, anxiety, shame, anger, and guilt—but also intense positive emotional states of exuberance, high energy, excitement, and uncharacteristic openness to experimentation and risk. Feelings such as these sound considerably more pleasant—but they, too, can derail good decision making during a divorce.

As you will read again and again in this book, you cannot avoid making choices. Refusing to choose what kind of divorce you will have is, in fact, a choice—one that will lead to a bad divorce. In the same way, making an uninformed choice equals choosing a bad divorce. So does making choices and decisions reactively, in the grip of strong emotion. Knowing that such intense emotions may take over unpredictably as you adjust to the ending of your marriage will help you anticipate and manage their impact on your ability to think clearly. Knowledge is power, and with knowledge about the emotional side of divorce you'll be better able to strip these strong emotions of their otherwise destructive force. Our experience tells us that understanding the connection between strong emotional states and bad divorce choices can help most people make better, more conscious, more informed ones.

THE CHALLENGE: MAKING GOOD DECISIONS AT A BAD TIME

When strong feelings take over, we quite literally cannot think straight—no matter how intelligent or competent we normally might be. Because divorce-related confusion and intense mood swings are so common, and because they tend to work against careful thinking focused on the best long-term outcomes, we have learned that people can rarely achieve their own "best divorce" working alone. They need the right professional advisors who can help them stay focused on that goal even when the roller coaster has once again swooped to the bottom. The collaborative divorce process provides coordinated resources that give divorcing individuals and couples the specific kinds of help they need to make good decisions, even—perhaps especially—at a very hard time.

In the past, people turned primarily to lawyers when they needed assistance in making decisions during a divorce. But lawyers' specialty is the law, and a divorce—to anyone other than a lawyer—is not primarily a legal event. It is a complex experience involving not only a legal transition but also enormously challenging emotional and financial changes. For most people we work with, these emotional and financial changes are at least as compelling as the legal aspect of a divorce that is the only domain in which traditional lawyers give their advice and counsel, and often far more so. Collaborative divorce, as you'll see, is the first way of getting help that will address all three aspects of your divorce: legal, emotional, and financial.

THE CHOICES YOU MAKE AFFECT MANY PEOPLE

If you're like most people, you'd probably say that your divorce is of concern only to you and your soon-to-be "ex," but in truth a bad divorce spurred by bad decision making has a much broader impact than you might think. If you have children—even adult children—you need to understand that they are the forgotten casualties in most divorces. Children of all ages are typically left out of the process, subjected to enormous life changes about which they receive little or no information and over which they are permitted to exert little or no influence. Their home and school may change, their contact with Mom or Dad may be restricted greatly, their financial welfare may be at risk—all without explanation or any opportunity for them to give input.

What's more, you (and your children, if you have any) have important relationships with many people outside your immediate family. In many divorces, battling adults who consider their divorce a private adult matter unwittingly foster conflicts and rifts that can make it impossible for those relationships to continue. They do not think about the impact that the divorce will have on children's relationships with their grandparents, aunts, uncles, and cousins whom they care about. Even if there are no children involved, most people who divorce have important relationships with friends and extended family, all of whom will be affected by the divorce. In conventional "old-style" divorces, these people often feel pressured to take sides, so that what one or both spouses thought was a solid web of supportive relationships may crumble and disappear in the face of divorce-related conflict. Similarly, coworkers and supervisors may become resentful of your reduced productivity and increased absence from work because of the legal and emotional demands of the divorce process. Collaborative divorce is the first way of getting help as your marriage ends that encourages you to pay attention to this important dimension of your divorce.

And, of course, your divorce takes place within a larger community. Is your son an important member of the football team? Does your daughter have the lead part in the school play? Were you a volunteer in the children's classroom or at the church or nursing home? If the time and energy you will have to commit to these pursuits during and after divorce will be reduced—and they probably will—the community you live in will be affected. Collaborative divorce is the first system of helping people through divorce that consistently brings concerns like these forward for your attention.

Our point in raising these questions is that your divorce affects far more people than you and your spouse might imagine, in ways that you might not yet be thinking about, and takes place in a community context in which your decisions can affect even people who are not especially close friends or family. The way to minimize the unintended negative effects of divorce is to be aware of all those who may be affected and to make good, careful choices that are the best for you and those you care about.

THE BEST DIVORCE FOR *YOU*

We assume that your goal is the best divorce you and your partner are capable of achieving. Such a divorce would protect your children, help you retain your dignity, preserve your finances, and allow you to have a cordial relationship with your spouse in the future. A good divorce builds your self-esteem. If that's the kind of divorce you want, here are some questions to consider as you choose who will help you through it:

- Do I want to get advice during my divorce from someone who believes that taking care of "number one" is the only agenda that matters when a marriage ends?
- Or would I rather be advised by people who believe that paying attention to healthy recovery from the divorce,

and to creating healthy new systems and relationships after the divorce, can be as important as paying attention to the bottom line?

- Do I want my divorce advisor to be someone who believes that nothing about my divorce is important unless the law allows judges to issue orders about it?
- Or do I want my divorce advice to come from professionals who believe that my own values and concerns should determine what's relevant in my divorce?
- Do I want my divorce advice to come from someone who believes that going to court is just another way of resolving divorce issues?
- Or would I rather be advised by someone who believes that staying out of court if at all possible is healthier for both adults and children experiencing divorce?

These are the issues to consider when you make your first choices about what kind of a divorce you want and who can provide the best help to get you there. People who don't think carefully about these questions tend to make hasty decisions that can result in an ugly divorce that no one really wanted.

A GOOD CHOICE: COLLABORATIVE DIVORCE

We know from long experience that only collaborative divorce—not old-style adversarial legal representation, and not a single mediator working with or without lawyers in the picture—views divorce as a complex experience requiring advice and counsel from multiple perspectives if it is to be navigated well. Collaborative divorce prepares you to deal with the emotional challenges and changes associated with divorce and provides the resources that can best help you make a healthy transition from married to single.

Collaborative divorce builds in important protections for children, too. It informs you fully about how your children are experiencing the divorce and what they need to weather the big changes in their family structure without harm. It helps protect your future relationship with your spouse by informing both of you fully—together, at the same time—about the financial realities of your marriage and divorce in a way that eliminates pointless arguments about economic issues. It also teaches you and your spouse new ways of problem solving and conflict resolution so that you develop useful skills for addressing your differences more constructively in the future. Further, collaborative divorce

- Helps you clarify your individual and shared values and priorities
- Helps you and your spouse reach maximum consensus
- Includes complete advice about the law without using legal rights as the sole template for negotiation and resolution
- Helps you and your spouse resolve serious differences creatively and without destructive conflict
- Helps parents improve their ability to coparent after divorce
- Builds in agreements about resolution of future differences after the divorce is over
- Focuses not only on resolving past differences but also on planning for healthy responses to current challenges and on laying a strong foundation for the future after the divorce is over
- Aims toward deep resolution, not shallow peace

WHY YOU DO NOT WANT AN "OLD-STYLE DIVORCE"

We're confident that, like the people we work with every day, you want to protect yourself and your loved ones from the havoc that an old-style divorce can wreak in your lives. Let's summarize the facts you now know about old-style divorce:

- It is based on the centuries-old belief that divorce is wrong and abnormal
- It seeks to find fault and mete out punishment
- It focuses on the past
- It is premised on conflict
- It is constrained by an arbitrary legal framework intended to resolve matters of right and wrong by the exchange of money
- It aims at a deal, not deep resolution
- It fails to take into account current understandings of how people are wired, what they need in times of change, what children need during and after divorce, and how families change and restructure

What's more, we know that old-style divorce is bad for individuals, families, and communities because

- It's expensive
- It's hurtful and damaging
- It's "one size fits all"
- It deems irrelevant many common concerns that are extremely important to most people because judges can't issue enforceable orders about them
- It focuses on the past
- It encourages unrealistic expectations on the part of both spouses about what should happen in the divorce
- It resolves disputes through competing predictions of what a judge would do rather than focusing on what you and your partner can agree on
- It won't provide essential help to you or those you care about
- The emotional and social costs are incalculable

Luckily, we live in an era when there is finally a better option—one that can end a marriage without destroying a family or setting into motion negative effects that can bedevil family members for a lifetime.

WHY COLLABORATIVE DIVORCE WORKS SO WELL

The reasons why collaborative divorce does such a good job of helping most people achieve their own "best divorce" are simple. Collaborative divorce addresses the financial and legal matters that must be resolved in any divorce, but it does so more effectively because it provides the built-in help of three professions, not just one. The design of collaborative divorce—with its team of professionals, its systematic attention to values, its emphasis on healthy relationships, and its focus on the future—takes into account the broad spectrum of what really matters to most people when their marriages end. It considers not only the two spouses but those around them who also matter to the divorcing couple and who will be both directly and indirectly affected by a good or a bad divorce: children, families, and even extended families, friends, and colleagues. It applies what we know about marriage and divorce from the realms of psychology, sociology, history, law, communication theory, conflict resolution theory, finance, and other realms in a very practical, useful, and concrete way.

COLLABORATIVE DIVORCE DEALS WITH WHAT
PEOPLE ACTUALLY EXPERIENCE IN DIVORCE

Unlike any other divorce conflict resolution process that has come before, collaborative divorce teams make constant use of vital information about how people are "wired," how we think, how our emotions affect our ability to communicate effectively and to process information, how we experience pain and loss, how we recover from the end of a marriage, what our children are experiencing and what they need in the divorce, and what the needs of each member of the family after the divorce are likely to be. In this way, collaborative divorce offers con-

Do You Want Your Divorce to Be Public Property?

Did you know that in most states, anyone can sit in on and watch divorce hearings and trials? Did you know that in thirty states in the United States, courthouse records are put online, making personal information from your divorce available to Web surfers, data collection companies, and identity thieves, as well as the media? Did you know that with few exceptions, anyone can go to the courthouse and have complete access to your entire court divorce file?

Although it's true that the parties in most old-style divorce cases do eventually settle, the court files are not purged of the embarrassing accusations and counteraccusations leveled along the way. All the personal dirty laundry and detailed financial data that were ever put before the judge remain on the public record—information that none of us would want our neighbors, our children, or identity thieves to have free access to.

Think about it: collaborative lawyers are the only divorce lawyers whose work is always conducted entirely outside the court system. Collaborative divorce files are never made part of any public record. When a couple reaches agreement in a collaborative divorce, their lawyers can ensure that only the bare minimum the law requires to process the legal divorce goes into the court file. They can ensure that your personal information is insulated from public records to the maximum degree permitted by law.

structive, comprehensive, multidisciplinary professional support that responds to the actual complexities of divorce as people experience it, rather than imposing an old-fashioned, limited institutional legal point of view as the sole perspective on a complex human experience.

HOW COLLABORATIVE DIVORCE
IS DIFFERENT FROM MEDIATION

When you first hear about collaborative divorce, you may think, "That's just like mediation." While it is a cousin of mediation, and while individual mediators often accomplish very good work with their clients, the mediation process itself compared to collaborative divorce is like checkers compared to 3-D chess. Through their very structure, collaborative divorce teams can consistently offer couples and families far more resources and far more powerful support for deep conflict resolution than any single mediator possibly can. Here are the important differences you need to know about:

Collaborative Divorce	Mediation
You and your partner each have your own specially trained collaborative lawyer as an advisor and counselor by your side at all times, helping you sort out and express your own concerns and priorities before helping you to reach an agreement.	One neutral mediator, working alone in meetings with you and your partner, helps you reach an agreement. Many mediators will not meet privately with clients outside mediation sessions to help them clarify and express concerns. Most states do not license mediators or require any specific training, credentials, or professional affiliation or degree.

Your legal advice is built into the heart of the negotiations, which are guided by collaborative lawyers whose sole job description is to help you and your partner reach fully informed resolution. You can terminate the process and go to court, but if you do you'll need new lawyers because the collaborative lawyers may not participate in adversarial litigation. One hundred percent of the effort of collaborative lawyers is devoted to settlement.	You must get your legal advice during mediation from independent lawyers who are not a central part of the conflict resolution process. Whether they do or do not sit in on mediation sessions, their job description includes going to court with you if mediation does not reach resolution. They are not fully aligned toward settlement as their sole job description and experience no consequences if they don't help you reach agreement.
You and your spouse each have a trained collaborative coach (a licensed counselor or psychologist) who will teach you and your partner how to communicate better during and after the divorce than you did before and will assist you to be a more focused, effective participant in legal negotiations.	No one teaches you how to improve your communications with your spouse during or after the divorce or how to be a more focused and effective participant in negotiations.

A specially trained child development specialist (a licensed mental health clinician) helps you and your partner understand your child's specific needs during and after the divorce and helps the child understand and communicate with the parents about the divorce.	No one helps the children express their needs and wishes or teaches you or your children what you need to know about the stresses and challenges children generally, and your children specifically, experience during divorce. So long as you and your partner reach agreement about dividing up time with your child, the job is done, whether or not the arrangement is likely to work well for your child.
A neutral financial consultant helps you and your spouse together to understand the family finances, prepares financial spreadsheets for use with the lawyers, and advises you and your team about financial and tax aspects of settlement options that arise during legal negotiations.	Mediators do not ordinarily bring financial expertise to help you and your spouse reach a shared understanding of the family finances. It's not the job of a mediator to teach financial skills, nor is it his or her job to help evaluate the long-term financial consequences of various settlement scenarios from an informed financial perspective.

WHY YOU OUGHT TO BEGIN WITH
COLLABORATIVE DIVORCE PROFESSIONALS

Here's what the presiding judge of the San Francisco Superior Court had to say about collaborative divorce: "I favor any system that best serves families and children, and from everything I've seen so far, the collaborative law approach is *the* best and the least litigious." From the very beginning, the process focuses on a positive outcome and minimizes the fighting. In a litigious divorce, the objective is to fight the good fight and win as much as possible. It doesn't take into account the emotional fallout, especially for the children. The effect in collaborative divorce is that parents and children suffer less and recover faster.

COLLABORATIVE DIVORCE IS NOT FOR EVERYONE

Collaborative divorce is the best approach to divorce that either of us has encountered. But we must be honest: it can't work miracles. You need to know its limits as well as its strengths. There are situations in which collaborative divorce may not be the best option, and it's important to take that fact into consideration when examining your divorce options. Collaborative divorce may not be a good choice when

- One or both partners have serious mental illness or drug or alcohol problems that aren't under control
- Domestic violence is occurring
- One or both partners lack the ability to participate fully and freely in the discussions that will lead to resolution
- One or both partners lack the capacity to make and keep commitments about behavior and follow-through, even with the help of collaborative divorce coaches
- One or both partners are prepared to lie in order to conceal information about finances

Of course, no other way of divorcing handles those challenges very effectively, either. Even conventional divorce representation can't make a liar honest, can't make an immature spouse behave responsibly, and can't cure mental illness or addiction. If you married someone with such problems, or if you have them yourself, your divorce will be challenging no matter how you proceed. Your own personal choice is to decide whether you would prefer to be in an adversarial divorce, which tends to bring out the worst in most people, or a collaborative one, which may or may not be able to bring out the best in you and your spouse but which tries to do so in ways that have worked for others. Since so much depends on what each of you is capable of, there are no guarantees.

But our years of experience with conventional and collaborative divorces have taught us that most people have what it takes to give collaborative divorce their best try. There is every reason to do so and seldom a strong reason not to. Collaborative divorce may be the single best thing you can do for yourself, your spouse, and your loved ones.

CHOOSING FEAR OR CHOOSING HOPE: JILL AND HOWARD'S STORY

Jill feels helpless, scared, and full of emotional turmoil. To Jill, her husband, Howard, has always seemed powerful and dominant and has been able to get his way because he can outlast her in an argument. She knows that mediation is not for her—she's afraid of losing control and humiliating herself if she sits face to face with Howard without an ally and advisor at her side. She is uncertain about whether she'll be protected sufficiently if she goes along with his urging to choose collaborative divorce.

Jill feels tempted to hire an old-style divorce lawyer who will take over all communications and negotiations, insulating Jill from any direct contact with Howard within the legal divorce process. But when Jill confers with a potential collaborative lawyer, that lawyer points out something that is easily overlooked at a time of overwhelming fear and confusion: the fact that she and Howard will need to be in communication constantly, now and for years to come, because they both love their young daughter. They will need to plan her custody and visitation schedule, holidays, school matters, medical appointments, camps, and so on. A gladiator lawyer may be able to insulate her while the actual divorce is being litigated, he tells her, but when the lawyer's file is closed, she will be entirely on her own and living with the aftermath. Further, he points out that an adversarial approach would prevent Jill from learning how to become more confident and competent in the parenting conversations that lie ahead for her and Howard.

Upon reflection following that meeting, Jill realizes that she would very much like it if Howard would agree to another round of marriage counseling. Choosing a conventional divorce lawyer, she fears, would probably close that door once and for all. And she also worries that if she retains a tough adversarial divorce lawyer to protect her, her husband might become so cold and withdrawn that it would affect his relationship with their beloved ten-year-old daughter, who misses him greatly since he moved out.

By reading the pamphlet given to her by the collaborative lawyer, Jill learns that in a collaborative divorce, she and Howard will work with divorce coaches to devise a sound, flexible, responsive parenting plan for their daughter as a first priority. This will necessarily bring them into more meaningful communication and problem solving about how to build the most functional relationship possible for them as divorced coparents.

Realizing the effect a bad divorce might have on their daughter makes Jill decide to give collaborative divorce a try. She and Howard have years of coparenting ahead of them. Without collaborative divorce coaching, they will have nothing to fall back upon after the divorce as their daughter grows older except the fear, anger, and avoidance that helped end their marriage. Their chances of parenting their daughter well together would look poor indeed.

Coaching will help Jill learn how to manage her strong feelings, build her self-confidence, and improve her communication skills. These are valuable self-caring skills she will take away from the divorce process and use for the rest of her life. Howard, too, will learn skills in the coaching process that can help him to communicate more effectively with Jill and with his daughter. With coaching, both of them will come out of the divorce far better prepared to guide their child effectively through her adolescent years.

2

TAKING A LOOK AT COLLABORATIVE DIVORCE

The dogmas of the quiet past are inadequate to the stormy present. The occasion is piled high with difficulty, and we must rise with the occasion. As our case is new, so we must think anew and act anew.

—ABRAHAM LINCOLN

One way to understand the sequence of events in a collaborative divorce is to compare it to building a house. There are all kinds of houses—big and small, simple and complex—but no matter what kind of house you require, the sequence of steps you'll need to take to get it built are the same, involving many choices at every juncture. Whatever kind of house you build, it starts with a foundation, moves through framing to roofing, and leaves the finish work until last. If you do your research, gather your information, take your time, and make good decisions relying on a well-chosen team of experienced building professionals, your new house can provide shelter and comfort for a lifetime.

How long does it take to build a house? And how many people must be involved to help you get it built right? It depends. Your answer may not be the same as your friend's or your sister's, just as your house may not be the same as theirs. If you want to build a house customized to fit your specific needs and those of your family, you'd do well to have the help of an architect, who will rely on information about you and everyone else who will live there before advising you about possible designs. Even if your house needs less custom work, you'll still need people skilled in digging foundations, framing, plumbing, roofing, tile work, roofing, painting, and many other specific trades if you want your house to have lasting quality and strength. If only one handyman/jack-of-all-trades had to do all the many tasks involved in designing and building your house, you'd probably end up with a structure that had walls and a roof, but would it meet all your needs? Would it have the best and most pleasing design? Would it have the kind of lasting strength needed to weather storms and aging? Probably not.

Similarly, when the time comes to choose who'll be on your collaborative divorce team, you'll need to consider your own specific situation, as well as how much of a budget you have for your divorce and how much importance you place on excellence of design and lasting strength of the ultimate results. One person alone can't do the job of a team of specialists. But exactly what mix of collaborative professionals is best for you may differ from what another couple settles on. You may begin with collaborative lawyers and, with their advice, decide to bring coaches and a child specialist onto the team. Another couple may begin with coaches, who will refer them to collaborative lawyers and a financial consultant. Wherever you begin, the job of your first professional helper will include advising you about the right mix of collaborative professional help for your own specific needs—the advice you'll need to choose the best team for your specific situation.

THE TEAM MEMBERS

A fully staffed collaborative divorce team will have two mental health professionals working as coaches, a child specialist, and a neutral collaborative financial consultant (typically a certified financial planner or certified public accountant with a Certified Divorce Financial Analyst credential or its equivalent). These professionals are all specially trained to work skillfully as a team with the two collaborative lawyers selected by the divorcing spouses.

Although it's always wise to consider the value of involving a complete collaborative divorce team, there are divorcing couples who decide that a full interdisciplinary team is not necessary for them, that two collaborative lawyers will be able to do the job without the rest of the team. Sometimes this is an accurate perception, but often it is not.

Let's take a look at what each team member does.

COLLABORATIVE DIVORCE LAWYERS

In a collaborative divorce, you and your spouse will each have your own collaborative lawyer. A good lawyer will do much more in a collaborative divorce than simply handle legal matters for you—he or she will handle a whole host of tasks. The lawyers' responsibilities include

- Advising their own clients about the divorce process, including the law
- Helping their own clients clarify and communicate effectively about goals, interests, concerns, priorities, and values
- Advocating for and with their own clients in all stages of the collaborative divorce process so that all concerns are addressed appropriately
- Working collegially with the other collaborative lawyer as guides and managers of the divorce negotiations

- Working collegially with other team members to manage conflict; gather, understand, and make use of information; expand options; and design and consider solutions
- Modeling and teaching collaborative conflict resolution skills
- Helping you and your spouse find creative, comprehensive, mutually acceptable solutions to all divorce-related problems
- Doing all tasks needed to complete a comprehensive settlement agreement and a legal divorce

Together, the lawyers for you and your spouse will help you hear each other's point of view and consider a range of options for resolution that have the broadest reach you and your partner wish to consider in terms of meeting the needs, concerns, goals, and priorities of each member of the divorcing family.

Collaborative lawyers are hired solely to help you and your spouse get to the best possible agreement, entirely outside the court system. While they will handle the necessary court paperwork to convert your divorce agreement into your divorce judgment, collaborative lawyers can never represent either you or your spouse in court against the other. Although your lawyer represents only you, not your spouse, your lawyer never becomes your spouse's adversary. Collaborative lawyers seek solutions that meet their own client's needs and are also acceptable to the other spouse, in order to reach a resolution that works for everyone. They each represent only their own client, but they both work toward the same goal: helping you and your partner devise informed, creative solutions that both of you can fully embrace.

Though the lawyers work individually with their own clients to prepare them for effective participation in all stages of their collaborative divorce, the work of sharing information and arriving at solutions is done in meetings that both lawyers and both spouses attend. You'll consult privately with your lawyer to help you clarify your needs and priorities before bringing them to the table for discussion, and the lawyers will confer with each other before meetings to ensure that the meetings are orderly and productive. But nearly all information sharing, options development, and negotiations involved in getting to mutually acceptable agreements take place in face-to-face "four-way" meetings attended by you, your spouse, and both collaborative lawyers. The lawyers never negotiate deals without both of you present at the table and actively participating in the negotiations.

Remember: your collaborative lawyer spends 100 percent of his or her time, energy, and creativity on helping you get to settlement. Your lawyer will never go to court on your behalf against your spouse, and will never testify against your spouse, even if the two of you leave the collaborative process and decide to hire conventional lawyers to take your problems to court.

Take the time to find the best collaborative lawyer you can locate, and encourage your spouse to do the same (see chapter 3). The best collaborative lawyers, in our experience, encourage their clients to take the long view and to work toward solutions that will still look wise fifteen or twenty years later. In the words of one of our colleagues, "I want to help you end your marriage in such a way that you can dance together at your daughter's wedding."

COLLABORATIVE DIVORCE COACHES

Collaborative divorce coaches provide a broad range of support to help you move constructively through your divorce, bringing perspectives and skills that only a mental health professional can offer. Collaborative coaches distinguish themselves from other similarly licensed mental health practitioners in the community with their special additional training and experience in communication skills, family dynamics, and issues relating to healthy recovery from separation and divorce. Coaches provide emotional encouragement, teach stress management and communication skills, explore parenting concerns, and help ensure that both partners' needs, concerns, and feelings are understood and expressed in constructive ways. They use an efficient, structured process for building up your competency, effectiveness, and resilience, all of which may be diminished as your marriage comes to an end. Also, they will teach you and your partner how to improve the quality of your communications and decision making as you move through the divorce negotiation process. They will begin to encourage you to think and dream about your personal futures and your future as coparents, if you have children.

Collaborative divorce coaching is different from life coaching. Although collaborative divorce coaches may at times work in ways that resemble "life coaching," life coaching is not a licensed profession and there is no standardization in the training life coaches receive. The collaborative divorce coach's mental health training, experience, and licensure requirements go far beyond what is required to work as a life coach. Collaborative divorce coaches undergo years of postgraduate study and clinical internships addressing family systems and human development, augmented by legally and professionally mandated continuing education to keep abreast of scientific advances.

Life coaching aims to help individuals identify and achieve their personal goals, matters your divorce coach may also help you with, because considering your future is an important part of the collaborative divorce process. But remember: the differences in purpose and training between life coaching and collaborative divorce coaching are big, and they matter. In collaborative divorce, coaches are working not just with individuals but also with a complex family system that is breaking down and reorganizing, often under highly stressful circumstances. Special training and experience in family dynamics are essential qualifications for collaborative divorce coaches.

You and your spouse will each have your own collaborative divorce coach to be your personal ally and helper. You will each meet privately with your coaches as well as in four-way coaching meetings. Your coaches will help you and your spouse recognize and change unhelpful communication patterns that are often in place as marriages end. If you have children, your coaches will help you discuss your concerns about parenting them effectively when you are living separately.

You will develop a plan for parenting with the help of the coaches, making use of the information provided by the child specialist.

Unlike psychotherapists or counselors, coaches are proactive. They will stay in regular contact with you during your divorce. This keeps problems from getting too big before they are addressed. Collaborative divorce coaches like to help you take preventive measures, making it important to contact your coach if you have questions or find that something is not working for you.

Coaches almost always add value to the process and outcome, as interests and priorities are clarified sooner, and communications are clearer. With the coaches' help, "meltdowns" on the part of either spouse that might have derailed constructive problem solving can be dealt with so that necessary conversations can be had about difficult issues. This work helps you participate far more effectively in the four-way meetings with your lawyers. If it turns out the coaches aren't needed after all, or if their work is finished quickly, they will step into the background, remaining available if and when they are again needed.

THE COLLABORATIVE FINANCIAL CONSULTANT

The collaborative financial consultant, who may be a certified public accountant or a certified financial planner, assists with the gathering of financial information and the preparation of provisional budgets and property division spreadsheets. What distinguishes these collaborative divorce professionals from other similarly credentialed financial professionals is their additional special training as Certified Divorce Financial Analysts or the equivalent, and their training and experience in how to work as a member of a collaborative divorce team.

Meeting jointly with their collaborative financial consultant, divorcing partners have the opportunity—face to face—to review their financial documents and information together, ask questions, resolve misunderstandings, and appreciate their differences in money management experience, values, and risk preferences. It's sometimes said that the area of differences that's the hardest for couples to discuss is not sex but money. Where that's true, it's not unusual for a couple to find that it is in the collaborative financial consultant's office (with the help of the coaches) that their first ever successful conversations concerning differences about money will take place.

Using the collaborative financial consultant as a single "point person" for gathering and sharing basic facts about the size of the marital financial pie, instead of doing this work separately in the offices of each spouse's lawyer, has the benefit of reducing distrust and developing accurate shared perceptions about the basic financial facts of the marital estate. For example, it's common for one spouse to feel that the other's spending is excessive. The financial consultant can take an objective look at the financial facts with both partners to see whether or not this is actually true. As potential issues are identified or "hot buttons" reveal themselves, the collaborative financial consultant passes this information on to the collaborative lawyers or the coaches. Collaborative financial consultants do not negotiate or resolve differences but do help identify them. They also work with you and your spouse to consider your financial future and various ways in which you can help ensure your financial stability as you move into your new life.

Acting as a resource for developing and exploring settlement scenarios and flagging tax implications, the financial consultant works with the collaborative lawyers to help both spouses reach a shared understanding of real-world financial limitations as well as possibilities for expanding the financial pie. If documents are missing or questions remain unanswered, the financial consultant lets the lawyers know. If one or the other of the spouses needs a basic education in checkbook balancing or budgeting, the financial consultant points this out and can provide the necessary skill training. This work allays fears on the part of both spouses because all financial disclosures are made together (rather than privately with one's own lawyer) and the work is not finished until all questions about family finances have been answered candidly and fully. The collaborative financial consultant assists in all aspects of financial information sharing and option development regarding both property division and determination of appropriate support.

Remember: your neutral financial consultant gathers, organizes, and presents your financial information; educates you about financial matters and planning; identifies issues that will need to be addressed by other team members; and helps develop and evaluate settlement scenarios in collaboration with your lawyers. The financial consultant may attend legal four-way sessions (which then become "five-way" meetings) but should never venture into negotiating issues or discussing possible terms of settlement with you or your spouse outside the legal five-way table. In the rare event that a collaborative divorce case terminates short of settlement and is taken to court, the financial consultant—like all the collaborative divorce team members—may not participate in any court proceedings between you and your spouse. Nor may the financial consultant provide investment services unrelated to the divorce.

The collaborative financial consultant is often helpful and sometimes indispensable as a team member but is not essential in every case. If you already have financial advisors managing your assets, advising about investments, handling your taxes, and so forth, your lawyers in some circumstances may suggest working with such an advisor instead of including a neutral collaborative financial consultant on the team. Just bear in mind that while specialized financial advisors can bring expert depth of knowledge, they don't generally bring the kind of information-sharing skills the collaborative financial consultant has. If resolving your financial issues will involve complex matters such as doing business valuations, allocating ownership of stock options, tracing marital and nonmarital property, or addressing bankruptcy or tax matters, your lawyers will definitely want the help of financial experts with specialized knowledge about how to handle such matters and may suggest that those specialists can also handle the more routine financial tasks of your divorce.

If you do call on such outside financial experts, it's important to remember that neither your personal accountant nor your business accountant nor a business valuations or other accounting specialist does what a collaborative financial consultant is trained to do: bring both partners together to gather and explain financial documents; to put together joint statements of marital property, debts, income, and expenses; to develop proposed budgets; and to project the financial implications of various settlement scenarios, in cooperation with other members of the team. If, however, yours has been a very short marriage or there are other reasons why the financial side of your divorce is extremely straightforward, your collaborative lawyers may recommend that they handle the financial disclosures and generate options for financial settlement without the assistance of a financial consultant on the team. Rely on your lawyers' advice about what mix of financial advice you and your partner should make use of during your collaborative divorce process, and give careful consideration to the particular skills that a collaborative financial consultant can bring to the table as you decide.

THE CHILD SPECIALIST

The child specialist focuses on your children's needs in the separation and divorce process. The child specialist is a licensed mental health professional with particular training and experience in family systems, child development, and the needs of children during and after divorce. Working in a short-term, focused manner during the divorce process to support the children during the difficult transition they face, the child specialist advocates for the children during the coaching process. Equally important, the child specialist ensures that each child has a safe, private place in which to ask questions, share feelings, express needs, and address problems related to the divorce. Adding vitally important information from the "child's eye view" to the foundation on which the parenting plans are built, child specialists give children a rare opportunity to voice their thoughts and concerns and to be heard on the issues that are important to them without having to feel divided loyalty. Divorcing couples who work solely with mediators or lawyers rarely if ever have available information of this quality and breadth

Children of Divorce:
There's Good News as Well as Bad!

While it's true that
* The first year of a divorce is usually brutally painful for children.
* 25 percent of youths from divorced families (compared with 10 percent from intact families) have serious emotional or psychological problems.
* Adult children of divorced parents generally feel they were scarred by the experience.

Studies also show that
* Most adult children of divorced parents have been able to build successful careers and families and meaningful lives.
* Some adult children of divorced parents have blossomed into mature, resilient, responsible, focused adults—because of, not despite, painful divorce experiences.

Nonetheless
* Even the children of divorced parents who were doing very well as adults believed they had been permanently scarred by their divorce experiences.

when they devise parenting plans, and it is their children who pay the price.

The child specialist brings important information about children generally and your children specifically into the coaching process, ensuring that the emotional needs and concerns of each child are considered by both the parents and the other team members. The whole team works together to plan how the adults will share the parenting responsibility. With the child specialist's participation in these discussions, the agreements that emerge from the coaching sessions have more balance and flexibility, because they take into account the changes in the family system from the children's perspective as well as the adults'.

Obviously, if there are no children, there won't be a child specialist on the team. But what about couples whose children are grown up? We know from experience and research that even adult children often experience pain, confusion, and conflicted loyalties when their parents divorce.

For example, in the case of our clients Jeffrey and Kelly, Kelly's coaching sessions centered on her deep desire to remain connected to Jeffrey's grown children (her stepchildren) despite her absence of a legal relationship to them. His daughter, Diana, was engaged to be married, and Kelly hoped to be involved in the wedding plans and to be accepted by both her and Jeffrey as the grandmother of any children that might be born. The collaborative divorce coaches suggested that the two adult children be contacted and invited to express their thoughts and concerns. Both Diana and Ted accepted that invitation and attended a special coaching session with Kelly and Jeffrey. "The coaching context allowed me to speak directly from my heart, making it clear how much I wanted Kelly's involvement in my wedding," says Diana. She also expressed a genuine desire to remain close to her stepmother after the divorce. Kelly was delighted to hear this.

TALKING TO YOUR SPOUSE

Now that you have a picture of who you might want to help you in your collaborative divorce and what they can do for you, perhaps you are convinced that collaborative divorce is right for you. But before you can speak to your partner about choosing collaborative divorce, if your partner is not yet aware that you wish to end your marriage, you must first speak to him or her about divorce itself. It should be a separate conversation, one that you prepare for with care. This is one of the most important conversations you will ever have, yet many people handle it badly, speaking from strong negative emotions such as rage or guilt. With a little planning, you can handle it better.

Here are some ideas that can help you improve how you handle this momentous step. Think about your deeply held ethical, religious, spiritual, and philosophical values. Then focus on those you particularly hope will infuse this difficult conversation. Perhaps they are dignity, honesty, and respect. Imagine how the conversation could take place if you stay aware of the great importance you place on those values. It can be very helpful to write out several different possible scripts that you could use, with word choice and tone. Whether you do so in writing or in your imagination, choose the way of expressing your thoughts and feelings that seems most comfortable to you and most consistent with those important values you highlighted, and practice it several times in private.

Before the actual conversation, take time to prepare yourself. Try to relax and clear your mind. Remind yourself to phrase all your statements from the "I" position, such as "I think . . ." or "I feel . . ." Speaking this way helps to keep inflammatory language out of the conversation and makes clearer what you are trying to communicate.

During the discussion, try to maintain composure and refrain from anger and blame, even if your spouse provokes you. If you think you may lose your temper, it is better to walk away than to respond in a manner that is destructive. Just be sure that you return to finish the conversation when you have regained your composure.

Plan ahead with regard to what you know about your partner's likely reaction when you explain that you want a divorce. If, for example, your partner has a bad temper and you suspect he or she may react physically when informed of the divorce, you could plan ahead by having the conversation in a public place or in your marriage counselor's office. If he or she tends to be depressed, you might want to let a friend or relative know that your partner may be in need of comfort and support after the conversation.

Once you've managed this difficult but necessary step, it's time to broach the subject of collaborative divorce with your spouse.

THERE'S NO "RIGHT" WAY TO TALK ABOUT COLLABORATIVE DIVORCE

You may be thinking, "If we couldn't agree during marriage, how could we agree during divorce?" It is natural during the early stages of a divorce to worry about how your spouse will behave as the marriage ends. Faced with such worries, you have a clear choice about how you yourself will respond. We have found time after time that people who opt from the start to be guided by their best hopes rather than their worst fears about the future have the greatest success in getting the co-operation of the spouses they are divorcing. Just as you have good reasons for your interest in collaborative divorce, so may your spouse.

Even if the communication between you and your spouse has deteriorated, make an effort to explain that you want to avoid the predictable emotional and economic toll of old-style divorce wars and that you are interested in reaching for the best divorce possible. Your spouse may be fearing the worst and may be relieved to hear of your interest in constructive, respectful divorce conflict resolution.

However, if your spouse is skeptical, he or she may need some persuading. How can you encourage your spouse to choose collaborative divorce? There is no one single right way to accomplish that task, but there are a number of useful approaches to consider. First, you can urge your spouse to educate him- or herself about collaborative divorce. You might put together a packet of information about collaborative divorce and give it to your spouse or ask a trusted friend to do so. Many collaborative coaches and lawyers have brochures and information packets; you could ask for an extra for your spouse. Or you could give your partner a copy of this book.

If your spouse is willing, ask him or her to call a collaborative divorce lawyer or coach. If you have already chosen a collaborative lawyer or coach, that person can send an introductory letter and information packet to your spouse, with Web links and the names of trained collaborative lawyers and coaches in your vicinity.

Your accountant may be someone your partner trusts who could suggest choosing collaborative divorce. (Conserving money and conserving assets as you divide them with an eye to careful tax planning and planning financial futures are characteristics of collaborative divorce that most accountants would value.) Or perhaps your pastor or spiritual advisor could help present the advantages of collaborative divorce to your spouse.

Finally, a counselor could help educate your spouse. If you and your partner are in marriage counseling, ask the counselor to explain the advantages of collaborative divorce to him or her at an appropriate time in the counseling process. If your children are in counseling, you could ask their counselor to explain to your partner the ways in which collaborative divorce protects children. The help of a good psychotherapist or couples counselor can be invaluable in helping your spouse to see the potential benefits of collaborative divorce. That said, we must caution you that not everyone in the mental health field is familiar with collaborative divorce and that therapists are just as vulnerable as anyone else to the myths surrounding divorce. Make sure that the person you choose to help you talk to your spouse is familiar with how collaborative divorce actually works.

ANSWERING YOUR SPOUSE'S QUESTIONS

Your spouse may have questions, such as "How much is this going to cost?" and "How long will it take if we do it this way?" We'll help prepare you with some answers. You'll see that it's not always possible to give definite answers to these understandable questions. You may better understand why that is so if we take a moment to explain how greatly people can differ in how they respond to a perceived crisis—such as an unanticipated or difficult divorce.

Remember the emotional roller coaster that you're on? Don't forget that your spouse is on the same ride. When faced with challenges—

internal or external—at the end of a marriage, people generally revert to their own personal "crisis mode," regardless of age, experience, education, wealth, sophistication, religious beliefs, and all the other factors that shape the decisions of millions of individuals who divorce each year.

For some—the lucky few—"crisis mode" means summoning up reserves of strength that they did not even know they possessed. For others, crisis evokes confusion, uncertainty, and emotional paralysis. Still others respond to crisis reactively, seeking comfort in immediate action—any action—in an effort to restore a sense of control and relieve the experience of helpless pain. To most of us, times of life crisis evoke both strengths and weaknesses that can surprise us, in patterns of ebb and flow that we may not understand or trust. The weaknesses can be particularly unsettling. Our clients often describe themselves in the most painful early stages of a divorce in words like these:

"This isn't like me. I just don't act this way. I hardly know who I am anymore."

"Looking back at my divorce, I can honestly say I was crazy. Some days I would feel great, as if the rest of my life was just opening up in front of me, and other days, *deranged* is not too strong a word for how I behaved."

"I had this terrible fear that if I didn't take decisive action to get this divorce over with fast, I'd come unglued and the pieces might never come together again."

Being aware of your spouse's emotional state can help you gauge when and how you should approach him or her to propose choosing collaborative divorce. Bear these different crisis modes in mind as you think about when and how to engage your partner's interest in collaborative divorce and how best to respond to your partner's possible concerns about it. If your spouse is easily angered or seems to be excitable and volatile, you might want to proceed slowly, as chances are good that he or she may later regret a hasty decision made while in that state. (Use the exercises at the back of the book to get a better sense of how these conversations with your spouse are likely to go.)

HOW MUCH WILL THIS COST?

Your spouse may be wondering about the cost of collaborative divorce, thinking, "Lawyers are expensive enough; how can we possibly afford all these other professionals?" The answer may seem paradoxical, but we know from experience that it is true: many couples save not only time and anguish but also money by including on their divorce team professionals skilled at working constructively with the welter of emotional issues that can arise during divorce. If you don't have the help of coaches, child specialists, and financial consultants when theirs are the perspectives that are called for, you can expect that tension and legal fees will escalate. Lack of the right kind of help can even cause one or both of you to turn to litigation in frustration.

When trained collaborative coaches help divorcing spouses deal with strong emotions and teach them how to communicate more effectively about divorce-related issues, the total cost of *all* the divorce-related professional services (including the fees of the collaborative lawyers and financial consultants as well as the coaches) will generally be much lower than if traditional adversarial lawyers had handled the case as a legal battle. Unresolved conflicts, fueled by miscommunications and unacknowledged powerful emotions, are the driving force behind high-conflict divorces and the high costs (both emotional and financial) that result.

Professional help that meets the needs of a restructuring family is not going to be cheap, but it is almost always more economical in the end than professional help that does *not* meet those needs. We do not mean to minimize the fact that you will be paying for the services you receive from your collaborative divorce team. It is true that couples who cannot afford any professional help at all in their divorces will not be able to afford the fees of a collaborative divorce team unless their community provides access to low-cost sliding scale collaborative divorce services. Each collaborative divorce professional will need to be paid at his or her respective hourly rate. As in any divorce mode, if your problems are complicated, your professional divorce services will cost more than if your problems are more straightforward. But for most couples, collaborative divorce is a very cost-effective way to solve their problems so that they stay solved.

HOW LONG WILL IT TAKE?

After "How much will this cost?," the most common question most people have about collaborative divorce (or any divorce) is usually "How long will it take?" Of course, this question really involves a handful of separate questions: How long does it take to become single under state law? How long will it take to devise a temporary and a longer-term parenting plan? How long will it take to complete the initial coaching work? How long will it take to arrive at a comprehensive settlement agreement that resolves all the property and support issues?

It isn't possible to predict in advance exactly how long any divorce will take or how long each of the smaller parts of a collaborative divorce will take, because as with "How much will it cost?," the answer depends on who the couple is, how much time each has had to accept the reality of the divorce, how emotionally stable and mature both partners are, how capable both are of following through with commitments, how well the couple communicates, how diligently each attends to collaborative "homework assignments," what their respective crisis modes are, how complex the financial and parenting aspects of the divorce are, and a host of other factors that can't be known beforehand. It's like asking how long it takes to get from Saint Louis to New Orleans: the answer depends on whether you walk, drive, or fly. You may take detours, or you may go directly. The weather may be sunny or stormy. Traffic may be heavy or light. In every collaborative divorce, we move from information gathering through consensus building and options development to resolution as efficiently as possible, but exactly how long the journey will take varies quite a bit from couple to couple and usually can't be predicted accurately in advance.

As to the legal aspect—the shortest time required before you can become a single person again—the laws of each state and Canadian province specify how long it will take. In some states, the time is very short—a few months or even weeks. Elsewhere you may have to wait longer before your marriage is legally dissolved.

Other factors pertain not to the law but to people's personalities. For example, some people like to solve problems at a "big-picture" level. They tend to be impatient with fact finding and want to get to resolution without touching the necessary bases along the way. Their team will advise them to slow down. That said, if you and your spouse are both big-picture types, your collaborative divorce may move from fact finding to resolution fairly quickly.

Other people need lots of information before they can reach resolution. We joke sometimes about people who like to calculate financial matters out to the tenth decimal place. That's an exaggeration, but not by much. If you or your spouse need maximum facts in order to feel comfortable moving forward, your divorce will progress more slowly. Also, sorting out complex problems always takes time. If houses, businesses, or collections need to be appraised, or if an expert in taxes or securities or vocational retraining needs to be consulted, you should expect these tasks to take some time if they are to be done well.

Of course, the greater the degree of emotional acceptance on the part of both spouses that the marriage is ending, the easier—and therefore the quicker—the divorce process will be. Trying to hurry a person who needs time to recover from the shock connected with the unexpected end of a marriage almost never works.

If your situation includes problems of mental illness or substance abuse, do not expect rapid resolution in collaborative divorce—or anywhere else. The slowest collaborative divorce cases we have ever handled involved two mentally ill spouses, severe disagreements about parenting, entrenched communication difficulties, extended travel by both partners, and complicated accounting and valuation problems. Cases as slow as this, however, are very rare.

The fastest collaborative divorce cases—usually involving short marriages with no children and few assets—may require three "four-way" meetings with the lawyers and one or two meetings with the coaches and financial consultant, if they are part of the team. Collaborative divorces that reach resolution this quickly are also relatively rare.

Meetings can be held as often as once or even twice a week, but most couples prefer at least two weeks between divorce-related meetings to allow time for emotional recharging and for the completion of homework assignments. If one or both spouses travel frequently, longer intervals between meetings may be necessary. Each divorce is different in this respect. Most people we work with require two or three four-way meetings with the coaches, four to six four-way meetings with the collaborative lawyers, and two or three meetings with the financial specialist, who may or may not also attend certain legal four-way meetings. These team members usually (though not always) work on parallel paths rather than one after the other. Most of our collaborative divorces involve work with the team over a period of four to twelve months.

Once in a while a professional team member's schedule (travel, vacations, health problems, work commitments, and so forth) can slow a divorce down. Ask questions if you have concerns about whether your case is getting the attention it needs.

Though collaborative divorce goes much more quickly than litigation, almost all clients we work with have unrealistic expectations about how long it will take to reach resolution and expect their divorces to be over far sooner than is possible. It's helpful to keep in mind that while you are in the process of a divorce, life doesn't stop. Over time, people's perspectives can change, and what once seemed like a vital sticking point to you or your partner—standing in the way of reaching resolution—may eventually feel less important. Time is a great healer, so although it's natural to want to get the divorce over with in a hurry, time is actually on your side.

The best advice we can give on keeping the process moving in a timely manner is to do your homework and be prepared for meetings, because good preparation helps move the process along. Simply thinking ahead about topics and issues and planning how to present your interests and concerns clearly will speed the process and cut costs. And if you can, try to relax about how fast the divorce is going. Collaborative divorce takes time because it involves a thorough examination of financial, legal, and psychological issues. If you try to hurry the process, you may very well miss opportunities to make the best choices—and you may end up with a shortsighted quick fix rather than a lasting solution. If real resolution—the kind of resolution that looks as good ten years from now as it does today—is your goal, you should be prepared to commit the time necessary to reach it.

YOUR REASONS FOR CHOOSING COLLABORATIVE DIVORCE MAY DIFFER

Even if you are skeptical that you and your partner will ever see eye to eye about much, collaborative divorce can still work. You and your spouse may have entirely different motivations for choosing collaborative divorce. For example, one of you may care a lot about the quality of relationships with extended family members after the divorce, while the other may care much less about that but may place a high value on privacy and on careful financial and tax planning. Even where there is little consensus about goals or values, many of our clients—both with and without children—simply want to remain dignified and look back on their own behavior during the divorce with self-respect. And even when they agree about nothing else, most couples with children share a desire to protect and do well by them.

Whatever their reasons, once a couple agrees on collaborative divorce, if they choose experienced team members to assist them they are likely to find the process and results satisfying. So long as both of you can respect your differences, honor the good-faith commitments of the collaborative process, and follow through with the tasks needed to reach resolution, you and your spouse will have the help you'll need to stay focused on getting to the best divorce the two of you are capable of.

MOVING FORWARD

Once you and your spouse are in agreement about giving collaborative divorce a try, it's time to start looking at the team players you'll need. In the next chapter, we'll look at who you'll need and what each person will do.

EVERY DIVORCE IS DIFFERENT

Please keep in mind that every divorce is different. Your own unique journey through the process will probably vary in certain details from the step-by-step explanation we will give you in the chapters that follow. For instance, some people begin with coaches, while others begin with lawyers or financial consultants. Some couples proceed on all three fronts simultaneously, while others have good reason for working intensively with one professional team member for a while before engaging in concentrated work with another.

What every couple can expect in their collaborative divorce is the coordination of resources by the members of your team to ensure that you are working with the right person at the right time on the right issues. What also remains the same is the road map of the process, beginning with information and moving through interests, values, consensus, and brainstorming before reaching resolution.

That is why, regardless of which professional doorway you use to enter the collaborative process, your team will consistently advise that until everyone knows and understands all basic factual information (gathered by all team members during fact-finding), it is a mistake to start talking about identifying priorities and options and reaching resolution (which takes place later). That's not true in other modes of divorce dispute resolution, and consequently couples using old-style divorce professional services frequently jump into discussing resolution much too soon because of their understandable wish to get the divorce over with quickly.

Wherever you begin in your own collaborative divorce, whether with lawyers or coaches or a financial consultant, you'll receive advice to take the stages in the right order. Starting with premature ideas about solutions often makes it much more difficult to reach resolution than it would have been with a strong foundation of facts, because often, what seem like differences of opinion about how to resolve an issue may actually be mistakes about underlying real-world facts that disappear when the full, correct information comes to light.

Ensuring that the work is done in the sequence that has proved most effective in getting to solutions is the job of your collaborative divorce team. But the details of each couple's pathway to resolution within that sequence will vary. For instance, even after you are deeply engaged in brainstorming work, if it appears that the real-world facts are changing (say, for instance, the stock market crashes), your team members will advise you to return to fact finding for a while, to understand what has changed. For example, you might need to reexamine with the financial consultant the basic facts about the value of an investment portfolio. You would return to brainstorming solutions only when your team was again confident that everyone's understanding of all the facts was correct and complete. They know that the sequence of the collaborative divorce process—gathering information, recognizing values and goals, reaching consensus through brainstorming, and then—and only then—implementing solutions—is a source of its considerable conflict resolution power.

CHOOSING COLLABORATIVE DIVORCE: ANDREW AND THERESE'S STORY

Whether to go with her best hopes or worst fears was a stark choice for Therese. An actress in a regional repertory theater company, Therese had been married for ten years to Andrew, the artistic director of the company. Andrew had been involved with other women throughout the marriage. Therese had been aware of some of these affairs and suspected others. Andrew seemed to operate on the philos-

ophy "Who are you going to believe—me or your own eyes?"
Even when his affairs were painfully obvious, he denied they were
happening. Though Therese wanted to save the marriage, primarily
because of their two young children, Andrew resisted any suggestion
of counseling—because, he later admitted, he did not see any point in
counseling unless he was prepared to admit conduct he was not ready
to be truthful about.

Andrew and Therese separated when Andrew became involved in
a protracted affair with another actress in a way so apparent that it became impossible for Therese to continue working in the company.
Therese assumed that since Andrew had lied to her for so long about
his liaisons, he would naturally lie and cheat in their divorce. Her
friends advised her to act swiftly and forcefully to protect herself financially.

Therese consulted Hank, an aggressive trial lawyer on the theater's
board of directors, asking for a referral to a tough divorce lawyer. She
had come to terms with the reality of the marriage ending but lived
her days and nights in dread of the impending vicious divorce battle,
which she feared would scar her children, ages three and seven. Yet she
knew that mediation would be impossible for her, and she was aware
of no other options.

Fortunately, Hank had just heard about collaborative divorce from
a legal colleague. He advised her to have a consultation with Jason, a
tough litigator, and also a consultation with his collaborative divorce
colleague, Charlotte. Therese did some basic research and then had
consultations with Jason, reputed to be the toughest divorce "bar-
racuda" in town, and then with Charlotte. Jason listened to Therese's
story of affair after affair and her fears about hidden assets, put his hand
over Therese's, and said, "Don't worry—I handle problems like this all
the time. We'll rip his lying lips off. First thing we'll do is get court orders to freeze all the bank accounts."

The interview with Charlotte could not have been more different. She asked Therese about the family finances and learned that one
trusted accountant had handled all their investments, taxes, and money
management throughout the entire marriage. With only a little dis-

cussion, Therese realized that the accountant had his fingers on all the information about the family's income, expenses, assets, and debts. Charlotte helped Therese evaluate whether she really believed Andrew was the type to have hidden bank accounts. The answer was surprisingly clear: no! Therese knew Andrew to be painfully honest about money. If anything, Andrew's feelings of guilt were causing him to give her more for current expenses than she could possibly need.

The conversation then turned to the children. With Charlotte's help, Therese saw that she was worried about how little time Andrew was spending with the children. He did have to travel for his work, but even when he was at home the children were seldom with him. He was, she felt, probably at a loss about how to bring the children into his life, given his increasingly serious relationship with his girlfriend— whom Therese disliked intensely. Alex and Therese would have to find a way to resolve that problem before he could be more involved with the children. Charlotte explained collaborative divorce coaching and how the coaches and child specialist could help Andrew and Therese communicate and make good decisions about these important child-related concerns.

Charlotte then asked a question that made Therese's mind up about choosing collaborative divorce. She said, "You've told me that the children are doing well but that they have seen Andrew only six or seven times in the two months since he moved out. So far as you know, what do they understand is the reason their father is gone from their daily lives?" Therese was shocked to realize that she'd been so focused on her own pain that she hadn't tried to imagine how the divorce looked and felt to them.

Therese gave Andrew a packet of information about collaborative divorce. He was immediately relieved to learn of Therese's interest in it. He had feared the worst, knowing that she had every right to be furious about his behavior. That she would consider a dignified end to their marriage in the interests of their children meant that he could hope to work out a way of becoming an active father to them again. And his fears that their accumulated investments would be spent in an embarrassing public court battle might—if they could work within the collaborative process—be put to rest, to the benefit of both of them and the children.

Therese made it clear when she gave the packet to Andrew that she'd participate in collaboration only if he were willing to work honestly with the coaches and child specialist, not just with lawyers. She explained what she'd learned about coaching from Charlotte: that it's not therapy. For Andrew, the potential benefits were attractive enough that he told her he'd be willing to learn more.

They were off to a good start. The possibility that they could end their marriage with greater dignity and integrity than they had been able to live it was now available to them.

3

ASSEMBLING YOUR TEAM

We don't accomplish anything in this world alone . . . and whatever happens is the result of the whole tapestry of one's life and all the weavings of individual threads from one to another that creates something.

—Sandra Day O'Connor

If I could solve all the problems myself, I would.

—Thomas Edison (when asked why he worked on a team of twenty-two people)

It's very helpful, as you deal with the ending of your marriage, to understand that a collaborative divorce proceeds according to a clear sequence. Think of it as a journey with a road map to a destination you haven't visited before. The journey has a beginning, middle, and end. Your professional team members will all be following the same map to guide you to the same destination. One couple's trip may be shorter, another's may be longer; one couple might make the trip entirely on the interstate highway, while another takes slower local roads; but the team members have made such trips many times before. They know what to expect in terms of alternate routes, detours, weather, and road conditions. One and the same road map will guide every team member's work in your case and will help each of you see where you are in the process at all times. There will always be an agreed-upon agenda for every collaborative divorce meeting that you'll know well in advance, and the work will nearly always move along more or less according to the steps and stages you'll read about in this and the coming chapters.

To make your journey as smooth as possible, you will need to choose the right professional helpers. In this chapter, we'll show you how.

CHOOSING YOUR COLLABORATIVE DIVORCE TEAM

Once you and your spouse have researched answers to your basic questions about the collaborative divorce process and have both decided that collaborative divorce is your best option, it's time to start putting together your team. (If you haven't yet felt the time is right to speak with your spouse about divorce, another way to begin is for you yourself to consult with a collaborative divorce coach or lawyer for guidance even before you ask your spouse to consider choosing it. That works, too. But eventually the time will come for both of you to select the members of the team.)

The next decision to make is which kind of professional help to start with. The answer will depend mainly on personal preferences and temperament—yours and your spouse's. Other factors to consider include the degree to which each of you has accepted the fact that the marriage is ending and your current ability to communicate with each other. (The exercises at the back of this book can help you assess these factors.) Beginning a collaborative divorce with lawyers can be difficult when emotional volatility is high. If you have a relationship in which arguments are intense and frequent, it might be better to start with coaches, who can guide you from the very beginning to communicate in more constructive ways. And if you have concerns about a child who is showing physical or emotional problems, or if you and your partner have differences of opinion or conflicts about parenting, starting in the coaches' offices can ensure that those issues get immediate attention.

Another reason why some couples prefer to begin with coaches rather than lawyers is that one spouse or the other has had either good experiences with counseling or psychotherapy in the past—or bad experiences with lawyers. Since coaches are mental health professionals, some people find them more familiar and less daunting to confer with than lawyers, and this makes them a better entry point into the divorce process.

If you begin with coaches, they will want you and your partner to retain your lawyers as a next step, so that your collaborative team will be organized and in place before the coaching begins. This is because the coaches need to know that your legal advice is going to be given right from the start by collaborative lawyers, not old-style divorce lawyers. For that reason, even if you start with coaches, full-scale collaborative coaching won't begin until both the coaches *and* the lawyers have joined your team.

Everyone going through divorce needs legal advice, and your friends and family will all be urging you to get an adversarial lawyer. On a bad day, at the bottom of the roller coaster, the temptation is to do so, and then tensions start to rise. But with collaborative lawyers on board, there is a system in place in which you will have a competent team member to tell you about the law and at the same time assist you with thinking through your decisions rather than using the law to escalate the fight.

Once the collaborative lawyers have been selected, couples who begin with the coaching process are likely to do important work with coaches and other team members for a while before shifting over to work more intensively with the lawyers. Divorces in which emotion runs high can benefit from this kind of triage so that you and your partner can address the areas of greatest pain and bleeding first. However, some "coaches-first" couples whose mutual acceptance of the divorce is greater may choose to initiate work on the legal side of the divorce at more or less the same time as they engage in coaching.

On the other hand, many couples begin their collaborative divorces with lawyers rather than coaches. Lawyers are probably the most familiar source of professional assistance during a divorce, and for many people, becoming familiar with the legal side of a divorce is an important way to relieve anxieties and fears. That's a common reason for beginning with lawyers. Or maybe you or your spouse reacts negatively to anything that even slightly resembles psychotherapy or counseling. In that case, you might be wise to choose collaborative lawyers as your entry point into the process.

Good collaborative lawyers will usually urge you and your partner to consider involving a larger team. Most collaborative lawyers will want you and your partner to have at least a first consultation with coaches, if they are available in your community, before the legal work moves forward. It's wise to do this, so that coaches will be available quickly if and when they are needed, even if you and your partner prefer to begin your divorce by working with your lawyers.

The important thing to remember is that there's more than one way to go about this process. We encourage you to consider all the options and to choose what will work best for you.

FINDING YOUR COLLABORATIVE LAWYERS

Collaborative divorce lawyers are experienced, licensed family lawyers, but they differ from other family lawyers in the community because of their additional special training and experience in collaborative family law and in working as a member of a collaborative divorce team.

How can you find collaborative divorce lawyers to help you and your partner with your divorce? You can locate potential collaborative lawyers in your area and find out quite a bit of information about them by going to the website of the International Academy of Collaborative Professionals, www.collaborativepractice.com. There, you will find a user-friendly international directory of collaborative lawyers who subscribe to the IACP ethical standards for collaborative practitioners. Many collaborative divorce lawyers who subscribe to the IACP standards of ethics are beginning to use this logo in their brochures and on their business cards, and if you see it in connection with a collaborative lawyer you'll know you are on the right track:

Though not all good collaborative lawyers are members of IACP, membership in that organization reflects a commitment to the highest standards of practice and is a handy way for you to identify well-qualified practitioners in your area.

If you live in a city, you'll probably find collaborative lawyers close by. If not, or if you and your partner now live in different locales, collaborative divorce is still an option. Because collaborative divorces take place entirely outside the courts, there is no need for your collaborative team to be located in your own community. So long as you and your partner are willing to travel and to use videoconferencing and other tools, you may be able to work with collaborative divorce lawyers wherever they may be in your state—or even out of state, provided that the collaborative lawyers make use of local counsel to ensure that everyone is aware of the relevant provisions of divorce law in your home state and to make sure your legal divorce is completed according to your state's law.

Once you've narrowed your search to three or four lawyers who seem like potential choices, interview several, if you can, before deciding whom you'll work with. You will want to be certain that the practitioner you select is well trained, experienced, capable, and a good "fit" with your own needs. Ask yourself the following questions: Does it make any difference to your comfort level whether you work with a man or a woman? What is your personal temperament? (If you are highly emotional, you might want to choose a person who is calm, thoughtful, and sensitive to your emotions.) Do you value rational efficiency and directness? (If so, pay particular attention to whether those qualities are present in the lawyer you are considering and avoid choosing someone who is more emotional or less organized in style.) If you're not sure about your preferences or style, and you are worried about whether you will choose well, your coach can help you understand what matters most to you.

The first conversation is a very good guide to how it would be for you to work with this lawyer. If your potential lawyer spends most of the time focusing on money, legal rights, and strategies, that will be the focus of the divorce process and you may get more of an old-style divorce, shadow-of-the-law settlement rather than deep conflict resolution. If the potential lawyer seems to be taking over both the problems and the approach to solutions, telling you not to worry because he or she will handle them, this lawyer is not likely to be a good team player and isn't likely to help you leave the divorce process with improved skills in solving problems with your ex-spouse on your own. A lawyer who spends plenty of time in the first interview listening to your concerns, finding out about the people who matter to you, understanding the reasons for the separation and divorce, and helping you anticipate the challenges you'll be addressing together from a constructive problem-solving perspective is someone who can help you achieve your "best divorce."

Another good reason to meet with more than one person before selecting the lawyer you will work with is that you need to have a good personal rapport with your lawyer for good collaborative teamwork. You'll be working together closely at times of potentially great stress. If it's not a good personal fit during that first interview, remember: the working relationship is not likely to get better as the tasks become more challenging.

Before making a final choice of your collaborative lawyer, find out how much training the person has had in collaborative divorce and collaborative law. One year of training in collaborative law is a good start, but more is better. If your prospective lawyer is just beginning to work as a collaborative lawyer, it might help if he or she also has experience in mediation. Making the shift from being a litigator to a collaborative lawyer takes time, training, and experience. In addition, look for someone who, if possible, has had training in how to work in an interdisciplinary team. Learning how to do teamwork with other professionals also takes time, training, and experience.

Also, find out if the person belongs to a local "practice group" of collaborative colleagues that meets regularly, conducts skill-building sessions, and provides mentoring and case conferencing. Practice groups work together to perfect their collaborative skills. They discuss common problems and help one another discover ways to solve them. In addition, practice groups build the kinds of trust relationships that make good teamwork possible. Collaborative lawyers (and other collaborative professionals) who are serious about learning to do the work of collaborative divorce well make the commitment to participate regularly in practice groups, because that's where the best "on the job" learning takes place.

Other information to get is how many collaborative divorce cases this person has worked on and whether those cases resulted in a completed settlement agreement using the collaborative process. Obviously, every new collaborative practitioner has to have a first case, and even the best and most experienced collaborative lawyers were beginners at one point. We aren't saying that you should never choose someone who is just beginning to learn this new way of working with divorcing couples, because in that case no new collaborative lawyers would ever learn to do this work well. At the same time, if all else is equal, you'll certainly benefit from working with a lawyer who has helped many couples move successfully through the collaborative process. If this is a journey to a destination you've never visited before, having a guide who knows where you're going and how best to get there has obvious value.

Finally, find out how long this person has been working professionally with divorcing couples. This criterion is very important. Although many lawyers are new to collaborative law and it may not yet be possible in your community to find a lawyer who has been doing it for many years, there is no reason why you should not be able to find a collaborative lawyer who has plenty of experience working with divorcing couples. Family law is a complex, demanding field of legal practice, and experience matters. All else being equal, you'll benefit from working with a lawyer who is seasoned by years of work in the field of divorce.

When you have chosen the lawyer you want to work with, you will sign a working agreement with him or her that defines your financial relationship and some elements of the lawyer's professional responsibilities to you. This is often referred to as a "retainer agreement" or "fee agreement." In some states (such as California), the rules of the state bar association require the lawyer and client to sign such a financial agreement at the start of the representation.

In addition, in many communities it is customary to give the lawyer a deposit retainer (a sum paid in advance, to be applied to your bill as services are rendered). There are several reasons why this is a good idea. First, it's never a good idea to run up large unpaid bills for any professional services, because that situation always gets in the way of good communication between you and your professional helper. Second, part of ensuring that you and your spouse participate in the collaborative divorce process on a "level playing field" is ensuring that all your professional helpers know that their services will be paid for. Many old-style divorce battles are fought about whether the nonemployed spouse will or will not have access to the resources necessary to secure legal counsel and other professional divorce-related help. That is not permitted in collaborative legal work, and, for that reason, ensuring that your lawyer and your spouse's lawyer are similarly situated with respect to compensation is important to the integrity of the negotiations. A retainer payment of this kind is not the same as a flat lump-sum divorce fee that pays for the entire divorce. Most deposit retainers are not predictions of how much your divorce will cost. Be sure that you and your lawyer are clear about these financial matters right from the start.

Next, your spouse will need to choose his or her collaborative lawyer. A very good approach is to ask your own lawyer for the names of collaborative colleagues with whom he or she works well. It's a fact that all else being equal, nothing is a better predictor of success in collaborative divorce than choosing team members who trust one another and have worked well together in the past.

If your spouse was the first to select collaborative legal counsel, the same principle works in reverse: you should give serious consideration to the lawyers suggested by your spouse's collaborative counsel, as they are people he or she works particularly well with. Of course, both you and your partner must choose freely, and each of you has every right not to follow either lawyer's suggestions. But couples benefit greatly from choosing lawyers who trust one another and suffer if they don't.

Occasionally couples who have a high level of mutual cooperation decide to interview potential collaborative lawyers jointly and to choose counsel for each spouse from a pool that both spouses feel comfortable with. (This is a novel concept for lawyers, who will need to ensure that you both understand and agree to this procedure in a way that meets ethical rules for lawyers, but it certainly can be done.)

However you and your partner go about it, the most important consideration is that both of you select experienced and capable collaborative lawyers who can work effectively together. If you do that, all should be well.

Once the two lawyers are on board, they'll find out basic information about your situation, confer with each other, and make recommendations about who could do good coaching in your divorce and who might serve you well as a financial consultant. They will recommend people whom they trust. Collaborative professionals never take referral fees; their goal is to help you find the right mix of skilled helpers who can work well with you and your team.

FINDING A DIVORCE COACH

If you and your partner are more comfortable beginning the process with coaches rather than with lawyers, the steps you'll take are very similar: do your research, narrow your choices to a short list, interview potential coaches, make your selection, and get referrals to possible coaches for your spouse who work well with the person you have selected.

As with choosing a lawyer, you'll want to begin your search for your coach by locating people in your community, region, or state who affirm their adherence to the mission statement, standards of practice, and ethical standards of the IACP. On the IACP website, you'll also find much information about potential coaches' education, experience, credentials, and training. Your coach may be a licensed clinical psychologist or social worker, a marriage and family therapist, or a psychiatrist.

Look for coaches who have participated in at least one, and preferably more, training in interdisciplinary collaborative practice. You'll also benefit by working with coaches who have prior training and experience as mediators and as family therapists.

Provided they have had the necessary training in collaborative divorce practice and otherwise meet the IACP standards for practitioners, potential coaches will bring similar skills to your collaborative divorce. However, as with any other team member, their experience matters. Find out how many collaborative divorce cases your prospective coach has participated in and how many of those cases resulted in a complete resolution of all issues through the collaborative process. As with lawyers, you may not yet be able to find coaches in your community who have been doing collaborative work for many years, but you certainly can expect to find a coach with ample prior experience in other kinds of divorce-related work that focuses on family systems. All else being equal, someone who has spent many years working with divorcing couples and families will bring a more seasoned perspective than someone who is newer to the work.

You'll want to interview prospective coaches, because, as with all the team members, you need to feel comfortable with this person who will guide you through your divorce process. Your coach needs to understand you and your goals, values, and concerns. In your first interview with prospective coaches, note how well you and the coach communicate with each other, whether you feel the coach focuses on subjects that matter to you, and whether the information you receive is presented in a way that is clear and understandable. Will you feel comfortable enough with this person to be able to talk about difficult subjects? Does this person understand and recognize your goals for the collaborative divorce process? These are important questions to ask yourself, because ultimately they will determine how effectively and comfortably you can work with your coach.

When all other issues are equal, consider using a coach of your own gender. Gender differences are often accentuated during a divorce, and you may find it helpful for that reason to have gender balance in the coaching process. You can discuss this subject with potential coaches as part of your decision-making process.

As with the collaborative lawyers, if you want the best possible assistance from your coaches, it's important that you and your partner select coaches who can work well together. Ask your prospective coaches for names of other coaches they work well with, and ask your spouse to find out the same information.

And as with the collaborative lawyers, once you've made your choice, you'll sign a fee agreement with your coach that clearly explains the financial aspects of his or her work with you.

FINDING A FINANCIAL CONSULTANT

The financial consultant needs to work closely with the two lawyers as well as with you and your spouse, and for that reason, advice from your lawyer and your spouse's lawyer is particularly important in making this choice. Choose a financial consultant whom the collaborative lawyers trust and respect and whose expertise they consider appropriate for the needs of your case. Many divorcing spouses already have a personal or business financial consultant or accountant. That person will be providing vital information during the information-gathering phase of your divorce, but it's important to understand that your current financial advisor serves a different role than a collaborative divorce financial consultant does. While your current advisor may assist in the divorce, he or she will not be a collaborative divorce team member in the sense that we are describing here. Your financial team member, if any, must be a neutral party with special collaborative divorce training who works only on your divorce-related issues and nothing else. Thus, the financial team member may not have a continuing professional relationship with either spouse or both spouses that is unrelated to the divorce. Nor is it ethically acceptable for a collaborative divorce financial consultant to provide ongoing investment or financial services after the divorce that are unrelated to divorce issues.

Often, the collaborative lawyers will recommend a collaborative financial consultant they consider to be a good choice in your situation, or perhaps several from whom you and your partner can select. You also can look for potential financial consultants yourself, though you must remember that your spouse and both lawyers will need to agree on the choice. As with other collaborative divorce team members, once you have your collaborative lawyers' recommendations about potential choices for this team member, you can do research about potential financial consultants on the website of the International Academy of Collaborative Professionals. Look for someone who affirms his or her adherence to the IACP mission statement and ethical standards and meets its standards for practitioners. Then look for the consultant's experience in the field of family law, as well as the training that the consultant has had in divorce financial planning and in collaborative divorce practice. Collaborative divorce financial consultants are usually Certified Public Accountants or Certified Financial Planners who have additional training in the collaborative team approach as well as in divorce financial planning. Sometimes your collaborative lawyers will recommend financial consultants with other credentials—for example, people who have served as expert consultants in the divorce area. As with all team members, a good indicator of commitment to excellence in the practice of collaborative divorce is active membership in a practice group.

In some communities you'll have a number of potential financial consultants to choose from, while in other communities the choices may be fewer. Where there are many choices, your collaborative lawyers will consider whether your financial situation is complex enough to need the tax and accounting expertise of a Certified Public Accountant, or whether a financial planner's skills are more what you'll need.

If your divorce finances are complex and require the services of a Certified Public Accountant but there is no collaborative divorce financial consultant in your community with that professional credential, you have several choices to discuss with your collaborative lawyer. You might retain a qualified accountant from a more distant locale, tailoring in-person and telephone or videoconferencing communications to meet your needs. Or you might retain an accountant in your community who can provide financial expertise but who lacks collaborative divorce training. In that event, you would have the more specialized financial services of an expert consultant but not the broader services of a trained collaborative divorce team member.

The most important considerations are that the financial consultant be able to meet the specific needs you and your partner have regarding the financial aspects of your divorce and that you and your collaborative lawyers agree that the person is right for the job.

As with the collaborative lawyers, once you've chosen your financial consultant, you'll sign a fee agreement that clearly explains the financial aspects of his or her work with you. Since this person is a neutral party whose work will be for both spouses, you'll both sign a fee agreement with the financial consultant.

FINDING A CHILD SPECIALIST

Any time a divorcing couple has minor children, it's wise to consider involving a collaborative child specialist. In many circumstances your coaches will advise that a child specialist's assistance is essential if, like most couples, your goal is to provide the best postdivorce parenting that you and your partner are capable of.

Some couples already have a marriage and divorce counselor who is helping them deal with parenting matters, and some children of divorcing couples are already seeing counselors or psychotherapists. Bear this in mind: just as your current financial advisor or accountant plays a very different role from the specially trained financial consultant who participates in a collaborative divorce team, so does the child specialist play an entirely different role from a marriage counselor or psychotherapist. In old-style divorce parenting negotiations, couples can get involved in difficult, destructive battles when a child's personal counselor or psychotherapist is drawn into the cross fire of a divorce. If the therapist's views conflict with those of either parent, the child may end up losing his or her trusted counselor. Child therapists, if they offer parenting advice at all, need to do so very cautiously in order not to alienate either parent—and, for that reason, many of them refuse to participate at all in disputes about parenting matters during divorce. Even when they do participate, it is difficult or impossible for them to be helpful without compromising their primary therapeutic relationship with the child. As for your own adult counselors or psychotherapists, you'll quickly see that they could not possibly present the perspectives or serve the vital functions that a child specialist performs on the team. It's a very delicate role. The child specialist is the voice of the child and speaks in that voice via the coaching process—because that has proven again and again to be the best way for all the vital information needed by parents and children during divorce to be fully presented in a way that can be heard and used constructively.

Your coaches will recommend one or more child specialists whom they consider to be appropriate choices, but it's important for you to be certain that the child specialist you work with has the right education, training, and experience for the job. In addition, the child specialist has to have a good working relationship with both coaches and a good rapport with both parents, as well as with your child or children. How quickly the child specialist is brought on board depends on where the greatest needs exist at the time the couple is putting together the team.

In making your choice, you will need to ask questions such as these about—or in conversation with—a recommended child specialist:

- What education have you had relating to divorce, children of divorce, and family systems?
- What experience have you had working with children of divorce of the age(s) of my child(ren)?
- What is your training and experience in collaborative divorce?
- Do you subscribe to the IACP mission statement and ethical standards and meet its standards for practitioners?

You and your partner both need to feel comfortable enough with the child specialist to trust that your children will be in good hands and that the information that the child specialist gathers and communicates will be reliable. If either of you does not feel sufficiently comfortable, it's better to find someone else than to attempt to persuade a reluctant partner to go forward with someone whose observations and suggestions must be received with a fully open mind by both of you.

Your children also should know that they have a choice in this matter. Some older children need the opportunity to meet with two or more potential child specialists before a decision is made. With younger children, let them know that if they are uncomfortable with your first choice, you'll look for someone else. With very young children, trust your own initial judgment as to whether your child appears to be at ease with the child specialist. The most important thing is for your children to understand that their views and feelings about this person matter.

As with the collaborative lawyers, once you've made your choice of a child specialist, you'll sign a fee agreement that clearly explains the financial aspects of his or her work with you. Since this person works not directly with either spouse but rather with the children of both of you, you'll both sign a fee agreement with the child specialist.

Once the child specialist is on board, if concerns arise later about any aspect of that person's work, it's always best to confer with your coaches or lawyers to address the concerns. Children don't do well with "revolving-door" professional help.

GETTING CLEAR ABOUT FINANCES AND RESPONSIBILITIES

In the first meetings with each of the team members you select, you will learn exactly what to expect from them in terms of their fees and responsibilities. Each lawyer, coach, financial consultant, and child specialist is an independent professional with no financial connection to the others. For that reason, you each need to work out your financial arrangements and other understandings with each of your team members separately. If it isn't volunteered, ask for an explanation of hourly rates, billing and retainer policies, and similar matters.

Also, make sure your professional team members explain how and when they will communicate with you and with other team members and how you will be billed for that time.

Written retainer or fee agreements that specify these matters should be signed with each professional. You'll sign a private retainer agreement with your own lawyer and coach. You and your spouse will sign joint retainer agreements with the child specialist and with the financial consultant, because each of these team members is accountable to both of you.

The specific form of the fee agreement will vary from community to community and from profession to profession. The logistical details are relatively unimportant; your team members will provide you with the particular fee agreements that are customary in their practices.

What matters is that you understand clearly your financial arrangement with each professional team member and that you have a fee agreement with each team member in writing, signed by both of you.

THE COLLABORATIVE TEAM AGREEMENT

At the beginning of any collaborative process, you and your partner together will sign one or more "participation agreements" with the members of your team. The participation agreements serve an entirely different purpose from the fee agreements. They relate to how the collaborative process itself will work. They specify the responsibilities and commitments of each professional and each spouse with respect to the actual work of a collaborative divorce. No work will be done in your divorce by any of the professionals—other than preliminary interviews with you—until these formal documents have been signed.

A participation agreement protects you. It establishes that the work of the collaborative team will be confidential. Since you are working with a team rather than with only a single lawyer, it's crucial that you clarify with your partner and all professional helpers what will and what will not remain confidential. There are several layers to this concept of confidentiality that you need to know about before you begin the process.

With your lawyer and your coach, you need to know whether there are any matters you can communicate to that professional helper in confidence, in the sense that you can be sure the confidence will be communicated to no one else without your specific consent. All lawyers, including collaborative lawyers, are bound by the "lawyer-client privilege," which means that if you tell something to a lawyer with the request not to disclose it, the lawyer may not violate that confidence without your specific permission. But because of the high value placed in collaborative divorce on disclosure of all matters that a reasonable decision maker would want to know before reaching agreement, the participation agreement will specify what will happen if you instruct the lawyer to keep secret something that the lawyer believes should be disclosed. The lawyer will either withdraw from further representation in that situation or, in certain circumstances, send out a notice terminating the collaborative divorce process. In either event, the lawyer will never disclose anything that you have stated is confidential (unless some provision of your state's law requires disclosure, which is a discussion beyond the scope of this book).

With coaches, you need to ask the same question: If I tell you something in strict confidence, will it be kept in confidence? In many states, coaches may be required to report child abuse and similar matters. Your participation agreement with your coaches will clarify this point and will inform you about any matters that state law requires them to report.

There is a different aspect to confidentiality that concerns matters addressed in collaborative negotiations involving the participation of your spouse and other team members. Confidentiality means something different in that situation. Your spouse will know everything that goes on in coaching or legal four-way meetings and in the collaborative financial meetings, because you'll both be participating directly in those events. But what if at some point one or the other of you decides to end the collaborative process and go to court? Before you begin the collaborative divorce process, you need to know that

- Settlement discussions in the collaborative four-way meetings will remain in the collaborative process and may not ever be used in court proceedings
- Documents prepared for settlement purposes in the collaborative process will be confidential and may not ever be used in court
- None of your team—the lawyers, coaches, child specialist, or financial consultant—may ever participate in any way in adversarial court proceedings between you and your partner

Those are vital, trust-building protections, and you need to know with certainty that they are in place before conversations begin. It is the collaborative participation agreements that govern all that and much more. Those documents also set out some of the responsibilities of the team members, as well as the good-faith participation commitments of all team members.

THE DOCUMENTS: WHEN ARE THEY SIGNED? WHO SIGNS WHAT?

Exactly how many documents will be signed, and how many people will sign each one, can vary quite a bit from locale to locale, but the principle is the same everywhere. You, your spouse, and each team member need to have signed written agreements about payment of fees. You, your spouse, and all team members also need to have signed written collaborative participation agreements that define what each team member will and will not do and what you will and will not do in the course of the collaborative divorce process. These documents state in writing what you can and cannot expect from the process and from each professional on the team and what they will expect from you and your spouse.

The most common way the necessary documents are taken care of—though not the only way—is that each member of the couple signs a separate fee agreement with his or her own lawyers and a separate fee agreement with his or her own coach, after each of these team members has been chosen. The coaches and lawyers sign fee agreements with their own individual clients, usually after the initial consultation and before further work proceeds. These fee agreements may also specify what the roles and responsibilities of that professional and the client will be, sometimes in general terms and sometimes quite specifically.

If a child specialist is involved, both spouses will need to sign a fee agreement, since they are both responsible for payment of that professional's fees. The terms of the child specialist's participation in the collaborative coaching process will be spelled out either in a separate participation agreement or as part of the coaching participation agreement that is signed by both coaches and both clients. Similarly, if a neutral financial consultant is involved, there will be a fee agreement with both spouses and either a separate participation agreement or an addendum to the legal participation agreement that is signed by both lawyers and both clients. Any neutral experts brought in to assist with specific issues—for example, real estate or business or art appraisers or vocational consultants—will be asked to sign an agreement showing their understanding that they, too, may not ever participate in litigation between you and your partner.

Although you may think this sounds like a lot of paperwork, it's only the description that sounds complicated. In fact, collaborative team members have done the paperwork many times and have standard forms and procedures ready for use. The papers will be explained quickly and efficiently and can be signed as soon as you and your spouse are ready to commit to the collaborative divorce process.

LOGISTICS

With different members of the team needing to meet at different times with different people, coordination is key. Different collaborative groups handle the logistics of scheduling differently. However the details are handled in your community, you should expect a series of appointments to be set in advance with any team member or members you work with, even if they need to be changed later.

MOVING FORWARD

Once all the paperwork has been taken care of, you're ready to begin the real work: gathering, sharing, and understanding the facts that will be important in your divorce, from all perspectives—yours, your partner's, your children's, and that of each of the team members. In the next chapter, we'll look closely at how all this will happen.

GETTING STARTED:
ALICE AND TODD'S STORY

Alice is uncertain about collaborative divorce. She has read about it and finds it appealing because she wants to expedite the end of her marriage to Todd. She knows that adversarial divorces can be expensive and slow. Also, she is close to Todd's mother and sisters and does not want to lose their friendship after the divorce, as she knows she would if the divorce became hostile. On the other hand, she worries about not being able to control the collaborative process. She knows that it doesn't permit unilateral actions and that it can't force Todd to cooperate with her ideas or to move forward as quickly as she'd like. He is living in the family residence, and he has no incentive to make progress in the divorce because he doesn't want the house to be sold. Alice needs her share of the house sale proceeds; it's the only source she knows of for money to buy into a new business partnership.

Like you, Alice has important decisions to make at the start of her divorce. She can make them well, or she can make them poorly. It is no exaggeration to say that she will experience the consequences of these decisions for the rest of her life. With collaborative divorce, she can choose to let her best hopes take the lead, refusing to let her worst fears occupy the driver's seat.

Alice's next step could be a consultation with a collaborative lawyer, with whom she can discuss her uncertainties about whether this is the right approach for her needs and priorities, which appear to be selling the house reasonably soon while preserving her extended family relationships. A good collaborative lawyer will give Alice wise counsel and accurate information about how well she could hope to achieve her priorities using the adversarial old-style divorce model and the possibilities using the collaborative divorce approach. Alice will learn from her prospective collaborative lawyer that in a litigated divorce, Todd might be able to delay a forced sale of the house for as long as several years. While he might also resist cooperating with a sale in a collaborative divorce, the collaborative process encourages cooperation—unlike the adversarial approach, which encourages opposition and resistance.

Instead of consulting with a prospective collaborative lawyer, Alice's next step could be a meeting with a prospective collaborative divorce coach. There she would get a different perspective about her options from what the collaborative lawyer might offer. A coach might initially focus on how effectively Alice and Todd have been communicating about the impending divorce, how well he understands her concerns, and how well she understands his. The coach might counsel Alice about the value of spending some time in coaching and really listening to each other's priorities, interests, and fears.

Whichever potential team member Alice begins with, she will be advised that when people agree to listen carefully and make a serious effort to understand the concerns brought to the table for resolution, they have a much better chance of finding solutions that will work for both of them than if they resort to battle. Wherever she begins—with a coach, lawyer, or financial consultant—the first order of business will be to help her decide in what way she has the best chance of addressing her concerns and achieving her goals.

Todd, too, will learn from his prospective collaborative lawyer or coach the difference between fighting with Alice in court about the sale of the house and having a constructive conversation at the collaborative divorce table about ways in which he and Alice might both be able to meet their needs in a settlement.

Assuming that both Alice and Todd choose collaborative divorce, they will work with collaborative coaches, collaborative lawyers, and the financial consultant to gather basic information, hear each other's concerns, and only then explore the possibilities for resolution. Alice, for example, might discover while working with the financial consultant that there could be ways—other than selling the house—to fund her partnership that Todd might be more inclined to cooperate with. Todd will bring to the table not simply a refusal to sell but an explanation of the real reasons why he does not want to. With that information on the table, other possibilities for meeting his underlying concerns can be sought. In this way, both Alice and Todd will be guided to look for a solution that could satisfy each of them.

Collaborative divorce will give Alice and Todd assistance from the three professional perspectives that can help them find solutions. This richness of professional conflict resolution resources brought to bear on the single agenda of finding solutions is found only in collaborative divorce. With it, Alice will have her best chance of meeting both of her goals—finding resources to start a new business and preserving important extended family relationships. Without collaboration, the chances of meeting her goals at all, much less within a reasonable time frame, will be slim.

Todd will also have his best chance of achieving his priorities with collaborative divorce. The job description for his collaborative professional advisors will include helping him understand what keeping the house really means to him—perhaps emotional stability in a time of rapid change, perhaps being able to remain in the same neighborhood, perhaps benefiting from a rising real estate market, or perhaps all three. More often than you might imagine, keeping the house is not the only—or even the best—way to meet the spouses' real concerns.

4

GATHERING INFORMATION:
A Look at the Role of the Lawyers and Financial Advisor

Not everything that can be counted counts, and not everything that counts can be counted.

—ALBERT EINSTEIN

There isn't any one right way to begin the actual work of a collaborative divorce. Once the team members are in place and the participation documents have been signed, most of your team may step back while you and your spouse begin working with one of the professionals. As you saw in chapter 3, you can begin with either coaches or lawyers. While some couples may work in tandem with both professionals, it is more common to start with just one.

In this chapter, we will examine how you get started on the first task of a collaborative divorce—gathering information—with your collaborative divorce team. We'll begin by explaining in greater depth the multiple perspectives brought by team members, and then we'll focus on how information gathering proceeds with lawyers and the financial consultant. Chapter 5 will examine how information gathering proceeds with coaches and the child specialist.

FIRST, THE FACTS

The search for lasting solutions to the complex problems facing a divorcing couple begins with a candid sharing of information about facts, priorities, values, concerns, and fears. That wealth of information, which is unique to you and your family, forms the essential foundation for all the collaborative problem-solving efforts that will follow. As with building a house, so with a collaborative divorce: the better the foundation, the more solid and long-lasting the structure that will rest on it. Accordingly, your team members will take time to gather and share as much information as possible, as thoroughly as possible, from multiple perspectives. They will help you and your partner pull together a great deal of information about your overall personal and financial situation that you have probably never examined before in such a thorough and organized way.

Though each divorcing partner will be familiar with individual parts of this picture, in our experience it's very rare for a divorcing couple to be able to master the entire array of pertinent facts without professional help. Although collaborative lawyers are accustomed to gathering information and helping clients understand certain parts of the big picture, and though they are skilled at helping their clients negotiate settlement agreements, they don't have the skills of financial or mental health professionals, who can put together pieces of the puzzle outside the frame of reference of most lawyers. For that reason, we know that lawyers can't usually do the jobs of an entire collaborative team on their own.

The members of the collaborative divorce team know how to gather important information from multiple perspectives relating to issues that matter to you, and they also know how to bring it effectively into the divorce conflict resolution process at a time, and in a

The Power of the Team

- A team is a group of people working toward the same goal: a cure for a disease, a design for a building, a high-tech solution to a computer software problem, or a plan for restructuring family relationships and systems after a divorce.
- Scientists and business leaders know that teams come up with better solutions faster.
- The same is true in divorce.
- We all have both strengths and weaknesses.
- When we work together as a team, the weaknesses of each member are balanced by the strengths of one or more other members of the team.

way, that is useful to you and your partner. When a team is involved, part of this information will consist of what the collaborative lawyers focus on: your particular needs, concerns, challenges, goals, and vision for the future, translated into concrete interests and priorities that you and your spouse can understand and appreciate. It also includes what the financial consultant focuses on: the detailed spreadsheets and supporting documentation showing assets and debts, income and expenses, and taxes. In addition, another component is information developed during coaching concerning which issues have emotional weight, where communication can be improved, which important personal hopes and values must be respected, and which parenting issues may have financial or other implications that the other professional team members should be aware of.

Having an interdisciplinary collaborative divorce team working together on information gathering greatly expands everyone's ability to reach consensus about the facts in a way that supports making well-informed decisions. Another great strength of the collaborative process is that the information-gathering phase is not done until all questions have been answered and everyone is satisfied about the facts. In this way, we eliminate arguments about easily verified information, reduce mistrust and suspicion, and focus everyone's energy on expanding options for solutions.

MORE THAN ONE KIND OF INFORMATION

In collaborative divorce, we pay attention to many kinds of facts, not just facts concerning real-world matters such as money and time with children. At the same time, we do not minimize the importance of good financial information. On the contrary; your team will help you reach an accurate and shared understanding of exactly what debts you have, what your assets are worth, what your income and expenses are, and where all the marital income went—all very common questions in divorce, and all fertile grounds for arguments when all information is not freely shared.

Through collaborative divorce, you'll both have access to the same information and have all your questions answered until both of you are satisfied. If there are gaps in the information or inconsistencies that cannot be satisfactorily accounted for, you and your lawyers will be made aware of this by your financial consultant, and it will be a problem that must be solved before solutions can be discussed. Disagreements about what was spent in the past and what should be spent in the future can be explored based upon a full analysis of past and current financial information prepared with your financial consultant's help.

Another kind of real-world information your team will take care to explore fully relates to the children, if you have them. The coaches—with the help of the child specialist—will help you gather and share information about how each child is doing at home, at school, and with friends. The concerns and priorities of the children will form part of the important information explored during coaching, allowing you and your spouse to address not only the children's divorce-related concerns but also any special needs they may have—whether medical, psychological, or educational. Even during marriage, spouses do not always agree about how to deal with such problems. At the time of divorce, coach-facilitated problem solving can elevate the quality of solutions for your children—often dramatically. Existing time-sharing and parenting arrangements can be explored not only from the perspective of whether they work for the adults but also from the perspective of how they are working for the children. Concerns and differences of opinion can be identified for further discussion as coaching continues.

But these "outer-world" facts, while necessary, are not sufficient as a foundation for reaching deep conflict resolution, which is the goal in collaborative practice and the only way to achieve your personal "best divorce." In order to accomplish this kind of conflict resolution, a second realm of "inner-world" facts must also be explored just as fully, and until that job is also completed, you are not yet ready to consider options for resolution.

Your collaborative divorce team will help both you and your partner clarify and explain the values, principles, and goals that each of you has for yourself and for other family members during and after the divorce. These are "facts," too—facts about the inner world of hopes and fears, ethics and beliefs, personal integrity and connections to others. This realm—we refer to it as the "inner estate" or "relational estate"—matters greatly to most of the people we work with. Judges can't issue orders about it and so it generally isn't on the radar screen in old-style divorces, but we know that it's vital to explore this information for real conflict resolution. Without it, how can you or your spouse possibly understand later on in the process why some proposed options for resolution will be appealing while others that seem equally reasonable will be rejected? Your team members will encourage you and your partner to share information from this inner realm in ways that can be heard and appreciated by the other spouse before you move to considering options for resolution.

VALUES AND "INVISIBLE ASSETS"

No one on your collaborative divorce team will tell you how much value you should place on the inner-world "invisible assets," but a good collaborative team will insist that *you* think about what value they have for *you* before you start to consider options for settlement. You may conclude in the end that getting more money out of your divorce settlement at all costs matters more to you than the price tag in lost "relationship estate" assets and opportunities, such as dancing together at grown children's weddings or sharing the pleasure of grandchildren's birthdays and graduations. But your team will make sure *you* think about the value of pushing for that last extra dollar if it may foreclose the possibility of rebuilding a functional family system after the divorce that will sustain the relationships that matter to you most.

THE LEGAL SIDE OF YOUR COLLABORATIVE DIVORCE

You and your partner will each begin the legal side of your collaborative divorce journey by meeting with your own lawyer, in preparation for participating in a series of legal four-way meetings. During these individual meetings, your respective collaborative lawyers will help you clarify how to think about, and how and when to discuss, the concerns that you feel are most pressing. Collaborative lawyers also encourage their clients to think about the qualities and principles that would characterize a good divorce process and outcome for each of them and to bring that information into the legal four-way meetings. The collaborative lawyers also invite each spouse to think and reflect about their highest hopes for him- or herself, for the other partner, and for any children, as we'll explain more fully later in this chapter.

THE FIRST FOUR-WAY MEETING WITH THE LAWYERS

After you and your spouse have each met once or twice privately with your respective collaborative lawyers, you'll attend the first legal four-way meeting. These four-way meetings are the heart and soul of the collaborative divorce process. At the legal four-way meetings, all the work of sharing and exploring information, identifying priorities, brainstorming options, and negotiating solutions is done face to face. Unlike conventional settlements in old-style divorces, in collaborative divorce the lawyers *never negotiate for you and never conduct negotiations without both you and your spouse being present.* Their job is to help both of you reach the point where you can, with your lawyer's help, explain what you need, listen to your spouse's needs, and work to find areas of consensus and agreement.

The first four-way meeting with the lawyers is unique because it is the only meeting at which the collaborative lawyers do most of the talking. The agenda for that meeting is to make sure that both of you fully understand how collaborative divorce differs from other types of divorce. It's crucial for you and your spouse to come away with a clear understanding of what will be expected of each of you in order for the process to work, and to understand the collaborative lawyers' special role within the collaborative divorce team.

You probably will have discussed much of this beforehand with your own lawyer, but sitting together in the same room with your spouse and the other lawyer and saying to each of these points "Yes, I understand" and "Yes, I promise" before you sign the formal collaborative divorce participation agreements forms a reservoir of good-faith understandings and commitments that you and your lawyers can go back and draw upon in those inevitable moments when negotiations become difficult or the process seems temporarily stuck.

At the first four-way meeting, you'll probably meet your spouse's divorce lawyer for the first time. It would be unreasonable to expect anyone to negotiate about worrisome issues with strangers, and that's why good collaborative lawyers postpone discussing specific divorce issues until a later meeting. By the end of that first four-way meeting, you'll have a sense of who your spouse's lawyer is, as well as how committed to the collaborative process your spouse seems to be. Your comfort level should be considerably greater than it was before you started the process, and then the work can begin.

GATHERING INFORMATION WITH YOUR COLLABORATIVE LAWYERS

The collaborative lawyers' primary task is to guide the negotiation process. At the start of their work with you, their job focuses on weaving the information that will be coming to them from you, your spouse, and the rest of your team—the collaborative financial consultant and the coaches—into a carefully sequenced series of discussions at the four-way legal table. These meetings begin by examining the wide range of facts that you and your spouse need to be aware of before you can be ready to clarify your objectives and brainstorm possible scenarios for resolution. The information-gathering and -sharing phase will include considering facts not only about finances and about how parenting the children will be arranged, but also about hopes, goals, values, needs, and priorities. To the extent that you and your spouse communicate about this inner realm, it will become possible to consider proposed solutions not only with finances in mind but also by how well they match up with your respective inner-realm concerns. Without such information, shallow peace is all that you are likely to reach, but with it you have the opportunity to work toward deep resolution.

One element of the "inner-estate" information gathering that your collaborative lawyers facilitate will be an invitation to you and your partner early in the process to make what some lawyers call "mission statements" and others call "statements of highest intentions." Your lawyers will probably suggest as an agenda item for the first or second four-way meeting with them that each of you describe in simple, broad, value-based terms what the "best divorce" would look like for you. This description should be general; it shouldn't include specific issues or outcomes. And it will go into the minutes of the meeting, so that everyone can refer back to it later when an upwelling of worst fears may cause you or your partner to lose sight of your best hopes.

Though fears about divorce are almost always oppositional in nature, involving expectation of harm as a result of the other partner's behavior, couples are often surprised and relieved to discover the degree to which their highest hopes overlap. Lisa and Hank discovered this kind of unexpected overlap during the "mission statement" phase of their second legal four-way meeting, easing both their minds and making them both less anxious about forthcoming negotiations. They found they both placed high value on making it possible for Lisa to remain a full-time parent until both their daughters graduated from high school. They understood that their mission statements were not an agreement that Lisa would in fact stay out of work for that long. Much more information about income and assets would be necessary before they could see if that would be possible. But just knowing that both of them wanted to explore solutions that could permit Lisa to do that was an important discovery about an inner value they shared. It would help give focus to the option development phase of their divorce and help them work toward solutions to achieve that shared goal. And it would help both of them see potential financial considerations for what they really were: simply financial considerations, not a smoke screen for a plan to thwart each other.

If Hank and Lisa had *not* been in agreement about that value, that too would have been useful, important information for the collaborative process. Highlighting their differing values on this point would alert the team members to an area where creative problem solving would be particularly important later in the process and make it possible for the team members to do a better job of guiding the discussion of issues relating to this difference.

Your collaborative lawyers will include these statements of principles and values in the minutes of the four-way meeting and will refer back to them at times of impasse or difficulties in negotiations, asking each of you to reflect on the degree to which recent efforts are or are not likely to bring you closer to the kind of divorce you described as what you most hoped for. They will form a touchstone for both the quality of your divorce process and the quality of proposed scenarios for resolution.

With coaches on your team, it is they who will do much of the "inner realm" information gathering, but collaborative lawyers will consistently encourage you to clarify and express this information at the legal four-way table and to explore it further with your coaches. How this is accomplished varies from couple to couple. What is always the same is that collaborative lawyers begin their work with you by gathering and focusing on the facts, both inner and outer, that are important for all to understand before good solutions can emerge.

UNDERSTANDING NEGOTIATIONS, UNDERSTANDING THE LAW

As well as helping you gather, clarify, and present essential information, your lawyers also will educate you. You and your spouse are the source of the information that you and your team need to have about outer- and inner-world facts, but your lawyers are responsible for providing certain other information that you'll also need to understand before you and your partner can move to the next phases of the collaborative legal process: developing options and reaching resolution. The lawyers' job description includes informing you about the law and teaching you about negotiating and conflict resolution—the techniques and methods you'll be using to move from information to solutions.

Before making any decisions, you and your spouse will learn more about certain legal concepts in your state and elsewhere. Your lawyers will help clarify what the law is and is not, so that you and your partner can carefully decide for yourselves the degree to which you do or do not want to rely upon it as a template for solutions. Good collaborative lawyers put the law into perspective as one tool for resolving disputes rather than treating it as the frame within which all negotiations and solutions must fit.

We all know that criminal law embodies deep principles about right and wrong, good and evil. "Thou shalt not kill" is a moral imperative that holds true in Kansas and Kenya, Boston and Beijing, and many couples mistakenly believe that the divorce law prescribed by the state legislature and dispensed at the courthouse is of the same order as "Thou shalt not kill." At the same time, as you saw in chapter 1, it's common for people to leave their marriages with a sense of shame and failure and a powerful need to lay blame. From watching TV dramas, many people mistakenly think that in court, judges will listen to the whole story and use the laws to award the stamp of approval that says "It wasn't your fault. You're the good person."

But nowadays, divorce law rarely addresses what's "right." It simply gets two people to a resolution. It might surprise you to learn that judges often dislike dealing with divorces because emotions run so strong and the law can do so little to help about what often matters most. Courts can't make a good parent out of a mediocre one. Courts can't fix hurt feelings or the sense of being wronged. Divorce laws for the most part address quantifiable questions such as "Who will pay how much to whom, and for what length of time?" and "How much time will the children spend with each parent, on what schedule?"

Judges are human beings. Because we don't want their personal biases to produce arbitrary results from one courthouse to the next and one family to the next, the family law code of your state aims to make sure all judges apply the same rules to answer those questions. But the specific rules in San Francisco may be very different from the rules in Boston, Miami, New York, or Vancouver—even for families with identical finances and similar issues. The family courts dispense predictability and consistency, not blame and exoneration, and provide a crude kind of dispute resolution that usually keeps divorcing couples from shooting each other. You need to know what the laws are in your state about matters you and your partner will be resolving, because that's part of achieving fully informed agreement to the terms of settlement you reach. But if you understand what the law is—and is not—you will see that there is no need for you and your spouse to be bound by it in the way in which a judge must be bound.

Experienced family lawyers know that any couple with good will and determination, working with skilled professionals, can usually do at least as well as—and often far better than—even the best judge to arrive at solutions that match the unique needs of their own situation. The law of your state is only one strand of information, and often not the most important one. Your collaborative lawyers will probably recommend that you put it aside once you understand it. You can use it as your "default" setting, something you can fall back on in negotiations if you and your partner can't come up with something more customized. But if you are like most couples, you probably can. Helping you understand why it may not be in anyone's interests to automatically make the law the main factor in how a settlement takes shape is part of the information your collaborative lawyers will provide.

Other kinds of real-world information your lawyers will provide include

- The procedural laws and rules for how to accomplish a divorce in your state
- The steps and stages in a collaborative legal process
- The way in which interest-based negotiation works and what role you, your partner, the lawyers, and the other team members will play in that process

The lawyers will work closely with each of you every step of the way, from gathering information at the start to finding solutions at the end. In the information-gathering phase of the work, your lawyer will help you

- Clarify your thinking and understanding
- Express your values, concerns, and priorities
- Ask and answer questions
- Organize and prioritize
- Prepare for meetings

- Complete homework assignments (outer-world assignments, such as locating documents, doing research about neighborhoods, schools, or jobs, and planning for reentry into the workforce; inner-world assignments, such as envisioning personal goals for the future)
- Recognize what has gone well in four-way meetings and what could be improved
- Decide whether other professional help is needed—whether from other team members or from expert consultants

The lawyers coordinate all information as it comes in and help you make sure that every question is answered through work with the most appropriate member of your team. They help you weigh the significance of various strands of information as you gradually identify goals and priorities for settlement.

GATHERING AND EXCHANGING INFORMATION WITH THE HELP OF YOUR FINANCIAL CONSULTANT

During the first or second four-way meeting, the lawyers may (depending on the complexity of the financial situation) refer you and your partner to a collaborative financial consultant to begin gathering and analyzing financial documents that will give a clear picture of your true financial history and current situation. Accurate, reliable, updated financial information must be gathered and shared and uncertainties and questions about finances must be fully addressed before you and your collaborative lawyers can begin to develop possible options for settlement. Divorce isn't easy, but most couples really do want to reach a financial settlement that is workable for both spouses. Once the facts are clear, seldom does either spouse insist on a scenario that is obviously unbalanced, unreasonable, or impractical.

Consequently, in collaborative divorces couples don't waste time arguing about basic financial facts that can be clarified by getting more and better data. And when challenges about finances do arise, the understandings that couples reach as they communicate about the "inner estate" tend to minimize any tendency on the part of either partner to be extremely selfish or unreasonable. Instead, the financial challenges in a collaborative divorce, when they arise, most often reflect real-world problems, such as

- Money that was barely sufficient to maintain the family under one roof cannot stretch far enough to sustain the same standard of living for two households
- Income is variable or cyclical rather than regular
- The spouses disagree about whether and how long one or both of them should be with the children rather than employed outside the home

These problems can sometimes be challenging to solve. However, it is much easier to consider solutions when everyone sees the facts accurately and when everyone understands both spouses' genuine needs and priorities. Helping you understand the financial facts accurately is the realm of the financial consultant.

USEFUL FINANCIAL INFORMATION

Your collaborative financial consultant, who is a neutral member of the team, will help you and your spouse organize your data about assets, debts, income, and expenses in a way that is most useful to the lawyers. This financial advisor can work with you and your collaborative divorce lawyers to devise ways of addressing short-term money and budgeting issues during the early months of separation and divorce that grow out of an understanding of your own specific needs and priorities rather than simply applying a standard formula, as a judge often must. (Of course, the formulas are always there to fall back upon if you and your spouse decide you prefer doing so to devising your own solution.)

The financial consultant is also able to address certain disparities in financial understanding. Does your spouse understand the income, asset, debt, and tax picture much better than you do? The collaborative financial consultant will help you, the less knowledgeable spouse, get up to speed on financial matters, teaching you what you need to know to understand your current finances and prepare yourself to manage money on your own, both now and after the divorce. If you are the more knowledgeable spouse, accustomed to managing all the family finances, your concerns may be allayed when you know that the collaborative financial consultant is helping your spouse learn how to manage money better.

Both of you will benefit from looking at the same financial documents, discussing questions, sorting out confusion, and removing suspicion in face-to-face meetings rather than having all information filtered through the voices of old-style legal advocates communicating about these matters in your absence. In addition, the collaborative financial consultant will help you and your collaborative lawyers take into account tax and other considerations that can help conserve your family's resources. While many family lawyers do understand these matters and can negotiate skillfully with one another about them, it is an entirely different task to help a couple understand and communicate accurately with each other about these matters—a skill that old-style divorce lawyers have no particular motivation to develop.

THE FINANCIAL CONSULTANT'S LONG-TERM ROLE

Later in the process, once the basic financial information-gathering work is done, the collaborative financial consultant may work closely with you and your lawyers to help you develop alternative scenarios for dividing and, if possible, enhancing the value of your assets. During the brainstorming and options development phase of the legal negotiating process, your collaborative financial consultant can provide detailed projections for the long-term economic consequences of various settlement scenarios. This can be very helpful in deciding how to divide

What If My Partner Hides Money?

Particularly if a marriage ended with one spouse's concealment of his or her involvement with another person, the other spouse may fear that the partner will lie about everything, even money. This is a common concern at the start of many divorces. If you are convinced that your partner is fundamentally dishonest—the kind of person who commits tax fraud, for instance—collaborative divorce is not for you.

But the fact is that lies about love affairs have no particular connection to concealment of money. Family law specialists know that fears about hidden assets are frequently expressed but infrequently validated, even after the most aggressive and costly audits. Your collaborative financial consultant can help you answer many common questions about where the money has gone. If yours is one of the rare cases where unanswered questions remain, your choices will include the option to leave the collaborative process and embark on forensic accounting to search aggressively for what is unaccounted for. Since in collaborative divorce your fears are tested in light of the facts, you'll take that step only if you learn that you need to, not because you are frightened and in the dark.

property, allocate income, and, if necessary, create inventive solutions to meet the financial needs of your children. Your collaborative financial consultant can help you avoid asset management errors that in the long term may cost your family money. Alternative ways of dividing even a small estate can sometimes make big differences in savings for the entire family. All this is information that enriches the eventual discussion of potential solutions.

And remember: what seems financially workable today may not be affordable just a few years from now. One tool most financial consultants can bring to settlement discussions is the ability to project the long-term consequences of various asset and income division ideas far into the future. These projections can demonstrate graphically whether it is or is not financially viable, for instance, for a homemaker spouse to hold on to an expensive family residence or whether there will be sufficient funds for both parties to remain in a community after a wage earner retires. This is why including a collaborative financial consultant as part of your collaborative divorce team can be so helpful in devising workable solutions that can last.

A WORD ABOUT TIMING

During divorce, it's common for couples to experience problems associated with timing differences. One of you may be far along the way to recovery from the loss of the marriage and feel that things are moving along much too slowly, while the other may still be in shock, unready to accept that the divorce is even happening, and barely at the first step of the five-step grieving process outlined in chapter 1. In addition, one or both of you will probably experience occasional episodes of the strong feelings and impaired thinking you also learned about in that chapter—episodes that can be recognized and managed with the help of your collaborative divorce team instead of pulling you down into impasse and battle.

All your team members—including your collaborative lawyers—will understand and follow a single road map through your divorce process, and at the same time they will help you recognize when it's necessary to leave the interstate highway for a while to take a break at a rest stop or travel an alternate route for a few miles. If one of you has an impatient day and demands to know why the divorce isn't over yet, the collaborative lawyer won't automatically jump in and try to make things move faster. If one of you is pushing for a particular issue to be resolved before the groundwork has been completed, the collaborative lawyer won't automatically jump in and try to change the next meeting's agenda. Instead, the focus will be on following an orderly, proven process that starts with gathering information, building consensus, expanding options, and only then moves to solutions—at a speed each of you can handle.

In short, a collaborative divorce team doesn't just give good advice, teach skills, and help you negotiate agreements. Your professional helpers are skilled "process managers." In a time of confusion and change, you can count on a clear divorce process that follows an orderly sequence.

MOVING FORWARD

If you begin your collaborative divorce work with the lawyers, you may spend time gathering information with them and perhaps also with a collaborative financial consultant. When the time is right, you'll shift your attention to work with other members of your team. Some couples will work with all team members simultaneously, while others will spend time first with one professional helper and then with another, depending on which subjects need attention in which order.

The important thing to remember is that when it comes to the collaborative divorce process, you have many choices, including choosing the order in which you will work with your team. In this way, a collaborative team resembles a jazz ensemble. The music that skilled jazz artists make cannot be scripted in advance. Each musician responds in the moment to every other musician, while working within basic shared ground rules and understandings about who will do what, when, and within what framework—the instruments, the key signature, the tempo. Sometimes everyone plays at the same time, and sometimes there are solos or duets. What becomes possible for a jazz combo is music of a different order from what any one of its members could make alone—yet it cannot happen at all without the specific contribution of each musician. In the next chapter you'll learn about working with the other potential members of your collaborative divorce team: the coaches and the child specialist.

AN OLDER COUPLE WORKS EFFICIENTLY WITH A SMALL COLLABORATIVE DIVORCE TEAM: RONALD AND MARTINE'S STORY

Ronald and Martine were married for six years before their marriage came to an end. This was a second marriage for Ronald, who was sixty-eight at the time they separated, and a third for Martine, who was seventy-three. Martine had inherited considerable wealth from her parents; Ron had only modest means.

Martine's son, a New York lawyer, had urged her to have Ronald sign a prenuptial agreement prior to the wedding. Her son had written up a very stringent agreement, and Ronald had signed it shortly before the wedding without paying much attention to its terms.

Ron left his employment a few years before retirement age to move where Martine lived and was not able to find work in his field in the small city near Martine's ranch. Martine was happy for Ron to take early retirement and happy to bear the lion's share of the expenses for their comfortable lifestyle, which included plenty of travel and entertainment. But their marriage was stormy, and over time they both realized that neither of them had sufficient motivation to make the kinds of changes that would have made it possible for them to be content together.

After Ronald and Martine both agreed that the marriage was over, Martine consulted with an aggressive divorce lawyer recommended by her son, but was repelled by the advice she received. She suggested, and Ronald agreed, that they should work with collaborative lawyers and attempt to end their marriage with dignity. Ronald consulted with Anthony, an experienced collaborative lawyer, and Martine retained Stephanie, a trusted colleague of Anthony's in the collaborative family law community.

It soon emerged that Ronald had made a series of highly risky investments in the early years of the marriage and had lost most of his retirement savings when the value of those investments fell. He explained that he had felt secure enough because of Martine's considerable wealth to make speculative investments, hoping to increase his own net worth over time, so that he could afford to buy her expensive gifts of the kind she often gave to him and so that he could pay for some of their travel and other lifestyle expenses instead of relying solely on his wife's money. Paradoxically, his desire to pay more of his own way had left him with not nearly enough retirement savings to support himself above the poverty level after he and Martine separated. Worse yet, he had run up more than $80,000 in credit card debt. Ronald was frightened and angry when he reviewed with his lawyer the terms of the prenuptial agreement he had signed. If the agreement were enforced as written, Ronald would have little more than his modest Social Security check to live on, while if it were set aside, Martine would probably be obliged to support Ronald after their divorce.

Early in the collaborative process, it became clear with the help of the collaborative lawyers that Martine was uncomfortable with and even somewhat embarrassed by the prenuptial agreement she had asked Ronald to sign. She understood from the advice of the aggressive litigator that it was possible she could end the marriage with no financial obligations at all toward Ronald, but she also understood from the legal discussion presented by both collaborative lawyers at the second four-way meeting that the prenuptial agreement might be set aside by a judge for a variety of reasons, should either of them decide to go to court. And regardless of whether it was or was not enforceable, Martine had no desire to see Ronald live in poverty. Ronald, for his part, had no wish to live as luxuriously as he had with Martine, but he also did not want to worry about whether he could pay for rent, food, or medicines. At the same time, he did not want to make demands or engage in back-and-forth haggling about specific line items in a budget. This seemed to him undignified and humiliating.

It was soon agreed, at the second legal four-way meeting, that the best next step for Ronald and Martine would be to work with a neutral financial consultant to develop a budget for Ronald. With the help of a financial consultant, both Martine and Ronald could focus their efforts on figuring out together what it actually would cost for Ronald to live in their community modestly but comfortably. Their consultant could also work with Ronald to see what he could hope to earn from the remains of his retirement funds if he invested more conservatively.

Ronald, Martine, and the two collaborative lawyers also discussed whether or not to bring coaches onto the collaborative divorce team. Martine and Ronald were in agreement: they did not wish to do so. Both of them felt that their marriage had been short, their communication was poor, and neither of them had the energy or motivation to improve the situation. They preferred to work as efficiently as they could with their financial consultant and to come back to the collaborative legal table as soon as they were ready, to see whether they could negotiate satisfactory settlement terms that would leave each of them feeling that they had ended their marriage appropriately.

For Ronald, a good collaborative divorce meant expressing his needs clearly and respectfully and having them treated with respect. For Martine, a good divorce meant putting behind them the toxic effects of an overreaching prenuptial agreement and being able to feel that Ronald had not been harmed economically by having married her. Both of them placed a high value on keeping their divorce private and civilized, as they traveled in the same small social circle and did not want to embarrass each other or cause their friends to have to take sides.

Ronald and Martine met twice with their neutral financial consultant, Elaine. Elaine's draft budgets were reviewed by Anthony and Stephanie, who each asked Elaine to clarify a few points and to ensure that certain cost and income projections were accurate. When everyone was satisfied with the draft budgets and income projections, Ronald and Martine gathered with Anthony and Stephanie at Stephanie's office for a third legal four-way meeting to brainstorm ways acceptable to Martine of ensuring that Ronald's financial needs were met. Elaine attended the meeting as well, transforming it into a "five-way" meeting. Ronald was particularly interested in paying off his consumer debt and finding ways of guaranteeing his basic living expenses, while not depriving Martine's son of capital that could remain part of his mother's estate. Elaine was able to help generate a range of possibilities, including the purchase of an annuity, a lifetime lease of an apartment that would continue to be owned by Martine, and similar concepts, and was able to give immediate advice about the tax implications for each of them of various options under consideration.

Ronald and Martine were highly motivated to find a solution and by the close of that third meeting worked out terms they both found acceptable. They were both relieved to be done with negotiating the financial terms of the divorce and to have achieved satisfactory resolution quickly, so that Ronald could move out of Martine's ranch and begin to establish a home and life of his own. The two lawyers prepared a settlement agreement and the necessary divorce papers, as well as the documents needed to implement the financial provisions of the settlement. At a final four-way meeting at Anthony's office, everyone signed the papers, and Ronald and Martine politely, though sadly, thanked each other for having been so considerate during the collaborative process. Although both were regretful and disappointed by their inability to make a success of their marriage, both felt that their goals and objectives had been met—and met well—through working with the collaborative team that fit their needs.

5

GATHERING INFORMATION:
A Look at the Role of the Coaches
and Child Specialist

If we don't stand up for children, then we don't stand for much.
—MARIAN WRIGHT EDELMAN

Not all couples begin the information-gathering work of their divorce with collaborative lawyers. Another option is to start with your coaches, especially if you feel too overwhelmed with emotion at first to do the clear thinking that the legal process requires. After all, the hardest part of a divorce can be learning to handle the intense emotions that so often accompany it. These emotions get in the way of clear thinking and fuel ongoing conflict, adding to the difficulty of communicating with your spouse about issues important to both of you. Because communication difficulties often contribute to a decision to divorce, it's common for couples to have trouble hearing each other clearly enough during divorce to discover potential good solutions, unless both partners take time to learn how to communicate in a clear, respectful, constructive, businesslike manner. Though improving communication is a good idea for any couple, it's in a sense optional for those without children. But where parents want the best for their children during and after the divorce, they *must* learn how to communicate clearly with each other—better than they did at the end of their marriage—for many years to come.

All of this work falls into the realm of collaborative divorce coaching, making it a useful place for some couples to begin. The tasks you'll undertake with your coaches could not be more important. Yet some divorcing individuals find the concept of collaborative divorce coaching unfamiliar or may even have reservations about it if they mistakenly consider it a kind of psychotherapy. Psychotherapy has its place in divorce, but collaborative divorce coaching is very different from psychotherapy or counseling. The coaching process is very focused, and though the work can be hard, it follows a clear structure that makes it extremely efficient and cost-effective. Because it focuses specifically on divorce-related tasks, most people accomplish the work of coaching more quickly than they would have imagined.

WORKING WITH COACHES

When you work with coaches, emotionally charged issues can be aired in the safety of coaching four-way meetings so that they are far less charged in subsequent meetings with the lawyers. While you may talk about issues that have to do with your legal negotiations in the coaching four-way meetings, the coaches do not function as mediators of legal issues (though they do help parents to devise parenting plans that then go to the lawyers for comment, approval, and incorporation into the ultimate settlement agreement). The purpose of the conversations with coaches is not to find solutions to legal issues but rather to help you address with your partner in constructive ways the emotional complexities that can interfere with clear thinking throughout the collaborative divorce process, particularly at the legal table. Your coaches will use their skills to help you and your partner learn both sides of effective communications—expressing yourselves clearly and listening deeply—so that when you are ready to consider options for resolution, both of you will be able to express yourselves more effectively, listen better, think more clearly, and be in a position to make the best decisions you are capable of.

During their work with you, your coaches—with your permission—will be sharing information as needed with other members of your team: your child specialist, your lawyers, and your financial consultant. This helps everyone on your team to be more effective in his or her work by giving each of them a better understanding of you, your family, your issues, and concerns. Your coaches can help you, your partner, and your other professional team members identify the needs, wants, issues, and conflicts that must be addressed not only in your parenting plan but also in the legal negotiations that will lead to a final framework for resolution.

When the coaches are the first team members you and your spouse meet with, they may work with you and your partner for a short time before you commence four-way meetings with the collaborative lawyers. You and your partner will agree on how to sequence the work with the coaches and with the lawyers—whether the legal process should slow down to permit more coaching or whether the coaching and legal work can proceed in tandem. The sequence varies from couple to couple. How much time in all will be needed with the coaches, in both individual and four-way coaching meetings, also varies from couple to couple. Typically, each partner may have three to five private meetings with his or her respective coach before gathering in coaching four-way meetings. (The timeline of a representative collaborative divorce case in Appendix B will give you a clearer picture of how much time one fairly typical couple spent in coaching sessions at various times during their collaborative divorce—but your divorce may be different from theirs.)

Your coaches will want you and your spouse to retain collaborative lawyers as soon as possible even if you don't have a legal four-way meeting for a while. Ethical collaborative divorce coaches won't let the coaching process continue for long without the assurance that your collaborative lawyers are signed onto the team and available to advise you when needed. You should expect your participation agreement with your coaches to specify that both you and your spouse need to retain collaborative lawyers before the coaching can move forward. This is an important protection for you and your spouse. The last thing you want is for either of you to run impulsively into the arms of an aggressive old-style divorce litigator on a particularly difficult day, when good collaborative lawyers could have worked with you and your coaches to help you regain perspective and continue on the path toward your best divorce.

It is especially helpful to start with coaches rather than collaborative lawyers if you and or your partner are in an emotional crisis at the start of your divorce. The coaches will listen to each partner's story of the divorce and help each of you gain more perspective so that you can begin to think more clearly. If you have children, they will help you focus on their needs by involving a child specialist whose participation will reassure your children and enrich your decision making about parenting. Your conflict and anger are very stressful for your children, yet in the midst of your own intense feelings and concerns, it is easy to overlook how your children are being affected by the divorce. For this reason, your coaches will usually advise involving the child specialist early in your divorce process, to prevent avoidable harm to your children.

A CLOSER LOOK AT HOW COACHING WORKS: DEVELOPING INFORMATION, BUILDING NEW SKILLS

Once you and your spouse have selected and retained your coaches, you'll each meet several times privately with your own coach, to clarify concerns and priorities, to develop new communication skills, and to build sufficient trust in your coach so that you are ready for the coaching four-way meetings.

Your coaches may ask you to fill out information sheets to give them important information about your marriage and your children.

Many coaches will do this during the first meeting with a new client, so that by the second meeting you and your spouse may each be ready to discuss with your respective coaches how they can best help you move through your divorce. Your coaches will ask you about your goals, both present and future. Your coaches will ask you to talk about issues that you may need to discuss in a structured way with your partner. As you present this information, your coach will begin to teach you new ways to talk about the issues that are most important to you so that your partner may be able to hear you better. Gradually, your coach will help you practice the hardest work of all: listening to and understanding what your partner is saying to you.

Often, your coach will ask you to talk about your marriage and your marital partner using questions such as these:

- What has your marriage been like in recent years?
- What has brought you to the point of divorce?
- What are the ways in which you have handled differences and disagreements during your marriage? What worked? What didn't?

There is no point in simply repeating old strategies for problem solving that have failed to work for you and your partner. Identifying them helps you avoid frustrating wheel spinning and the repetition of familiar old arguments, both during and after your divorce. You can't change your partner, but, with your coach's help, you may be able to see your own contribution to a destructive pattern, and with that information, you can choose to change your own behavior. Of course, your spouse will be learning the same perspectives with his or her coach. This work alone can have a dramatically positive impact on problem-solving communications.

Your coaches won't focus only on the difficulties. There is value in regaining a more balanced perspective about what was good as well as what was bad in the marriage that is ending because your memory of your marriage will be a permanent part of your internal life history. It can be difficult to recall the good times as a marriage comes to an end,

but an emotionally skewed recollection that includes only the negative is a false life history that will impede your own recovery from the
divorce crisis and your ability to move forward constructively with
your life. Your coach will help you recall what is worth remembering.
Coaches will also encourage you to think about your own future and
dream a little about what kind of life you want for yourself. The dramatic changes in your life that occur when a marriage ends actually
open up a great opportunity for positive change, if you're willing to do
some dreaming and planning.

Your coach may then focus more specifically on improving communications, with questions such as these:

- How well do you think you and your partner are pres-
  ently communicating about important divorce issues?
- What particular aspects of interactions with your partner would you like to change as you address divorce decision making?

Most people faced with ending an intimate relationship have
problems communicating. Even when they manage to talk to each
other in a rational, contained way, it can still be challenging to arrive at
mutually acceptable decisions. That's because during marriage or any
intimate relationship, couples devise ways to communicate about difficult problems that ordinarily depend on intimacy to work well, while
conversations about divorce take place at a time when the emotional
task is to separate—to give up intimacy. Divorcing couples need, but
rarely have available on their own, new ways of solving problems associated with divorce—matters such as dividing assets or parenting children—that do not require intimacy in order to reach resolution. That
is why even the best-intentioned efforts to solve problems at the time
of separation and divorce can so readily end in outbursts of anger and
tears. These conversations are painful because they cause both partners
to come up forcefully against the reality that their intimate connection
is ending. Coaching helps divorcing partners learn ways to resolve
problems together that are businesslike and detached. Practicing this

kind of nonintimate problem solving in coaching makes it possible to do it at the collaborative legal table and—even more important—after the divorce is over and life moves on.

This kind of businesslike communication in the service of making decisions and resolving problems is particularly important for couples with children, who will need to confer about them in order to be good parents during and long after the legal divorce. Parenting is never easy, even for couples who live together. It requires clarity, coordination, and consistency. Sorting out what really matters from what you can let go is a skill you'll learn in coaching that will stand you in particularly good stead not only with your ex-spouse but also with your children when they become teenagers.

IN COACHING, YOU'LL LEARN LIFE SKILLS THAT YOU'LL USE ALL YOUR LIFE

As you work with your coaches on the information-gathering and value clarification process, you will be cultivating new tools that most couples find to be of great value during and after the collaborative divorce process. When you work with the divorce coaches, you and your spouse (separately and together) will receive skilled help in

- Becoming aware of and managing your strongest emotions
- Learning to separate thoughts from feelings
- Thinking through highly charged issues
- Learning ways to talk to each other about difficult problems in a businesslike manner
- Setting short- and long-term goals for yourself, your children, and your coparenting relationship

During these sessions, you will learn techniques that are very effective for managing the inevitable conflicts with your partner—

conflicts that may continue to arise long after the divorce decree has been entered. If your intense feelings about the divorce—and the persistent bad habits and difficult patterns of communications with your ex—are not addressed now, they certainly won't go away just because you have a divorce decree. As the saying goes, "If you keep on doing what you've been doing, you'll keep on getting what you've been getting."

At times of crisis (and divorce surely qualifies as a crisis for most of us), we human beings are generally far more open to change than when life is moving along predictably in well-worn channels. For that reason, we are not being naïve or falsely optimistic when we emphasize in collaborative divorce that with the help of the coaches, you have nothing to lose and everything to gain by considering this difficult passage as an opportunity to learn how to make changes that can substantially improve your life after the divorce.

As the philosopher Friedrich Nietzsche observed, "What does not kill me makes me stronger." By choosing to focus on the positive possibilities of this sometimes unwelcome and always challenging life transition, you are very likely to improve the prospects for yourself and your children long after the divorce is over and life moves on. Your coaches will help you keep your focus on positive outcomes—how to plan for them and how to make them real as life moves on.

HOW COACHES WORK WHEN CHILDREN ARE INVOLVED

Coaches teach you techniques to help yourself reduce conflict and stress, so that you can be more available to your children. The coaches will also help you and your spouse plan how and when to talk with your children about the divorce, as we'll explore more fully later in this chapter.

If you have already separated, the coaches will ask about the children's understanding of what's happening and how you are arranging for them to have time with both of you in an age-appropriate manner. If you have no shared parenting schedule, the coaches will help you work out a temporary arrangement under which each of you have parenting time. (Later, with the help of the child specialist, you and your coaches will develop a better-thought-out plan that ultimately will become part of your divorce settlement agreement.) Taking the time to do a good job with a temporary parenting arrangement is vital. Children become quite distressed if a parent simply disappears from their daily lives without an explanation that makes sense. This is an extremely stressful time for your children, and all too often they don't know what is going to happen to them. They may fear the worst. Children need to know that there is a plan for them, and for regular contact with both parents, that they can rely on—and parents need to ensure that the plan is honored consistently. Finding ways to help you address these immediate needs in the best way you and your partner can manage is the work of the coaches.

After ensuring that your children's immediate needs for information, stability, and contact with both of you have been addressed, your coaches will help you plan constructively for shared parenting after separation so that you and your partner can ensure that the divorce goes as smoothly as possible for your children. Divorce is always a cataclysmic event for children, no matter how well it is managed—but you have the ability, working with your team, to help your children weather this period of rapid change as constructively as possible. Without this kind of help, many well-meaning parents simply have no way of understanding their children's experience of the divorce. Other parents hope that if a child is not complaining, not depressed, and not doing badly in school, everything is fine—unlikely as that actually is. Many parents who use other settlement modes that do not include coaches and child specialists mistakenly assume that arriving at a deal about time-sharing that both parents can live with is the same as doing the best they can for their children. The price for these well-intentioned but shortsighted ways of thinking about children in divorce is paid primarily by the children themselves. The work of the coaches is to help you and your partner do better than that for your children—much better.

TALKING TO CHILDREN ABOUT DIVORCE

Helping parents talk with their children about divorce is one of the earliest and highest priorities in the coaching process. Telling your children their parents are getting divorced is a conversation most parents dread, and some put it off for as long as possible. This is understandable, as it is often hard to find the right words, and if you are very angry or upset and don't want to say the wrong thing, keeping quiet may seem like the best solution. Your coaches will help both of you understand why this is a mistake: children are like sponges, and they pick up emotional information even before they can talk. Chances are they already know more than you imagine about your marital breakdown and may have made up stories to help them understand what is happening that can be much worse than the truth.

Almost all children know something about divorce, much of it wrong and a good deal of it pretty scary. Children may jump to the conclusion that they will have the same bad experiences they have heard about from friends or seen in the movies or on TV. In other words, they are not immune from the myth that divorce necessarily means war. If you can tell them together that you plan to divorce in a noncombative, collaborative way (without fighting), it helps them to see that you will both still be acting as good parents for them.

Coaches can be invaluable in helping parents speak with their children appropriately about divorce. For example, if you are the one who wants the divorce while your partner does not, it's quite natural to feel defensive and it can be difficult to keep that defensiveness from seeping into what you express to the children. Or if you don't want the divorce, it can be very difficult to separate your own sadness or feelings of betrayal from what your children feel and perilously tempting to enlist them as allies and try to bid for their loyalty—without even seeing that this is happening. Some parents carry a desire for honesty to inadvertently destructive extremes, telling children far more about the breach between the parents than they can understand or should be burdened with. Others, in the guise of giving their children a voice in what happens, insist that their children make choices and decisions that place them squarely between their parents and cause painful feelings of divided loyalty and betrayal. Your coaches will help you and your partner sort all this out and learn effective ways of talking honestly and appropriately with your children in ways that protect them and help them feel well cared for.

In the exercises section at the end of this book, you will find materials that will give you a better idea of how coaches help parents learn to talk with their children about divorce. If your own divorce is moving more rapidly than your ability to mobilize a collaborative divorce team and it becomes necessary to speak with your children about a separation before you and your partner have coaches to help you do it well, these exercises can help you avoid some obvious pitfalls and errors.

If you and your spouse have already decided on a collaborative divorce but haven't yet begun the process, you can still tell your children that both of you are committed to moving through this change in the least painful way possible. You can explain in ways that your children can understand that you will have plenty of help to solve problems and make decisions in the best possible way. You can tell them you will have coaches to help you when you are sad or mad and lawyers who promise they will only help solve problems and never encourage people to fight. You can assure them that they, too, will be part of the process and will have a person to talk with, since the divorce is going to change their lives, too. This person, who has helped many other children through divorces, will be like a coach for them who can talk with them about divorce problems and figure out solutions.

Getting into the collaborative divorce process quickly is important if your children are already having to adjust to a marital separation. Children need to know that they will not be asked to choose between parents and that they will have a part in the decision making about their lives. All children are deeply affected by divorce. Knowing that their ideas and concerns will be considered gives children greater self-esteem, as it sends the message that they are people whose opinions matter. There is no better way to make such assurances concrete and real for your children than offering them the opportunity to work with a child specialist.

With your team's help, both you and your spouse will be able to send consistent, reassuring messages to your children that their parents are in charge of the situation and are working together to solve divorce problems even if they don't yet have all the answers. Don't make promises about what will happen if you don't yet know—and at this early stage of the divorce you may well not know. Children are better off not being given false assurances. They can tolerate the unknown as long as they know that their parents are working to create a plan. Above all, parents need to talk to their children in constructive ways that tell the truth and avoid blame and judgment of the other parent—not just once, but repeatedly. Even if your first conversations with your children must take place before you and your spouse commence work with your collaborative divorce team, you will have ample opportunity to rehearse with your coaches what will surely be ongoing conversations with your children, so that you can save them needless anxiety about their futures.

COACHES BRING INFORMATION AS WELL AS GATHERING INFORMATION ABOUT PARENTING

Your coaches will not only gather important information about how your children are doing and how well shared parenting is working; they will also give you and your partner important information you'll need in order to reach good decisions about parenting after the divorce. Recognizing that differences in parenting styles and values can actually benefit children is extremely helpful during the stress of divorce, helping a couple appreciate why it is so important for both parents to remain in frequent, continuing contact with their children.

For example, one parent may be more emotionally sensitive to the child, while the other may provide tough love when it is needed. One parent may be action-oriented while the other may be more reflective. Children need different things at different times. In studies of parents, it was found that fathers tended to challenge children to push beyond their zone of comfort, while mothers tended to be more protective. In old-style adversarial divorces, such differences become the breeding ground for custody battles in which parents accuse each other of insufficiency, but in collaborative divorce your coaches will help you appreciate that two parents provide a valuable balance. They will work to help each of you be the best parent you can be, by clarifying the role that each of you played with the children during the marriage and identifying ways to strengthen what each of you can offer as a parent after your divorce, when both parents won't be available to the children on a daily basis.

GATHERING INNER-WORLD INFORMATION WITH YOUR COACHES

Like all collaborative divorce professionals, your coaches focus not just on the past and the immediate present. They put great emphasis on planning for the future, and good future planning in a divorce requires communicating a great deal of accurate information about goals, hopes, values, concerns, priorities, and fears. Toward that end, the coaches will ask you to think about questions like these:

- What do you think is most important for your children as you move forward?
- What are your highest hopes for your children as they grow up?
- What are your highest hopes and goals for your own relationship with your children after your divorce?
- What kind of coparenting relationship do you think would be best for your children after the divorce?
- What do you want for yourself in the future?

- What are your goals for your relationship with your soon-to-be ex-spouse after your divorce?
- Who are the friends and extended family members who matter to you, and what can you do now to ensure that your goals for your continuing relationship with them are realized?

Questions like these are at the heart of the divorce-planning process when you select collaborative divorce, though they never appear on the agenda at all in an old-style divorce. They are questions about the "inner estate." Developing this kind of information early in the collaborative divorce process builds a strong foundation for making good decisions later in the process. Couples are often amazed to find the degree to which their values and aspirations, for themselves and for their children, mirror each other's. Seeing this makes most couples feel more confident that it will be possible to arrive at consensus and agreement, even on issues where differences exist.

INNER-WORLD GOALS AND THE MISSION STATEMENT

Early in the coaching process, your coaches will encourage you and your partner to create a joint "mission statement." Whether or not you and your spouse have children, your joint mission statement will reflect the values and principles that will guide you to end your relationship with integrity and dignity and with a focus on the future. The process of creating it has two parts: writing the mission statement of what the couple wants, then listing some specific actions to help them achieve it. This joint statement is similar in purpose to the individual statements you'll bring to the legal four-way table. If you started out your divorce with the collaborative lawyers, your joint mission statement in the coaching process can be an elaboration of what each of you may have already brought forward as individual statements of your highest intentions at the legal four-way table.

Many couples find a surprising degree of congruence between

their values, goals, hopes, and dreams for the future as they create the coaching mission statement. It is used actively in later stages of the divorce process, to help measure both behavior and outcomes against the values and principles that the mission statement sets forth.

MISSION STATEMENTS INVOLVING CHILDREN AND PARENTING

The joint mission statement makes broad affirmations about your wishes and dreams for yourselves and your children. You can't achieve what you have not thought about, so this is the best time to use your imagination to create an image of your future that would include your own fulfillment and happiness and a constructive and supportive relationship with your former partner as parents of your children. Parents who live apart still can be good parents, but it requires planning. This future-focused planning and dreaming of new opportunities in your life is the hallmark of the new-style divorce and will be a key part of your recovery process. It is a big part of developing both your mission as parents and your overall mission for yourself.

Although the mission statement is very personal and individualized, couples with children often include statements such as these:

- We want to provide our children with loving support and the structure they need to grow and develop
- We want our children to have the opportunity for a good education and as many options for developing their talents as we are able to provide
- We value and respect our children's individuality and their wishes and desires, and we want their voices and views considered as we plan for the future
- We want our children to have warm relationships with their grandparents, aunts, uncles, and cousins on both sides of the family and intend to make it a priority that this happens

- We want to share with our grown children the major life passages that happen in all families, and we will act in ways that make our children comfortable with including both of us

Doing what is required to follow through on these best intentions can be challenging, particularly where children are involved. Often, putting the mission statement into practice requires spouses to put the children's needs before the adults'. Coaches help parents see that this is simply the work of good parenting, whether you are together or apart. It is easy to forget during the tensions and stresses of a divorce, when a couple finds reason to differ on many issues, that parents who remain married to each other experience many of the same tensions and stresses as they negotiate about how to raise their children. Of course, intimacy makes it easier and divorce makes it harder, but this is a difference of degree, not of kind. Even good parents who had relatively little difficulty putting the needs of the children first during the marriage may falter now and then during divorce, simply because the situation is so painful. Your coaches will encourage both of you to keep this in mind: the sooner both of you can once again put your children's needs first, the better it will be for your children. The development of a mission statement helps most couples take a very big first step in that direction.

Although the mission statement will contain broad, sweeping statements of principle, most mission statements where children are involved also set forth more specific voluntary undertakings about parental standards of behavior. The statements also usually include at least a few specific steps that a couple agrees to take to start them on the road to implementing those broad principles. Even a few concrete steps in a mission statement help a couple begin to build new habits of collaborative joint parenting. For example, many couples include commitments such as these:

- We will plan in advance so that Isabel can spend her usual summer week with grandparents and cousins

- We will respect any new partner either of us has and support a positive relationship between that person and the twins
- We will take the responsibility of telling each other when we become romantically involved so that neither Joseph nor Teddy has to keep a secret or inform the other about this new person
- Each of us will tell the other before we invite another adult to stay with us overnight when the children are with us

These statements may pertain to all children in the family, or there may be specific statements about specific children, depending on the family circumstances and the differences in the children and their ages.

Composing a joint mission statement with your coaches gives both of you the opportunity to think ahead about events that will challenge you to make good choices about your behavior as you divorce and as you cope with rapid change following the legal divorce. For instance, Aaron and Rita expected that both would probably find a new partner not long after their divorce. Both placed a high value on making sure that new lovers, partners, or spouses would not be seen as enemies by their children or by each other. Their joint mission statement included this shared principle: "We plan to agree beforehand about when, where, and how new people will be introduced into our children's lives so that new relationships do not become a source of conflict for us or our children. We share a commitment to work with the coaches any time we need help with this." As it did for Aaron and Rita, your joint mission statement can help you and your partner clarify what to aim for and what to avoid in joint parenting after the divorce.

As they develop their joint mission statement, many couples recognize the truth that it's difficult—sometimes impossible—to plan well for good parenting after a divorce without also working together on financial and legal strategies for achieving that shared vision. This is another way in which the joint mission statement supports good decision making in a collaborative divorce. It lays a strong foundation for constructive planning about shared economic support that meets your children's needs as you and your partner define those needs. For example, one couple we worked with included this in their mission statement: "We will confer every six months to budget appropriately for agreed-upon extracurricular activities for Rosie."

Devising guiding principles for how you and your partner want to behave in the future will help you make better choices in all aspects of your divorce—choices that protect your children's interests by enhancing the quality of shared decision making between you and your soon-to-be ex-spouse.

MISSION STATEMENTS FOCUSING ON ADULTS

Sharing information about nonmaterial values and goals in order to write a joint mission statement with your coaches has great value for childless couples, too. For example, couples without (as well as with) children may discover in coaching that both partners place high value on

- Behaving well
- Ending the divorce amicably
- Maintaining contact with extended family
- Honoring what was valuable in the years of the marriage
- And even allowing an opportunity to forgive each other for the failure of the marriage

Their mission statements often include provisions such as these:

- We value our connections with each other's extended family and want to sustain those connections for each of us, both now and in the future
- We want each of us to continue to enjoy friendships with the people who have been our shared friendship

network during our marriage, and to act in ways that
support such friendships for each of us
- We want to be able to look back on how we handled
our divorce with a sense of dignity and self-respect
- We want to be able to meet as friends after our divorce

Discovering unexpected areas of agreement about values such as
these, while learning to understand and respect your differences as you
separate, can ease the healing process, helping you rebuild your life
after the divorce with far greater clarity and confidence.

GATHERING AND EXCHANGING INFORMATION
WITH YOUR CHILD SPECIALIST

Divorce is at best a disruptive and disturbing experience for children,
even though it may also be the best or perhaps the only option for the
adults. Children experience great distress during divorce even in cases
where divorce is necessary to protect the safety of the children. Even
children who appear to be managing well during their parents' divorce
are generally going through the most difficult experience of their
lives.

"I'M FINE"

Your child may say he or she is fine, and it may even sound true. After
all, it is tempting for a parent to accept such a statement at face value,
particularly if no obvious difficulties have arisen, because you may
have plenty of pressing problems to attend to as you come to grips
yourself with the changes and challenges of divorce. But think about
it. Are *you* "fine"? Probably not. You're going through one of the most
challenging and confusing experiences of your life—and you're an
adult, with an adult's understanding of the world and an adult's perspective on relationships and emotions.

Collaborative Divorce Provides the Help Children Need During Divorce

Kids need:	Collaborative divorce provides:
More and better information about the divorce than parents can usually provide for them (the typical parent spends only ten minutes explaining the divorce experience to his or her children)	As much support and information for the children as for the adults during and after the divorce, through the coaches and the child specialist
A strong ongoing relationship with both parents and skillful, attentive parenting by both mother and father	Particular emphasis on helping both parents understand the real needs of their children, and coaching them to become the best coparents they can be, during and after the divorce
Financial stability	Wise financial counsel and planning for the future as well as conservation of scarce resources during the divorce itself

Your child, too, is experiencing a confusing, distressing loss and has only a child's understanding and perspective to bring to the situation.

Children have coaches for sports, tutors for academic work, and school counselors for guidance about important educational and life

What Young Children Say About Divorce

You'd be disturbed to learn how divorce looks to children. Here's what some normal, healthy kids told psychologists at the Yale Child Study Center:

What is divorce?
- "Divorce is when Mom and Dad hate each other and your family is dead." (3.4-year-old)
- "It's when someone signs a paper, someone leaves home, and then kids cry." (5-year-old)

What do you know about lawyers?
- "The big problem with lawyers is that they don't help Mom and Dad stay friends, but they take your money. I'll never like them." (4.1-year-old)
- "I talked to one once, and I thought she listened, but she took care of the money, not me." (5.2-year-old)

What suggestions would you give to lawyers and judges?
- "Keep that gray tape for people's mouths in the court hall so they don't say stuff that hurts people's feelings." (2.4-year-old)
- "Don't scare people about not seeing each other anymore. It's too scary to think you can't see your mom or dad anymore. God decides that, not people."(6.4-year-old)

choices. So here are some questions to you as a parent: children are suddenly living in two houses where there was one, with parents suddenly preoccupied by the collapse of the most important intimate relationship of their lives—perhaps even distraught by the circumstances under which the marriage has ended. Their contact with both parents may no longer be a regular, daily event but a tension-fraught transition requiring a journey across town or further. Do you think it is possible that such children have no problems? Might they benefit from the help of a knowledgeable person as they come to terms with this enormous change in their lives?

INVOLVING CHILDREN CONSTRUCTIVELY

All other approaches to divorce that we are aware of, even if they can meet the needs of the adults, lack a built-in mechanism for involving the children in a constructive way. They are left outside the process and given neither a voice nor a meaningful chance to participate in the decisions that will affect them. The collaborative divorce team approach assures children that their needs and concerns matter and that through their own representative, the child specialist, their voices will be heard and their questions will be answered.

The child specialist starts by meeting with both parents to hear their perspectives and concerns and then meeting with the children—privately, unless they are very young. The children thus have the opportunity to talk about the divorce with a neutral, trained, sympathetic person in a safe environment. In this environment, children generally ask questions and express concerns that they feel uncomfortable discussing with their parents because of fears about taking sides or about making life more difficult for already distressed parents.

Next, the child specialist will meet with you, your spouse, and both your coaches in a "five-way" meeting to discuss your children's concerns and needs, while providing perspectives about what is working for your children and what could be improved. This discussion gives you the chance to consider this important information as you develop a plan for parenting your children from two separate households. The child specialist's observations—which are descriptive, solution-oriented, and never judgmental—are invariably seen by parents as very helpful.

In our experience, parents who have harbored secret fears about potential conflict with their partner concerning how to share custody of the children almost always find the child specialist's information comforting. It reduces disagreements and expands the openness of both parents to potential solutions that they can both embrace as being best for their children.

THE CHILD SPECIALIST'S WORK
WITH CHILDREN AND PARENTS

The child specialist's work is not psychotherapy. It's not intended to deal with extreme emotional disturbances but emphasizes divorce-related changes and challenges. Working privately with your children in a focused, short-term way, the child specialist keeps their needs and concerns in the forefront during the divorce. In the process, it also gives them an independent voice, one that can provide you with important insights that you might otherwise miss as you gather and understand the information.

The child specialist's work, like the work of all collaborative divorce professionals, is confidential and does not go beyond the collaborative divorce process. The child specialist is not allowed to testify for or against either parent in any court proceedings brought by one against the other.

With the involvement of the child specialist, the collaborative divorce approach goes far beyond the conventional idea that child-related issues can be resolved by a piece of paper laying out the rules for shifting children back and forth between two houses. Such agreements for time-sharing do matter, but they are only the tip of the iceberg. Your team's goal will be to bring together all the information and perspectives that will help you reach shared agreement about how to coparent your children in the best way the two of you are capable of.

THE FIVE-WAY MEETING AND THE PARENTING PLAN

At some point in the coaching process, the time will be right for the five-way meeting with the child specialist, during which a parenting plan is developed. For the sake of the children, this is generally done as soon as possible. In our experience, nearly all parents find this meeting with coaches and the child specialist valuable and even enjoyable. At this meeting, they will engage in constructive conversation with someone who is as focused on their children's needs, concerns, and interests as they themselves are. The parents can talk about challenges their children are facing with a specialist whose sole objective is to help them address those challenges in the most constructive possible way, based on accurate information about the children and on the best professional perspectives about how to help children who are experiencing divorce. If the conversation turns to areas that either or both parents have difficulty talking about, the coaches are there to support each spouse in the new communication skills and stress management techniques that are being learned during the coaching process.

In this meeting, there is ample opportunity for everyone to ask questions concerning the needs of the children and the advantages and disadvantages of various plans for how the children can spend time with both parents. The intention is to help both parents make plans and decisions that will allow each of them to give the best of what they have to offer their children as coparents.

Consequently, although differences about parenting children often lead to the bitterest and most destructive old-style divorce battles, we find in collaborative divorce that even couples with very different perspectives on parenting can reach consensus and agree on parenting plans that satisfy both of them. The difference is that in old-style divorce custody battles, strong emotions drive the divorce process, so that every disagreement between the parents becomes a magnet for the feelings of guilt, shame, and blame that we described in chapter 1. In old-style divorce, every difference in parenting style— differences that can become benefits for the children when they are understood and valued—is recast as a deficiency or danger. When this happens, each parent may feel that he or she must be the champion of the children, the sole defender against insufficient or bad parenting by the other.

In contrast, in collaborative divorce, parenting differences become the subject of discussion and are put into perspective by the coaches and child specialist. Every parent knows that it's always possible to do better with children. In collaborative divorce, each parent is helped to build on strengths and address weaknesses, and thereby to improve what both parents can offer the children. Where the emotional challenges are great and the differences are deeply entrenched, the process of arriving at a mutually acceptable parenting plan in a collaborative divorce may take longer, but in our experience, no couple has ever terminated a collaborative divorce because of inability to reach agreement about a parenting plan.

In collaborative divorce, the parenting plans that emerge from the coaching five-way meeting with the child specialist look quite different from the custody agreements reached in old-style divorce negotiations and trials. We begin with an entirely different set of assumptions. In old-style divorce, the goal is to look at the past and use it as a template for allocating each child's time with each parent for the rest of their lives. Once those old-style divorce orders are issued, it can be quite difficult for either parent to change them. But that approach fails to take into account what research tells us that divorcing families actually will experience. When arrangements about children don't match real life, the arrangements must be changed or the children will suffer. Divorcing families are undergoing rapid change that does not cease simply because a paper is filed at the courthouse. For that reason alone, the old-style divorce approach to custody doesn't work. Finances change, new babies are born of subsequent marriages, parents move— life goes on, but fixed old-style divorce custody orders treat change as a problem, not a natural fact. Even more important is the obvious reality that children grow and change even as the divorce progresses. Very young children and teens require far more communication and co-ordination between parents than is usually required in the middle years. As children's needs change, good parents make adaptations—but old divorce custody orders don't readily permit this.

For all these reasons, creating a permanent parenting plan at the time of your divorce makes very little sense. That's why, in collabora-tive divorce, coaches and the child specialist help both parents see that good parenting after a divorce requires ongoing communication about the children's needs, the children's financial support, and the scheduling of time with both parents—all of which can be addressed best by assuming that change will happen and building in ongoing re-views at regular intervals. In the collaborative process the goal is the opposite of a fixed custody schedule. Instead, your team helps you plan how you will make good decisions to ensure that good parenting will continue as change occurs.

WHAT WILL BE INCLUDED IN A PARENTING PLAN?

A calendar that tells you and your children which parent is taking re-sponsibility for them in a given time period will be developed at the coaching five-way meeting. But your parenting plan will include much more than just a calendar; it will address all concerns that either of you have brought to the coaches and that the children have raised with the child specialist, whether or not a judge can issue enforceable court orders about them. The parenting plan will build in a provision for reviews at agreed intervals depending on the ages and anticipated needs of your children, as well as on request when unexpected changes arise in the lives of the children or adults. The plan will include com-mitments about how and when you will conduct these reviews, on your own or with the help of the coaches when necessary. Where fi-nancial implications may be involved, the parenting plan will include agreements about returning to the collaborative lawyers for assistance.

THE INFORMATION THAT LEADS
TO YOUR PARENTING PLAN

You may be wondering how you and your partner can possibly reach agreement about such difficult matters. After all, entrenched disputes about parenting your children may be one of the big reasons your marriage is ending. It may be the source of the bitterest arguments as you and your partner separate. We can assure you unequivocally: the step-by-step process you'll follow with your coaches and child specialist, supported by the work of your collaborative lawyers and financial consultant, works.

The joint mission statement you and your partner will have written with your coaches' help constitutes the touchstone for your parenting plan. During (and after) the five-way meeting with the child specialist, your coaches will help you match your shared aspirations for your children's future with the information the child specialist brings *from* the children and *about* the children: about their current development, temperament, strengths, and challenges. You and your spouse will hear about the children's worries and concerns, likes and dislikes, and some of their ideas about possible living arrangements that they think might work for them.

Collaborative divorce brings the children's concerns and thoughts to the table for consideration during the discussion that leads to a parenting plan. It's easy during a divorce for parents to worry about allocating time with their children solely in terms of each adult's having "enough" of what looks like a scarce resource when compared to the unlimited time they had with their children before the separation. Well-meaning parents can easily overlook the fact that time with peers is extremely important for children of all ages. As children grow older, it's a central part of their development to become more involved with friends, to make their own decisions about activities, and to organize their schedules themselves. Adjusting to these independent needs of a maturing child can be challenging even for intact families. Where divorce is involved, it's perilously easy for parents to confuse their own desires with the needs of the children or to overlook the children's independent scheduling concerns altogether. And where the child's desire for contact with friends appears to conflict with a parent's vision of how to divide up time with the children, the real-world aspects of the problem become complicated by conflicting feelings of loyalty. Consequently, few children feel completely comfortable expressing their own needs about scheduling matters to their parents during a divorce. The child specialist voices these needs.

The child specialist will ensure that the views of the children are heard regarding what time they want to spend with each parent and what time they need for themselves. This conversation may include looking at one or more calendars of possible parenting arrangements that the children have developed with the help of the child specialist. The child specialist has carefully explained that these are ideas that will be considered but ultimately the parents will decide. Children as young as five can have ideas about scheduling, and by the time they are teens their opinions are well defined.

Many parents arrive in the collaborative divorce process with an adult-centered belief that the only fair outcome is for the children to be split fifty-fifty between the parents—as if they were a retirement fund or a loaf of bread. This rarely is because they are uncaring, but more often because parents are fearful of becoming marginal figures in their children's lives. With coaching and the input of the child specialist, nearly all parents relax and become open to constructive discussion of what might work best for the children, considering all concerns and views that have been brought to the table.

SCHEDULES AND CALENDARS
IN YOUR PARENTING PLAN

After this five-way meeting with the child specialist, parents and coaches can complete the plan for parenting, including the first of

COLLABORATIVE DIVORCE

what will be for most families many calendars for sharing parental responsibility. This initial calendar usually addresses the first three to six months—seldom longer. This is because once the focus of discussion has shifted to where it should be—the needs of growing children in light of rapidly changing family circumstances—few parents will want the initial calendar to remain in place much longer than six months before they review it to assess how well it is working and make any needed adjustments. While many couples find they can do this review process themselves, some will need the coaches' help the first few times they do it. For couples who have had particularly challenging conversations as they devise their parenting plan and initial calendar, it can be reassuring to build into the plan an agreement to return to the coaches for the first review—perhaps even to set up an appointment with the coaches, even if the couple doesn't actually end up using it when the time comes.

Specific calendaring and review provisions may depend on when the five-way meeting with the child specialist takes place. Parents need to plan children's summer activities and vacation schedule well before the school year ends. When both parents work and the children will need care and supervision, this becomes even more critical. If the five-way meeting with the child specialist takes place in March or April, the initial calendar that becomes part of the parenting plan and settlement agreement will need to include detailed arrangements for the first summer. If the initial calendar and parenting plan are put in place in the fall or early winter, the plan might include provisions for a first review to take place three or four months before school ends so that the first round of summer planning can be done with the help of the coaches. All of these considerations become a part of the parenting plan the parents work out with the coaches and then bring to the lawyers for review and ultimate incorporation into the final comprehensive divorce settlement agreement.

THE COLLABORATIVE LAWYERS
AND THE PARENTING PLAN

The parenting plan that is designed with the coaches and child specialist won't be considered done until both parents are fully comfortable with it, at least as a trial plan. And it will not become a formal agreement between the parents until the lawyers have had an opportunity to review and discuss it with their clients separately and, if need be, at the legal four-way table. The collaborative lawyers don't engage in strategic maneuvering about the parenting plan to try to "get a better deal" for their own respective clients—though that's often what old-style divorce lawyers do with mediated child custody agreements. Instead, the first job of the collaborative lawyers is to ensure that each parent understands fully what the parenting plan involves and that it fully addresses that parent's concerns. It is rare for lawyers to find problems with these issues, because the work of the coaches is to ensure that all concerns and priorities have been fully discussed in working out the parenting plan. Coaches have the right skills to do that job very effectively. And the collaborative professionals support the role of the collaborative lawyers in ensuring that the parents do fully understand and embrace the plan before it becomes part of the final divorce settlement agreement.

The second job of the collaborative lawyers with respect to the proposed parenting plan is to make sure it includes resolution of all points that should be addressed. Once in a while, something is overlooked. For instance, the proposed calendar for holidays may have overlooked a religious observance that one of the parents values. Or it may have neglected to address how the parents should communicate about unanticipated work-related travel. The lawyers will usually resolve such issues only if they are very straightforward and readily addressed. If that's not the case, they will point out to the couple and the coaches that a little more work needs to go into the plan.

The third job of the collaborative lawyers is to ensure that the language of the proposed plan is completely clear, so that it will pass muster as part of the final divorce judgment submitted to the court. Coaches and child specialists don't always have the ability to write up agreements in a way that eliminates all ambiguity. That's a skill that lawyers excel at. Sometimes, neither the parents nor the coaches notice a language problem that the lawyers will readily see. This is not just technical legalistic thinking. Confused language can sometimes mask a lack of full and complete resolution, and without such resolution there may be a problem waiting to happen. In that case, parents don't yet have an agreement that will last. The lawyers work with each other, and with their clients and the coaches, to make sure that the agreement says exactly what both parents have agreed to—clearly, understandably, and with no confusion. Usually this part of the work is completed very quickly. If it takes more time, that's because more work was needed to get the job done right. If we compare the work of the coaches and child specialist to the work of a diamond cutter, the work of the lawyers can be thought of as the careful final polishing to make sure that the qualities of the plan are as unequivocal as possible, with no rough edges or unclear terms.

WHERE DO YOU GO FROM HERE?

If you chose to start with coaches, here is how the information-gathering work of your team will proceed once the information-gathering work of the coaches is complete and a parenting plan (if there are children) has been worked out. You will meet individually from time to time with your own lawyer, who will help you clarify your thinking, sort out any confusion, understand information, complete "homework" assignments, and identify and prioritize your interests. And you, your partner, and the other collaborative lawyer will gather in four-way legal meetings to share and review financial information and begin discussing interests, goals, and priorities, as you saw in chapter 3.

If the emotional roller coaster causes temporary problems that interfere with constructive work at the legal table, your lawyers will suggest a brief pause while you and your partner return for a little more coaching. Couples with emotional or substance abuse problems or other barriers to constructive problem solving may need extra coaching throughout the collaborative process, while partners who both fully accept the idea of a divorce and who are able to communicate well and to manage their emotions without undue difficulty may not go back to the coaches at all as the legal process unfolds.

As the information-gathering phase continues at the legal table, your lawyers may advise bringing in neutral experts for specific purposes, such as to appraise collections, houses, or businesses, or to advise about career development. You and your lawyers will continue to work with your financial consultant to ensure that account balances are updated, taxes are attended to, cash flow is managed and accounted for appropriately, and assets and debts appear accurately on property division worksheets.

Eventually, you, your lawyers, and the other members of the team who are involved will agree that the information-gathering phase appears to be complete. Then, and only then, will you and your collaborative legal counsel move into the brainstorming process, expanding the options for addressing issues that need resolution before you can reach a framework for comprehensive settlement.

It's a nuanced, customized process, thanks to the continuous collaboration between team members. Sometimes the lawyers will be in a brief holding pattern, waiting to hear from the collaborative financial consultant about financial facts. Meanwhile, you and your spouse may also be meeting with coaches for additional work on undoing the self-defeating communication habits that can cloud good judgment and block clear thinking. Working with the right professional at the right time to bring in the necessary information or strengthen the necessary skill or understanding is how your collaborative divorce team helps you and your partner avoid the emotional meltdowns that can prevent divorcing spouses from being able to discuss facts and concerns constructively at the legal table.

HOW LONG DOES INFORMATION GATHERING LAST?

Information gathering continues until the collaborative divorce team has helped a couple reach the most extensive consensus they are capable of achieving. Don't misunderstand us: reaching consensus is not the same thing as reaching agreement. Agreement comes much later. Consensus means that each partner has a shared understanding of exactly where you are aligned and exactly where you differ, based on full and complete information about the inner- and outer-world facts of your specific situation. Consensus building focuses the problem-solving efforts that will follow exactly where they are needed.

EXPANDING AREAS OF CONSENSUS

Before problem solving can begin, the members of your team will work with you during their involvement in the information-gathering phase to expand the areas of consensus between you and your partner. A couple reaches consensus when they have

- Dispelled any remaining confusion or misunderstandings about facts
- Shared truthful information about concerns, values, goals, and priorities
- Identified as many areas as possible where they are actually or potentially in accord with each other's values, goals, and priorities
- Identified as many areas as possible where their differences can be accommodated without undue difficulty
- Clarified any differences between them that will be more challenging to resolve

Reaching consensus about goals and priorities includes real-world matters such as where you want to live, what kind of work you will be doing, how much money you will be earning, and where the children will go to school. It also includes the inner realm: matters of personal integrity, hopes, dreams, relationships, and so on. Consensus means that each partner fully understands the goals, priorities, and concerns of the other so that they can identify maximum areas of agreement and overlap—for example, "I see that we both place a high value on Mom remaining in the house until Junior graduates from high school"—as well as understanding areas of difference—for example, "I see that I place a higher value on Junior's having a parent available after school even during high school because of my concerns about adolescent escapades, while you are less concerned about that and place higher value on having more income available from both of us so that Junior's college fund will be larger when he needs it."

You can realistically expect to achieve a broad, overlapping consensus with your spouse about outer-world facts, because most outer-world facts can be pinned down if you keep on gathering and sharing information—which is exactly what your team will insist upon. Unless someone is committing a fraud, you'll be able to figure out where money went and what you've both got to show for it. You might disagree about whether the money given to your brother-in-law was a gift or a loan, but you will know when it happened and how much is involved, as well as the reasons each of you has for your difference of opinion. And you'll reach consensus about inner-world values and priorities about the divorce. Whether that consensus includes recognizing a broad area of overlapping interests and values or recognizing a broad area of differences, you'll understand what matters most to each of you.

You've seen how each member of the collaborative divorce team potentially contributes to the information-gathering stage of a divorce. With your team's help, you and your partner will reach maximum areas of consensus about both outer-world facts and inner-world values and aspirations before considering resolution. Once consensus exists, fear generally recedes and confidence that a solution might be found grows. Each potential option for resolution that is ultimately considered during settlement negotiations can then be measured by

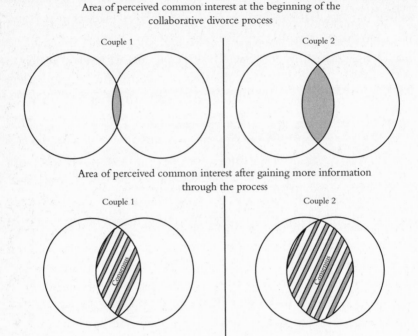

Area of perceived common interest at the beginning of the
collaborative divorce process

Couple 1   Couple 2

Area of perceived common interest after gaining more information
through the process

Couple 1   Couple 2

Figure 1. Consensus About Shared Values and Principles

Your collaborative divorce team uses the information-gathering process to help you
and your spouse recognize what matters to each of you, and to see where your
values and principles match up. Couples differ in the extent of their shared goals,
values, and principles. Where the overlap is less, more brainstorming to expand options will be essential before negotiating settlement. Where the overlap is greater,
solutions tend to become apparent and less effort is needed to explore alternative
options before negotiating settlement. The divorce team helps you and your spouse
expand consensus about both matching values/principles and differing values/
principles. Both kinds of consensus help couples reach resolution.

how well it fits the facts and values that you've reached consensus about
during the information-gathering phase of your collaborative divorce.
Using this foundation, your ultimate settlement agreement can truly
resolve (rather than paper over) divorce issues because it will represent
your best effort to respect the deepest values of each of you regarding
matters such as

- Parenting your children
- Preserving your relationships with friends and extended family
- Acting with integrity
- Honoring your life history
- Using and conserving your resources
- Rebuilding healthy new family systems

MOVING FORWARD TOWARD RESOLUTION

After building consensus, your team will help you and your partner move on to brainstorming options for resolution on matters about which differences are more significant and the pathway to agreement is less clear. In the next chapter, we'll look at how brainstorming happens on a practical level.

COACHING OPENS THE DOOR TO CREATIVE PROBLEM SOLVING: JEFF AND SARAH'S STORY

Jeff is the chief executive officer of a midsize, privately owned manufacturing company. His first divorce was memorably difficult, and he is still bitter about how drawn out and hostile the court proceedings were, how intrusive and seemingly endless the document production demands from his ex-wife's lawyer were, and how embarrassing it was to have his business colleagues drawn into the fight over money (not to mention how high the legal fees rose). Jeff wants to protect his own interests as he sees them. He wants this divorce to be different: contained, private, efficient, and speedy. Most of all, he wants to ensure that the prenuptial agreement that he and his wife, Sarah, signed will not be attacked.

As you can see, Jeff has formed strong views about what should and should not happen in this divorce—*before* any collaborative discussions with Sarah have begun. His goals may or may not all be achievable, either in collaboration or anywhere else. Sarah may or may not feel sufficiently protected by the terms of that prenuptial agreement to honor it willingly in the divorce. And resolving Sarah's concerns may or may not be possible at the rapid speed that Jeff envisions.

A collaborative conflict resolution approach starts with a look at the facts of Jeff's and Sarah's current situations with respect to the prenuptial agreement. Sarah may have long-standing resentments about the agreement itself—regardless of its legal enforceability—that Jeff may disagree with but certainly would benefit from knowing more about. She also may have fears about her financial situation after the divorce that Jeff might accept as valid if they were explained well. And Sarah may or may not fully appreciate the "scorched earth" divorce experience that led Jeff to want that prenuptial agreement in the first place or his sense of justice and fair play attached to honoring an agreement that he believes was fair.

Jeff and Sarah are both starting out with some powerful fears and resentments about central features of the divorce that is about to begin. At the same time, it is not at all certain from a legal perspective whether their prenuptial agreement would or would not be enforced under the laws of their state if the matter were taken to court. Their lawyers will educate both Jeff and Sarah about that legal context and about the often distressing testimony that must be presented in order to resolve such matters via litigation. Ignoring their fears and resentments and focusing on their situation solely as a legal problem would be a recipe for war, and for that reason, good collaborative lawyers will begin by inviting Jeff and Sarah to bring collaborative divorce coaches on as part of their professional team. Sarah and Jeff will be guided by their coaches to speak more frankly about their powerful underlying feelings than they may have been able to do during their marriage.

By communicating their feelings about the prenuptial agreement clearly, in a safely facilitated, focused process, Sarah and Jeff have a good chance of defusing the destructive power those feelings would otherwise exert. Almost certainly, Sarah and Jeff will be able to think far more clearly about priorities, choices, and long-term consequences after coaching than before. Only then—when the coaching process has fully aired the underlying emotions driving their initial positions about the prenuptial agreement—will Sarah and Jeff move on to examine their respective financial circumstances with their lawyers and collaborative financial consultant, and only after that work is done will they move on to explore with the help of their collaborative lawyers and their financial consultant the impact of the prenuptial agreement—as well as other possible settlement scenarios—on the postdivorce circumstances of each of them.

This systematic process of developing and examining financial and emotional information before leaping to solutions holds open for Sarah and Jeff the possibility of finding areas of consensus and potential agreement that could be far more creative, and far more satisfactory to both of them, than what a court could do or what the terms of their prenuptial agreement might dictate. Although there are no guarantees about outcomes, what *can* be promised to Sarah and Jeff is that using the collaborative divorce process to free themselves from knee-jerk reactions to strong feelings, so that they can examine their options thoughtfully with a full understanding of the facts, will give them their best chance of finding mutually acceptable ways to avoid a war—a goal both of them have recognized that they share.

6

REACHING RESOLUTION

To accomplish great things, we must not only act, but also dream; not only plan, but also believe.

—ANATOLE FRANCE

Once you and your partner have reached consensus about where you have values and priorities in common, where they are consistent, and where they differ, it is usually apparent which issues will be easy to resolve and which will require more effort. Particularly where there are difficult issues—matters on which you seriously disagree with your partner, matters as to which there seems to be only an "either-or" solution, matters on which emotions run high—you and your team will probably make use of brainstorming to expand the range of possible options for resolution.

BRAINSTORMING OPTIONS FOR RESOLUTION

Perhaps you are new to the concept of brainstorming, or perhaps you have participated in brainstorming sessions in your work. As you may know, the term has a specific meaning when we use it in connection with problem solving and conflict resolution. As used in collaborative negotiations, brainstorming is a technique we use to expand options for resolving particular problems or issues about which you and your partner disagree.

WHERE AND HOW BRAINSTORMING TAKES PLACE

Brainstorming can take place in legal or coaching four-way meetings, as well as in meetings that include more of your professional helpers, depending on the issue at hand. For instance, brainstorming ideas for a parenting problem involving the needs of a child might take place at a coaching five-way meeting attended by the child specialist, while brainstorming what to do with the family residence would take place at the legal negotiating table, at a four-way meeting, or perhaps a five-way meeting attended by the financial consultant.

Brainstorming has nothing to do with the traditional negotiations of old-style divorce, in which each side, working separately, exchanges a sequence of offers and counteroffers arrived at privately with one's own lawyer. In collaborative brainstorming, your team leads you in a structured but freewheeling process in which you are both invited to imagine every conceivable way of resolving the particular problem, practical or not, acceptable or not, reasonable or absurd. The team writes down all ideas—no matter how strange or unappealing they may be—as rapidly as possible, with the rule that no one is permitted to discuss the ideas or criticize in any way.

The goal of brainstorming is to imagine every conceivable way to solve the problem. We often urge each spouse to include ideas that he or she would not under any circumstances agree to, and we remind both partners that they should even come up with ideas that they would never give a moment's serious consideration to. This kind of brainstorming can free both partners from the stifling effect that pre-conceived notions about what's acceptable or not can have on creative thinking.

BRAINSTORMING SESSIONS

Though the specific ideas of a brainstorming session are unique to each divorce, each session follows a pattern. During the brainstorming session, any member of the team—spouses, coaches, or lawyers—can toss out an idea at any time. Though the professionals often try to encourage the spouses to take the lead, if the flow of ideas starts to wane, they sometimes offer absurd ideas just to keep the creativity going.

Let's suppose that Ken and Caroline are considering the advantages and disadvantages of agreeing that after the sale of their home, they will move to homes close to each other. In a brainstorming session, we'd encourage Ken and Caroline to think of as many advantages and disadvantages of coordinating this decision, as well as not coordinating this decision, as they can. Their list might include ideas like these, in addition to the one each started out with (Ken: "We should each move where we please; it's none of your business where I live!"; and Caroline: "We should both move to condominiums near where my sister lives because it will help both of us and the kids if we do.").

Advantages of both living where Caroline suggests:

• The children can walk from one home to the other
• Caroline's sister can provide emergency backup
• The children can play with their cousins easily
• Housing is affordable
• There is plenty of green space and playgrounds
• The school is within walking distance

Disadvantages:

- Ken and Caroline's sister dislike each other
- Caroline and her sister sometimes don't speak to each other
- The neighborhood school is not a very good one
- The noise of the freeway is loud
- When Ken or Caroline begins dating, it could be awkward being under each other's noses
- The commute to Ken's job would take forty-five minutes longer than at present

Advantages of not moving together to the vicinity of Caroline's sister:

- Ken and Caroline can each move exactly where they want
- Each can have more privacy from the other if they live further apart
- The children will be better able to let go of fantasies that Ken and Caroline will reconcile
- Ken and Caroline could research other locales that don't include the problems with her sister

Disadvantages:

- The logistical problems of ensuring regular time with children will be greater
- No family support system would be readily available
- The children wouldn't have extended family available on demand
- The children wouldn't be able to visit either parent whenever they wanted
- School projects and homework would be harder to coordinate

Once a brainstorming session gets into full swing, people usually begin to enjoy the challenge of thinking of more and more ideas to put on the list. In this instance, upon reflection Ken and Caroline can see from their first brainstorming list that they are mixing up several separate issues: Should they try to live close to each other? If so, should they both locate near Caroline's sister? If not, does it make sense for Caroline to move there even if Ken does not? They could continue brainstorming with those more refined questions, or they could at any point decide they had finished. Or they could try a different kind of brainstorming to generate more options by responding to the question "How many possibilities can we think of for where all or some of us could live after the house is sold?"

Brainstorming clarifies issues, brings values to light, and expands the range of possible solutions. As you can see from the case of Caroline and Ken, the issues about which couples can brainstorm are unlimited. Anything they are willing to discuss can be clarified in this way with the help of their team—even if it is a topic, as with the one we've looked at here, that a judge could not issue orders about.

The next step involves weighing each of the ideas on the list to decide whether it's worth considering seriously. Remember that in the first part of the collaborative divorce process, Caroline and Ken will already have learned a great deal about the goals and priorities each of them has for the divorce and the interests and concerns that need to be addressed in a divorce agreement. They also will have in their early four-way minutes one or more mission statements setting out their highest intentions for self, children, and spouse—qualities by which a proposed resolution can be measured. Each of the brainstormed ideas and considerations can be tested and weighed to see whether it meets the identified interests and concerns of one or both of the spouses, and whether it measures up to the ideals set forth in the mission statements. Many of the brainstormed ideas may be put aside as unworkable or frivolous, but many may survive this first examination and remain on the list as possibilities to be considered further.

Now, if an acceptable resolution still isn't apparent, the next step could be a "foursquare" analysis of each of the surviving ideas. Here's how the foursquare process works. Let's assume that one of the surviving ideas from a brainstorming list that Ken and Caroline generated is that Ken and Caroline would move close to each other, but in the city rather than near Caroline's sister. The idea would be written at the top of a page on a flip chart or a board. A grid would be drawn, and the brainstorming would continue in each of the four categories:

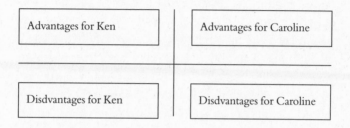

The team would encourage Ken and Caroline to consider not only the financial and practical repercussions but also those having to do with principles and values that they have already identified as important to each of them. This process fleshes out the many considerations that can help a couple decide together whether a possible solution does or does not pass muster in terms of what matters most.

For instance, maybe both of you want a child to remain in his or her public school for a certain period of time into the future. Any scenario that creates financial or other consequences that would require the child to move out of the area during that timeframe would not meet the test. That doesn't mean the idea is automatically out of the question; it does mean that it does not measure up to a value both partners have already agreed is important. Or there may be an elderly parent whose needs for care have been identified as important by both spouses. Any solution that would make this more difficult would need to be considered carefully in light of the fact that it does not match that shared priority.

It often happens that this kind of extended brainstorming reveals possibilities that both partners are willing to consider. But before deciding on the best resolution, more information might be needed. For

Where Does the Law Fit In?

Your collaborative lawyers will definitely advise you about the law that a judge would apply to your case if you took it to court. But they will also encourage both of you to understand that you are free to choose solutions that are much more customized than what a judge is allowed to do. They will help both of you see that divorce law is about reliable guidelines and rules for getting disagreements resolved, rather than about justice. And they will help both of you appreciate how different the outcomes would be in court for couples exactly like you who happen to live in another state where the judge is required to apply different laws to the same kinds of facts. They can put the law into perspective rather than letting it limit your creativity.

instance, a tax advisor might be consulted, to make sure that tax consequences of various possible solutions are clearly understood. Input about real estate values and current rental rates might be important. If more time is needed to gather that information, more time will be taken.

As you can see, brainstorming at this point in the process—after inner information (about values, hopes, goals, and priorities) and outer information (about schools, finances, child care, work commute, and so forth) have all been shared and understood and maximum consensus has been reached—can jump-start creative problem solving, because everything important about the decision is out on the table.

HOW MUCH BRAINSTORMING WILL WE DO?

How much brainstorming you'll do in your collaborative divorce will depend on the particular challenges you and your partner face, the extent and intensity of your differences, and your skill in addressing them. Brainstorming will be used in your work with your coaches to help you resolve the terms of your plan for parenting and with your lawyers as you approach resolution of issues at the legal table. Couples who face their fears directly, who communicate effectively about the legitimate concerns that can be masked by those fears, who look at all the facts unflinchingly, and whose values and priorities match reasonably well are likely to have success at reaching solutions that both can accept. These couples can expect the brainstorming phase to be relatively brief because their need for a formal system to expand options will be less. Such couples may find that there is no need for negotiations as such, because the obvious solutions may quickly become apparent.

Couples who are less candid about sharing inner and outer information, who are more attached to fear-driven quick fixes or more entrenched in their differences about values or principles, will probably need a more structured and extensive formal brainstorming phase in order to develop their options. They may need to spend more time, go into more detail, and evaluate many more possibilities before finding the solution that they both can accept.

REACHING RESOLUTION

Finally, when this formal brainstorming process has been used for all issues that need it, it's time to discuss solutions. With the breadth of possibilities that brainstorming reveals, minds tend to open, points of view usually become less rigid, and solutions to even very challenging divorce-related differences start to seem possible.

Brainstorming helps you and your spouse make creative use of your differences rather than just be divided by them. For example, you and your spouse may want different assets for different purposes. One of you may want liquid assets in order to start a business, while the other may want the security of real estate. One of you may want to move as soon as possible to a new location, while the other may value remaining in a familiar neighborhood. One of you may be willing to take less money if it can be advanced right now; the other may be willing to wait longer in order to receive more. One may value safety and security above all, while the other may be a risk taker who is willing to gamble on speculative investments. We can create value and expand options by making positive use of differences such as these.

A formal brainstorming session that considers every possible option can be the catalyst that pulls together all the preceding work and brings couples to deep conflict resolution—what some of our clients call "the Zone." Clients who leap to the first solution that comes to mind or who remain attached to one position without considering others can still negotiate a compromise divorce settlement—a "shallow peace"—but they rarely arrive in the Zone. That is why so much of the conflict resolution work of your collaborative professional team is devoted to the groundwork: sharing information, arriving at consensus, and expanding the range of solutions to be considered. Deals can be made without that groundwork, but without it you aren't likely to get to deep resolution. The groundwork leads to systematic understanding of what's true for yourself and what matters most to your spouse and your children. Couples who do this work discover their common ground and sometimes find that it is greater than they imagined possible at the start. They find the possibility for more where at first there seemed only the certainty of less.

Of course, sometimes even the best effort at brainstorming can't lead to deep resolution. In that case, we can always fall back upon old-fashioned horse-trading to reach a compromise that each spouse can accept. But that's only if we can't do better. In collaborative divorce, we start by trying to find solutions that meet the identified interests of both spouses, resorting to trade-offs only as a last resort. In contrast, horse-trading compromise is where old divorce bargaining begins and

The Story of the Orange

The story of dividing the orange can help you understand the importance of exploring what matters to each of you before jumping to solutions.

Imagine that the entire marital estate of Sharon and Paul consists of one ripe orange. Conventional negotiators would "know" that the reasonable, evenhanded way to divide that estate is for each of them to get half an orange and would try to get to that solution quickly. If Sharon's lawyer were particularly aggressive, she might try to get more of the orange for her client and be proud if she succeeds.

Suppose the orange is divided 51 percent to Sharon and 49 percent to Paul. Sharon's lawyer now asks why Sharon looks so glum about that great result. And Sharon says, "I like to make potpourri; I was actually hoping to get all the peel." Meanwhile, Paul's lawyer asks him why he's so disappointed; after all, his share is only 1 percent less than half. And Paul replies, "I really like orange juice; I was hoping to get all the pulp."

If their lawyers had asked questions at the start about what dividing the orange really meant to Sharon and to Paul, each of them could have received 100 percent of what they wanted.

ends, because in old-style divorce bargaining, each spouse tends to remain wedded to the first idea each one had, and the lawyers tend to define their job as trying to bring about that particular outcome, regardless of whether or not it's the best for all concerned. In contrast, your collaborative divorce team will do its best to help you and your partner reach the best quality outcome the two of you can achieve, for yourselves and any children.

WHEN A HOUSE IS MORE THAN A HOUSE: ADAM AND SUE'S STORY

It may make it easier to see how the resources of the collaborative divorce team can help you reach deep resolution if we take a closer look at a very common divorce-related question:"What are we going to do with the family residence?" It's common in traditional old-style divorce negotiations for both partners to arrive with fear-driven decisions already in place about the big issues that will need to be resolved. For instance, it's not unusual for the person who handles the finances to be convinced that the house has to be sold or there won't be enough money for both husband and wife to buy replacement housing after all the marital property has been divided. Just as common, a spouse who has spent years as a homemaker and parent may become panic-stricken if she so much as thinks about selling the house, because in a period of rapid and possibly unwelcome changes, the familiar home and neighborhood can be much more than just a place to live; they can be a vital emotional "security blanket."

Let's look at how one couple and their collaborative divorce team approached this problem. Adam was an executive in a local supermarket chain, while Sue had left her job as a fabric designer after the birth of their second child eight years before to be a full-time parent and homemaker. Their divorce was Adam's choice, not Sue's. Adam and Sue began the divorce process by selecting collaborative lawyers. Each of them made it very clear during the first meetings with their respective lawyers how important it was for the house to be either sold (according to Adam) or awarded to Sue in the divorce (according to Sue). Adam and Sue, in other words, entered the collaborative process with fixed—and opposing—decisions in place about one of the most valuable assets they owned. In old-style divorce, this could have been a recipe for war.

Fortunately, they had selected collaborative divorce. Sue and Adam's collaborative lawyers helped them choose other team members—coaches and a financial consultant—and their team members helped Adam and Sue begin the first phase of work—gathering and sharing information. As is customary in collaborative divorce, each of their team members echoed one consistent message to Adam and Sue every time their fears pulled them into worrying about whether the house would be sold or not: "It's much too soon for that discussion; you need much more information before you can make good decisions about the house." In a collaborative divorce, every team member encourages every couple to stay away from making final decisions until all the facts, both inner and outer, are on the table.

Their coaches worked with Sue and Adam individually and together, to help them clarify and explain what keeping or selling the house would mean for each of them after the divorce. Adam was certain that if Sue kept the house, all he would get in the divorce was debts, plus retirement funds that couldn't be touched until he was much older. Without a house sale, how would he be able to afford to buy housing anywhere near where his children would be living with Sue? And how would he ever get back into the home ownership market with housing prices rising so rapidly? He'd be a renter, not an owner, and rental housing was pretty scarce in their neighborhood. If he lived very far from Sue, he feared he'd become a minor figure in his children's lives because they would not be able to visit him on their own. His dream solution was that he and Sue would sell the house and buy condominiums reasonably close to each other's, and the children would be able to bicycle to and from each parent's home and school on their own.

Sue's coach helped her to understand how worn out and over-stressed she had become as the marriage broke down and how much the house had come to symbolize peace and security to her. Sue was surprised when she saw how emotionally charged the house issue had become and how difficult it was for her to think clearly about the advantages and disadvantages of keeping it versus selling it. Whenever she and Adam talked about the subject on their own, feelings of panic swept over her and led to a meltdown in which Sue would cry over Adam's pushiness, while Adam would storm out in anger because of Sue's closed-mindedness. Sue and her coach worked together privately for several sessions to help Sue understand her feelings and clarify her thinking about the house before both coaches and spouses came to the table for a four-way conversation.

At this point, the coaches and collaborative lawyers conferred briefly and recommended that Sue and Adam take some time with the financial consultant to investigate

- How their cash, investments, and debts might be divided if the house were or were not sold
- How much it would cost if they both bought condominiums in nearby neighborhoods with good schools
- What other sources of money might be available for Adam to buy housing if the home were not sold
- What each of their monthly housing costs would look like now as well as in a few years if they decided to sell—or not to sell—the family home

Only after Sue and Adam completed this work with their coaches and financial consultant did their lawyers conclude that they were ready to gather together at the legal four-way table. There, the lawyers helped Adam and Sue bring together what they'd learned separately in coaching and together with their financial consultant before moving on to a brainstorming session.

Before beginning the formal brainstorming process, their lawyers helped Sue and Adam reflect upon what concerns were most important for each of them in resolving the house question. Adam and Sue focused on their shared understanding of basic financial realities such as current house costs, rental costs, maintenance expenses, real estate market factors, other sources of cash for housing purchase, income, expenses, and taxes. They also reviewed each other's concerns about the children's anticipated schooling, how they would coparent the children, and their plans and hopes for the future—when and how Sue would complete retraining in her field, when she would return to work, and when Adam hoped to retire and start the business he had long dreamed of.

As Adam and Sue explored the facts and listened deeply to each other's concerns, it became possible for Adam to hear and appreciate why Sue hesitated to move and for Sue to hear and appreciate Adam's concerns about money, housing, and parenting. As they did this at the legal four-way meeting, it became clear to them and to their collaborative lawyers that other possibilities for the house might exist for Adam and Sue in addition to the two they had started out with.

The brainstorming process that followed allowed them to consider, for better and for worse, the impact on each of them and their children that would result from every conceivable solution they and their lawyers could imagine for handling the family residence. Here are some of the possibilities—some potentially useful, others not—that emerged during the legal brainstorming process:

- The house could be sold now or later
- It could be rented out
- Sue could keep it
- Adam could keep it
- They could co-own it
- They could agree to a deferred sale
- Sue's occupancy could reduce Adam's support obligation

This is only part of the list they came up with. Sue and Adam's lawyers encouraged them to imagine every conceivable option, even ones they would not consider accepting under any circumstances. Adam and Sue then worked with their lawyers to test the expanded lists of possible house solutions against their "mission statements" developed earlier in the process, to see how well each possible solution measured up. Because they respected and cared about each other and their children, no solution would work for them that failed to honor each other's key concerns.

Neither Adam nor Sue could have handled this kind of brainstorming and options development when they first arrived in their collaborative lawyers' offices. But their coaches taught them stress

management and communication skills and their financial consultant
helped them weed out misunderstandings and misconceptions about
their economic situation, so that by the time they were ready to brainstorm solutions, they were able to reach resolution about the house
very quickly.

Adam and Sue, like most of our collaborative clients, became more
flexible and realistic as they absorbed the information they needed
about finances, concerns, and priorities. They were able to consider
solutions that wouldn't have occurred to either of them without the
help of their collaborative divorce team. For them, the solution that fit
both of their needs and priorities turned out to be a deferred sale of
the house in eighteen months, after their older child finished middle
school.

Solutions like the one Adam and Sue eventually settled on are
what we mean by "deep resolution." These "deep peace" solutions become possible when we start by paying close attention to the actual
concerns and financial realities of two specific people, looking for
maximum areas of consensus and overlapping interests and priorities,
before the decision-making process. They are far superior to "one-
size-fits-all" solutions imposed by judges or quick-fix decisions made
in the grip of fears about the future that are not grounded in reality. A
deep resolution is one in which both partners can honestly say, "I can
live with that. That works for me." When problems are solved in this
manner, they *stay* solved.

7

ATTAINING THE NECESSARY
SENSE OF CLOSURE

What we call the beginning is often the end and to make an end is to make a beginning.
The end is where we start from.

—T. S. ELIOT

By the time you and your partner reach a complete framework for agreement, you'll have accomplished a great deal of work and you'll be well on your way to the best divorce you can possibly achieve for you, your spouse, your children, and your loved ones. At that point, you will be justifiably proud of what you have accomplished. But the process won't be quite done. A few tasks will still remain, which we will address in this chapter.

FINISHING THE JOB

Once you and your partner reach terms of comprehensive settlement, some important tasks remain before the job is finished. After all, divorce is a legal matter, and the agreement that you and your spouse reach must be made legally binding. Therefore, your lawyers must do the following:

- Your collaborative lawyers will carefully prepare a legally binding settlement agreement that will become part of your divorce judgment
- That agreement will set out all the terms of resolution you and your partner have agreed upon, clearly and understandably, including your parenting plan
- Your lawyers will prepare the papers required by the courts to complete the legal side of your divorce and will help you process them through the court system
- The lawyers will help you complete other important paperwork, such as title transfers, changes in beneficiaries, retirement fund transfers, and so forth

In old-style divorce, all this work takes place by e-mail, fax, and mail without you and your spouse meeting again face to face unless your local court system happens to require both of you to appear in court when the judge issues the divorce decree. But in collaborative divorce, you'll be encouraged by your team to gather in a last four-way meeting to sign the settlement agreement and other key divorce documents.

A LOOK AT THE PAPERS

Let's look more closely at the paperwork your lawyers will prepare at this point in your collaborative divorce, as the legal divorce process comes to a close. Your lawyers will help you handle all the necessary details so that you

- Have a clear, binding agreement with your partner
- Get a divorce judgment and become single
- Properly transfer ownership of assets and responsibility for debts

Your divorce agreement will be prepared by the collaborative lawyers, with one of them writing up a first draft and both lawyers discussing and revising it until they are sure it accurately reflects exactly what you and your partner agreed upon. They will ask you to review it, too, so that you can ask questions, make suggestions, and make sure the written agreement is correct. In addition, they will insert provisions that may seem somewhat legalistic and weren't discussed during negotiations. While they may appear unfamiliar, these provisions will ensure that your agreement is a binding contract and that it complies with all state laws and addresses all appropriate tax matters.

In this respect, your lawyers are doing what all good divorce lawyers would do. The difference is that in old-style divorce, lawyers often use the process of arriving at a final written settlement agreement as an opportunity to push for more concessions or take advantage of misconceptions or oversights on the part of the other lawyer. During a collaborative divorce, the lawyers discuss in a constructive way with you and your partner any unresolved matters that may come to their attention during the process of writing up terms of agreement. And as agreed on in the first four-way meeting, your collaborative lawyers are committed to point out errors or oversights and never to take advantage of them.

Why? Because, as you will recall, the goal of the collaborative divorce process is not a "quick-fix" deal. The goal is a resolution that will last, that will help both of you and your children meet the changes and challenges that so often arise after the divorce decree has been entered. Taking advantage of mistakes is shortsighted. It doesn't resolve conflicts; instead, it ensures that conflicts will continue.

PLANNING FOR THE FUTURE

There is another big difference between a collaborative divorce agreement and an old-style divorce agreement: it doesn't just wrap up the loose ends of the past; it sets out plans, intentions, and commitments about good-faith behavior for the future. Old-style divorce settlement agreements and judgments after trial tend to focus exclusively on terms and provisions that a court has the power and ability to enforce. Your collaborative agreement will include those same provisions about property division, support, and parenting, in the form of enforceable terms of a contract between you and your partner, which will also be issued as court orders, where appropriate. But a collaborative divorce agreement in most cases will go further, into the realm of good intentions that depend on integrity, not the threat of legal enforcement. Courts lack jurisdiction to address many matters of great importance. The laws about this vary from state to state, but you'll find that often divorce courts cannot make orders about matters such as

- Payment for college education
- Shared decision making concerning adult children with disabilities
- Grandchildren
- Stepchildren
- Support of aged parents
- Psychotherapy for a family member with emotional problems
- Religious education and observances
- How to discipline children

For example, Brenda and George, a couple in their early sixties, divorced after a fifteen-year marriage. George had been a dedicated stepfather to Brenda's daughter Rachel, who now was married and had a young son, Jackie, whom George adored. Neither the court nor Brenda herself had the power to guarantee George's continuing access to the child, but through the collaborative divorce agreement, the chances are good that George will continue to see Jackie, because in their settlement agreement Brenda promised to do all she could to support that relationship.

Amy and Victor, whose daughters were twelve and ten when they divorced, both cared greatly that when their girls turned thirteen, their Bat Mitzvah ceremonies would be attended by both sides of the family. While a traditional court agreement could not have addressed this issue, their settlement agreement included commitments about how they would work together to ensure that the occasions would be happy for the children and their extended families. Similarly, Larry and Joyce included in their settlement agreement some mutually agreed upon ground rules for their teenage son's use of automobiles that they both felt were extremely important. Despite the fact that all these various promises lie outside the realm of a judges' jurisdiction, the final collaborative divorce agreement makes them all possible.

Just because a judge cannot force you to abide by certain important commitments is no reason why you and your spouse should not be encouraged to make them and no reason to expect that you and your partner will not honor them. Quite the contrary: our experience confirms that the vast majority of couples who move through the collaborative divorce process and promise each other in writing as part of their settlement that they will behave in a certain manner in the future want to honor their promises, and do so. For most people, looking their partner in the eye and saying "I agree" is more than reason enough to do what was promised. That is why your coaches and lawyers will encourage you and your spouse to make agreements about using collaborative team resources as much as possible to handle future disagreements—a "conflict resolution plan"—rather than filing motions in court.

Your agreement will also incorporate the terms of your parenting plan, which includes enforceable matters (such as where the children will live, what their last names will be, where they will spend holidays, and so forth) as well as good-faith promises about behavior that depend on personal integrity (such as respecting each other's privacy, encouraging the children to love both parents, conferring in advance about introducing new intimate partners to children, and so forth).

YOUR CONFLICT RESOLUTION PLAN

Your conflict resolution plan is a document that you will be able to come back to again and again in the future to help guide you when conflict arises, as it almost inevitably does. Many couples see the wisdom of agreeing in advance that they will review, refine, and adjust their parenting agreements from time to time on their own and with the coaches' help as children grow and circumstances change. Good parenting includes making adjustments to life's changes, both big and small. Attending to small changes as necessary builds habits and skills that can make adjustment easier when larger changes must be faced. Your team will help you build understandings into your settlement agreement about when to return for help, because waiting for a full-blown problem to explode before asking the team's help is like waiting until you've had a heart attack to get medical care instead of getting regular checkups. After all, raising children through adolescence to adulthood is one of life's very challenging endeavors, even for couples who remain married. Those couples still have an intimate connection that helps them stay in harmony and focus on constructive solutions when they disagree about how to handle parenting issues. You and your divorced partner won't have that intimacy to lubricate the friction when you see problems differently. You'll benefit from planning ahead to expect differences and from having a method you can fall back on if you can't reach agreement on your own.

Where children are involved, most collaborative divorce agreements that have had the benefit of oversight by coaches and a child specialist include a section that we sometimes refer to as a "maintenance plan" or "checkup schedule." This is not a separate document. It will be a part of your collaborative divorce settlement agreement—the one that is included in your divorce judgment. Many couples include an agreement to return to the collaborative divorce coaches for "maintenance" at short intervals during the first eighteen to twenty-four months after the legal divorce is completed. Such an agreement might read something like this: "We will return to our coaches every six months for a period of two years following signing this agreement to review how well our parenting plan is working for us and for our children, and to consider possible improvements." After that, the plan might include a promise to return to the coaches once a year for another year or two, and thereafter only if one partner or the other requests it. Other couples might prefer a commitment to return to coaching only if either of them feels he or she can't handle a particular challenge alone.

Sometimes couples discover during these planned coaching "checkups" that the existing arrangements for shared parenting of the children are working just fine. More often, they conclude that the arrangements need some fine-tuning, which is easily accomplished with a little help from the coaches. Sometimes, the changes required are big and the challenges are greater than what the coaches alone can address. At such times, couples can call upon the resources of any team member who can help: the collaborative lawyers, the child specialist, or the financial consultant.

USING YOUR TEAM TO ANTICIPATE, FORESTALL, AND RESOLVE CONFLICT

Most collaborative divorce agreements go on to provide that—barring an emergency affecting the safety of a child—neither partner will resort to old-style divorce motions asking a judge to make a decision until he or she has first made a good-faith effort to resolve the problem with the help of the team. This is an example of a promise that may or may not be considered enforceable by a judge in your locale but has great value nonetheless. It's the kind of promise that nearly all people want to abide by if they understand it at the time they make it and make a serious personal commitment to honor it.

The conflict resolution plan is a useful tool for couples both with and without children. It can address not only parenting differences but also possible changes that might affect support and property arrangements. For example, support arrangements for children can benefit from planned periodic reviews with the lawyers, and these reviews can be written into the settlement agreement. What worked for young preschoolers will almost certainly not work for adolescents. One of the essential conditions for good parenting is adequate, stable financial arrangements between parents when circumstances change, and the conflict resolution plan provides steps you can take to deal with those changes as they arise. In some cases, the original support agreement may have been structured for maximum tax deductibility where minor children as well as a parent were receiving support. When a child reaches adulthood, the support arrangements for the parent and any remaining minor children may need to be revisited with careful attention to tax consequences. If a supported spouse remarries, spousal support (also called alimony or separate maintenance) normally terminates. A review to address tax concerns as well as child support may also be needed.

Perhaps a supported spouse is pursuing education to develop a career or to get vocational training or retraining. Many agreements include plans to reconvene to adjust support depending on progress toward completion of the educational plan or success in finding employment. Or sometimes a "paying" spouse may change jobs, become unemployed, become disabled, or retire. A good conflict resolution plan includes an agreement to return to collaboration before anyone resorts to traditional motions in court about such matters.

One partner or the other may want or need to move to another locale, with resulting changes in the need for support or ability to pay. An aged parent may become dependent on either the paying or the supported spouse. Either former spouse may remarry and/or set up a home with a nonmarital partner and/or have other children with someone else. The future is impossible to predict, but with a good conflict resolution plan in place, you will know how you and your partner will make decisions when life's surprises occur.

Another common situation that the conflict resolution plan can anticipate has to do with co-ownership and sale of the former family residence or other valuable assets that remain jointly owned after the legal divorce. It's not unusual for a divorced couple to disagree about matters such as these:

- Is a certain repair or improvement necessary to keep the property up or not? Who should pay for it?
- What happens to agreements about upkeep and/or sale if one of us runs into financial hard times?
- What property management company shall we retain to manage renting our cabin at the lake?
- How shall we handle requests from friends and relatives to use the vacation home, especially if one person's relatives want it more often?
- When shall we list the property for sale?
- What shall the listing price be?
- Whom shall we choose as a real estate agent?
- What improvements need to be made in order to get the best selling price for the property?
- Which offers are acceptable and which are not?
- What counteroffers should be made?
- What price would be reasonable if one of us wants to buy instead of selling on the open market?
- Would either of us be willing to consider "creative financing" in order to allow the other to remain in the house or buy it?

Another area of predictable change you can plan ahead about arises when divorcing partners either want to, or feel obliged to, continue co-owning a business after their divorce. For example, Kevin and Cindy had created a very successful business consulting firm that helped medium-sized and large businesses all over the world design programs to make their companies more attractive to middle- and upper-level managers and executives with children. Cindy was the "outside" person who was talented at getting new contracts and keeping clients happy, while Kevin was gifted at running the home office smoothly, delivering on contracts, and keeping their own workforce happy and productive. Neither of them could do the other's job, and neither of them wanted a new business partner. They felt reasonably confident they could continue as business partners after their collaborative divorce. At the same time, they knew that having a conflict resolution plan to rely upon in the event of disagreements would protect the business and the employees of the business, as well as the long-term economic interests of each of them and their children.

We have seen other couples agree to jointly co-own and operate a winery, a horse-breeding ranch, and a number of other businesses after collaborative divorces—an unusual result in conflict-ridden old-style divorces. We know that the process of deep conflict resolution that collaborative divorce offers, together with the support of a conflict resolution plan in the divorce agreement and the availability of the collaborative team after the divorce judgment, is what makes these ongoing business partnerships possible.

HOW YOUR CONFLICT RESOLUTION PLAN WILL HELP

Planning ahead for change and conflict in your divorce agreement will help you and your partner cope with challenges in many specific ways during the period of rapid change and consolidation that you can expect after the divorce.

First of all, the discussion that results in the inclusion of checkups and conflict resolution plans in the divorce settlement agreement helps both partners reach consensus in advance about their priorities, values, and concerns should such problems arise. That discussion helps them recognize in advance where they are aligned and where they should expect possible differences of opinion, so that they can invoke their agreed-upon conflict resolution plan early, before tempers flare. For instance, most couples with young children spend time exploring values and priorities having to do with introducing new intimate partners.

Second, discussing the conflict resolution plan carefully as they work on terms of resolution at the end of the legal divorce process helps them avoid making certain innocent blunders after the divorce because of ignorance about what matters to the other partner. For example, couples who are encouraged by their team members to anticipate likely areas of challenge can learn, to their surprise, that having a support check arrive exactly on time is much more significant to one of them than the other could have imagined.

Third, the plan reminds them of the spectrum of coordinated resources they can call upon should a difference arise—not just the lawyers, but the coaches and financial consultant as well.

WHEN AND HOW TO USE YOUR TEAM

Working with the coaches is wise when the problem is strong emotions, hot buttons, and difficulties communicating clearly when something changes, whether anticipated or not. The coaches also can help either or both of you clarify your own thinking and priorities. And whenever children are involved, the coaches are a first resource for reliable feedback and support in devising solutions that can work well for the children as well as the adults. This kind of "as-needed" assistance from your coaches is easily obtained because they already know you and your partner well. One or both of you can request a return to the coaches for a session or two to work on a specific issue that you are having difficulty resolving. Or they can help both of you "tune up" your communication skills if arguments have temporarily replaced constructive problem solving. They also can help you figure out what other professional resources might be needed. For instance, if either ex-spouse or a child develops emotional difficulties or substance abuse problems, the coaches can suggest where and how to get help.

The child specialist is the best resource when the voice of the children needs to be heard in order for wise solutions to emerge. When the children's needs or wishes seem to be changing, most conflict resolution plans include a return to the coaches, who will, when appropriate, involve the child specialist as another voice in the coaching process. Differences of opinion about the best interests of children almost always trigger strong feelings and make communications between the adults more difficult. The child specialist is the advocate for the children but isn't the professional whose skills are best suited to help the adults reach resolution in the face of their different opinions about change. For that reason, if you and your partner run into difficulties about parenting your children, you'll return to the coaches rather than going directly to the child specialist. If the coaches feel that the situation could benefit from clear information about what's actually going on with your children, they can easily bring the child specialist back for brief assistance in resolving the problem.

Your collaborative lawyers are the team members to call upon when changes may call for adjustments to financial arrangements about support or when differences about how to handle property or tax matters are involved. You or your partner simply contacts your collaborative lawyer, describes the problem, and asks for a brief return to the collaborative four-way table to brainstorm options, expand consensus, and reach resolution. If the help of the financial consultant or an accountant or appraiser would be a plus in order to generate necessary factual information, the collaborative lawyers will recommend that. And they are always the right team members to draft new or modified legal language changing the terms of your original divorce settlement agreement or to help you and your partner reach new legally binding contracts or agreements.

Sometimes, a visit to the financial consultant can help a divorced couple manage a change. If, for example, one of the former spouses has encountered financial problems that make it difficult to honor an agreement to share equally the expenses of a co-owned piece of real estate, the consultant might be able to suggest alternative financial scenarios that could get you through the period of scarcity. Either of you can request a brief return to the financial consultant for this kind of assistance with divorce-related issues—but only with divorce-related issues. Your financial consultant may not become the private advisor of either of you regarding matters unrelated to your divorce settlement. Usually, the financial consultant will want you to involve the collaborative lawyers so that you can translate the financial advice into new agreements that both of you understand fully and can commit to.

A couple who has completed a collaborative divorce and committed to a conflict resolution plan as part of their divorce agreement has usually learned quite a bit in the process about managing strong emotions and communicating clearly about differences. And at the same time, the professional team members have learned a lot about the couple: how they process information; what their basic values, priorities, and concerns are; how they handle emotionally charged discussions; how readily they reach resolution. Consequently, when team members are called in for help following the divorce, the work with them tends to be efficient and quick.

At the end of this chapter, you'll read about how Eileen and Andy planned for resolution of potential future conflicts. Their conflict resolution plan is typical of what many couples include in their settlement agreements. Andy and Eileen planned for how to resolve differences not only about parenting but also about support that could arise in connection with Eileen's eventual completion of her education and return to the workforce. Your team will help you anticipate changes that predictably lie ahead for you, your partner, and any children and will help you agree on steps you will take to reach agreement when those changes and others cause you and your spouse to disagree.

UNTYING THE KNOT AND TYING UP THE LOOSE ENDS

Though the divorce agreement is the fruit of all your efforts in the collaborative divorce, there are still loose ends that must be addressed. A future-oriented document that you can rely on often during the tumultuous months and years following the entry of your divorce judgment, the agreement is the most important paper your lawyers will prepare for you. But it's not the only one.

Whether or not your state permits uncontested divorces to be processed through the courts entirely by mail, there will be required court forms that your lawyers will prepare for you and help you process through the court. These forms differ from state to state. They tend to be routine in nature.

Similarly routine in nature, though sometimes more complicated, are the documents that change ownership of assets and responsibility for debts. Some of these vary from state to state, while others are uniform across all states. Some are less than a page in length, while others may consist of page after page of legalese. Some need to be signed by judges and other third parties or filed by a court clerk, while others don't. Because all these various forms and papers merely put into effect the resolutions in your settlement agreement, you won't need to engage in much discussion about them, but your lawyers will put time and energy into doing them properly for you.

For instance, transferring title to an automobile generally involves very simple paperwork—perhaps just a signature on a single form you already have in your possession. Transferring the title to a house may be more complicated; the deed needs to be carefully drawn, and there may be tax documents that need to be filed with the county tax collector, as well as other papers specific to your locale. Shifting retirement funds from one spouse to the other is always a highly technical matter. The papers need to be done exactly right, or serious tax problems can result. In some circumstances, actuaries may need to be involved, while in others, lengthy court orders must be prepared and signed not only by you and your spouse but also by the retirement plan administrator as well as the judge. As you can see, your lawyers will have work to do at this stage in order to make sure that your financial agreements are implemented as you intend.

THE SIGNING CEREMONY

When all the papers have been prepared and are ready to be signed, your collaborative lawyers will usually suggest a final gathering at a four-way meeting to review and sign all the papers. Unless your state requires you and your spouse to come before a judge before your marriage can be dissolved, this ceremonial final gathering at the

Going to Court in a Collaborative Divorce

The absolute rule in a collaborative divorce is that your collaborative lawyers and other team members may never participate in adversarial court proceedings between you and your spouse. So what if your state law requires you and your spouse to appear before a judge in person before your divorce decree will be granted? Do you have to go alone? And if the collaborative lawyers go with you, how does that fit with the strict rule that they aren't permitted to participate in court proceedings?

Answer: you don't have to go to court alone. The collaborative lawyers can go with you if a court appearance is required because no opposition is involved. This court appearance is the sole exception to the "never go to court" rule for collaborative lawyers.

lawyers' office will be the last face-to-face meeting in your legal divorce process.

WHY A SIGNING CEREMONY?

Although it may seem odd to have a ceremony that recognizes the end of a marriage, experience tells us that gathering together for a last meeting of this kind has many benefits.

First, your lawyers can review the written settlement agreement with both of you together so that any confusion or concerns can be sorted out. That means you won't have to discover something you don't understand while reviewing the document at home and have to set up another appointment to have your questions answered.

Your lawyers can review with you and your partner the normal changes and "speed bumps" that are likely to arise after the legal divorce is finished, during the period of rapid change and consolidation as you and your ex settle into your new lives. If you worked with coaches, they will have done this work with you earlier at some length, but whether or not you worked with coaches, a review as you sign your agreement is always wise. This helps you have a clear sense of what lies ahead and will keep you from being too distressed when these normal changes take place.

You and your partner can review and confirm face to face the plan you've agreed upon for resolving future conflicts. This cements good will and increases the chances that you will both stick to what you have agreed to and that you will follow through on your commitments.

Your lawyers can take time to congratulate each of you about moments of grace, generosity, flexibility, and creativity, as well as remind each of you how far you have come since the divorce process began. This can let you end on a positive note that you can take with you as you start a new chapter of your life.

You and your partner both can use this occasion as a marker of the end of a major chapter in your lives—a fitting "bookend" to a chapter that began with the ceremony of marriage. Time and time again, we have seen that the closure this affords a couple has great psychological benefits.

After all, your marriage may be ending, but the years you spent together will remain an important piece of your personal life history. If your marriage was like most we have seen, it had good moments as well as bad. Being able to look back with acceptance of the good as well as the bad is a gift of wholeness to yourself and your children, if you have them. The family album contains photographs of this chapter. Though it may always be somewhat poignant to look at them, you'll do so with much greater comfort and integrity if you have ended this last chapter consciously and well.

The final four-way meeting can be an important element in ending the marriage well, emotionally as well as legally. Unlike making an appearance before a judge in a busy courtroom or signing papers alone or at your lawyer's office as the final event of your marriage, this final four-way meeting is always personal, always constructive, always focused on what was done well during the divorce and on planning well for the future. That makes it an event you will be able to look back on with some sense of pride and personal accomplishment.

We humans seem to be hardwired to want clear beginnings, middles, and ends, so that we can experience a sense of completion about the major transitional events of our lives. Transitional ceremonies such as the final signing four-way meeting give us a sense of order and integrity. They help us close the books on one chapter of life and to embark wholeheartedly on the next, without regrets and a sense of unfinished business. Just as we meet human emotional needs when we have christening and naming ceremonies, First Communion and Bar Mitzvah ceremonies, graduations and retirement dinners, weddings and funerals, there is an emotional need that is met by the closing four-way meeting.

Just as you might decide to skip a christening or graduation or funeral, you could certainly decide you don't want a closing ceremony. But showing up and participating with intentionality seems, in our experience, to help couples move forward with life, while not doing so can leave people dangling emotionally, with nagging feelings of something left undone.

WHAT HAPPENS IN A SIGNING FOUR-WAY MEETING?

For many couples, the final legal four-way meeting represents the intentional crossing of a bridge into the future. Particularly for couples without children, this last legal four-way meeting could be the last time they deliberately meet face to face. Whether or not that is so, the planned gathering to review what was accomplished, to anticipate what is likely to come, and to sign the papers that will end permanently the marital relationship that all couples enter into with such profound hope and vulnerability is by its very nature a ceremonial occasion.

How it is handled will make a difference, for better or for worse, in how both members of a couple look back on the ending of their intimate connection. For that reason, collaborative teams often encourage their clients to consider how to imbue the event with personal meaning.

Without such a meeting, the marriage that may have begun with so much ceremony and ritual ends with nothing more than a solitary flourish of pens in separate offices. Even in jurisdictions where a divorcing couple must appear in court for the judge to announce that the marriage is dissolved, the event is anticlimactic and unsatisfying. Each spouse waits separately with his or her lawyer—often in a courtroom crowded with lawyers and clients arguing motions—until their case is called by the court clerk. They come forward, sit at separate "counsel tables," and are each asked under oath the formulaic questions required under local law for the judge to be able to say, "Divorce granted." Whether such a court appearance is required or not, no meaningful event of any kind takes place to mark the momentous fact that a marriage has now come to a final, irrevocable end.

Your collaborative divorce professionals know that as sad as the failure of an intimate relationship may be, there can be genuine satisfaction in ending it gracefully and well. When there is no felt recognition that something important and valuable has come to an end, we feel incomplete, up in the air, unsettled.

AN OPPORTUNITY TO CREATE PERSONAL MEANING

You may be a very matter-of-fact, no-nonsense sort of person who likes to stick to basics and move forward efficiently. Spending time reflecting on personal life history, acknowledging the end of one life cycle and the beginning of another, or allowing space for recognition of complicated feelings may sound foreign to you, perhaps even uncomfortable. Rest assured: if all that you and your spouse want to do in your final legal four-way meeting is sign the necessary papers and move on, that's what will happen. If those jobs are done consciously and well, a ceremonial closing will have taken place that can actually help you and your spouse "close the books" on the past and move more consciously and with greater ease into the future.

Consider, though, that this last meeting puts closure on an enormously important chapter of your personal life history that began on your wedding day. Perhaps your wedding was a simple, matter-of-fact occasion, a civil ceremony at city hall followed by a private celebration between you and your spouse. You may want to do something just as simple on the day of the final legal four-way meeting.

But for many people, their wedding day was a carefully designed ceremonial event of great personal significance. Perhaps the bride and groom and their attendants wore elaborate formal garb and spoke their vows in an enormous cathedral or hotel ballroom. Perhaps they gathered with friends on a mountaintop to participate in a ceremony they had designed themselves with great imagination and care. Perhaps they even spoke their marriage vows on horseback or surfboards. The particular vows spoken by bride and groom may have been cloaked with ancient religious authority or echoes of ancient family rituals, or may have been highly personal or poetic affirmations of hope and intention. It may have been the first marriage of very young people or a second or third marriage of widowers or divorcés.

Whatever your marriage ceremony was like, we are convinced that honoring what was good about the marriage that is ending can have great value for our clients and their children. We do this throughout our work with divorcing couples who choose collaborative divorce, and we do this with particular attention at the time of the final legal four-way meeting.

Your team will help you think in advance about whether to include any particularly meaningful personal elements in that final legal four-way meeting, or perhaps in a special meeting with the coaches if that is more comfortable. This is an opportunity for personalizing the last day of the marriage that can never be repeated.

We close this chapter with examples of ways that couples we have worked with have made meaningful personal closings of their last legal four-way meeting. Some of these "ceremonies" are simple indeed, while others are more complicated or spiritual in nature. What seems awkward or forced to one couple may be for another couple a major step toward healing and moving on. Think of the final legal four-way meeting as your opportunity to close your marriage with a sense that you conducted yourself well.

- Claudia prepared a list of things Paul had done during their fifty-year marriage that had enriched the life she had shared with him, their two children, and their many grandchildren. As Paul listened, he was spontaneously moved to thank Claudia for the support, companionship, and rich home life that their marriage had given him. He acknowledged the growing independence and competency she'd exhibited during the year of collaborative coaching and negotiations, moving from dependent homemaker to capable manager of her own life and finances. It had been a challenging journey for Claudia, from her initial despair at Paul's unexpected request for a divorce to her comfortable presence at this last four-way meeting. When the papers were ready to sign, Claudia looked directly at Paul, held her hand across the table to him, and said, " I want this divorce." He grasped her hand and replied, "I also want this divorce." They passed the necessary papers back and forth for signature, paused to look at one another quietly, and for a moment both had tears in their eyes. Claudia then suggested that everyone have a glass of the champagne she had brought. Each lawyer proposed a toast to the work that Claudia and Paul had accomplished. As they left, Claudia and Paul hugged briefly and a few more tears were shed.
- Andrew and Lisa had chosen collaborative divorce because they believed it was the best way to ensure that their children's needs would be attended to as they ended their marriage. They and their children arrived at the final legal four-way meeting as a family. The children

sat on the couch and watched as the lawyers recounted the accomplishments of the parents in the process and emphasized the careful plans both parents had made for the welfare of the children, both now and in the future, including their agreement to come back for fine-tuning of the parenting plan as the children grew older. At the end Lisa and Andrew praised each other as parents, then turned to the children and promised to include them whenever decisions needed to be made about their lives and interests. Before leaving, the children hugged both parents. They appeared perhaps not happy, but certainly at peace with the divorce.

- Suzanne had requested a divorce from Alex, her high school sweetheart, because they had grown apart over the twelve years of their marriage and she felt they had little in common anymore. She arrived at the final legal four-way meeting with a full carryall bag, and after the necessary papers had been signed, she asked Alex whether it would be okay if she conducted a brief divorce ritual. He agreed. She lit a candle and read a short poem with a powerful message about endings and beginnings. She pulled out a small wrapped gift, which she handed to Alex, saying simply, "I forgive you for the rough spots—I hope you can forgive me—and I wouldn't have given up our relationship for anything, even if I'd known in advance how it would end."

A FINAL MEETING:
EILEEN AND ANDY'S STORY

The final legal four-way meeting in Eileen and Andy's collaborative divorce took place in Pauline's conference room, at the round table where Eileen and Andy and their collaborative lawyers had gathered from time to time for their legal meetings over the preceding five months. A month earlier, after four of these four-way sessions, full terms of agreement had been reached that satisfied both Eileen and Andy. The two lawyers, Pauline and David, had then gone to work, preparing and revising the final settlement agreement to everyone's satisfaction.

Attached to the agreement was the parenting plan that had been worked out with the help of the collaborative divorce coaches and child specialist, as well as a property division spreadsheet prepared with the help of the collaborative financial consultant. The legal forms required by the court were ready, too. It was time to complete the legal part of the divorce by signing the agreement and other papers and sending them to the court. On the table were neat packets of documents with copies for everyone, as well as light refreshments of fruit, cheese, and crackers.

Pauline opened the meeting by reading briefly from the minutes of the second legal four-way meeting the broad general statements of values that Eileen and Andy had each made early in the collaborative divorce about what kind of a divorce process and agreement would represent a success for each of them. Together, Pauline and David reviewed some of the challenges that Eileen and Andy had faced during the process as they gathered information, shared priorities and values, and brainstormed options for resolution.

Each lawyer noted moments of grace and generosity that had occurred during the divorce process and congratulated both Eileen and Andy for a job well done—for arriving at a comprehensive agreement that matched their own values, priorities, and concerns. They invited Eileen and Andy each to comment on how well the process had worked for them.

Both Eileen and Andy mentioned how nervous they had been at the first legal four-way meeting and how reassuring it had been to spend time getting comfortable with the other lawyer and the collaborative process before jumping into the information-gathering phase. They also both expressed surprise and relief that after working for a relatively short time with their coaches, they had been able to devise a good parenting plan without getting bogged down in old arguments about differences in their parenting styles.

Eileen thanked Andy for his unexpected willingness to step in and help with extra transporting and caring for the children during her mother's final illness, which had occurred as the divorce process unfolded, and as she did so, all could see her tears well up. Andy, obviously moved, in turn thanked Eileen for being willing to consider a range of alternatives about when and how to sell the family residence—something he had initially thought was a closed subject for her. For Andy, this openness to other options was the key to devising a housing and asset division solution that would allow him to live near the children and therefore to remain involved in day-to-day parenting.

Next, the two lawyers reviewed the specifics of the final settlement agreement with Eileen and Andy, pointing out several provisions that had required flexibility and creative thinking on everyone's part. They reminded Andy and Eileen that during the next three to five years—if they were like most divorcing families—many changes would take place, some of which might involve differences of opinion, and they reviewed with Eileen and Andy the specific steps both had committed to take to resolve any future disagreements that might arise, outside court. Andy and Eileen each expressed optimism that they would be able to work out any problems that might lie ahead, particularly since the collaborative divorce coaches would remain available.

Their parenting agreement called for a review of their time-sharing plan after a year, to see whether it needed any adjustment. Since Eileen would be finishing her college degree program and entering the workforce around that same time, the lawyers invited her and Andy to consider at that same point whether there had been any financial changes significant enough to require adjustments to the support arrangements and, if so, to return to the collaborative lawyers at that time for help.

Then Pauline and David circulated the settlement agreement and the court forms for signature, giving all those present copies for their files. Eileen and Andy were clearly relieved to have reached this point.

Yet both hesitated to bring the meeting to a close. Both of them obviously needed something more to acknowledge the significance of this moment for them. Pauline suggested a toast to their perseverance, their commitment to full disclosure, and their abiding faith in the integrity of collaboration. With their agreement she opened some wine, and the meeting ended on a relaxed note. As Andy and Eileen left the office, Andy and David shook hands and everyone else exchanged spontaneous hugs. The sense of completion was palpable. Andy and Eileen were deep in animated conversation as they left together.

8

EXPECTING AND DEALING WITH CHANGE

To exist is to change, to change is to mature, to mature is to go on cre-
ating oneself endlessly.

—Henri Bergson

Problems, disagreements, and bumps in the road don't stop simply because a divorce agreement was signed and a judgment was issued.
They keep on coming, sometimes more rapidly than ever, during the
period immediately following a divorce. But with collaborative divorce, you'll be prepared. It's the only mode of divorce conflict resolution that does not regard the work of your professional helpers as
finished just because a court enters a divorce decree.

Your team knows that some of the biggest challenges most couples
face will arise in the months and years after traditional lawyers close
their divorce files. Unlike those lawyers, your team will remain available to you and will encourage you to make use of their resources after
your divorce decree is entered, as part of how you think about your divorce. While the signing of a piece of paper is a legal event, completing

the reconstruction of new family systems after the divorce is a much longer process. Because changes and challenges are a normal part of the divorce process, collaborative divorce builds understandings into your divorce agreement that detail how you and your ex-spouse will resolve differences as these changes arise. Part of what makes the agreement such an important document is this anticipation of future problems and the inclusion of a road map for resolving them.

With it, you know what to expect from yourself and your partner when these anticipated changes occur, and also when an unexpected bump in the road interrupts the smooth forward movement in your life. Instead of making angry trips back to the courthouse, couples who reach collaborative divorce agreements know that when these changes happen, it's time to roll up their sleeves and get to work on solutions.

EXPECT CHANGE: IT'S NORMAL

If you were wondering why your best friend's divorce involved so many bitter trips back to the courthouse after the divorce was over and how it is that we can be so confident it won't happen to you in a collaborative divorce, here's the reason: court orders dictate rules for future behavior based on what happened in the past. Looking backward, those orders can't encourage flexibility to adjust to changes—even though we know that change is normal and is going to happen at a rapid pace in most families during the years immediately following the divorce. For example, the reality is that very few couples follow the terms of divorce judgments about children for longer than about eighteen months after the entry of judgment. Instead of fighting about it, we encourage you to expect—and work constructively with—change.

COMMON CHANGES

Every family travels its own unique path after the legal divorce is over, but some patterns of change are common. Children grow up and their interests and needs shift, throwing off schedules and arrangements. Younger children may no longer want to study ballet or gymnastics or piano or play soccer or swim, despite their parents' intense differences of opinion and struggles to reach resolution about these matters at the time of the divorce. Similarly, older teens may resist a carefully tailored time-sharing plan because they want and need unstructured time with their friends.

Someone may lose a job; someone may be transferred to another state; someone may become critically ill. Most divorced people form new intimate relationships within a few years after the divorce; they may remarry and start second families. These and other changes that often take place during the years following a divorce can be rich fuel for ongoing battles.

Knowing that these developments are on the horizon and recognizing that they may trigger strong feelings helps to soften the impact of these events if and when they do occur. Having a plan for how you will manage those events if they happen will add to your confidence—both now and then. A well-crafted collaborative divorce agreement includes such a plan, in the form of general principles and steps you and your partner will employ to handle these difficult but normal challenges. With such a plan in place, adapting to change can be much smoother and more manageable. If finding an acceptable adjustment to existing arrangements proves difficult on your own, you will have a team of coaches, a child specialist, a financial consultant, and collaborative lawyers to call upon who know you and your family and who can help as needed.

WHEN PROGRESS STOPS

If you are like nearly all the couples we have worked with, your conflict resolution plan is all you'll need to achieve resolution in times of change and disagreement. After all, you were able to reach agreement about very difficult issues with the help of your team at a time when both you and your partner were probably far more emotional and less resilient than you will be as time passes. Even if your differences are great and emotions are running high, nearly all couples find that they can reach resolution with the help of the right team members. Steve and Jenny, whose story you will read below, illustrate how even a couple with very challenging problems can use their conflict resolution plan to reach resolution.

But what if, for some reason, your conflict resolution plan is not sufficient? What if you return for help from your team and you still cannot reach agreement with your ex-spouse about how to deal with a change that affects the terms of your divorce agreement? It's simple: you always have the option of terminating the collaborative divorce process and using conventional "old-style divorce" conflict resolution techniques: motions, court proceedings, and hardball legal-template settlement negotiations. In our experience, few couples decide to take this course, but if necessary, it's always available.

STAYING ON TRACK WHEN EMOTIONS RUN HIGH AFTER THE DIVORCE: STEVE AND JENNY'S STORY

Now remarried to other spouses, Steve and Jenny chose collaborative divorce eight years ago to end their twelve-year marriage. Steve was a widower with two young sons when he and Jenny married. After two years, they had a daughter, Lynn. Their marriage ended stormily when Jenny became involved in an affair with a coworker, and the divorce process that followed was fraught with intense emotional outbursts on both sides. Steve was hurt and angry, Jenny guilty and defensive.

Lynn, who was ten at the time of the divorce, found the upheaval in her family life terribly confusing and upsetting. The boys, who were adults at the time of the divorce, were furious at Jenny for hurting their father and sister. In spite of the strong currents of negative feeling, Steve and Jenny had agreed from the start that the highest priority in their divorce was to do their very best as parents to Lynn. Though the divorce process was difficult, their entire collaborative divorce professional team—coaches, child specialist, financial consultant, and collaborative lawyers—helped them through the rough patches, until they reached a complete divorce agreement they could both live with.

However, completing the divorce did not make their problems disappear. Jenny and Steve returned four times during the first year following the divorce decree to work with their divorce coaches about difficult challenges in coparenting Lynn.

For instance, Steve reacted with barely contained outrage when Jenny announced only weeks after entry of the divorce judgment that she would be moving in with her boyfriend. Steve demanded that Lynn live with him full-time while Jenny gave her attention to managing her new relationship and handling a promotion at work.

Jenny at first rejected that idea as an unthinkable admission that she was a bad parent, but the coaches and child specialist helped her see how little time she actually was available to Lynn during the workweek. After some challenging coaching sessions, she agreed that, at least for a while, Lynn would live with Steve during the week and spend weekends with her.

Because they had resolved that difficult problem through honest, clear communications focused on information about Lynn's needs rather than through a fight aimed at persuading a judge, neither Steve nor Jenny became overly concerned about who was the "good" parent, and neither felt that these changes in their parenting arrangement would be irreversible. They remained able to pay attention to how Lynn was actually doing instead of being blinded by fears about one or the other gaining control over Lynn.

Soon afterward it became evident to both parents that Lynn was suffering. By now, they understood how unhelpful it would be simply to blame each other for Lynn's pain. Instead, they arranged for her to return for further talk with the child specialist, who determined that Lynn was seriously depressed. The arrangement that had seemed a promising solution to Jenny and Steve was not working for Lynn. She felt hurt and abandoned, believing that her mother wanted to be with the new boyfriend, not with her. Through the child specialist, Lynn was able to make this clear to Jenny.

The time had come, Jenny realized, for serious self-reflection. Working with her coach, she concluded that big changes were needed if parenting Lynn well was really a priority for her. She would need to move to her own apartment and cut back to part-time work, even if it meant accepting a demotion, in order to spend more time with her daughter. But Steve strongly opposed Jenny's plan. He argued that for Lynn to make another change in her primary residence so soon would only create further upheaval in her life.

Steve's coach helped Steve to differentiate his continuing anger at Jenny from his genuine commitment to Lynn's welfare. With the child specialist's help, he saw how much pain it was causing Lynn to feel abandoned by Jenny. To him, Jenny seemed unstable and unreliable, but with his team's help, he was able to accept the proposed change for Lynn's sake, if Jenny would agree to remain in her own apartment and not include any other adults in her household for at least a full year. With that understanding, Steve and Jenny reversed the schedule so that Lynn would be with Jenny during the week and with Steve on weekends.

Six months later, Steve met a woman he cared about and told Jenny he planned to ask her to move in with him. This precipitated another visit to the coaches. They reminded Steve that while neither he nor Jenny had any right to be involved in decisions about the private life of the other, they had agreed on the importance of stability for Lynn and their parenting plan included reaching mutual agreement about how and when Lynn would be introduced to new adult partners.

It took several more sessions for Jenny and Steve to reach resolution: neither of them would have a live-in lover until at least a full year after this current series of conversations. They would alternate full weeks with Lynn to give each of them time for their private lives as well as sustained parenting time with Lynn. They also agreed to insulate her completely from all new adult relationships for the time being. As both Jenny's and Steve's new relationships ended before the year was up, both parents felt considerable relief that Lynn had been spared involvement with either person.

By the time that year ended, things were finally beginning to settle down. When Steve's son Edward graduated from college at the top of his class, his entire extended family—Steve, Jenny, and Lynn, along with Jenny's parents and both sets of biological grandparents— attended the ceremony. All the adults who had been close to Edward as he grew up were able to take pride in his valedictory speech. Edward was grateful he could celebrate this event with all the adults who mattered to him—unlike his best friend, Adam, whose parents' continuing bitterness years after their ugly divorce had made it impossible for him to invite both to the graduation. A year later, Edward's brother, Malcolm, was married—and again, the entire extended family gathered to celebrate. The wedding photographs show happy adults whose focus is on sharing joy with the young couple.

However, when Lynn turned fifteen, new challenges arose. Steve remarried and Lynn—already a difficult teenager—became moody, demanding, and disobedient. Her grades dropped, and she began to skip school. Steve brushed off Jenny's efforts to talk with him about Lynn's problems, dismissing them as normal teenage behavior. To Jenny, it seemed that Steve didn't care.

As provided in their divorce agreement, Jenny asked Steve to return for help from the coaches, and Steve agreed. It took only one session for them to devise new ground rules for Lynn's behavior in both their homes. These changes provided the very boundaries and limits that Lynn needed. She has done well in high school, is about to graduate, and will go away to college in the fall.

Jenny recently reported to her coach that all the adults involved in Lynn's life will be attending her high school graduation and that Jenny herself plans to remarry in the fall. She expressed great appreciation for the guidance and help that the coach had given her at critical times. Although she wasn't always happy with what she heard there, Jenny knows those coaching sessions were a lifeline to rational thinking for her at a time when her judgment was poor. She looks back on the period right after her divorce as a time when she was "close to crazy" and wonders now how she could ever have considered moving in with a new lover so soon after leaving Steve.

Without the support and help of the collaborative team, she is certain her mistakes—and Steve's, too—would have been far more damaging to Lynn than they actually were. They achieved the best divorce they were capable of—a far better process and outcome than they had initially imagined to be possible.

Steve and Jenny faced an unusually challenging series of problems during this "rapid change and consolidation" phase of their collaborative divorce—some of them predictable, others less so. Each in their own way was somewhat impulsive, somewhat reactive, and somewhat immature in temperament, qualities that are often magnified during separation and divorce. If Steve and Jenny could manage to remain in constructive problem-solving mode during the five tumultuous years following their collaborative divorce, we think that with the help of a collaborative divorce team, the chances are reasonably good that you can, too.

MATURE HANDLING OF DIFFERENCES AFTER DIVORCE: ELLEN AND PETER'S STORY

Ellen and Peter went through a collaborative divorce, ending a twelve-year marriage. Peter has considerable inherited wealth and was willing to build into their divorce agreement financial and other terms that would allow Ellen to earn an M.B.A. so that instead of returning to middle school teaching, she could have greater earning power and maintain her standard of living even after her alimony eventually terminated. In return, her alimony was to end sooner than it otherwise would have.

But after two years, Peter became concerned because Ellen had not yet completed her degree. She had taken a semester off and was then pursuing less than a full-time program of studies. He felt taken advantage of and became angry. He had already paid for quite a lot of education, but the prospects of the alimony ending as planned in their settlement agreement were looking slim to him.

Peter and Ellen had also built into their divorce agreement a con-flict resolution process that they could both rely on if problems arose. That conflict resolution plan had two stages:

First, Ellen and Peter would confer and see whether they could reach agreement about their differences. They did confer, but Ellen got upset and angry at what she considered his pressure and his lack of sympathy. After this meeting, Peter felt frustrated and at a dead end.

Second, if this did not resolve the problem, their conflict resolu-tion plan provided that at the request of either of them they would re-turn either to the collaborative lawyers or to the collaborative coaches for help. Peter met with his collaborative lawyer as agreed.

Peter's lawyer scheduled a four-way meeting that included Ellen and her collaborative lawyer. Their agenda was to discuss why Ellen hadn't met the anticipated schedule for completing her degree. It be-came apparent during this meeting that Ellen was depressed and her energy was low. She reported that she had been quite ill with Lyme disease and that the treatment would take a full year to complete. The two collaborative lawyers, with Ellen's consent, scheduled a confer-ence call with her physician, who told them that Ellen was likely to be debilitated for some months but that her prognosis for a full recovery after a year or so was excellent.

Ellen shared that belief. But she privately told her lawyer she was feeling overwhelmed by the emotional impact of the disease and her lost time in her master's program. She was having difficulty speaking straightforwardly about her situation with Peter, both alone and at the legal four-way table.

The two lawyers conferred, and at their suggestion, Ellen and Peter participated in two coaching sessions, which gave each of them a much-needed opportunity to communicate their concerns and fears clearly. Only then did they return to the legal four-way process, where they found that they were far more able to discuss the situation and what to do about it than had been possible before the coaching.

They renegotiated the terms of their financial agreement in a way that satisfied both of them. Ellen would be allowed a full year from the date of their new agreement for treatment, with no expectation that she would take courses unless she felt able to do so. However, after that year she would have to maintain a full-time program and complete the degree on time. If she did not follow through, Peter would have no further obligation to pay for her tuition, and under some circumstances (detailed in their new agreement) she might even be obliged to reimburse him for the tuition he had already paid. Alimony would end one year after she completed her degree or five years from the date of their original divorce decree, whichever came first.

Both felt that all their concerns had been clearly expressed and heard with respect. Both felt satisfied with this resolution. Ellen and Peter remained friends and are reasonably optimistic about the future. Peter's adult daughter from a prior marriage is expecting her first child, and Ellen and Peter are both gratified that they will be able to share this happy event as cograndparents.

The friendship between Ellen and Peter mattered a great deal to both of them. Their work in collaborative divorce protected the survival of that friendship in a new form after their divorce. Their conflict resolution plan anticipated possible changes and challenges after the entry of their divorce judgment. It provided an agreed-upon mode of resolution, so that neither Ellen nor Peter overreacted when both were distressed in the face of an unanticipated change. The ready availability of their team helped them move quickly to adjust their agreement in response to changed circumstances. Quick response to change allowed them to keep their focus where they both wanted it to be: on building future lives that would work for both of them.

Ellen and Peter were careful not to allow misunderstandings or emotional reactions to dictate how they addressed their differences. Their collaborative divorce agreement is not just a dusty piece of paper in a court file. Instead, it's a living document that continues to help them weather both predictable and unexpected challenges. It is an agreement that will last.

9

MOVING ON:
Life After It's Really Over

Peace is not an absence of war. It is a virtue, a state of mind, a disposi-
tion for benevolence, confidence, justice.

—BARUCH SPINOZA

In collaborative divorces as in conventional divorces, no questions are
asked more often than "When will we be done?" and "Is it over yet?"
You've seen that many storms remain to be weathered with your team
during the challenging period of change following the divorce decree.
Eventually, even that phase of your divorce comes to an end—not dramatically, but quietly. With reflection, one day you'll realize that your
collaborative divorce is at last well and truly over. Your new family system has settled into stability, your relationships with friends and family
have survived the crisis of divorce, and your disagreements with your
former spouse are few.

We can't tell you exactly when this will occur. For some couples
with short marriages, no children, financial independence, and few

ongoing family ties, this can happen quickly. For others, such as Steve and Jenny (the couple you met in the last chapter), navigating the shoals of rapid change continues for years and the team will be called in to help with some regularity.

You'll know you're approaching completion when, instead of riding the emotional roller coaster we described in chapter 1, you are spending most of your time back on the ground. You'll recognize that your collaborative divorce is finally over when most of the time you feel like the person you were accustomed to being before your marriage came to an end. The fog of confusion and anxiety has cleared. You don't feel overwhelmed by change or by the need to make major life decisions before you are ready. You have energy for yourself, your work, your children, your family, and your friends. Your life has settled into new patterns that are starting to feel familiar and stable. You know what to expect from life most days. You feel optimistic again.

LOOKING BACK, LOOKING AHEAD

What happens after you've made peace with your divorce? We devote a short chapter of this book to a subject that will be a very long chapter of your experience: the rest of your life. You might wonder why we include it at all in a book about collaborative divorce. After all, the collaborative divorce is now over.

The reason we now focus on it briefly is simple: when couples embrace the collaborative divorce process and make full use of its resources for deep resolution of conflict, planning for the future, and the protection of relationships during a challenging life passage, we see a difference in the quality of their lives after the divorce is over. From the beginning, they are encouraged by their professional helpers to expect and aspire to a dignified, respectful, civilized ending of their intimate connection. And that is what nearly all couples who work with collaborative divorce teams do achieve.

It's common for people to step back at this point and reflect on their divorce as a complete experience that has now drawn to a close. In a sense, it's like a scrapbook that the divorced spouses thumb through, shut, tie with a ribbon, and put on the shelf. In doing so, they tend to sum up, consciously or not, the personal experience of that life passage in fairly simple, broad-brush terms: "Not so bad," "Better than I expected," "Amazing," "Hard work but worth it," "I learned so much," "We did it!," "What a relief," "I'm so grateful for the help we had," and so forth.

From then on, when the thought of the divorce passes through their minds, it's the quality of the experience that they tend to recall, together with a few emblematic moments in the divorce. In collaborative divorce, couples choose and expect a process that reduces conflict and aims for highest shared intentions. Consequently, the memories that flash into their awareness when the subject of the divorce comes to mind are largely moments of accomplishment—the times when a difficult challenge became a constructive solution.

If your experience is like theirs, at this point in your divorce your quick mental picture of yourself and your partner during the divorce process will tend to be of two people working hard to maintain dignity and mutual respect—and for the most part succeeding. If you chose to have a final signing meeting, you'll almost certainly remember that as one of the emblematic moments.

We don't want to claim too much. Couples whose marriages were brief and whose interest in continuing a connection is negligible will of course benefit from the coordinated skills of the team during their divorce. For such couples, the period of changes and challenges after the divorce decree may be very brief. They may not need the help of a team after their legal divorce is done, and they may recover from the stress of the divorce quickly. Even those couples, however, take away from their collaborative divorce into the rest of their lives something that other divorce modes don't usually provide: a memory of having done it carefully, completely, and constructively. This, we know, serves people well as they move forward into new relationships.

For people with longer marriages and more challenging divorces, we have seen that collaborative divorce makes a much bigger difference in the quality of life after the marriage is over. Putting on the imaginary shelf a mental scrapbook about their divorce experience that includes dignified behavior and a constructive process and acceptable outcome for every challenge leaves people far stronger, more optimistic, and more able to embrace what life brings them than people for whom the mental divorce scrapbook is largely a record of fear, suspicion, overreaction, miscommunication, anger, struggle, and disappointment—the old-style divorce scrapbook.

Our collaborative divorce clients for the most part emerge with their integrity intact, with renewed confidence about family and relationships, and with the possibility for creative extended family systems that can grow out of respect and friendship with the former intimate partner.

The story below illustrates how life after the collaborative divorce for one such couple took a direction that enriched the lives of many people—a direction that would have been beyond their capacity to imagine had they chosen an old-style divorce.

LIFE CAN TAKE SURPRISING TURNS AFTER A SUCCESSFUL COLLABORATIVE DIVORCE: PAUL AND NANCY'S STORY

Paul and Nancy ended their ten-year marriage four years ago. When they married, Nancy was thirty-four and Paul was forty-two; both of them were ready to start a family. Their marriage ended after five years of stressful fertility treatments, when it became clear that Nancy couldn't bear a child. Paul wanted a child that was genetically his; Nancy was not willing to use a surrogate mother. They were out of options. After years of emotional and physical struggle, Nancy was almost relieved when Paul finally asked for a divorce.

She and Paul chose collaborative divorce because both valued a civilized, respectful end to their intimate relationship. Nancy wanted her connections with Paul and his family to continue as friendships. Paul wanted to be as kind as possible to Nancy so that he could continue to pursue fatherhood with as little guilt as possible.

Paul's sister Beth, a professor at the local college, was Nancy's closest friend. The two women had a tradition of traveling together on vacation each year, often accompanied by Paul's mother, a still-youthful widow.

At first Paul resented his mother's and sister's intention to continue their friendship with Nancy, but with coaching he accepted how pointless it would be, and how difficult for everyone, if he tried to force his relatives to take sides. With his coach's help, he saw that his own guilty feelings about ending the marriage were leading him to suppose—wrongly—that the women would gang up against him if they all remained friends. In fact, Nancy and he were not enemies, and there was no reason why the rest of his family should not remain her friends, just as he hoped to do.

With the air cleared in coaching, the divorce negotiations with the collaborative lawyers went smoothly. Nancy and Paul divided their property without difficulty. Nancy moved into the apartment complex where Beth lived, and the three women continued their cherished tradition of annual vacations together.

Soon after the divorce, Paul met and married a young Japanese woman. While he was on an extended business trip in Japan with his wife, his mother was critically injured in an automobile accident. She required daily care in her home during her lengthy rehabilitation period. Together, Nancy and Beth provided the help she needed to recover.

Within eighteen months of Paul's remarriage, he became the father of twins. Although he was hesitant because of how odd it might look to other people, his mother and sister encouraged him in the idea of asking Nancy to be his children's godmother. His wife agreed. After only a little reflection, Nancy was pleased to accept. Nancy is in no hurry to remarry; she is enjoying her life as a single woman with an extended family she cares about. Nancy, Paul, and Paul's mother and sister all refused to allow their negative emotions at the end of the marriage to unravel a rich web of relationships that enriches life for all of them.

They are all moving forward with life in a way none of them could have imagined at the time of separation. It is collaborative divorce, with its respectful, integrity-based conflict resolution, its emphasis on valuing relationships, and its focus on the future, that opened the door to these possibilities.

10

COMMON QUESTIONS AND CONCERNS

All people facing divorce share some common questions and concerns. Some will arise in connection with unique situations, but they will still be variations on common themes, such as difficulty controlling emotions or breaches of trust. We will look at both kinds of concerns in this segment of the book, where we apply the ideas you've read about in the previous chapters to answering the kinds of questions and concerns we hear every day, especially from potential clients who are contemplating embarking on the collaborative divorce process. We've grouped these questions and concerns into three sections: "Thinking About Collaborative Divorce," "Talking to Others About Collaborative Divorce," and "Understanding the Process Better." Feel free either to jump to the segment that seems likeliest to address the pressing issues on your mind right now, or to start from the beginning.

THINKING ABOUT COLLABORATIVE DIVORCE

My husband just told me he wants a divorce. He suggested collaborative divorce and wants me to get a lawyer, but I am so overwhelmed with grief and pain I don't feel ready to deal with this at all. What can I do?

This is a difficult time, but as well as being a crisis it is also a valuable window of opportunity. Your husband is ready to move forward, having already—on his own—dealt with his own feelings about ending your marriage. You, on the other hand, have been hit with a double whammy: first, the shock of an unexpected and immense loss, and second, the need to enter the unfamiliar and possibly frightening arena of a legal divorce process. People in the earliest stages of loss of an intimate partnership—whether by death or by divorce—often experience periods of denial ("This can't be happening to me!") and depression ("I am too overwhelmed by feelings of grief to handle any of this right now").

However, there is some good news. First, after a while you will feel better, and you'll gradually feel much more ready to handle the demands of the divorce. Second, your husband is suggesting a divorce mode that will allow both of you to proceed only as fast as is comfortable. Once both of you have collaborative lawyers and coaches, it may be possible to agree that all will initially proceed at a slow pace while you adjust to this unexpected and unwelcome change in your life. That's one example of why it could be to your advantage that he wishes to proceed via collaborative divorce. Ignoring his request could result in frustration on his part and could lead him to an "old-style" divorce litigator. That's not likely to be in your best interests.

First, tell your husband that you want to consider the idea. Even if you are upset and don't feel you can deal with anything right now, you can let him know that you are open to the possibility. By reading this, you have already taken a step in the right direction and you can tell him that.

Second, give attention to helping yourself feel better. How you can help yourself move forward depends on how you personally find comfort when things get tough in your life. For some people, getting organized helps them feel more competent and less helpless. If you are like that, you might want to set up a divorce notebook with several sections in which you can organize different kinds of material relating to the divorce. One section could be for research about potential collaborative lawyers and coaches. You may not be ready to interview team members, but just the fact that you are doing this preliminary work will show your husband you are taking his request for a divorce seriously. In this section of your notebook, you can file printouts of website information for various lawyers and coaches, as well as notes of any telephone contacts with their offices and notes of meetings with them. Later, you can use this notebook to organize copies of papers your coach, lawyer, and financial consultant give you. Other useful sections could include

- A planning section where you write down concerns, goals, priorities, and discussion points
- A section for your own written reflections about the divorce process, not to be shared with anyone else. It's been shown that simply writing for ten minutes a day—without any specific goal or purpose and without censoring what you put down—is strong medicine for depression and anxiety. You can use that section for some of the written exercises you'll read about later in this part of the book. Or you could dedicate a separate notebook or journal to this

During challenging times, some people benefit greatly from talking with others. Make time with friends and ask them just to listen without giving advice. Tell them about your feelings and how you are coming to grips with what is happening. If no one is available to be with you, use the telephone.

These approaches and others you'll read about below will gradually help you recover your composure. When you are ready to take a concrete step, consider suggesting to your husband that you'd feel more comfortable beginning the divorce process with coaches rather than lawyers. The sooner you are able to take this step, the better, because meeting with your first team members is the initial step in confirming that yours will be a collaborative rather than an adversarial divorce. Your husband is much further along in the divorce recovery process than you are and is likely to crave forward movement. Getting started with coaches will reassure him that something concrete is happening. And the coaches can help each of you handle the significant differences in your current feelings about the divorce.

I understand that I can expect help from my coach in dealing with the emotional shock of this unexpected divorce, but I am not ready to interview any professionals—including coaches. It's just too painful to talk about the divorce right now. Is there anything you can suggest that I can do now, on my own, to help me reach the point where I can talk to potential team members?

Yes, there are a number of techniques that you can use on your own. Here are some you can easily do, no matter how bad you are feeling. They can't replace the highly nuanced and focused help your coach will provide, but they are proven ways of calming and steadying yourself at times of crisis, confusion, stress, or emotional overload. Use them both now and throughout your divorce process.

Establish a daily routine. When life feels out of control, it helps to know that your day has a regular structure. Planning how you will spend your time will definitely help you function more effectively. At a time when mental turmoil and forgetfulness are common, using something as simple as a day planner will ensure you remember your doctor's appointments, lunch with a friend, and the "to do" list of more general tasks you need to attend to. If you see these tasks written down in black and white, you're more likely to follow through on them—and if you follow through, you'll begin to feel more competent again.

Get physically active. Take twenty minutes each day to walk, run, or ride your bike if at all possible—alone or with friends you can talk with. Exercising even lightly for twenty minutes each day reduces the stress that comes with any major life change. If you exercise at an aerobic level, you'll interrupt the body's "fight-or-flight" response to stress and experience physiological changes in your bloodstream that can actually alleviate depression. Research has shown that regular strenuous exercise can sometimes work better than drugs for combating depression and anxiety—and the only side effects are better physical health and greater energy.

Spend some time by yourself each day. You are going to be called upon to make major decisions with long-standing effects on both yourself and everyone you care about. More than ever before in your life, you need time to reflect without distractions. Simply ensuring that you have time to be alone can make a big difference in the quality of your responses and decisions. Many people do their best thinking and reflecting in conjunction with their daily physical activity.

Get outdoors and into nature. Unlike exercising in a gym, being outside allows you to use your senses of sight, smell, hearing, and even touch to help you put into perspective intrusive thoughts and feelings about your divorce. Pay deliberate attention to your surroundings, using all your senses. If you notice yourself worrying or reliving painful moments, don't try to push away those thoughts. Instead, simply broaden your attention to include seeing trees or clouds, feeling the warmth of sunlight or the sharpness of a breeze, smelling plant life, hearing the buzz of insects or children playing. As you relax and notice the life around you, your awareness will broaden and you'll begin to experience your personal concerns as one important but small part of a bigger picture.

Focus your attention on a repetitive activity. Almost any repetitive physical activity will calm you, not only as you do it but for some time afterward as well. Put aside at least ten or fifteen minutes each day—perhaps at a regular time—for an activity of this kind that you enjoy. For example, you could groom or play with your dog or cat, prune shrubs in your garden, water houseplants, chop wood or weed the grass, sharpen knives, or do woodworking or needlework. The greatest benefits come when you give your full attention to such activities rather than doing them mindlessly, so don't watch television or talk on the phone at the same time. Instead, concentrate on doing just this one thing.

Use deep breathing to relax. When your body's "fight-or-flight" response kicks in—which it will when you are upset or anxious—one physiological effect is that your breath shortens as your muscles tighten and get ready for action. You can learn to notice when your breathing is taking place only in your chest; that's a good indicator that you're in "fight-or-flight" mode. Happily, you can use your breath to regain mental and physical composure. Here's how it's done: concentrate on drawing your breath more deeply into your abdomen, easily and effortlessly. Whatever your breath rate is, consciously slow it a little. You can do so by counting: first, inhale to a count of four, then exhale to a count of four. Gradually increase the count to five, six, or more. Mentally follow your breath as it goes deeper and deeper into your body on the inhale, and notice all the abdominal muscles that are involved as you exhale fully and completely. This is a technique you can use anytime, anywhere. As you be- come more practiced at using your breath to relax, you'll be able to do it without anyone noticing.

Watch what you drink. Coffee, strong tea, cola, and other high-caffeine beverages can exacerbate the distressing emotions you are feeling and make it harder to regain a balanced perspective. Likewise, drinking alcohol can be problematic. When you are upset, even small quantities can worsen the situation by making clear thinking even more difficult and by decreasing your control over your actions. If a situation is coming up when you need to be at your best, pay particular attention to what you drink immediately beforehand.

I am trying to be guided by my best hopes rather than my worst fears, but I keep having setbacks. I find myself lying awake late at night imagining all the bad things that could happen once I tell Bill I want a divorce. These fears are keeping me from moving forward with a collab- orative divorce, though I know it's what we need. What can I do?

It's difficult to keep a positive perspective during the early phases of a divorce. Since you anticipate being the one who will request the divorce, it's natural that you would fear a bad reaction from Bill, who may not be expecting this. Even if it turns out that you both agree that your marriage should end, and even if you both agree on collaborative divorce, it's realis- tic to expect that each of you may have some emotionally challenging times during the divorce process. But while it's useful to understand how normal it is to worry about how Bill will react, it's not helpful to lie awake night after night envi- sioning worst-case scenarios. The more you can learn to loosen the grip of runaway negative emotions, the more capacity you'll develop to keep those feelings in perspective and prevent them from wreaking havoc in your divorce.

Collaborative divorce coaches emphasize redirecting your attention toward thoughts that build confidence and emphasize positive possibilities. One of the best places to start is with your own values, as we've suggested above. You could make a list in your notebook of all the values and qualities that have meant most to you in your own life and that you admire in the lives and character of others. These might include trust, honesty, integrity, courage, resilience—and many more. You can, of course, add to this list over time.

Next, choose a short reading, poem, or inspirational quotation about that value or quality that is meaningful to you. Write it out in your notebook, and also place it in a prominent place where you will see it often each day. When you feel challenged by negative thoughts or runaway emotion, reread your selection. Just doing that will gradually affect how you think, feel, and act. As each week goes by, use the above method to focus on a different value or quality that matters to you. If you're like most people we work with, you'll notice your mind gravitating more and more frequently toward the ideas and values embodied in these readings. You'll literally be "changing your mind."

Another useful idea is to take note of what you are choosing as reading material. What you read is food for your mind. Consider adding biographies and memoirs about people who embody what you'd like to see more of in yourself right now—for instance, people who have been courageous and optimistic during great adversity or who have created unexpected and fulfilling life pathways for themselves instead of remaining in constrained circumstances.

You say you know you need a divorce, yet you seem to be limiting your sense of the possibilities that lie in store for you by concentrating on potential difficulties. Imagination is a powerful tool. Have you tried imagining what your life could be in the future? Start to think about that. Plan how you want your life to be in as much detail as possible, or envision alternative scenarios that might be fulfilling. After all, you surely have some goals for yourself beyond simply getting out of your marriage, whether you've imagined them in detail or only envisioned an undefined better future. Doubtless when you were young, you had dreams for yourself that did not fully materialize. Now is a great time to revisit those old dreams, updated a bit to fit your older self.

Your professional team will encourage you to include much more on the collaborative divorce agenda than just ending your marriage, incorporating ideas such as old dreams and goals into your thinking. They will help you move through the divorce in ways that build self-esteem and a fuller sense of what you're capable of. They will encourage you to focus not only on tying up loose ends from the past with your spouse but also on how you want to shape your life after the divorce. You could use your notebook or a journal to begin imagining, thinking, and planning in this direction. Apart from anything else, this expanded and more balanced perspective should help you be more decisive about taking the necessary first steps with Bill.

I'm persuaded by your point that we all absorb ideas that romanticize marriage and demonize divorce. But it's awfully hard for me to see whether I myself hold these false beliefs. I'd like to pay some attention to this before my divorce moves along very far. How can I smoke out these hidden attitudes?

You can do some self-reflective exercises to help you recognize beliefs and attitudes about marriage and divorce that you might not have noticed before. Doing so will help you now as well as later, at every step through your divorce. Use these techniques on your own, and also expect your collaborative divorce team members to raise this subject if they notice unwarranted mistrust, combative assumptions, guilt, or other destructive beliefs or feelings associated with myths about divorce that interfere with constructive problem solving during the divorce process. Our own habitual attitudes tend to be invisible to us and elusive to grasp, but they are usually apparent to experienced collaborative professionals.

Here are two ideas to help you shine light on your hidden beliefs:

Isolate your feelings on divorce. Put aside twenty minutes for quiet, reflective time and, after relaxing and calming your mind, notice any thoughts, feelings, and attitudes that arise when your mind turns to divorce. Notice the images and pictures that flash through your mind under the mental heading "What I Know About Divorce." Are they pictures of people cooperating and solving their problems respectfully? People arguing? Hiding valuables and emptying safe-deposit boxes? Throwing china plates? Weeping? If you are getting better at noticing your own feelings and emotions, pay attention to which ones arise in you as these images of divorce move through your field of attention: Fear? Sorrow? Worry? Relief? Anger? Do you have thoughts in connection with what arises—perhaps disapproval? Pity? You might jot down these images, feelings, and thoughts in your notebook.

Find the source of those feelings. Do they come from your church, your friends, the media? Do any relate to close relatives or your own childhood? Are your feelings strongly personal and deep, or more generalized? How helpful do you imagine these embedded feelings and attitudes will be in your own divorce? What are they priming you to expect?

It's not just you who carries unhelpful beliefs and feelings about divorce. You will want emotional support from the people close to you when you are feeling vulnerable or when the changes associated with divorce are especially distressing. Unfortunately, well-meaning friends and relatives all too often give extremely bad advice because of the powerful effects of their own unexamined attitudes, beliefs, and feelings about divorce. You'll need to watch for members of your support system who encourage antagonism and a "strike first" mentality. Even counselors and psychotherapists can fall prey to this way of thinking and urge inappropriately aggressive or mistrustful behavior that is not in your best interests.

The ideas you have read in chapters of this book may be new, unfamiliar, and possibly even confusing to the people around you. Explain to them why you've chosen collaborative divorce and ask that they keep their negative advice to themselves, as it is not helpful. Suggest other, more positive ways that they can provide encouragement to you during hard times, and limit your exposure to people who continue to be unsupportive of what you're doing.

I'm reading this book because I'm unhappy in my marriage and thinking about divorce, but I can't seem to reach a decision. Is there anything I can do to get clarity?

Collaborative divorce is unique in that embarking on it can sometimes turn out to be the first step to putting your marriage back together. Unlike old-style divorce, collaborative divorce begins with information about facts, goals, hopes, and priorities before addressing solutions to divorce-related issues. The information that you gather for the purposes of collaborative divorce is explored in a respectful, constructive dialogue aimed at mutual understanding. Such discussions can occasionally turn in the direction of reconciliation rather than divorce.

But to experience such discussions, you first need to take the steps that will bring on board a collaborative divorce team. Here are some suggestions that may help you decide whether discussing divorce with your husband is right for you at this time—or whether you might want a private consultation with a collaborative lawyer or coach. Writing is probably the best way to clarify your thoughts. Begin by calming and clearing your mind, using the techniques we've suggested earlier. The following exercise works best if you read through it first. Then write your thoughts and feelings about each of these points in your notebook. Write down whatever comes to mind, without worrying whether it is appropriate or reasonable. Don't censor yourself, and don't evaluate what you write. Take as much time as you need, and let your thoughts fly. See what comes up when you are completely honest with yourself.

Writing Exercise 1

1. Divide a notebook page into two columns. In one, jot down all the reasons you can think of for ending your marriage. In the other, jot down all the reasons you can imagine why your partner might want a divorce.

2. On a fresh page, make three columns. In the left column, list every problem area in your marriage that relates in any way to possible reasons for considering divorce. In the middle column, next to each problem, write down how divorce will resolve the problem or change it for the better. If divorce alone won't address the problem, note that, too. Next, imagine that you don't divorce. What ways can you envision of addressing each problem

if you remain with your spouse? Write those down in the right column. (Remember that divorce alone won't usually solve problems related to children—they will persist after divorce unless they are addressed.)

3. On a new notebook page, make two columns. On the left side, list each of the collaborative divorce professionals—collaborative lawyers, coaches, child specialists, financial consultants—who could help you on your divorce team. On the right side, opposite each member of the team, write down how that particular professional might help you, your spouse, your children, and anyone else you care about with any of the problems and concerns you've identified. This can help you decide whether to have a private consultation, and with whom.

Remember: in collaborative divorce, you can explore divorce as a possible solution to your problems without fear of damaging your relationship. Often, a preliminary conversation with a coach or lawyer turns to the question of whether a divorce is truly what you and your partner need and want. Collaborative professionals will not assume that divorce is necessarily the best solution even if that is what you ask about, and they will avoid giving advice that encourages mistrust or fear. We have consulted with people considering divorce and then not heard from them again for six months or a year because they went back to working on their marriages. The pace and sequence of a collaborative divorce allow sufficient time for couples to change their minds about divorce if that's appropriate. The members of your team can shift gears and help you address your concerns within your marriage if you and your partner decide it's worth another try from a new perspective.

People sometimes decide to divorce because of exhaustion after seemingly endless repetitions of the same old arguments about the same old problems. For some couples, once coaching builds up better communication skills and once they begin exploring with their lawyers what their true interests and needs are in the divorce, the possibility emerges that their problems can be addressed within the marriage. Perhaps a postnuptial agreement can establish new parameters for how money will be managed, thereby addressing entrenched disagreements about finances—a common cause of marital discord. Perhaps the child specialist will help parents see that a child has unaddressed special needs and that with the right resources for the child, fights between the couple about parenting may diminish. A partner who hasn't been open to marriage counseling may discover during coaching that talking about problems isn't as difficult as he or she had feared.

Reconciliation is not the goal of collaborative divorce. But the collaborative process allows the possibility of reconciliation in ways that are usually foreclosed very quickly in old-style divorce. The collaborative divorce process can readily incorporate final efforts to save a marriage when both spouses wish to do that.

My husband, Stuart, and I are in our late forties and have two teenage sons. I've filed for divorce because I discovered that he has been having an affair for almost a year with a nineteen-year-old girl who does bookkeeping for his auto shop. Now that it's out, guys at the shop have told me things that make me wonder if I ever knew anything about my husband's character—such as that he's given his girlfriend expensive gifts and that he took her to Las Vegas for a weekend while I was vacationing with our sons. Since the boys were born, we've just managed to make ends meet, trying to put aside money for the boys to go to college. I am beyond anger—in a state of disbelief and shock. But I don't want my sons to be harmed any more than they already have been, knowing their father has been playing around with a girl hardly older than they are. Do you recommend that people in a position like mine consider collaborative divorce? My family is telling me that I should get the toughest lawyer I can find and make Stuart pay.

Yours is a terribly painful situation that presents difficult choices. We won't tell you that you should choose collaborative divorce—or that you should not. Stuart is the man you married, and, whoever he really may be in terms of character and values, Stuart is the man you have to divorce. One thing is certain: behaving badly yourself is not going to improve matters for yourself or your sons. Another certainty is that using lawyers and the courts to try to extract revenge almost never brings satisfaction—but it always brings a high price tag. The money you spend on a legal battle is money you definitely won't have for other purposes, and the results of such battles are generally uncertain at best—especially if you live in a "no-fault" state.

In the end, your own values and priorities should guide your choice of professional helpers and what mode of divorce you will use. Since you must surely be reeling from what you're learning, the most important thing you can do right now is slow down so that you have time to think clearly and choose wisely. You also need to be particularly alert to what advice you heed from friends and family. People who care about you are likely to be so outraged on your behalf that they will urge aggressive and provocative behavior in retaliation for Stuart's betrayal. Whether that will bring you anything of value—either now or five or ten years down the road—is something only you can decide.

Collaborative divorce is not necessarily precluded, but it would involve certain risks. If Stuart owns the auto shop and controls the books along with his young girlfriend, one real risk is that you might never know whether and to what extent money is being hidden from you. By the same token, though, you might never know even with the most aggressive divorce lawyer and expensive forensic accountant. It would make sense for you to get some preliminary advice about how this problem would be addressed both by collaborative lawyers and by a more traditional lawyer. Find out what the difference in legal and accounting fees might be if you worked collaboratively or conventionally, and see how that cost measures up against what Stuart's business has earned in the past. Listen to the advice you get from each perspective, and pay careful attention to your own level of comfort with what you hear.

If Stuart is an employee, the financial side of the story will be less challenging to unravel. But you still must consider whether you would be able to sit at a table with Stuart and two coaches, or two collaborative lawyers, and work on solutions constructively and with dignity. If that seems impossible, you might meet with a coach and explore further whether there is any point in considering the collaborative approach.

In the end, what matters is that the divorce be handled in a way that satisfies you, given the situation you find yourself in. Just because it's in your power to search aggressively for hidden money does not necessarily mean you should do so, or that you will find it even if Stuart has hidden it, or that the cost of hunting for it will ever be justified in terms of what is learned. One cost will definitely be professional fees. Another cost is that any possibility of professional help that could assist Stuart to mend what must be a seriously damaged relationship with your sons would probably disappear. At this moment, you may want to write Stuart out of your life and theirs, but wishing won't make it so. He will remain in the picture. Your sons' connection with their paternal grandparents and other relatives is also going to be affected by how your divorce unfolds.

Whether you have sufficient motivation and energy to focus on making the best of this bad situation, whether you prefer to cut your losses, or whether you prefer to fight are all issues you must weigh in terms of your own personal values and priorities. Whatever you decide, Stuart is, for better or for worse, a part of your own life history, too. Even if you decide you can't handle collaborative divorce, you can still refrain from needless retaliation, which we've never seen lead to anything good. How you end this chapter and whether you do it in a way that measures up to your own value system is a choice that will have ramifications for you, your sons, and other family members for years to come.

TALKING WITH OTHERS ABOUT COLLABORATIVE DIVORCE

I need to tell my wife that I want a divorce, and I want to make sure that the conversation goes well, because I really want her to agree to a collaborative divorce. How do I do this without messing it up?

The first conversation with your spouse about divorce is one of the most important conversations anyone can have, yet most people handle it badly, impelled by powerful, unexamined negative emotions of the kind you read about in chapter 1. You're well on your way to addressing this challenge constructively simply by posing the question, because it demonstrates your understanding that how the conversation will unfold depends on you as well as your wife. You can't dictate her reactions or make her choices, but you can choose to behave in ways that are more likely to elicit a calm, considered response from your wife. There is no guarantee that these suggestions will lead to a reasonable, constructive conversation, but they will help you avoid ways of communicating that are guaranteed to produce the opposite result.

Before talking with your wife, prepare yourself by reflecting on how she is likely to react. Things to consider:

1. How prepared is she for the news?
   - Have you ever talked about or threatened divorce?
   - Has she ever suggested to you that she was thinking of divorce?

2. What is her style of handling difficult conversations?
  • Does she tend to be highly emotional?
  • Does she fly into a rage?
  • Does she respond with silence?
  • Does she appear to handle things and then fall apart
    later?

Once you know how you might expect her to react, you can plan accordingly so that you can avoid causing needless distress to others. If you have children, be sure they are not around and that they will not come home unexpectedly. Decide if you need to have the conversation in a public or private place. You might want to alert your wife that you need to have a serious discussion with her and agree on where and when it will happen. But don't get into the conversation itself while you are discussing when and where to have it.

When it's time for the conversation, take some time to prepare. Effective communication on difficult subjects is a two-step process. First, you'll need to pay attention to relaxing yourself and clearing your mind so that you can think effectively. No one can think well in a "fight-or-flight" state of mind, and as this conversation is likely to be stressful, that's the state you'll probably be in unless you take steps to ensure you're not. We've already provided a number of ideas about how to do so, in answers to questions above in this section. Use those techniques in connection with this conversation.

Second, once your body and mind are relaxed, you'll need to focus on the positive, reflect on your options, anticipate likely problems, decide how to express yourself in the best possible way, and practice doing so before the conversation. Preparing systematically for this important conversation is like training for an athletic event: it improves your chances of achieving your objective. In this instance, preparation increases the odds that you'll do it well enough that your wife will be willing to give serious consideration to collaborative divorce. You'll do better if this planning takes place in more than one session—just as you'd train more than once for a marathon.

Put yourself in the most positive frame of mind possible, both when you plan this conversation and just before you actually initiate it. Research has shown without doubt that if your mind focuses on the positive, your behavior soon afterward is likely to be affected for the better—and conversely, if you focus on the negative, your performance may be affected for the worse. An excellent place to begin accentuating the positive is with values. Reflect on the values you want to invoke during this important conversation, and write them down. Preparing yourself in orderly steps like these gives you a strong foundation to rely upon even if your wife becomes upset or argues about what you have to say. Think about the following questions:

What values are most important to you? Think about and write down the ethical, philosophical, spiritual, and/or religious values that you consider most important as touchstones for resolving differences with others.

Rely on your past experiences. Recall a distressing incident that recently occurred in your marriage in which you had a choice about how to behave. Did you stop to think before you acted, or did you react impulsively, in the grip of strong emotion? Reflect on how well your behavior during or after that incident matches those deeply held personal values you noted.

Consider the "ripple effects" of your behavior during that incident. How did your behavior affect the other person/people involved? If you have children, how have they been affected by what happened during and after this incident?

Doing things differently. If you could "rewind" the incident, would you choose to behave differently? If so, how would you choose to act? In what ways would this different behavior be a better match with your most significant values?

Revisit your list of significant values. Imagine that you are looking back on this important first conversation about divorce, just as you have looked back on an interaction that didn't go well and about which you have now envisioned a better way you could have done it. From this perspective, which of your values do you want to see embodied in your behavior when you look back on the first conversation about divorce? Imagine saying what needs to be said to your spouse in a way that embodies those highest values.

Work out several ideas. It's a good idea to write out several possible ways you could express important ideas, paying attention to word choice and tone—not because you're going to recite a memorized speech, but because this will help you have in mind better words and phrases and will help you avoid ways of speaking that could cause difficulties.

Practice makes perfect. As a last step, it helps to practice in private speaking some of the more challenging parts of the conversation aloud, for the same reason: under stress you'll be better prepared to spontaneously invoke positive ways of expression and better able to avoid unintended provocation.

My husband, Jack, and I agreed about six months ago to end our marriage. He kept suggesting that we consider collaborative divorce, and in fact I liked the idea, but I kept putting off finding a lawyer. I was busy coping with the kids and the stresses of Jack's moving out. He handed me divorce papers a few days ago that were prepared by a lawyer who represented one of his friends in a very nasty divorce. I am really scared and don't know what to do. Is it too late for collaborative divorce?

It may or may not be too late, but you have nothing to lose by finding out whether Jack is still open to collaborative divorce. He hasn't proceeded very far yet with his old-style divorce lawyer. Jack's original choice of collaboration was a good one, and he probably is still interested in collaborative divorce, although he may also have some concerns that will need to be addressed.

Depending on how things have been going between the two of you, the simplest way to find out might be to ask Jack. Planning this conversation carefully in advance to give yourself every advantage of clear, constructive communications will be very important. Make use of the preparation techniques outlined earlier in this section.

Before asking whether Jack might still be open to collaborative divorce, you could begin the conversation with one of the most powerful tools in the entire collaborative divorce toolbox: an apology. Even though you have many good reasons to explain why you got started with the divorce process more slowly than Jack wished, justifying yourself isn't the same as apologizing. An apology simply says—in your own words and in your own way—"I'm sorry. I can see that my slow response really bothered you. That's not what I intended. Is there anything I can do now to make amends? I really appreciate that you wanted to do our divorce respectfully and with dignity, and that's what I want, too. I hope it's not too late." Particularly as there are children involved, it's important that both of you do all you can to avoid destructive litigation. You might want to point this out to Jack. If the emotional temperature is such that you're not sure about such a direct approach, you could ask a family friend or trusted relative or a clergyperson or counselor to talk about the situation with Jack.

Another first step you could take to check out whether collaborative divorce is still possible would be to do what Jack originally asked: interview and select a collaborative divorce professional. Since Jack has served you with divorce papers, you probably should begin with a collaborative lawyer. Find out whether that lawyer has ideas about how he or she—or someone else—could broach the subject with Jack in a way that doesn't violate the rules of legal ethics in your state. Even though your first meeting should be with a collaborative lawyer, if Jack does agree to proceed with a collaborative divorce, it would be wise to meet with coaches right away to make sure that you and Jack clear the air and get off to a good start in the collaborative process.

I try my best to stay respectful and dignified when I talk with my wife, Jane. But we both have a lot of anger right now, and she knows exactly how to push my buttons. She even seems to take perverse pleasure in making me lose my cool. We are just getting started with our collaborative lawyers, and we are still living under the same roof because money will be tight until the house is sold. Jane and I are still deciding whether or not we should include coaches on our team. Communication these days is impossible, but there are things we simply have to talk about—mainly, bills and spending. Is there anything I can do right now that will help me get through necessary conversations without a meltdown?

Your situation is challenging. In circumstances like yours, we can't say strongly enough how valuable it will be to have a full team helping you. You have both chosen collaborative divorce, which means that, on better days, you know the value of making good choices and good decisions. However, you will have a hard time getting through the divorce process and achieving your personal "best divorce" without the resources of a team. You need coaches, because you both have strong emotions that are interfering with communication and surely will interfere with constructive problem solving. And you'll also benefit from a collaborative financial consultant, with whom you and Jane can sit down to look at your cash flow and to consider how to deal with limited resources on a temporary basis, until longer-term decisions can be made with the help of your collaborative lawyers.

Until you have coaches on board, we can teach you a few techniques to help you understand and manage your strong feelings—such as anger—that may arise as both of you adjust to the end of your relationship. Don't expect miracles—you'll need expert coaching before you can start tackling some of the really big issues. But you can begin mapping your own negative emotional reactions now. That mapping will give you a head start on the work you will do with the coaches. It will also help you start to do better interacting with Jane even before the coaching begins. Try some of the following techniques:

Vent—but not constantly. While ventilating anger can be an important step, it is better to do it once or twice with a trusted friend who will just listen, and then let it go and focus on moving forward. If you find yourself venting all the time, it may end up becoming unproductive and negative. Another approach is to write out all your anger, blame, and resentment once or twice and then burn or shred the paper you wrote it on.

Take the time to reflect. Self-reflection can help clarify your thinking when it's clouded by strong feelings. This is particularly important in connection with issues that you need to talk about with Jane. If you're ready to do so, the suggestions that follow provide a structured way to reflect upon and understand your feelings better so that their destructive power can be lessened.

Writing Exercise 2

1. Divide a page into four columns and label them as follows:

   - **Observed words and actions.** In this column you'll note down exactly what you saw, heard, or otherwise experienced with your five senses during any interaction with your partner or when any issue has arisen between you and your partner.
   - **Thoughts.** Here, you'll note down what you were thinking—what ideas were going through your mind—as your senses picked up information during that interaction.
   - **Feelings.** This is the place to note your own physical and emotional responses to what you observed during the interaction, as well as your emotional responses to your own thoughts.
   - **Wants.** In this column you'll write what you want for yourself in connection with this issue or situation.

2. Now choose one single interaction or issue. Use the four columns to sort out all of the many things that were going on at one time as you moved through that situation. Stick with this one situation until you have finished the entire sequence of steps.

   - **Column 1: Observed words and actions:** Describe each action you saw and exactly what you heard that upset you. If there was physical contact, describe exactly what took place physically—not how it felt to you but exactly what occurred. Include body language (such as rolled eyes or a raised eyebrow). Most couples communicate much of their meaning in gestures that the other may not pick up on consciously until attention is focused on it. Being conscious of how you react to body language helps you to be more aware of its impact on others. Body language speaks louder than almost all other forms of communication and can lead to serious misunderstandings. In collaborative divorce, as your coaches help you and Jane to communicate more clearly, you'll learn to recognize your own triggers and provocative signals.

- **Column 2: Thoughts:** Set out as specifically as you can what you were thinking when you heard or saw what you wrote in column 1. For example, "When I saw you pulling into my driveway at 8 P.M., I thought, 'You are late again, and you just don't respect any agreements.' " Or "When I heard you shouting, 'You are so stingy' during our phone conversation, I thought to myself, 'I don't know how to make you understand that we just don't have the money for luxuries like perfume.' " Or "When I saw you get that certain smile, I thought, 'You know you've got me upset, and now you're satisfied.' "

- **Column 3: Feelings:** Write down the precise emotion you experienced during the interaction; for example, anger, sadness, frustration, confusion, fury. If you can't find the right word for the emotion you were experiencing, you can describe your physical sensations, such as "I felt sick to my stomach" or "My throat constricted and tears welled up." If you find yourself writing, "I felt *that . . .*" you are writing about a thought, not a feeling. Put it into column 2, the thought column.

- **Column 4: Wants:** Take it one more step in the fourth column and say what you want. For example, "I want to be able to express to you in a way you can understand that money is tight without coming across as trying to make your life miserable." Or "I want to be able to count on your being on time." Or "I want you not to roll your eyes when I am telling you something that is important to me."

You can do this process whenever you feel the need to blame your partner or to ventilate strong feelings. It will help you to clarify exactly what happens in your mind and body during the course of your strong emotional reactions. The more you do it, the more you'll develop an early-warning system that permits choosing *not* to allow your negative emotions to take over.

How can I talk to my relatives and friends about my choice of collaborative divorce in a way that they can understand?

It is difficult or impossible to keep a divorce secret for very long. It is better for your relatives and friends to hear the news from you than to get it secondhand. Remember, you are not obliged to answer all their questions. When in doubt about how much to share, wait. You can reveal more later, but you can't unsay what's already been said.

It is important for most families to know about major changes in your life. How wide you go in the family circle depends on the closeness of your extended family. Since you are taking an approach to divorce that they may know nothing about, you will need to tell them about the process and what they can expect. Make sure everyone understands your commitment to a dignified, respectful divorce right from the start.

For example, here's what one divorcing husband and father told his family: "I want you to know that Marilyn and I intend to remain cooperative and friendly after the divorce. I don't expect that you will need to change your relationship with her—in fact, for the sake of the children, I want you to remain on good terms with her. Please don't think you need to sever your connection with her in order to be loyal to me. That's the last thing either of us wants."

Here are some ways to let people know about the divorce:

- Set aside a day to call all friends and family members you want to tell personally. Remember how quickly gossip travels
- Conference all your siblings on one call so you don't need to repeat yourself and all of them will hear the same information at once
- Write to or e-mail all the people you want to tell
- Ask your coach or lawyer for brochures you can share with anyone who wants to know more, or refer them to the IACP website, www.collaborativepractice.com

I have tried to talk with friends and family about collaborative divorce, but they all think I'm a fool to "be so nice" to my husband, as he cheated on me and did other terrible things. Since we have no children who would benefit from our keeping our relationship harmonious, they think I should turn the divorce over to adversarial lawyers and be done with it. But I'm not doing this for him, I'm doing this for me, because I want to be able to look back at this period with self-respect. I feel so alone—how can I get support for handling my divorce in a way that feels right to me?

It's common to feel alone during the early stages of a divorce, but in today's age of technology, there's no need to choose between confiding in people who don't appreciate your values and going it alone. You can use the Internet both to connect with people online and to arrange to meet in the real world.

Lisa, a client of ours who has been coming to terms with a similar situation, recounted how an online support group was a lifeline during her darkest moment. One Christmas Eve, Lisa discovered that her husband had been unfaithful to her, living a double life with a series of other men throughout their marriage. In a split second, her entire world was shattered. Some-how, she got her husband to leave the house to stay elsewhere, and she managed to get to her computer and type the words "divorce support" into a search engine. She was led to an on-line divorce support group, where she tapped out her story. To her surprise, she immediately received a flood of encouraging responses from strangers who were themselves coping with the pain of infidelity.

On Christmas morning, Lisa was still reeling from the un-expected turn of events, and didn't know how she'd be able to get through the day. Another person in the online support group, Elinore, told Lisa, "Here's what you're going to do. You're going to take a walk, because it will do you good. Then, when you're back, you're going to e-mail me and tell me how it went."

Lisa went for the walk. It was raining and she was crying, but she told us that just knowing that Elinore—a complete stranger, but a supportive one—was out there somewhere waiting for her e-mail was an enormous comfort. Lisa says that in the months following, her online support group has been a lifesaving source of encouragement, information, and humor. Whenever feelings overwhelm her—even at two in the morning—others are online whom she can turn to, who understand exactly what she's going through. By luck, the group happens to encourage collaboration and taking the high road and discourages gossip and bad-mouthing the soon-to-be ex-spouse, focusing instead on emotional self-care.

You, too, might want to join an online support group. In-vestigate before jumping in, to be sure it's not one that en-courages an adversarial approach or otherwise doesn't seem to reflect your values. And use all the appropriate cautions that a sensible person would employ when communicating with strangers. It's possible to give and receive plenty of valuable support without providing identifying information about who you are or where you live.

Or you could start or join a real-world support group where you meet with other people who are also going through collaborative divorce. Online sites such as www .craigslist.org can help you get the word out and learn whether such groups already exist in your vicinity. Churches, community centers, and community colleges may offer workshops or courses about surviving divorce where you can meet people going through similar struggles who might like to form a support group with you. You could even make it a book group, where you read and discuss this and other books on divorce to help you get through the process. There's really no need to go it alone.

My husband, Donald, refused marriage counseling when I kept suggesting it toward the end of our marriage. How can I expect him to consider collaborative divorce coaching—isn't it similar to therapy?

Because coaches are licensed mental health professionals who may provide psychotherapy or counseling to people outside collaborative divorce, it's not unusual for people to conclude that coaching will be similar to therapy. But it is quite different from therapy, and you need to be able to explain those differences to your husband. Here are some points to understand:

- Coaching is short term, while psychotherapy may last for many years
- Coaching aims to help you do a better job with divorce-related challenges, while psychotherapy aims at personal insight and inner growth and change
- Coaching aims to help you do a better job of communicating with your partner and therefore assumes that you will share most of what is discussed with the others in your collaborative divorce process, while individual psychotherapy assumes that what is discussed will remain private between you and your therapist

You might use metaphors to help illustrate the differences. For example, collaborative divorce coaching can be compared to working with an athletic coach or trainer to enhance individual and group performance in a team sport, while psychotherapy can be compared to working with a physical therapist to get more mobility and strength in an injured muscle.

Many men in the business world have been coached as executives to improve their management skills or have had career coaches to help them move up the ladder. These men have no trouble accepting the idea that a coach improves your performance in a given area so you can function at your best. This same idea applies to the divorce coach.

UNDERSTANDING THE PROCESS BETTER

I am still confused about how it can possibly cost less to have an interdisciplinary collaborative divorce team than to have only collaborative lawyers for our divorce. How can that be?

You're not alone in asking this question. Until you experience it, you may remain somewhat skeptical that this can be so. The explanation begins with the reality that it's difficult for individuals and couples to assess accurately the kinds of problems they will encounter during their divorce. After all, as you've read, emotions have a way of erupting and derailing constructive negotiations unexpectedly. Confusion about finances can easily morph into mistrust and paranoia. Fear about the future can inflate the importance of relatively small matters. A new adult relationship can temporarily set a divorcing spouse back in the divorce recovery process or cause nasty disputes about when and how to introduce the children to the new partner.

These are normal, predictable events in a divorce. Without the right help to address them, they can cause legal fees to escalate, because a single lawyer—even a collaborative lawyer—lacks the right tools to do the best job of dealing with all these challenges. Your collaborative lawyers will do the best they can to steer you back into a constructive discussion, but if the help of coaches, a child specialist, or a financial consultant is what's really needed and you don't get it, you can't expect the kind of deep resolution that will solve the problem fully and stop the conflict. At best, you may achieve a compromise solution that glides over the real problem (allowing it to resurface later); at worst, you and your spouse may become polarized to the point of ending the collaborative divorce process. Either way, your legal fees will be higher—often much higher—than if you'd obtained the right kind of professional help at the right time.

The right help at the right time doesn't sweep conflict under the rug or push you to a quick-fix deal. It can teach you something you didn't previously know, give you information or perspectives you didn't previously have, develop skills you previously were lacking, and provide an agreed-upon structure for dealing with future issues of the same nature. Not only will you really resolve the problem, you will also take away personal skills you can use later when new challenges arise, so that your future costs for professional help on divorce-related issues will also be lower.

In other words, you are getting added value for your money. Collaborative divorce teams often help divorcing spouses move into a new life better prepared than they ever could have been without those resources. The time and money spent on the services of coaches and other collaborative professional helpers doesn't just resolve the problems that are troubling you now. Those services can save you from big expenses later. A divorce is a life-changing event. Cutting corners in how you meet its challenges may be the most expensive thing you can do.

*My brother is an aggressive business trial lawyer. I told him about my
interest in collaborative divorce. He raised a question I couldn't answer: "Isn't there a danger your collaborative lawyer will push you into
accepting a settlement agreement that is less than you're entitled to?
After all, the lawyers are out of a job if you don't agree to a settlement.
How can you be sure a collaborative lawyer will get you the best possible deal?"*

Your brother means well, but his question is so permeated
with old-style divorce beliefs and misunderstandings that
it will take a little sorting out to help you answer this for
yourself. (Don't worry about persuading him that collaborative divorce is a good idea. Focus on what makes sense
to you.)

Your brother is viewing collaborative divorce through an
old-style divorce lens. As you saw in chapter 1 of this book,
there is a lot more at stake during your divorce than just getting the largest share of everything. Your brother's concept of
the best possible deal is getting the maximum advantage on
every issue compared with what could have been achieved in
court. That's not how collaborative divorce professionals look
at conflict resolution. In collaborative divorce, you begin with
what matters to you personally and then find professional
helpers whose philosophy, values, skills, experience, and commitment make it likely that they can help you achieve your
personal goals in a way that matches those personal values.

By invoking a more conventional legalistic perspective,
your brother is measuring success by quantity: how much
money you will get, how many hours or days or weeks of the
children's time will be yours, whether you will get all the family silver or have to divide it up—you get the picture. He's not
paying attention to the costs, both obvious and not so obvious,
of this so-called best deal: runaway legal fees, lost time at work,
greatly delayed recovery from the trauma of divorce, permanent damage to the ability to parent children, continued conflict long after the divorce is over, and more.

Let's clear up another misunderstanding. Yes, the collaborative lawyers are "out of a job" if you or your spouse terminates the collaborative divorce process short of an agreement. But they will move on to work with other clients who need their services. If your lawyer advises you inappropriately about settlement negotiations for reasons unrelated to your needs and interests, your problem is not that you have chosen collaborative divorce, it's that you haven't chosen a good collaborative lawyer. Exactly the same problem would exist if you had chosen a poorly qualified or unethical old-style divorce lawyer who gave you bad advice that put his or her own self-interest ahead of yours.

There is no logical reason to think that a collaborative divorce lawyer will pressure you unduly to reach an agreement. In fact, there's far more reason to have that worry about old-style divorce lawyers. After all, it's generally agreed that only about 5 percent of all divorces culminate in full trials. The rest, bitter and civilized alike, eventually end in a settlement agreement—including those handled by old-style divorce lawyers whose idea of preparing for settlement is to prepare vigorously for trial, filing aggressive motions and intrusive discovery demands and requesting extreme and provocative forms of legal relief. Why doesn't your brother worry about how much pressure such an old-style divorce lawyer would apply to persuade you to settle on the courthouse steps, on the eve of trial—the point at which many old-style divorce lawyers thrust terms of settlement upon angry, reluctant spouses? Has he mentioned to you that many old-style divorce settlements finally happen at that point because the clients have run out of money during the pretrial preparation period and can't afford to pay their lawyers to go to trial? Is he warning you about how much money old-style divorce lawyers make when they do go to trial and therefore how little personal incentive they may have to contain conflict and help you and your partner reach agreement?

Our point is not that old-style divorce lawyers are less ethical than collaborative lawyers. Rather, it is that unethical practitioners—whether collaborative or old-style, whether lawyers or doctors or psychotherapists or dentists or plumbers—may put their own self interest ahead of their clients' interests, whatever the services they offer. Ethical practitioners stay alert to where their own self-interest diverges from that of their clients and work hard to put their clients' interests first.

In your divorce, decide what matters most to you, and then find an ethical, capable practitioner whose philosophy and approach can help you achieve your goals. If getting the biggest possible piece of the financial pie is what matters most to you, don't choose collaborative divorce. But if your goals are more evenhanded and balanced, remember: the collaborative model involves you every step of the way, postpones making decisions until everyone is ready to do so, and makes sure that all concerns have been discussed fully and respectfully and addressed to the greatest extent possible. Compare that to old-style divorce, in which the lawyers negotiate with each other about what they consider most important and then try to persuade their clients to accept what the lawyers consider a good settlement. Ask yourself where the greatest risk lies that you might be pressured to accept a settlement that doesn't meet your real needs.

Why should I choose a model in which I could lose my lawyer if my wife and I can't reach agreement? Why can't my lawyer go to court with me? I like everything about this approach except for that one thing—is it really so important?

Yes, this feature of the collaborative method is vitally important.

Lawyers have to work hard to become skilled at working collaboratively. Nearly everything they are taught in law school and learn on the job in their conventional work teaches them to fight hard and win at all costs, and to prepare aggressively for trial as the best way to "win big" for their clients. Adversarial behavior is familiar and comfortable for lawyers; they don't experience it as a catastrophe if settlement negotiations end and the case goes to court. Going to court is what old-style divorce lawyers do when settlement negotiations stall, and lawyers who are good at litigation aren't put off at all by doing so. Finding out what Judge Jones has to say about an apparent impasse is the logical next step for lawyers.

But for divorcing families, taking an issue to court can lead to irreversible harm. As one family law judge has said, "If anyone leaves my courtroom happy, I've made a dreadful mistake." So when an apparent impasse arises, the stakes are different and much graver for you and your family than they are for the lawyers who offer old-style divorce services.

It's not that any lawyer deliberately sets out to cause harm. But lawyers can be impatient. Conventional lawyers often value efficiency too greatly and fail to appreciate that *how* you and your partner get to a solution—and whether you both agreed to it rather than having it imposed on you by a judge—can matter as much as, or more than, the specific terms of a divorce decree. Conventional lawyers also place greater emphasis on legal rights and entitlements and less emphasis on what happens to children and the quality of family relationships after the divorce than you would if you knew as much as they do about the collateral damage caused when divorce disputes are taken to court.

You may be thinking that you will get less effective help from your lawyer with collaborative divorce because your lawyer is not permitted to take your divorce issues to court if negotiations stall. In fact, the opposite is true: you will get more. Because conventional lawyers are taught that the best way to settle a case is to prepare aggressively for trial, as much as 95 percent or more of the fees you pay your old-style divorce lawyer may be devoted to preparing for an event that nobody wants and that actually happens less than 5 percent of the time: a trial. With a collaborative lawyer, 100 percent of the work is devoted to an event that happens about 95 percent of the time—settlement.

Moreover, conventional lawyers may be very skilled at litigation, but few can offer the array of effective, client-centered conflict resolution skills provided by a good collaborative lawyer. That means that when the going gets rough, a collaborative lawyer is more likely to help you get through the difficulty and get back on track to constructive problem solving. An old-style divorce lawyer typically runs out of useful skills and alternative approaches much sooner, declares the impasse insurmountable, and sees less reason not to take a matter to the judge than a collaborative lawyer would. You'll stay at the negotiating table longer with collaborative lawyers, your lawyers will work at all times to help you and your partner find acceptable solutions, and you'll have the resources of a diverse collaborative divorce team to help you get past challenging points in the process.

Nothing prevents old-style divorce lawyers from staying at the table in the face of an impasse to help you and your partner solve problems—nothing except habit and an adversarial mind-set filled with "demonized divorce" assumptions and beliefs. Your collaborative lawyers, in contrast, see what at first glance looks like an impasse as a normal aspect of collaborative conflict resolution that calls for extra imagination and effort from everyone on the team. They just roll up their sleeves and get to work.

Remember: what looks like an impasse rarely causes collaborative divorce cases to terminate and go to court. Couples almost always can find solutions with their team's help.

Then why do collaborative divorce cases terminate and go to court?
First, you should know that only a small percentage of collaborative divorce cases terminate short of a full settlement

agreement. We don't have scientific statistics, but collaborative lawyers everywhere report that only about 10 percent or fewer of their collaborative cases end short of full agreement. Thus, the odds are slim that you and your partner will fail to arrive at a mutually satisfactory collaborative agreement if you're both motivated to resolve your differences consensually.

Some couples with serious problems, such as mental illness, drug or alcohol abuse, or violence, may be unable to sustain important commitments of the collaborative process, such as good-faith participation and follow-through or respectful and constructive efforts to reach resolution. Or it may simply be too difficult for one or both partners to face each other directly at four-way meetings, even with the support of coaches and collaborative lawyers. Sometimes, these couples find that "friendly negotiations" can work for them. Lawyers experienced in mediation and/or collaborative law can represent these spouses and can negotiate on their behalf, lawyer to lawyer. Though the risk of the backward slide to court always exists in that situation, and the advantages of the collaborative team are absent, lawyers can nonetheless sometimes manage to hammer out a deal that both partners can accept without going to court.

Couples who leave the collaborative process to fight in court generally do so for one or more of these reasons:

- Entrenched psychiatric or substance abuse problems
- Domestic violence
- Inability or unwillingness to control impulsive emotional reactions during or between collaborative meetings
- Inability to participate in good faith, ranging from passive-aggressive refusal to engage in constructive problem solving, through refusal to attend meetings, all the way up to and including dishonesty and concealment of money

- Unreasonable goals that cannot be achieved in a consensual process because they are so skewed toward excessively narrow self-interest that there is no reason why the other spouse should consider agreeing to them
- Collaborative divorce professional helpers who lack sufficient understanding, experience, or skills to help people through major challenges when emotions run high

Can my husband and I work with just one lawyer and just one coach? We're both pretty reasonable and cooperative and want to save money where we can.

Yes and no. The two of you are free to choose any configuration of divorce professional helpers that fits your needs. But it's not a collaborative divorce without two collaborative lawyers, and if you wish to include collaborative divorce coaching, there must be two coaches as well.

In most states, you'd need to choose a mediator if you wanted to work on divorce-related legal issues with only one conflict resolution professional, because it's generally a violation of professional ethics for one divorce lawyer to represent both spouses. A divorce lawyer—including a collaborative lawyer—serves as advisor and ally to only one partner.

While no ethical rules prevent mental health professionals from providing joint counseling to a couple, it's important to understand that the collaborative divorce model is a specific model—and by definition, when coaching is included, this model requires each spouse to have a coach of his or her own.

Often, the people who have the training and skills required to be collaborative coaches also provide custody mediation or joint divorce counseling to some of their clients. A person who is a custody mediator in one divorce and a divorce counselor in another may be serving as one spouse's collaborative coach in yet a third divorce. The important thing to remember is that mediation, counseling, and coaching are distinct and different processes. One and the same person may be qualified to do all three, but what you get with each process is very different.

Why is it so important to have two coaches, rather than one? Because your coach is not neutral. Your coach is an ally and helper who gets to know you and has the task of helping you privately so that you are better prepared to function in the four-way coaching and legal meetings. If you happen to be the spouse with greater emotional volatility, you're going through an unusually challenging series of conversations, or you're stuck on a particular issue, you'll leave the four-way table to work privately with your coach until you are ready to return to constructive problem solving. The same goes for your husband and his coach. These are individual relationships with one's own helpful ally, similar to the relationship you'll have with your lawyer. Your coach is working to help you be the best you can be, during and after the divorce. Certain important coaching conversations may concern what you yourself can do to make the process work more effectively for you. Such conversations often include sensitive personal information about doubts, feelings, and emotional reactions. The same is true of certain coaching sessions your husband will have with his coach. Experience has shown that if a single coach tries to do the job with both spouses, it's common for one or both partners to imagine that the coach is favoring one person over the other and it can become difficult or impossible for the coach to be effective. In addition, when two people are at very different stages in their emotional recovery from the loss of the marriage or have widely divergent values and perspectives relating to parenting decisions, it's important for each to have a trusted ally at the coaching four-way meetings who provides reminders and supportive help at the precise moment it's needed. A single neutral person can't do that job, either.

Unlike coaching, joint marriage counseling with one counselor can work, because there the goal is to bring two people together. But collaborative coaches help you and your partner to separate, to learn communication skills that do not depend upon intimacy, and to build lives apart from each other. To be done well, much of this work needs to be done with each of you individually.

The situation with respect to the two collaborative lawyers is similar. One and the same person may be qualified to be a collaborative lawyer, a mediator, and a litigator, and may provide one or another of these services to different clients. The person is the same, but the job description is quite different, depending on whether it's mediation, collaboration, or litigation. A lawyer acting as a mediator must remain neutral. If the emotional playing field between the spouses is not level, their negotiating skill or familiarity with financial facts differs greatly, or one or the other is failing to follow through with homework or keeps canceling meetings, a mediator can't take one person aside for more than a short time to help that person get back to constructive problem solving and can't go very far to redress imbalances in the ability to assert interests at the table. Nor do mediators schedule private meetings with just one client to prepare him or her to participate more effectively in reaching resolution. Those are advocacy jobs, ill suited to the role of a neutral person. A mediator who does try to work individually with one spouse risks ceasing to be regarded as neutral by the other spouse. But those are jobs that every collaborative lawyer is responsible for doing with each individual client.

Thus, it's not collaborative divorce if you both work with one lawyer-mediator, and similarly, it's not collaborative divorce if—as sometimes happens—one spouse hires a lawyer while the other prefers not to do so. The reasons for this vary—sometimes one spouse is a lawyer and wants to represent him- or herself, or sometimes one spouse is not comfortable with the idea of having a lawyer. In that situation, even if one partner hires a person trained as a collaborative lawyer, if the other has no lawyer it will not be a collaborative divorce. Why? Because it takes two. The job of the collaborative lawyers isn't just to get you to a deal. It includes working privately with each of you to help you clarify and express your concerns and interests at the table, fulfill homework assignments, and participate constructively in the ultimate conflict resolution discussions. Then, they work collegially with each other to ensure that the four-way meetings proceed respectfully and constructively. If your husband doesn't have a collaborative lawyer, there is no one who can do those jobs with him when the need arises.

Furthermore, much of the power of collaborative legal work lies in the fact that neither lawyer can go to court and therefore both lawyers must work hard to help their clients find a way through apparent impasses in negotiations. If you were the only spouse represented by a lawyer, how could it reasonably be expected that you would fire your lawyer and find a litigation lawyer if your husband—who had no lawyer—became upset during an apparent impasse and decided to go to court? In that situation, there would be no one in the picture who could remind your husband of the risks of abandoning the collaborative process to take the divorce to court and no one who could invite him to return to constructive thinking about solutions.

That's why the essence and definition of a collaborative divorce is that there must be two lawyers, and, if there are coaches, there must be two of them as well.

You and your husband may be able to handle all your concerns working with a single neutral mediator, and, depending on your issues, that kind of professional assistance may be sufficient for you. Or, like some couples, you can decide that only one of you will have a lawyer to help you arrive at a settlement, while the other will be unrepresented. Remember, though, that with a collaborative team, you and your husband will both be encouraged to plan carefully for the future, not

just be guided to a quick deal. You'll have the benefit of communication skill training, exploration of money issues with a
trained financial expert, built-in information from and about
your children, and many more "value-added" features that no
single mediator or lawyer can provide.

EPILOGUE

"Change is the law of life. And those who look only to the past or present are certain to miss the future."
— John Fitzgerald Kennedy

In the process of reading this book, you may have come to the same realization that we did in writing it: this is not just a book about divorce. *Collaborative Divorce,* both the book and the journey, is actually about practicing peacemaking as the guiding principle for building a resilient, adaptive family system that works for all the people concerned after a marriage ends.

We know—because we have worked with so many clients who have shown us this—that the doorway to peacemaking in divorce is to move away from law as the sole organizing principle of resolving disputes. When law is put into its proper place, divorcing couples can learn to speak truthfully and listen for understanding as pathways to deeper resolution. Truth and reconciliation have provided new and moving pathways to peace at the global level, and they are proving also to be the way to peace in the restructured family after divorce. Collaborative divorce is the doorway, and deep conflict resolution is the pathway that it will open to constructive possibilities for you, your partner, and any children you may share, in the unknown terrain beyond your present family structure. We continue to be amazed at the ability of divorcing couples to embrace life-affirming choices, make changes, and follow constructive new pathways when the professionals who work with them all hold out that expectation, guide them along the way, and encourage them when they falter. Another truth we know from experience as well as from research: the decision to make peace in your divorce does not necessarily have to begin as a mutual choice. Each partner in a marriage that is ending has great power to change for the better what will happen in the divorce by making choices, one at a time, that call forth constructive change in return. By making peace in the family as you divorce, you make it possible for yourself and the others you are permanently connected with to emerge from the divorce passage stronger and healthier, with new family systems in place that can help all members flourish after the divorce.

Families are where children are raised. Behaving with respect, dignity, and integrity, seeking consensus, aiming high, and divorcing well—these are not simply private choices. Every divorcing couple is deconstructing a fundamental unit of our society as they end their marriage. When a family breaks apart without attention to the quality of what will replace it, children cannot be raised well. In the words of the psychiatrist and peace activist Jean Shinoda Bolen, "The world is small. A deprived and abused child soon becomes an adult, and, as an enraged adult with the power to harm others, may do just that."

When more than half of all marriages end in divorce, it is of concern to every one of us that those who divorce are helped to do it as well as they are able, so that our children, the next generation, are reared with the capacity to value and sustain intimate relationships— and can themselves grow up to raise healthy children.

The couples you have read about in this book chose collaborative divorce. They committed themselves to a process that transformed their lives and the lives of their children and families for the better at a time when the old paradigm for divorce told them to fear and expect the worst. Every couple who aspires to the best divorce they are capable of is teaching by example in our community and in our culture how to bring about deep resolution and real peace.

Choosing to move through the divorce passage in this way as a peacemaker is a personal decision that has a ripple effect through all your world. As Michael Lerner, a highly respected social theorist, theologian, and philosopher has put it, "Change will come whether we want it to or not, and what we will have to do is to try to make change our friend, not our enemy. But probably most profoundly and importantly, the changes that will count the most are the millions of changes that take place on the individual level as people reject cynicism, as they are willing to be hopeful once again, as they are willing to take risks to meet the challenges they see around them."

Your divorce, chosen or not, offers you the opportunity to be a peacemaker. Peace begins at home—even or especially when home is fraught with tension and fear of the unknown and even when home is in the process of rapid redefinition, as is so often the case for couples whose intimate relationship is ending. Ancient wisdom teaches that a journey of a thousand miles begins with a single step. For you and your partner, your children and extended family, and the society we all share, we hope this first and most important step will be to consider collaborative divorce.

APPENDIX A:
Understanding the Flow
of a Collaborative Divorce

The family:

John and Marsha were married for fifteen years and had two children, Lisa (13) and Charles (10) when Marsha decided to end the marriage shortly after the Christmas holidays in 2004. From her perspective, the marriage had become distant and John seemed to spend all his spare time (including the most recent Christmas vacation) golfing with male friends rather than with her and the children. John was stunned and saw no reason for a divorce. Both are employed. They own a home and two vacation properties. They have no significant debts, and their finances are not complex.

The collaborative divorce process:

Marsha's first meeting with collaborative lawyer. She learns about collaborative divorce and brings home a materials packet and a list of collaborative professionals, which she gives to John. January 20, 2005 (1 hour)

Marsha then calls a coach to get the collaborative divorce process moving. She thinks John drinks too much, she wants to protect the children, and coaches seem like a good place to start. January 23, 2005 (5 minutes)

John calls a coach at Marsha's urging and agrees to participate in an exploratory joint meeting of both spouses and both coaches. Coaches talk by phone and schedule a joint meeting date. January 25, 2005 (10 minutes)

Marsha and John meet with both coaches, discuss the collaborative divorce process, and sign the collaborative divorce participation agreement with the coaches. They both agree to contact a child specialist recommended by the coaches. February 10, 2005 (1 hour)

John meets immediately afterward with his own coach, who urges him to engage a collaborative lawyer. February 10, 2005 (1 hour)

Marsha also meets afterward individually with her coach. February 10, 2005 (1 hour)

John's second individual meeting with his coach. He doesn't want a divorce and hopes the coaches might persuade Marsha to reconsider. February 15, 2005 (1.5 hours)

Marsha's second individual meeting with her coach. Marsha is clear that this marriage is over for her. February 17, 2005 (1.5 hours)

Marsha calls the child specialist, confers by telephone, and makes an appointment for her and John to meet jointly with the child specialist. February 21, 2005 (1 hour)

John's first meeting with a collaborative lawyer. February 22, 2005 (1 hour)

Coaches' conference call. February 22, 2005 (15 minutes)

Brief status conference call between coaches and both collaborative lawyers. February 23, 2005 (15 minutes)

Coaches send written questionnaires completed by the parents to the child specialist. Brief conference call between coaches and child specialist. February 23, 2005 (15 minutes)

Collaborative lawyers meet separately with their respective clients to prepare for first four-way meeting. February 24, 2005 (1 hour each meeting)

First legal four-way meeting: both lawyers and both clients. Procedural ground rules and negotiating theory discussed and formal collaborative agreements signed. Homework assignments given. February 26, 2005 (1.5 hours)

Lawyers have brief conference call with financial consultant.
February 26, 2005 (15 minutes)

John and Marsha meet jointly with child specialist.
February 27, 2005 (1 hour)

Lawyers' conference call re whether there are any legal concerns that need to be discussed with clients before the clients can address with coaches a possible move by John. Lawyers then briefly confer by telephone with coaches to confirm no necessity for prior legal four-way meeting.
February 28, 2005 (25 minutes)

John and Marsha meet jointly with financial consultant and are given homework: gather financial data.
February 28, 2005 (2 hours)

Marsha's third individual meeting with her coach. She has been arguing with John for weeks about wanting him to move out of the house and find an apartment. She wants to remain in the family home with the children.
March 1, 2005 (1.5 hours)

Team conference call (lawyers and coaches) re how all can help with managing tensions in home and facilitating clients' decisions about living situation.
March 2, 2005 (20 minutes)

Financial consultant organizes documents, prepares spreadsheets, and calls clients with questions before e-mailing draft spreadsheets to clients, lawyers, and coaches.
March 3, 2005 (3 hours)

John meets with his coach to discuss relationship with Marsha and moving forward with more functional living arrangements.
March 6, 2005 (1 hour)

Marsha calls lawyer about wanting
the process finished ASAP. Lawyer
counsels Marsha with perspective
on realistic timing in a consensual
conflict resolution process and
advises conferring with coach about
reasons for differences between
John's emotional readiness to
negotiate and Marsha's.
March 6, 2005 (45 minutes)

Children meet individually and jointly with child
specialist: child specialist then has conference call
with coaches.
March 8, 2005 (3 hours)

John meets with his coach to prepare
for a coaching four-way meeting.
March 10, 2005 (1 hour)

E-mail from coaches to
lawyers re tensions children
are experiencing in the
current living arrangement
and behavioral impacts.
March 11, 2005 (20 minutes)

Marsha meets with her
coach to prepare for a
coaching four-way meeting.
March 11, 2005 (1 hour)

Financial consultant updates spreadsheet data
with new financial statements from clients and
sends to clients and attorneys in preparation for
forthcoming five-way meeting (clients, lawyers,
financial consultant).
March 18, 2005 (1 hour)

Four-way meeting including John, Marsha, and
both coaches; separate meetings between each
client and coach before and after four-way session.
Agreement reached that John will move out of
family residence as soon as he finds an apartment.
March 24, 2005 (2 hours)

Conference call between coaches and child
specialist about need to bring children's perspectives
into a joint coaching session before parents
physically separate. E-mail from coaches to lawyers
and child specialist summarizing the conversation.
March 28, 2005 (20 minutes)

Child specialist meets with each child individually
for more discussion of the family changes.
March 30, 2005 (2 hours) followed by conference
call with coaches (15 minutes)

Five-way meeting of coaches, child specialist, and
parents, preceded by premeeting between coaches and
child specialist, and followed by separate meetings
between each parent and coach.
April 7, 2005 (3 hours)

Conference call between
lawyers and financial
consultant re need for
additional analysis of
financial data before
scheduling five-way
meeting.
April 12, 2005 (15 minutes)

Four-way meeting between parents and
coaches addressing concerns and plans for
effective joint parenting after physical
separation.
April 12, 2005 (2 hours)

John moves into a rented town
house near the family residence.
April 14, 2005

Financial consultant does additional work requested by lawyers with occasional telephone queries to clients.
April 14–18, 2005 (1.5 hours)

Four-way meeting between parents and coaches to plan shared parenting schedule for next months and summer.
April 19, 2005 (1.5 hours)

E-mails from lawyers and from coaches to other team members summarizing results of recent five-way and four-way meetings.
April 20 and 28, 2005 (30 minutes)

Child specialist and children meet regarding their concerns about transitions between the two parents' homes and about planning for the summer. Lisa angry at Mom and wants to try living with Dad, at least for summer.
April 24, 2005 (1.5 hours)

Five-way meeting with clients, lawyers, and financial consultant concerning income, expenses, assets, and debts.
April 27, 2005 (2 hours)

Four-way meeting with clients and lawyers to brainstorm options for property division and support solutions, preceded by individual meetings between each client and lawyer before four-way meeting.
May 16, 2005 (3 hours)

Four-way meeting of parents and coaches concerning children's concerns and requests. Agreement is reached regarding schedule for the summer and children's concerns, including agreed-upon children's activities and camps and vacation time with each parent.
May 26, 2005 (1.5 hours)

Conference call involving lawyers, coaches, and child specialist to identify issues
needing attention from various professionals in order for clients to reach
comprehensive resolution and settlement agreement.
May 29, 2005 (15 minutes)

Four-way meeting with lawyers: coming to resolution
and confirming final framework for settlement.
Individual meetings between each lawyer and client
preceding four-way meeting.
May 30, 2005 (2 hours)

Lawyers draft and revise settlement agreement and
ensure that terms reflect clients' actual intended
resolution of all issues. Lawyers prepare forms needed
for entry of legal divorce judgment.
June 1–17, 2005 (3 hours)

Final legal four-way meeting: reviewing accomplishments,
reviewing terms of agreement, signing agreement, signing
papers required for legal divorce. Meeting ends with a
wine toast to a job well done.
June 18, 2005 (2 hours)

Lawyers process final papers through the court, distribute
copies, and assist with title transfers and related details.
June 19–30, 2005 (1 hour)

Parents return to coaches for progress review of how shared
parenting plan is working for themselves and the children. Minor
schedule adjustments and plans for the fall agreed to.
July 28, 2005 (1.5 hours)

↓

Marsha calls coach to report she wants to have her boyfriend, Mike, move in with
her. The parenting plan included an agreement to return to coaching before
introducing new adult relationships to children. Coaches confer via conference call
and arrange to schedule individual and four-way coaching sessions.
November 30, 2005 (30 minutes)

↓

Four-way meeting with coaches to discuss potential impact on children if Mike moves in with Marsha. Discussion includes possible agreements between John and Marsha about when and how to introduce new adult relationships to the children. Marsha agrees to postpone decisions until after holidays.
December 5, 2005 (1.5 hours)

John meets with his coach to discuss managing his feelings and how he wants to handle this change.
December 8, 2005 (1 hour)

Marsha meets with her coach. She resents the need to confer with John about her own life. The coach reminds Marsha of the high value she has always placed on parenting the children well and points out that the focus of coaching is not to restrict the lives of the adults but to consider the needs and concerns of the children.
December 15, 2005 (1 hour)

Four-way meeting with coaches to discuss constructive ways of introducing the children to Marsha's serious relationship with Mike.
January 5, 2006 (1.5 hours)

As agreed, children meet with child specialist to talk about what it will be like when Mike moves in with them. Child specialist has conference call with coaches.
January 14, 2006 (1.5 hours)

Coaching four-way meeting. John and Marsha have difficult but honest discussion about children's concerns and John's anxieties that results in an agreed-upon plan to defer Mike's move until March.
January 16, 2006 (1.5 hours)

Mike moves in with Marsha in early March. As agreed, John and Marsha meet with coaches twice during the period March through June to check in on how children are doing. Both children and adults seem to be doing fine.
March–June 2006 (2 hours)

APPENDIX B:
A Collaborative Divorce Team
Participation Agreement

What follows is a typical collaborative divorce team participation agreement that is used in substantially this form in the San Francisco Bay Area. It is a composite document reflecting the efforts of many collaborative lawyers and coaches from many communities over many years. Collaborative lawyers, coaches, financial consultants, and child specialists in your community may use a participation document similar to this one or several such documents—or theirs may be quite different. But the purposes served by participation agreements are the same: to ensure that couples choosing collaborative divorce take time to discuss and understand what the roles of all members of their team will be and what is expected of all participants, including the clients.

PRINCIPLES AND GUIDELINES
FOR COLLABORATIVE PRACTICE

I. INTRODUCTION

    1.01 The essence of "Collaborative Divorce" is the shared belief of the participants that it is in the best interests of the parties and their family to commit themselves to avoiding adversarial legal proceedings and to adopt a conflict resolution process that does not rely on a court-imposed resolution. Collaborative Divorce relies on an atmosphere of honesty, cooperation, integrity, and professionalism geared toward the future well-being of the parties and their children.

1.02 One of our major goals in adopting Collaborative Divorce is to minimize, if not eliminate, the negative economic, social, and emotional consequences of the traditional adversarial legal process to the parties and their family. In signing this document the divorcing parties commit themselves to the Collaborative Divorce process and agree to seek a better way to resolve their differences justly and equitably.

II. NO COURT OR OTHER INTERVENTION

2.01 By electing to treat this matter as a Collaborative Divorce case, the parties and their Collaborative Divorce Professionals are committing themselves to settling all divorce-related issues without court intervention. The parties agree to give complete, full, honest, and open disclosure of all information having a material bearing on the case, whether requested or not, and to engage in informal discussions and conferences for the purpose of reaching resolution of all issues. All legal, financial, and mental health professionals working in this matter as a Collaborative Divorce team, as well as all appraisers, evaluators, and other consultants retained by the parties, will likewise be directed to work in a cooperative effort to resolve issues without resort to litigation or any other external decision making process.

III. LIMITATIONS OF COLLABORATIVE PRACTICE

3.01 In choosing Collaborative Divorce, we—the divorcing couple—each understand that there is no guarantee of success. We also understand that we cannot eliminate concerns about disharmony, distrust, and irreconcilable differences that have led to the current circumstances. While we all are intent on reaching a cooperative and open solution, we understand that our actual experience in our Collaborative Divorce may fall short of that goal.

3.02 Even though we have chosen Collaborative Divorce, we—the divorcing couple—understand that each of us is still expected to protect his or her respective interests and not to lapse into a false sense of security in the assumptions and expectations each holds about the other, the collaborative lawyers, or the Collaborative Divorce process. Subject to the requirements of applicable law and good faith commitments of these Principles and Guidelines, each of us may continue to act in our own respective best interests, even where those interests diverge from the other party's interests.

IV. PARTICIPATION WITH INTEGRITY

4.01 As participants in the Collaborative Divorce process, all signatories to these Principles and Guidelines are concerned about protecting the privacy, respect, and dignity of all involved, including parties, lawyers, coaches, financial specialists, child specialists, and the consulting professionals, and each of us agrees to uphold a high standard of integrity. The parties and all Collaborative Divorce professionals specifically agree that they shall not take advantage of inconsistencies, misstatements of fact or law, or others' miscalculations, but shall disclose them and seek to have them corrected at the earliest opportunity. In the event a Collaborative Divorce professional discovers inconsistencies, misstatements of fact or law, withheld information, or miscalculations by a party or by any other professional, the Collaborative Divorce professional shall inform that person of the discovery and remind him or her of the obligations under these Principles and Guidelines to make the required disclosure. In the event a Collaborative Divorce professional discovers that she or he has made a misstatement of law or a miscalculation, he or she shall disclose and correct the same. In the event a Collaborative Divorce professional discovers that another Collaborative Divorce professional has made a misstatement of law or a miscalculation, she or he shall inform the other Collaborative Divorce professional of the discovery and request disclosure and correction.

V. COLLABORATIVE DIVORCE TEAM AND OTHER PROFESSIONALS

5.01 Each divorcing party shall retain a Collaborative Lawyer and a Collaborative Divorce Coach. Unless otherwise agreed, the divorcing couple (with the advice of the Collaborative Lawyers) will retain a Collaborative Financial Consultant to assist in their evaluation of financial considerations and, if they are parents, will retain a Child Specialist (with the advice of their Collaborative Divorce coaches) to give support and a voice to their children during the divorce process.

5.02 In addressing questions about sharing the enjoyment of and responsibility for their children, the parents and all Collaborative Divorce professionals shall make every reasonable effort to reach amicable and well-informed solutions that promote the children's best interests. The parents agree to act quickly to resolve all differences related to their children in a manner that will promote a caring, loving, and involved relationship between the children and each parent.

5.03 *Other Professionals.* In securing additional professional assistance, the parties shall ordinarily retain joint neutral experts and specialist consultants as recommended by the Collaborative Lawyers and/ or Collaborative Divorce Coaches. While neither party and neither Collaborative Lawyer is precluded by these Principles and Guidelines from consulting privately with separate experts or consultants, each such expert or consultant shall be directed to follow the spirit and direction of these Principles and Guidelines, and, when appropriate, to collaborate with each other, meet and confer, and, if possible, render joint statements on the matters in question. The divorcing couple agrees not to retain separate experts or specialist consultants without advising their respective Collaborative Lawyers of their intent to do so, during this Collaborative Divorce process.

VI. NEGOTIATION IN GOOD FAITH

6.01 The parties understand that even with full and honest disclosure, the Collaborative Divorce process will involve vigorous good faith negotiation. Each party will be expected to take a reasoned approach on all disagreements and disputed matters and, where such approaches differ, each party will be encouraged to consider modifying his or her approach in order to reach a resolution of all disputed matters. While the parties shall be informed by their Collaborative Lawyers about applicable law and about the litigation process, neither a party nor any Collaborative Divorce professional will use threats of going to court as a way of forcing settlement.

VII. ABUSE OF COLLABORATIVE PROCESS

7.01 A Collaborative Lawyer shall immediately either withdraw from or terminate a Collaborative Divorce case upon learning that her or his client is knowingly withholding or misrepresenting information having a material bearing on the case or otherwise acting so as to undermine or take unfair advantage of the Collaborative Divorce process. Examples of such behavior include: the secret disposition of marital, quasi-marital, or nonmarital property, failure to disclose the existence or the true nature of assets and/or obligations, ongoing emotional or physical abuse by either party, secret preparation to engage in litigation while appearing to participate in a Collaborative Divorce process, or withholding a secret plan or intention to leave the jurisdiction of the court with their children. Each divorcing party shall clarify separately, in writing, with his and her respective Collaborative Lawyers whether the lawyer will withdraw from or terminate the Collaborative Divorce process in the event his or her client abuses the process.

7.02 Both divorcing parties understand that the Collaborative Lawyers each represent only one party and not both parties. Both parties understand and acknowledge that neither Collaborative Lawyer owes a legal duty to a party he or she does not represent. Nothing in these Principles and Guidelines shall be interpreted to mean that either party could ever have a claim against the other party's lawyer with respect to any aspect of Collaborative Divorce, including, without limitation: disclosures, negotiations, and/or terms of settlement.

7.03 All understand that the ultimate sanction against professionals who abuse the Collaborative Divorce process, or condone and/or encourage such abuse by clients, is the diminution of that professional's reputation in the legal community, including the judiciary.

VIII. DISQUALIFICATION BY COURT INTERVENTION

8.01 The parties and their Collaborative Divorce professionals shall sign these Principles and Guidelines, and such other documents as their team members request, including but not necessarily limited to fee agreements, a Coaching Agreement, and a Stipulation and Order Re: Collaborative Divorce, and agree to be bound by their terms and provisions.

8.02 The parties understand that their lawyers' representation is limited to the Collaborative Divorce process. Thus, while your Collaborative Lawyer is your counselor and advocate, he or she cannot ever represent you in court in proceedings against your divorcing spouse, nor be named or remain as your lawyer of record on any document filed with the court.

8.03 None of your Collaborative Divorce team members, including the Collaborative Lawyers, Collaborative Divorce Coaches, Collaborative Financial Consultant, and Child Specialist, and none of the other jointly retained experts and specialist consultants participating in your Collaborative Divorce, may ever assist you in court proceedings against your divorcing spouse, nor give evidence in such a matter.

8.04 In the event a party files adversary documents with the court, all Collaborative Divorce professionals will be disqualified from further representing or assisting their respective clients, and the Collaborative Divorce process will automatically terminate. Upon termination of the Collaborative Divorce process, all Collaborative Professionals will be disqualified as witnesses and their work product and the work of all other jointly retained experts and consultants will be inadmissible as evidence in any adversarial court proceeding.

IX. WITHDRAWAL OF LAWYER

9.01 If a Collaborative Lawyer deems it appropriate to withdraw from the case for any reason, he or she agrees to do so by a written Notice of Withdrawal to the parties, their coaches and lawyers, and the financial and child specialists, as well as any other participants and, if a Stipulation and Order has been filed, to the court. This may be done without terminating the status of the case as a Collaborative Divorce case.

9.02 The party losing her or his collaborative lawyer by virtue of withdrawal may continue in the Collaborative Divorce process by retaining a new collaborative lawyer who will agree in writing to be bound by these Principles and Guidelines.

X. ELECTION TO TERMINATE COLLABORATIVE PROCESS

10.01 If a party decides that the Collaborative Divorce process is no longer appropriate and elects to terminate the status of the matter as a Collaborative Divorce case, she or he agrees to do so by sending a written Termination Election to all other parties, Collaborative Professionals, and other participants and, if a Stipulation and Order has been filed, to the court. Similarly, if a Collaborative Lawyer deems it necessary to terminate the Collaborative Divorce process, a written Termination Election shall be sent to the recipients noted in the preceding sentence.

10.02 The termination of the Collaborative Divorce proceeding shall occur automatically in the event a party deems it necessary to initiate an adversarial court proceeding to protect his or her property, self, or children, unless both parties and all Collaborative Divorce team members agree otherwise in writing.

XI. PROFESSIONAL FEES AND COSTS IN COLLABORATIVE DIVORCE

11.01 Both divorcing parties understand that all Collaborative Divorce professionals are independent of one another and have no financial connections or fee-sharing or referral fee arrangements with one another. They also understand and agree that each professional team member must be paid separately for his and her services in this Collaborative Divorce, pursuant to terms set out specifically in separate fee agreements with each team member.

11.02 Because imbalance in payment to the parties' respective coaches or lawyers can adversely affect one party's access to advice and counsel as compared to the other party, both parties agree that the coaches' and lawyers' fees will be kept current. The Child Specialist and Collaborative Financial Consultant and other jointly retained expert consultants will also be paid in a timely manner. Any disagreements about ultimate responsibility for payment of such fees will be resolved as and when other financial issues are resolved. Each divorcing party understands that no Collaborative Divorce professional can continue to provide services without being paid.

11.03 The Collaborative Divorce professionals will confer with one another from time to time by telephone, in person, and via email, in service of ensuring full and complete disclosure of material information and in service of ensuring an effective Collaborative Divorce process. Each professional will bill for time spent in such communications as set out in his and her separate fee agreements.

11.04 Each party should ensure that he and she clarifies with their respective Collaborative Divorce coaches and lawyers how private confidential communications will be handled by that professional.

XII. SELECTION OF NEW LAWYER; ADDITIONAL FEES

12.01 Once the status of the case as a Collaborative Divorce matter is terminated, the Collaborative Lawyers agree to assist their respective client in the selection of new lawyers.

12.02 The parties understand that in retaining new lawyers in the event of the termination of the case's status as a Collaborative Divorce matter, each of them will incur further professionals' fees—including but not necessarily limited to lawyers' fees—that may equal or exceed those paid during the Collaborative Divorce process.

XIII. PLEDGE

13.01 All parties, lawyers, coaches, financial specialists, and other consulting professionals hereby pledge to comply with and to promote the spirit and written word of this document.

Parties:

Dated: _____   _____
                                      Wife

Dated: _____   _____
                                      Husband

Collaborative Divorce Professionals:

_____   _____
Collaborative Lawyer for Wife   Collaborative Lawyer for Husband

_____   _____
Collaborative Divorce Coach for Wife Collaborative Divorce Coach for
                                      Husband

_____   _____
Collaborative Financial   Child Specialist Consultant

Other Professional Consultants and Experts:

_____   _____
Real Estate or Other Appraiser   Actuary

_____   _____
Vocational Consultant   Certified Public Accountant

_____   _____
Other   Other

ACKNOWLEDGMENTS

Pauline Tesler's Acknowledgments

I want to thank my husband, Peter Sandmann, whose intelligence, good humor, and support of every kind—particularly his patience about my frequent absence from our law partnership—made it possible for me to learn enough about collaborative legal practice to have something to say in a book, and my daughter Leia, who never complained and always tolerated my periods of over-commitment with grace and humor.

Warm appreciation to my coauthor and friend, Peggy Thompson—a visionary who has always known what should happen next, including this book.

I owe a special debt of gratitude to Angeles Arrien, who showed me how to make use of wisdom from many cultures and many centuries in my daily life and work. Her teaching opened important doors, including this one. Jan Johnston first showed me the difference between winning and being of use to divorcing clients, thereby making it impossible for me to continue being a litigator—for which I belatedly thank her. My extraordinary colleagues on the IACP board of directors and in my own Bay Area practice group—affectionately known as "the Green Group"—have taught me more than I can ever thank them all for. The superb collaborative lawyers with whom I've worked on cases during the past year—notably John McCall, Larry Wilson, Jenni Jackson, and Madeleine Simborg—have been patient, supportive and collegial beyond all expectation, in ways that allowed me to finish this manuscript. Julie MacFarlane, Bernie Mayer, Don Royall, David Hoffman, Sue Hansen, Norma Trusch, George Richardson, James Pirrie, Susan Gamache, Nancy Cameron, Stu Webb, John McShane, David Weinberg, Bruce Winick, Susan Daicoff, Talia Katz and a host of other dearly valued colleagues have taught me more than you can imagine and you all have been great fun to work with—please forgive me for not naming each and every one of you. The many lawyers who have been kind enough to invite me to their communities to teach and to learn from them are an international community of pioneers who are changing our profession from the bottom up and the top down in ways that are long overdue. They deserve great credit, as do the courageous divorcing couples who helped us create this new and better way of moving through divorce.

Peggy and I can't begin to thank these people sufficiently, for without each of them this book wouldn't have made it to print: our agent, Sue Herner, whose confidence in us hasn't wavered and who has helped us far beyond her job description; our amazingly dedicated and patient editors at ReganBooks, Anna Bliss and Matt Harper; Sharon Goldinger, who got us started; and Elsa Dixon, our gift from the universe.

It's past time that I thanked my parents, James and Gertude Tesler and my grandmother, Leah Bluestein Glaser and the entire Glaser clan for raising me to believe I could accomplish whatever I wished, and Mike Tesler, for being the best of brothers.

Finally, my love and appreciation go to Jean Shinoda Bolen, Grace Dammann, Toni Triest, Carole Robinson, and Isabel Allende, sisters on the journey.

Peggy Thompson's Acknowledgments

I wish to acknowledge the help and support of my husband, Dr. Nurse, who has worked alongside me to develop and promote the use of the collaborative divorce model from the very beginning, and who has supported my work with his love and advice. My son, Eric, who has provided technical support for me from an early age, as well as artistic and design advice as he has developed his expertise, and my daughter, Sonya, who supported me by taking over many of the household duties and contributing a child's and emerging adult's observations and thoughts that brought to my attention important issues. Also to my grandmother, who taught me from an early age to be independent and persistent, and my aunt and uncle, Blevins and Marjorie, who give me support when I most need it and who believe in me. Special warm appreciation to my friend, colleague, and coauthor, Pauline Tesler, for all her work and dedication both along the road we have traveled together and in the endeavor of this book. Much appreciation goes to all those who have participated along the way in thinking and rethinking both the theory and practice as it has developed—especially Nancy Ross, LCSW, without whose dedication and support I might have given up. I also wish to express my appreciation to all the dedicated members of the collaborative communities across the country have stimulated my thinking both in trainings and other contexts, raised important questions that helped to polish and refine the model, and offered their continued support. Last, but not least, to all the children of divorced families who inspired me to create a better solution for them.

INDEX